Early Sculptural Art in the Indian Coastlands

Early Sculptural Art in the Indian Coastlands

— A Study in Cultural Transmission and Syncretism —

(300 BCE – CE 500)

Sunil Gupta

Foreword by
S.P. Gupta

D.K. Printworld (P) Ltd.
New Delhi

Cataloging in Publication Data — DK
[Courtesy: D.K. Agencies (P) Ltd. <docinfo@dkagencies.com>]

Gupta, Sunil, 1961–
Early sculptural art in the Indian coastlands/
Sunil Gupta.
xxix, 210 p. 25 cm.
Includes bibliographical references. (p.)
Includes index.
ISBN 812460438X

1. Sculpture, Ancient — India. 2. Coastal archaeology — India I. Title.

DDC 732.44 22

ISBN 81-246-0438-X
First published in India in 2008

Published and printed by:
D.K. Printworld (P) Ltd.
Regd. Office: 'Sri Kunj', F-52, Bali Nagar
Ramesh Nagar Metro Station
New Delhi-110 015
Phones: (011) 2545 3975; 2546 6019; *Fax*: (011) 2546 5926
E-mail: dkprintworld@vsnl.net
Website: www.dkprintworld.com

Dedicated to

Shashi Asthana

Foreword

HERE is an interesting book on Indian Art History penned by Dr Sunil Gupta of the Allahabad Museum, Allahabad, who is also editing with me the *Journal of Indian Ocean Archaeology*. It deals with an old subject but from an entirely new perspective. Hence we have reasons to welcome it. So far Indian Art History has been looked upon either in the framework of chronology, political dynasties, regional manifestations, religious architecture, as works of art and aesthetics, or as products of architectural engineering, etc. Each and every approach has its own merits and demerits since each one emphasizes only one aspect of the history of Indian art and architecture at the cost of other aspects. This book also places emphasis on one aspect of the history of Indian art — that of the coastal regions. This is an aspect which had not been adequately and exclusively dealt with anyone earlier. Therefore, this book may be useful for not only all serious scholars but also for the students of art history.

The book tries to reveal the role that the Indian Ocean Rim Countries, including India, played in the dissemination of Indian art and architecture, including the Indian art motifs, from the third century BCE onwards. The author has given not only the old data of the west Indian coast, but has also collected new data from his own explorations and added many new things for our knowledge.

This book also takes us beyond the Indian coastline, into Oman and other West Asian countries. It also takes us to the eastern coastline of India and also beyond along the eastern Indian Ocean Rim Countries. Therefore, the scholars of Indian art history will have something new to add to their knowledge even on this count.

However, one particular aspect, which I feel, should have been there in order to make the story complete. It is the coastline and hinterland of Goa. In recent years, Goa has been explored by archaeologists, both extensively and intensively. Even articles have been written and published by serious researchers like Prof. (Ms.) Pratima Kamat and Prof. V.K. Mitragotri in journals like *Purātattva* and *Journal of Indian Ocean Archaeology*. But unfortunately, these findings have as yet not found their rightful place in the full-length books of history of Indian art. I am summarizing here these findings with the hope that anyone writing in future on the subject of history of Indian art may reproduce these photographs and write more on them.

There are two major groups of works of art in Goa. One that relates to what is called "Petroglyphs" or Rock Art. These are mainly deep engravings of the outlines of figures done *in situ* on huge rock-surfaces, although high reliefs are also included in it. And the second relates to individual sculptured stone stele depicting Hindu gods and goddesses, which may have been once kept in temples for worship. The former is generally dated to the late Neolithic–Early Bronze Age, around 3000–1000 BCE although no one is sure about the dating of these petroglyphs. When I visited and saw them a few years ago, I was simply amazed and thrilled since these were engraved deeply on the flat exposed surface along a narrow flowing river called Kuśāvatī. The rock is laterite in its primary context. I gathered that every year in the rainy season these engravings get submerged in the muddy waters of the flooded stream. The site is named Pansaimol. It is located in the Sanguem *tāluka* where Pirla mines are active and the secondary lateritic deposits are still under digging for commercial purposes. It sometimes leads to dangerous situations for the conservationists of these rarest of the rare works of art. The area coverage of these engravings at the site is 10 m. x 70 m.

The rock-engravings include large human figures, both male and female. Animals depicted are both extinct and living, and include the zebu bull, wild goat, bison, antelope, wild goat, hyena, monkey, dog, etc. Besides these, there are symbols of fertility like cross, concentric circles, rectangles, labyrinths, footprints and X-rayed forms of animals, such as the *neelgai*. This shows that culturally they were primarily hunters and gatherers.

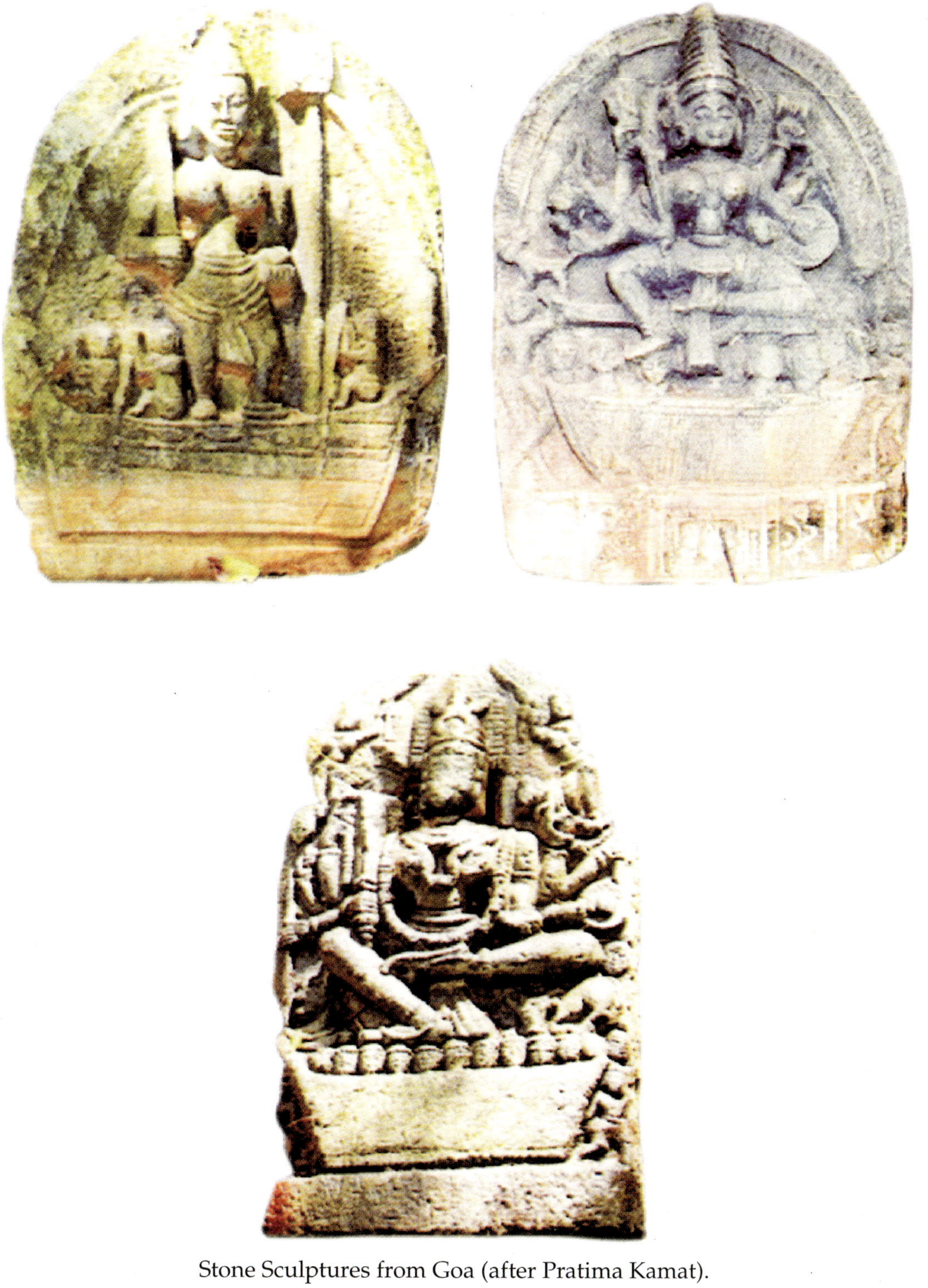

Stone Sculptures from Goa (after Pratima Kamat).

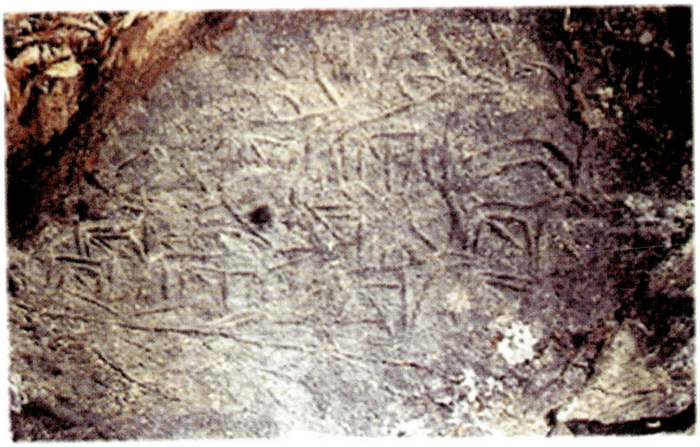

Rock-engravings of wild animals etc. In a herd at Pansaimol, Goa (after Pratima Kamat).

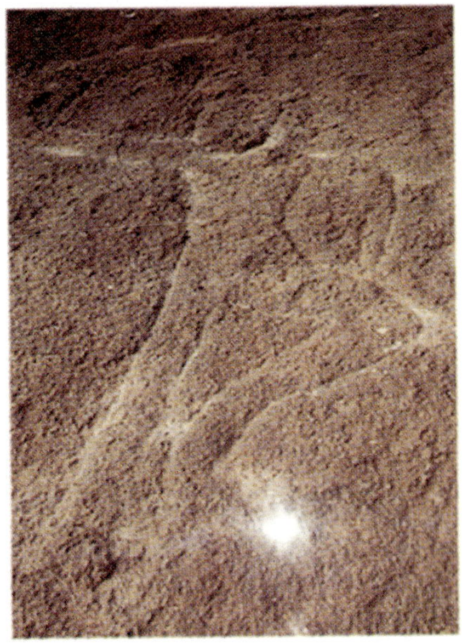

Rock-engravings of a Dacing Girl(?) At Pansaimol, Goa (after Pratima Kamat).

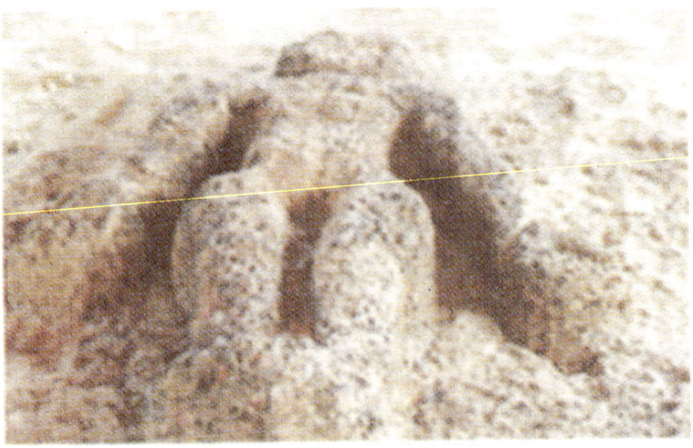

Rock-engravings of a Mother-goddess in relief at Kajur, Goa (after Pratima Kamat).

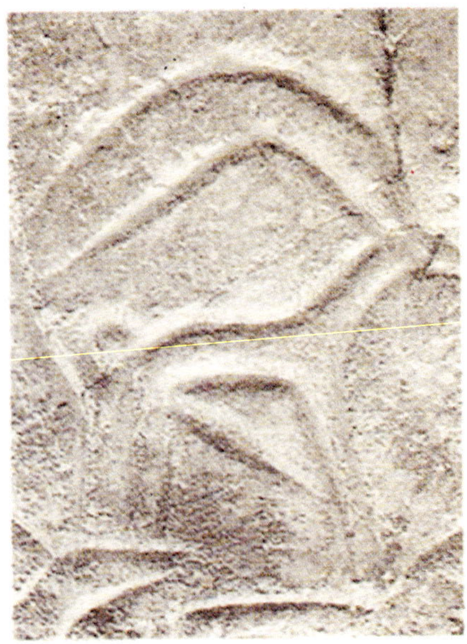

Rock-engravings of an amtelope at Pansaimol, Goa (after Pratima Kamat).

On a branch of the same river, some 20 km from Sanguem township, is the site of Kajur. Here a huge horizontally laid abstract figure of nude mother-goddess has been engraved in high relief. However, there are around two dozen more engravings similar in content and character to the Pansaimol engravings.

Belonging to the late medieval and the continuing traditions, are some of the rare sculptures carved out of dark schist stone. These sculptured stele come from the temple sites located in the forests along the river named Mhdei (= Mahādevī) in *tāluka* Sattari. The sites, discovered in the hinterland from Bondir to Ganjem, were connected with the sea, hence they played an important role in the maritime trade with West Asian and East African countries. The sculptures depict various female deities such as Gajalakṣmī, Saptamātṛkās, Śānta-Durgā, Mahiṣāsuramardinī, etc. the last being most popularly depicted. Amongst the male deities are Kārttikeya and Rāma. There are some figures of *bhikṣu*s or *muni*s also in the compositions. The peculiarities of these sculptures lie not so much in the depiction of these traditional deities but in their associations, motifs and purposes.

To begin with, most of the female deities are associated with boat or *nāva* motif, i.e. the deities are seen seated on a pedestal, raised from the central part of a large boat. Sometimes they are seen sitting inside the boat or on the corner of a boat, or sitting on an animal using the boat as *howdāh,* i.e. a seat kept on the back of an animal. Hence, it is more than clear that these deities were worshiped by the sea-farers of Goa.

Secondly, on many occasions the boats have human beings sitting inside. But since the boats are deep, only their heads can be seen in a row.

Thirdly, at a few other times, the whole human figures, generally in sitting posture, are also depicted.

It is due to these factors that these goddesses, particularly Mahiṣāsuramardinī, who is more popularly worshiped than any other goddess, are called 'the saviours of sailors', or the "Boat Devī" or "Nāva Devī". Some of the sites, where these sculptures have been found, are Sanvarde, Guleti, Dhamshe, Bhuipal, Nagvem, Zarme, etc.

One can, therefore, see the process of adoption, adaptation and transformation of traditional Hindu deities in the coastal region of Goa.

Taking an overall perspective, it is reiterated that the work at hand explores a theme which has never been dealt before in a holistic manner, i.e. taking into account the *entire* Indian coastland. This book dispels the notion that all great art flowered in the interiors of India. In investigating the early sculptural art in the Indian coastlands, a wider framework is introduced into the debate, that of the Indian Ocean. In this sense, the book can be placed in the emerging genre of global studies of art.

S.P. Gupta

Preface

THE idea of authoring a book exclusively on early sculptural art in the Indian coastlands needed some justification deeper than being merely convinced of the academic utility of the venture. Of the latter I was not in doubt. The opportunity lay in the "peripheral" nature of the theme. As has been the case with mainstream Indian archaeology, the scholars of early Indian art traditions have viewed the coastlands as being in the margins of the cultural efflorescences which happened in the interiors of the subcontinent. The classical schools of Indian sculptural art that sprang up at Mathurā, Gandhāra and Sārnāth in the first half of the first millennium CE, have become axioms in the study of early Indian sculptural art. No discussion on early sculptural art can be complete without reference to one or other of the schools. While the coastlands were not bereft of the influences of the great schools of art, it needs to be realized that the littoral regions of the subcontinent were cultural melting pots in their own right, often transcending the art of the interiors. The grand architecture and bold reliefs in the rock-cut cave of Karla close to the western coast is in stark contrast to the spartan precincts of the early rock-cut caves in Bihar. The role of the coastlands as disseminators of art is evident in the unique Amarāvatī Buddha figures whose likenesses were transmitted across the Bay of Bengal to different parts of South-East Asia. In the same vein, we can speak of the stone slab from Yemen depicting human and animal figures reminiscent of the Nāgārjunakoṇḍa friezes. To me, the coastlands have never represented the periphery. As staging areas of long distance maritime exchanges, the Indian coastlands have long mediated between the far civilizations of the Indian Ocean world (Egyptian, Arabian, Persian, East African and South-East Asian) and the Indic cultural sphere.

All this must have made for a great amount of interactivity. The early art of the Indian coastlands seems to have been born out of a robust eclectic spirit. How else would you explain the carvings of the Vedic gods Indra and Sūrya in the Buddhist rock-cut sanctuary of Bhaja? Who took the sensuous bronze figure of a dancing *yakṣī* of the Sāñcī tradition to the remote coast of southern Oman in the second century CE? Does the ninth-century Buddha figure from a Viking burial in Sweden denote an exotic import or an artefact of greater significance? These images of transmission, absorption and syncretism are the wellsprings of my inspiration. This brief work is an attempt to understand the process of give and take which characterizes all artistic activity. Such a quest also fits the larger civilizational themes I have been pursuing through a decade and a half; themes of long distance contact, exchange and trade in the early Indian Ocean world.

This monograph would not have seen the light of day but for the encouragement of Dr S.P. Gupta, Chairman of the Indian Archaeological Society, whose seminal works *Roots of Indian Art* and *Elements of Indian Art* convinced me that archaeology and art are not as disparate as they appear. On this occasion I express my gratitude to Prof. D.P. Agrawal (formerly of the Physical Research Laboratory, Ahmedabad) for introducing me to archaeology and to Prof. V.N. Mishra, my PhD Supervisor at the Deccan College, Pune, for encouraging me for seven long years to complete my thesis on the archaeology of Indo-Roman sea trade. I would like to give my regards to Shri K.N. Dikshit for facilitating my work in the Indian Archaeological Society. I am thankful to my Chairman, Professor Radha Kant Varma for his support for my academic pursuits. My colleagues in the Allahabad Museum were forthcoming with their ideas and advice for which I am grateful. In particular, I benefited from Dr S.K. Sharma's views on Greek art. I am thankful to Dr Sri Ranjan Shukla for discussions on the Mathurā school of art. Dr Prabhakar Pandey gave me an overview of the terracotta art of the Gangetic Valley. I was also benefited by the ideas of my colleague Shri Arun Wankhede on the nature of early Buddhism. I also thank my colleagues Dr D.K. Kesarwani, Dr Ajay Mishra, Dr R.K. Mishra and Shri Waman Wankhede for their constant encouragement. I am thankful to the staff of the museum's library, Shri Kamlesh Tripathi and Shri Dhiresh Joshi who never hesitated to find me the most inconspicuous reference. Ms Vandana Sinha at the American Institute of Indian Studies (Gurgaon) helped me retrieve the right photographs in a short time from the valuable photo-archives of the institute. Dr Sila Tripati of the National Institute of Oceanography, Goa responded quickly to my call for photographs of the Buddha heads from Lakshadweep. I foundly recall the grueling exploration of the Karnataka Coast in the company of my friend Dr S.K. Aruni. Shri Rajneesh of Syncrotek Computers put all his energies in making the illustrated maps and scanning the photographs within a short period of time. I also thank my publisher Shri Shusheel Mittal and Shri Rajendra Agarwal for all the critial inputs made in the book.

To my wife Charu, a very special thank. Nothing would have been possible all these years without her support. My son Revant and daughter Anahita provided those moments of distraction that gave welcome relief from dour scholarship. For my parents' blessings, I remain forever grateful.

Allahabad **Sunil Gupta**
March 19, 2007
Caitra Sudi Ekam, 2064

Contents

	Foreword by S.P. Gupta	vii
	Preface	xiii
	Acknowledgement	xix
	List of Maps, B/W Photographs and Colour Plates	xxi
	Key to Transliteration	xxix
1.	Introduction	1
2.	Epicentres of Early Indian Sculptural Art	9
3.	Routes of Transmission	21
4.	The Western Coastland	37
5.	The Southern Coastland	53
6.	The Eastern Coastland	77
7.	Spread of Art Overseas	89
8.	The Indianization of South-East Asia: A New Perspective	101
9.	Conclusion	117
	Figures & Colour Plates	123
	References	195
	Index	201

Acknowledgement

The following scholars and institutions are acknowledged for use of photographhc material:-

- Allahabad Museum for Plates: 4, 5, 22, 23, 37, 42.
- Institute of Archaeology, London for Plates 43, 44 & 45
- American Institute of Indian Studies (Gurgaon) for Figures: 8, 9, 15, 16, 17, 18, 19, 20, 21, 22, 29, 30, 31, 32, 33, 34, 36, 41, 42, 45, 49, 50, 52, 53, 54, 55, 56, 57, 58.
- Bangkok National Museum for Plates. 38, 39, 40, 46, 47.
- Institute of Maritime Studies, Bhubaneswar for Plate 48.
- Bergen Museum for Plate 41.
- Asher (1980) and Varendra Research Institute for Figure 47.
- Cimino (1994) for Figures: 2, 8, 39, 61, 63 and Plates 3, 20.
- Craven (1986) for Figures: 2, 10, 11, 62.
- Rao (1966) for Figures: 23, 24, 25, 26, 27.
- Archaeological Survey of India for Figures: 12, 14, 38, 40, 43, 44, 48, 51 (sourced from Indian Archaeology û A Review)
- Marg and Kolhapur Museum for Figure 13.
- The French Institute, Pondicherry for Figure. 37.
- Tamluk Museum for Figure. 46.
- Naseema Mohamed (2002) and Department of Culture, Government of Maldives for Figure. 59.
- A. Skjolsvold in Quagliotti (1998) for Figure. 60.
- Doffelmeyer (1999: 38-52) for Figure. 64.
- Le May (1956) for Figure 65.

- Dr. Raj Somadeva, Department of Archaeology, University of Kelaniya, Sri Lanka for Figure. 66.
- Dr. Sila Tripati, Centre for Marine Archaeology, NIO, Goa for Plate 26.
- Rest of the photographs and maps are by the author.

List of Maps, Figures and Plates

Maps

Map 1 : Location of early *stūpa* sites in India with special reference to Andhra Pradesh.

Map 2 : Map showing the line of diffusion of Early rock-cut caves.

Map 3 : Location of major schools of sculptural art in ancient India.

Map 4 : Map showing the major trade routes in early historic India.

Map 5 : Find places of Early Sculptural Art on Route A.

Map 6 : Find places of Early Sculptural Art on Route B.

Map 7 : Find places of Early Sculptural Art on Route C.

Map 8 : Find places of Early Sculptural Art on Route D and Route E.

Map 9 : Find places of Early Sculptural Art on Route G.

Map 10 : Find places of Early Sculptural Art on the Western Coast.

Map 11 : Find places of Early Sculptural Art on the Southern Coast of India and Sri Lanka.

Map 12 : Map showing the Roman coin find places on the northern Andhra coast.

Map 13 : Map of Karnataka coast.

Map 14 : Find places of Early Sculptural Art on the Eastern Coast of India and Bangladesh.

Map 15 : Illustrated map showing spread of early Indian sculptural art overseas.

Map 16 : Map of the Bay of Bengal Interaction Sphere.

Black and white Photographs

fig. 1 : Didārgañj *yakṣī,* sandstone, third century BCE, Patna Museum.

fig. 2 : View of Sāñcī Stūpa.

fig. 3 : Medallion from Bharhut, second century BCE.

fig. 4 : Figure of Parkham *Yakṣa,* Mathurā, second century BCE.

fig. 5 : Buddha image of the Mathurā School.

fig. 6 : Viṣṇu image of the Mathurā School.

fig. 7 : Buddha image of the Gāndhāra School.

fig. 8 : Slab depicting the Amarāvatī Stūpa.

fig. 9 : Frieze showing ascent to heaven with turban of Buddha, Amarāvatī, second century CE.

fig. 10 : Standing Buddha of the Sārnath School.

fig. 11 : Seated Buddha in *dharmacakrapravartana* pose from Sārnath.

fig. 12 : Limestone slab from Ṭer showing Amarāvatī influence.

fig. 13 : Bronze figure of Poseidon from Brahmapuri.

fig. 14 : Stone image of Buddha from Candraketugaṛh.

fig. 15 : Sūrya–Indra panels, Bhaja Cave, second-first century BCE.

fig. 16 : Indra on Elephant? Bhaja Cave, second-first century BCE.

fig. 17 : Sūrya on chariot? Bhaja Cave, second-first century BCE.

fig. 18 : Gajalakṣmī panel at entrance of rock-cut cave at Junnar, first century BCE.

fig. 19 : Pillar capitals at Kārle showing animals and human figures, first century CE.

fig. 20 : Buddha image at Kanheri, sixth century CE.

fig. 21 : Figure of male in kaolin from Ṭer, first century CE.

fig. 22 : Portrait of Scythian in terracotta, Ṭer, first century CE.

fig. 23 : Terracotta imitation of stone image of Kaniṣka in

Mathurā, Amreli, Gujarat, second century CE.

fig. 24 : Viṣṇu image from Amreli, stone, second century CE.

fig. 25 : Image of four armed goddess, stone, Amreli, first-second century CE.

fig. 26 : Image of Vaiṣṇavī, stone, Amreli, first-second century CE.

fig. 27 : Stone image (fragmentary) of Mahiṣāsuramardinī, stone, Amreli, fifth century CE.

fig. 28 : Highly decorated pillars in Junāgaṛh Cave, Gujarat, second century CE?

fig. 29 : Gaṇa image in green schist, Devnīmorī, fifth century CE?

fig. 30 : Decorative frieze from Kesanapalli showing Bodhi tree, limestone, second century BCE?

fig. 31 : Decorative motif showing *srivatsa* from Jaggayapetta, limestone, second century BCE?

fig 32 : Buddha, Amarāvatī, white marble, third century CE.

fig. 33 : Buddha, limestone, Nāgārjunikoṇḍa? second-third century CE, Andhra Pradesh Goverment Museum.

fig. 34 : Garbhagṛha, Śivaliṅga, granite, second century BCE, Parasurāmeśvara Temple, Gudimallam, Chittoor district, Andhra Pradesh.

fig. 35 : Wheel like plan of *stūpa* from Andhra Pradesh.

fig. 36 : Mālāvāhakas, limestone, Amarāvatī, second century CE.

fig. 37 : Terracotta head of *yavana?* discovered at Erode, Tamil Nadu.

fig. 38 : Terracotta head of a lady? from Kañcīpuram, fifth century CE.

fig. 39 : Headless figure from Arikamedu showing Hellenistic/ Roman influence.

fig. 40 : Terracotta figure of Indra on elephant, Candraketugaṛh, second-first century BCE.

fig. 41 : Elephant toy cart, terracotta, mouldmade, first century CE, Candraketugaṛh, Burdwan University Museum.

fig. 42 : Gaṇeśa sculpture, stone, cave X (Gaṇeśa Gumphā), Verandah, rear wall, Udayagiri–Khaṇḍagiri complex, Puri district, *c.* 5–25 BCE (?)

fig. 43 : Terracotta figure of Lakṣmi, Candraketugaṛh, first century BCE.

fig. 44 : Terracotta figure of a female deity with elaborate headdress, Candraketugaṛh.

fig. 45 : Female figure with mirror (part of bigger image), terracotta, mouldmade, first century BCE, Candraketugaṛh, Burdwan University Museum.

fig. 46 : Terracotta head of Buddha from Tilda, fifth century CE.

fig. 47 : Viṣṇu figure in stone found in Māldā, West Bengal, fourth century CE.

fig. 48 : Hellenistic sculpture from Bengal, Terracotta, first-second century CE.

fig. 49 : Elephant carved on rock face, third century BCE, Dhauli, Orissa.

fig. 50 : Free standing elephant, Gaṇeśa Gumphā, exterior, Udayagiri–Khaṇḍagiri, Puri district, last half of first century BCE, sandstone.

fig. 51 : Sandstone bust of *yakṣī* recovered from Udayagiri, second-first century BCE.

fig. 52 : Gajalakṣmī, cave 3 (Ananta Gumphā), Udayagiri–Khaṇḍagiri, 50–25 BCE.

fig. 53 : Yavana soldier? cave 1 (Rānī Gumphā), Udayagiri-Khaṇḍagiri, sandstone, 50–25 BCE.

fig. 54 : Pillar fragment from palace site, with figure of dwarf *yakṣa* and Scythian soldier, Nāgārjunikoṇḍa, Guntur district, National Museum, third century CE?

fig. 55 : Dvārapāla, holding a spear in right hand and shield in left (shield–Scythian influence), Vihāra Cave 18, Bhaja, Pune district, first century BCE.

fig. 56 : *Yakṣī*, Jayavijaya Cave (no. 5), Udayagiri–Khaṇḍagiri, first century BCE, sandstone.

fig. 57 : Frieze showing hunting scene, Rānī Gumphā no. 1. Udayagiri–Khaṇḍagiri, fifth century CE.

fig. 58 : Seated Tīrthaṁkaras and Devīs, cave 8 (Bārābhujī Gumphā), Udayagiri–Khaṇḍagiri, Puri district, fifth century CE.

fig. 59 : Head of Buddha statue excavated from a *stūpa* in Thoddo Island, Maldives, third-fourth century CE.

fig. 60 : *Buddhapāda* from Vadu Island, Gaaf Atoll (Maldives Islands), second-third century CE.

fig. 61 : Statuette of *Yakṣī*, bronze, Khor Rori, Dhofar, Oman, first-second century CE.

fig. 62 : *Yakṣī* image from bracket of gateway at Sāñcī, stone, first century BCE.

fig. 63 : Marble plaque showing Indian influence, Manakha (Yemen) second-third century CE.

fig. 64 : Viṣṇu image from Chaiya, Thailand, stone, fifth–sixth century CE.

fig. 65 : Amarāvatī type Buddha image in bronze from Kedah, Malaysia, fourth–fifth century CE.

fig. 66 : Plaque showing influence of Amarāvatī art, found at Tissamaharama, Sri Lanka, third century CE.

Colours Plates

Pl. 1 : Aśokan Pillar at Allahabad, third century BCE.

Pl. 2 : Early historic mound within Bharuch city.

Pl. 3 : Figure of Eros from Junnar, Maharashtra, first-second century CE.

Pl. 4 : Headless Buddha(?) image from Kauśāmbī showing Gāndhāra influence.

Pl. 5 : Pañcajūḍā figurine from Kauśāmbī, terracotta, first century BCE.

Pl. 6 : Caityagṛha at Kārle, first century CE.

Pl. 7 : Horse-shoe entrance of Kārle Cave.

Pl. 8 : Brāhmī inscription mentioning *yavana* donors at Kārle, first century CE.

Pl. 9 : Pillar surmounted by lion capital at entrance of Kārle cave, first-second century CE.

Pl. 10 : Mithuna figures, entrance of Kārle Caitya Cave, first century CE.

Pl. 11. : *Yakṣī* figure at the entrance of Kārle Cave, first-second century CE.

Pl. 12 : Stūpa carved in relief inside a rock-cut cave at Caul, first century CE.

Pl. 13 : Janjira creek viewed from the rock-cut caves at Kuda.

Pl. 14 : Buddhist rock-cut caves at Kuda viewed from the beach head.

Pl. 15 : Stūpa carved in relief inside a rock-cut cave in Kuda, first century CE.

Pl. 16 : Stūpa carved in the round inside a rock-cut cave at Kuda, first-second century CE.

Pl. 17 : Decorative balustrade at Kuda imitating wooden architecture, first-second century CE.

Pl. 18 : Buddha image carved inside a rock-cut cave in Kuda, sixth century CE.

Pl. 19 : Site of early historic Kamrej on the banks of the river Tāpti.

Pl. 20 : Ivory figurine of western Indian origin found at Pompei, Italy, first century CE.

Pl. 21 : Lakulīśa image on decorated brick, Karvan, Baroda, sixth-seventh century CE.

Pl. 22 : Terracotta bust of a nobleman from Kauśāmbī (Uttar

Pradesh) having red polish and glaze, first-second century CE.

Pl. 23 : Terracotta bust of Śiva from Kauśāmbī (Uttar Pradesh) having red slip, first-second century CE.

Pl. 24 : Fragments of Red Polished Ware vessels from Nevasa (Maharashtra) and Kauśāmbī (Uttar Pradesh), first-second century CE.

Pl. 25 : Early historic site of Arikamedu (Pondicherry) on the banks of the Ariyankuppam river.

Pl. 26 : Buddha-heads from Andhroth Island, Lakshadweep, fifth century CE.

Pl. 27 : View of the Śarāvatī river from Haigunda Island.

Pl. 28 : *Yakṣa* image of stone inside a sacred grove on Haigunda Island, Uttar Kannada Dist., Karnataka, fourth century CE.

Pl. 29 : Close up of *yakṣa* figure on Haigunda Island.

Pl. 30 : Viṣṇu image flanked by Buddha figures outside the village of Haigunda.

Pl. 31 : Stone sculpture of Viṣṇu, Haigunda Island, third-fourth century CE.

Pl. 32 : Buddha image to the left of Viṣṇu figure, Haigunda Island in fifth-sixth century CE.

Pl. 33 : Buddha image to the right of Viṣṇu figure, Haigunda Island in fifth-sixth century CE.

Pl. 34 : Śivaliṅga found in a field in Haigunda Island, fifth century CE?

Pl. 35 : View of Malpe creek as it opens into the Arabian Sea.

Pl. 36 : Apsidal temple dedicated to Śiva, Udyavara, Dakshin Kannada.

Pl. 37 : Terracotta toy cart. Kauśāmbī, first century CE.

Pl. 38 : *Dharmacakra* in stone, seventh-eighth century CE, Bangkok National Museum.

Pl. 39 : Decorated stone column, Dvarāvatī period, seventh century CE, Bangkok National Museum.

Pl. 40 : Bodhi tree carved on stone plaque, sixth century CE, Bangkok National Museum.

Pl. 41 : Metal figure from Viking site in Norway resembling a Buddha figure.

Pl. 42 : Carnelian bead in shape of a dog from Kauśāmbī (Uttar Pradesh), Early centuries CE.

Pl. 43 : Agate beads from Ban Don Ta Phet, Thailand, fourth-third century BCE.

Pl. 44 : Carnelian beads from Ban Don Ta Phet, Thailand, fourth-third century BCE.

Pl. 45 : A glass "beryl" from Ban Don Ta Phet, Thailand, fourth–third century BCE.

Pl. 46 : Kṛṣṇa lifting mount Govardhana, stone, Bangkok National Museum, sixth century CE.

Pl. 47 : Personification of Garuḍa, Stucco, Bangkok National Museum, sixth-seventh century CE.

Pl. 48 : Elephant in stone on Kayama Hill, Puri District, Orissa.

Key to Transliteration

VOWELS

अ *a*	आ *ā*	इ *i*	ई *ī*	उ *u*	ऊ *ū*
(but)	(palm)	(it)	(beet)	(put)	(pool)
ऋ *ṛ*	ए *e*	ऐ *ai*	ओ *o*	औ *au*	
(rhythm)	(play)	(air)	(toe)	(loud)	

CONSONANTS

Guttural	क *ka*	ख* *kha*	ग *ga*	घ *gha*	ङ *ṅa*
	(skate)	(blockhead)	(gate)	(ghost)	(sing)
Palatal	च *ca*	छ* *cha*	ज *ja*	झ *jha*	ञ *ña*
	(chunk)	(catch him)	(john)	(hedgehog)	(bunch)
Cerebral	ट *ṭa*	ठ* *ṭha*	ड *ḍa*	ढ* *ḍha*	ण* *ṇa*
	(start)	(anthill)	(dart)	(godhead)	(under)
Dental	त *ta*	थ *tha*	द *da*	ध* *dha*	न *na*
	(path)	(thunder)	(that)	(breathe)	(numb)
Labial	प *pa*	फ* *pha*	ब *ba*	भ *bha*	म *ma*
	(spin)	(philosophy)	(bin)	(abhor)	(much)
Semi-	य *ya*	र *ra*	ल *la*	व *va*	
vowels	(young)	(drama)	(luck)	(vile)	
Sibilants	श *śa*	ष *ṣa*	स *sa*	ह *ha*	
	(shove)	(bushel)	(so)	(hum)	
Others	क्ष *kṣa*	त्र *tra*	ज्ञ *jña*	ळ* ḷ	ॠ* *ṝ*
	(*kṣatriya*)	(*triśūla*)	(*jñānī*)	(*play*)	

अं (ं)*ṁ anusvāra* (nasalisation of preceding vowel) like *saṁskṛti*

अः *visarga* = *ḥ* (aspiration of preceding vowel) like (*prātaḥ*)

ऽ *Avagraha* consonant #'consonant (like:- *ime 'vasthitā*)

Anusvāra at the end of a line is presented by m (म्) and not ṁ

HINDI LETTERS (extras)

ँ = *ñ*	ं = ṅ	ड़ = *ṛa*	ढ़ = *ṛha*
(*candrabindu*)	(*anusvāra*)		

* No exact English equivalents for these letters.

1

Introduction

THE emergence of all art is tied to deeper civilizational processes. It is universally observed that high art has flourished in places that emerged as hubs of power and privilege: capitals of kingdoms, large urban centres, crossroads of trade, far off places associated with the lives of saints and spiritual beings or else places associated with mythological narratives such as my own city of Prayag, Allahabad. With respect to India, forms of "high" art first appear in the third millennium BCE when the Bronze Age Haṛappan or the Indus-Saraswatī Civilization was flourishing. The Haṛappan Civilization (3000–1800 BCE), characterized by town planning, high craft skills and widespread trade, represents the first cycle of urbanization in India. Before that, the many settlements of the pre-Haṛappan cultures flourishing in the piedmont regions of Baluchistan and Sindh between 4000 and 3000 BCE anticipated the high art and craft of the Harappans. The lissom figure of a female dancer created in bronze, the calm visage of the so-called bearded "priest-king" in limestone and the exquisite unicorns, bulls and mythological beings carved in intaglio on the seals are expressive of the fine aesthetic sense and high craft skills of the Harappans. The second cycle of urbanization, marked by the rise of the first Iron Age polities (*mahājanapada*s) in northern India, commenced around early first millennium BCE in the Gaṅgā Valley, nearly a thousand years after the decline of Harappan cities. It is the second urban phase that concerns us here, the mature stage of the Early Historic period, broadly covering the time span from 300 BCE to CE 500.

Two phases of sculptural art can be observed in the latter period. The first phase was dictated by monumentality and architecture and is reflected in the stone work of the Mauryan period (fourth–third century BCE). Well-known examples of Mauryan art are the famous Didārgañj *yakṣī* (*fig.* 1) and the elephant figure at Dhauli in Orissa (*fig.* 55) and the polished sandstone pillars inscribed with the edicts of Emperor Aśoka (Plate: 1). In the second-first century BCE we see constructions in stone of major Buddhist *stūpa*s at Bharhut, Vaiśālī, Sārnāth, Kauśāmbī, Bodh-Gayā, Sāñcī, Amarāvatī, etc (*Map* 1, *fig.* 2). The Buddhist *stūpa*s showcased the indigenous Indian art in the form of *yakṣa* and *yakṣī* figures and depiction of *Jātaka* tales in panels (*fig.* 3). The figures of men and women were carved in low relief, high relief as well as in the round. The Buddha was shown in aniconic form by way of symbolisms like his own feet (*pāda*) (*fig.* 60), his seat under the *bodhi* tree (*fig.* 30), his turban (*fig.* 9). The carvings in the rock-cut caves in Bihar (Lomas Ṛṣi Cave at Barābar near Bodh-Gayā) and on the eastern (Thotlakoṇḍa, Salihundam) and western coasts (Bhaja, Bedsā) also anticipated the classic sculptural art that flowered in the BCE–CE transition (*Map* 2). Concomitantly, Brāhmanical icons also began to occur in the last centuries BCE, as seen in the figures of Kṛṣṇa and Balarāma on the coins of the Bactrian king Agathocles (178 BCE) and the Śiva image at Guḍimallam from Andhra Pradesh dated to the second century BCE (*fig.* 34).

The second phase in ancient sculptural art commenced with the appearance of many more Brāhmanical images as well as Buddhist and Jaina religious imagery during the BCE–CE transition. This was the outcome of a general shift from aniconic to iconic forms of worship. This shift was no less than a revolution in Buddhist and Brāhmanical religious thought. In the Vedas, Indra, Sūrya and all other gods were worshipped as celestial powers, divine energies with the power of life and death. Initially, these gods were eulogized in the literary and oral traditions and not in the visual arts. Though these energies began to be shown as earthly beings (Indra in the Bhaja relief and on terracottas of lower Bengal), the rise of religious theism, expressed in worship of the divinity in anthropomorphic medium, completely changed the nature of the Brāhmanical, Buddhist and Jaina faiths. There seems to have been an element of competition among the various

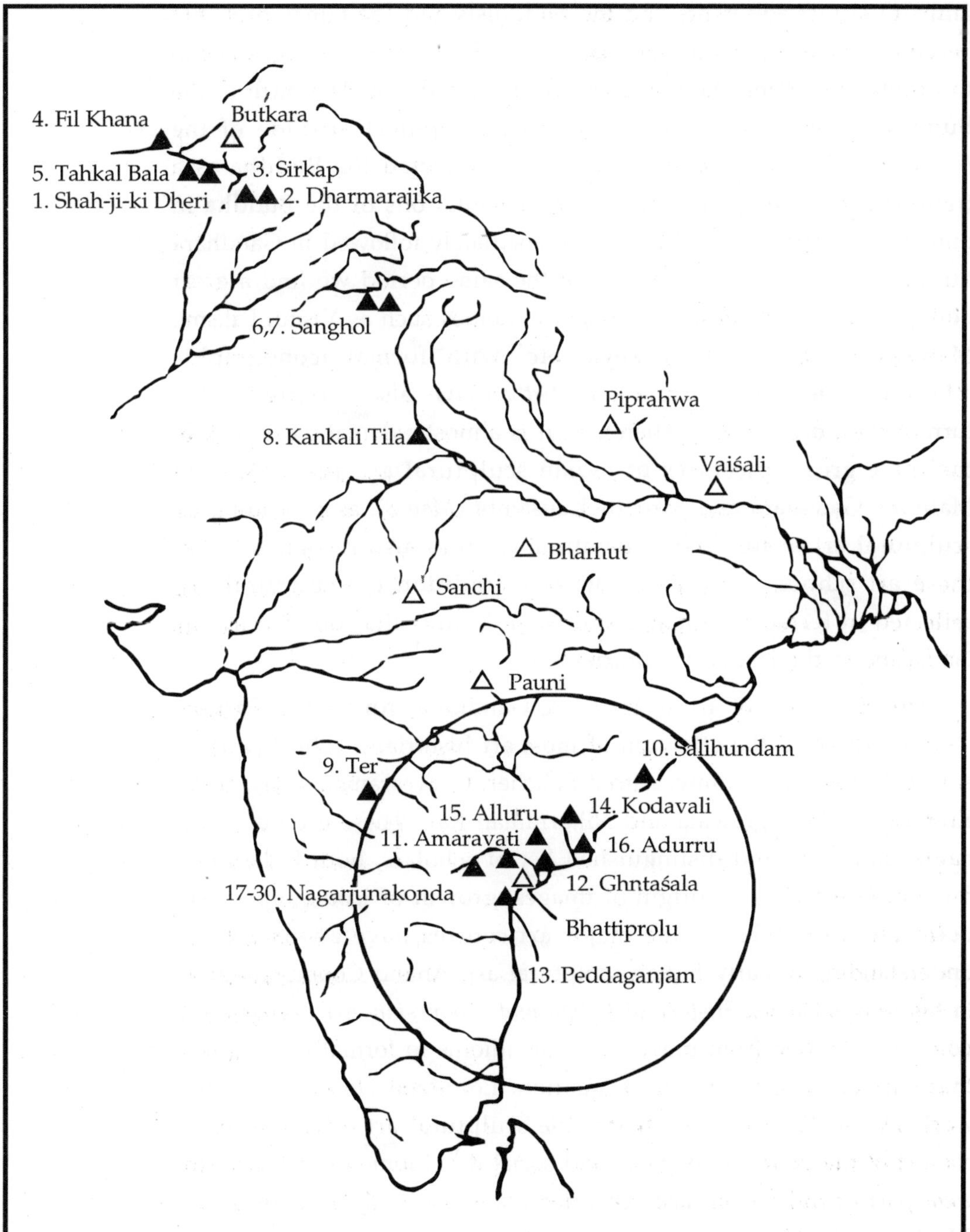

Map 1: Location of early *stūpa* sites in India with special reference to Andhra Pradesh.

faiths to attract adherents and the Buddhists and the Jainas probably became convinced of the new path when Brāhmanical images began to proliferate among the populace and pose a threat. The birth of the Buddha image lies in the changed philosophical attitude of the *Mahāsaṁghika* sect of Buddhism which projected the Buddha as a transcendental being. The earliest representations of the Buddha in human form appeared in Mathurā, immediately followed in Gandhāra during the BCE–CE transition. It is in the same period we find a great multiplication of images of Brāhmanical deities such as Viṣṇu, Lakṣmī, Mahiṣāsuramardinī, Kārttikeya, etc. with formal iconographic attributes. The images of the Jaina *tīrthaṁkara*s also appeared at the turn of the Common Era. Therefore, it is almost axiomatic to speak of the three great epicentres of Indian sculptural art, the schools of Mathurā, Gandhāra and Sārnāth–Kauśāmbī (*Map* 3), as pervading all sculptural art of the first millennium CE. It is also recognized that these art schools drew from the rich tradition of sculptural art, reflected in terracotta images and *yakṣa* figures that dot the Indian landscape in the last two centuries BCE.

The epicentres of art — Mathurā, Gandhāra, Amarāvatī, Sārnāth — have attracted the attention of most art historians: John Marshall, Anand K. Coomaraswamy, Alfred Foucher, C. Sivaramamurthy, Stella Kramrisch, V.S. Agrawala and Niharranjan Ray. These are but a few names in a long and distinguished list of scholars, both Indian and foreign. Researches on origin of images, growth of iconography and delineation of styles of the major art centres have advanced our understanding of early Indian sculptural art. Anand Coomaraswamy, in his seminal work *History of Indian and Indonesian Art* explores the point of transition from universal Vedic idioms to formalized imagery that happened in the BCE–CE transition. Lohuizen De Leeuw in her work *The Scythian Period* situates the sculptural art of Gandhāra in context of the political, religious and social developments in the north-west part of India from last centuries BCE to the middle centuries CE. S.P. Gupta, in *The Roots of Indian Art* traces the absorption of foreign (Achaemenid, Greek and West Asian) art motifs which contributed to the rise of Early Historic sculptural art from 300 BCE.

However, the sustained focus on the "epicentres" of art has also bred a certain inclusiveness in appreciation of early sculptural art. What lay beyond the famous schools of art, in the "peripheral" coastlands for instance? Were the coastal regions static in terms of art activity, mere recipients of the classical art styles from the interiors? How much of the sculptural art of Mathurā, Pāṭaliputra, Gandhāra and Sārnāth–Kauśāmbī spread to the littorals? Did the coastlands also develop their own styles in sculptural art? Did coastal art exhibit syncretic qualities? Did "reverse" transmissions take place from the coastlands into the interiors? In this study, the early sculptural art of the Indian coastlands is not viewed as marginal to the classical forms that developed in the interiors. In fact, the Amarāvatī school of art emerged on the eastern coast of India, in the estuary of the Kṛṣṇā Valley. The Buddha figures of Amarāvatī became the models for Buddha images created in South-East Asia in the mid-first millennium CE. In this sense, the Amarāvatī school became an epicentre disseminating its style across the Bay of Bengal. Though much has been written about early sculptural art on the Indian coastlands, the researches have been fragmentary, restricted to a certain part of the littoral. An overview of early sculptural art on the Indian coastland would, hopefully, fill the gap.

The choice of the coastlands is also inspired by the notion of interactivity. All ideas, including expressions of culture, change as they encounter new situations. Of course, powerful classical forms of art also influence and mould local/regional art traditions. The theme of transmission, absorption and syncretism is basic to notion of interactivity. The coastlands are viewed as cross-cultural realms, places most conducive for absorption of new ideas and for syncretic manifestations. As I shall attempt to show, the early sculptural art traditions on the Indian coastlands were influenced by the classicism of the interior as well as by art influences from overseas. There was also the role of local and folk traditions, prominent in many areas, particularly in the south.

The principal themes taken up in this monograph are:

- To trace the spread of the major styles of ancient Indian sculptural art from the "epicentres" to the "peripheries," i.e. from the hinterland to the coast.
- To specifically focus upon the spread of major religious iconographic forms like that of Buddha, Jina, Śiva, Viṣṇu, etc.
- To see how the indigenous styles on the Indian coastlands mingled with the classical art forms.
- To trace the infusion of overseas art (Graeco–Roman, Parthian, etc.) with the classical art forms on the Indian coastlands.
- To distinguish between the aniconic and iconic forms of worship and their reflection in early sculptural art.
- To trace the spread of secular art themes like royal portraiture, costumes and coiffure to the Indian coastlands.
- To explore the relationship between art and trade.
- To observe the spread of early Indian sculptural art overseas. To review, in particular, the concept of "Indianization of South-East Asia" on the basis of recent evidence from archaeology and art.

To delve further, it is necessary to articulate the notion of sculptural art and the stylistic features of the main schools of sculptural art which flourished in India at the turn of the Common Era. It is clarified that by sculptural art I mean creations in all possible media: stone, bone, metal, terracotta, stucco, etc. I shall, like many others, continue to use the dynastic labels for broad periodization, though not happily, to trace the growth of early sculptural art. The Didārgañj *yakṣī* was a product of the Mauryan Age around third century BCE, and the highly decorated moulded terracottas can be attributed to the succeeding Śuṅga period (second–first century BCE). The Buddha figures of the Mathurā and Gāndhāra schools, which first appeared perhaps 50 years before the beginning of the Kuṣāṇa period (first–third century CE) were different in delineation from those produced in the succeeding Gupta period (fourth–sixth century CE). In the Deccan, the main dynastic art was that of the Sātavāhanas in the BCE–CE transition (third century BCE–third century CE). The Sātavāhanas were succeeded by the Ikṣvākus in the eastern Deccan (third–fourth century CE). The Ikṣvākus created the great architectural complex of Nāgārjunakoṇḍa on the banks of the river Kr̥ṣṇā during the third-fourth centuries CE. In western India, particularly in the littoral state of Gujarat, the Western Kṣatrapa dynasty of Scythian stock held sway from the first century BCE to fifth century CE. After defining the styles of the major schools and delineating the main art categories (aniconic, iconic, secular), the discussion will move on to the "routes of transmission." It is assumed that ancient sculptural art was transmitted along established trade routes through which also moved the practitioners of religions, erecting or carving edifices of and for the gods and goddesses of their choice and beliefs. Thereafter, three successive sections on the western, southern and eastern coastlands reconstruct the early sculptural art of the Indian littoral regions and attempt to show how classical, local and overseas idioms mingled at the edge of the Indian Ocean. The section on spread of art overseas is followed by a critical review of the old idea of "Indianization of South-East Asia" and the need to interface archaeological and art historical evidence to properly understand this powerful phenomenon of cultural transmission and acculturation. Before I move on there are two notions of territory which need to be clarified. This book restricts itself to the coastlands of India. This is not to deny the role of the larger outlier of the subcontinent. The littoral states of India comprised the main staging areas of cultural interactivity and are therefore convenient categories of analysis. Second, the coastlands are not strictly defined. I do not mean that I am only studying art found on the beaches and sea-facing locations. The idea is to approximate to the sea, in this case the Arabian Sea and the Bay of Bengal. Therefore the sense of what constitutes a littoral is conveyed at the beginning of the key chapters on the western, southern and eastern coastlands.

dynastic art was that of the Sātavāhanas [illegible] dated [illegible] third century [illegible] succeeded by [illegible] Ikṣvākus [illegible] century [illegible] The [illegible] complex [illegible] lands on the banks of the river Kṛṣṇā during the [illegible] fourth century [illegible] particularly [illegible] in Gujarat, the Western Kṣatrapa [illegible] [illegible] routes [illegible]

[illegible]

[illegible] not mean that I am only [illegible] found on the [illegible] the [illegible] approximate [illegible] Therefore the scope of [illegible] at the beginning of the [illegible] chapter [illegible] northern and western [illegible]

2

Epicentres of Early Indian Sculptural Art

ANY understanding of the syncretism and originality in the early sculptural art of the Indian coastlands needs an anchoring point, a frame of reference which makes it possible to go back to the basic conceptions. The very concept of sculpture is broadly defined in this work as "the art of making objects or figures using solid materials, for example, by carving stone or shaping clay." The act of creatively carving and shaping is not confined to figures but also includes features which are overtly architectural. The rock faces that were cut into large monastic spaces by Buddhists and Jainas in the BCE–CE transition can be viewed as ambitious sculptural ventures. This idea is brilliantly articulated by Percy Brown (1983: 19),

> These rock hewn forms are expert achievements but (by their very nature) they involved no constructional principles, nor do they display any functional properties, their columns signify no adjustment of support to load, the arches carrying no weight, nor do they counteract any thrust, in the whole operation no structural intelligibility is required, as no problem of this nature arise (in any rock-cut architecture form). *In a word, rock-cut architecture to all intents and purposes is not architecture, it is sculpture, but sculpture on a grand and magnificent scale.* (italics and brackets mine).

Also, the rock-cut sanctuaries had various functional and decorative elements which constitute mainstream sculpture, such as the hut carved within the Mauryan period Lomas Ṛṣi cave in Bihar, the images of the Vedic gods Indra and Sūrya in bold relief in the Buddhist rock-cut cave at Bhaja in western India or the *stūpa*s carved in the Buddhist cave groups along the western coast. The earliest rock-cut caves are found in the group of hills that rise from the Gangetic plains in Bihar. In his book, *Roots of Indian Art,* S.P. Gupta traces the growth of rock-cut architecture. To quote:

> The first stage of rock-cut caves and polishing the stone with Mauryan polish arose in Magadh itself, in the Son Bhandar cave of Rajgir, from where it goes to Barabar in Mauryan times; lastly to Bhaja and eastern *ghāṭ* caves in post-Mauryan times; to Kondivte and Guntapalle, only the cave form goes, not the polish.
>
> — Gupta 1980: 306-07

This spread from the interiors to the coastlands, delineated by Gupta in a map (*Map* 2), would have taken nearly 200 years from third century BCE (Mauryan times) to first century BCE. Early rock-cut caves also appear in the deep south, in Tamil Nadu and Sri Lanka. The caves in the deep south were spartan affairs, like those in the Barābar group, and were made by Jaina, Buddhist and Brāhmanical mendicants who had arrived from northern India. These early caves have been dated to the second-first century BCE on the basis of Tamil–Brāhmī inscriptions (*Encyclopaedia of Indian Archaeology*, vol. I: 151). However, these caves were simple ones. It is observed that the conception of rock-cut caves matured faster on the western (Maharashtra) and eastern (Andhra) coasts of India; with sculptures in bold relief, the columns with capitals and the decorative facades a far cry from the austerity of the early rock-cut caves in the Gangetic Valley. The earliest of the rock-cut caves near the coastlands, such as the Jaina Udayagiri–Khaṇḍagiri group in Orissa (second–first century BCE) and the Bhaja and Pītalkhora caves dug by Buddhists (second–first century BCE) are embellished with *aṣṭamaṅgala* signs, *yakṣī* figures, *mithuna*s and *dvārapāla*s, etc.

Besides rock-cut sanctuaries, the other forms of architecture with strong sculptural features are *stūpa*s, frieze/panels as well as pillars and *sanctum sanctorum* or *maṇḍapa*s of early temples.

Stūpas

The free standing *stūpa*s were large constructs having a central drum with hemispherical top (*aṇḍa*) surmounted by a upright (*harmikā*) and parasol (Kārle). The architecture of the early *stūpa*s at Bodh-Gayā, Bharhut, Sāñcī and Amarāvatī was unique (*fig.* 2). A *stūpa* was

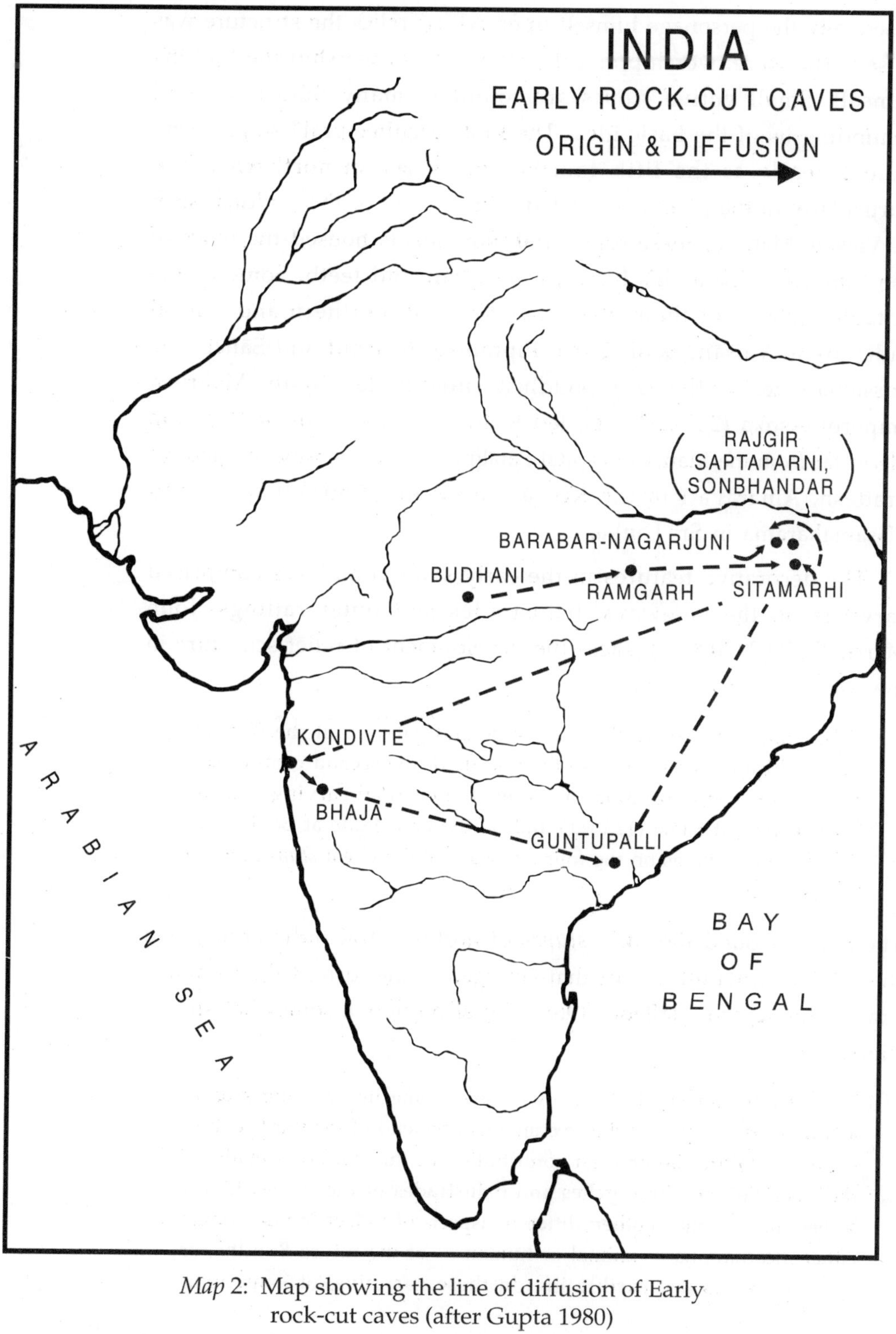

Map 2: Map showing the line of diffusion of Early rock-cut caves (after Gupta 1980)

essentially the personage himself upon whose relics the structure was raised. Therefore, worshipping the *stūpa* was to worship the Buddha himself. Small votive *stūpa*s are found in many Buddhist sites, reminding us of the basic idea. The first "architectural" *stūpa*s were built as early as the fifth–fourth century BCE in northern India, particularly in the places associated with the life of the Buddha, such as Vaiśālī. Many of these sepulchral monuments housed the relics of the Buddha, such as his bones, ashes, hair and teeth. Some of the notable remains of the early *stūpa*s found in northern and central India are at Vaiśālī, Bodh-Gayā, Piprahwa, Bharhut and Sāñcī. The missionary zeal of the early Buddhists, fired no less by the Mauryan emperor Aśoka (269-232 BCE), led to the establishment of *stūpa*s in places far from the Mauryan capital Pāṭaliputra, such as Sāñcī in Madhya Pradesh, Amarāvatī in the Kṛṣṇā Valley and Anurādhapura and Tissamaharama in Sri Lanka.

The decorative features in the early *stūpa* complexes comprised carvings on the gateways, balustrades and outer railings. John Marshall (1960/2000: 7) traces the development of relief sculpture in the *stūpa* sites. To quote:

> oldest among these are the balustrade and gateway of the Bharhut *stūpa*, which are assignable to the middle of the second century BCE. Then follow, in chronological order, the original carvings on the Second *stūpa* at Sāñcī (125 BCE) and on the balustrade at Bodh-Gayā (75 BCE), the carvings on the four gateways of the Great *stūpa* at Sāñcī (50 BCE). . . .

The reliefs around the early *stūpa*s of north-central India anticipated the full-blown sculptural art that emerged at the turn of the Common Era. In this regard, Hallade (1968: 179) also offers a somewhat similar view:

> The early Indian or Sāñcī style was developing in the Ganges basin and the northern part of the Deccan about the end of the third century BCE. In sculpture the greatest contribution of this period is made by the bas-reliefs on the porches and balustrades of the *stūpa*s. Lively scenes succeed one another; different aspects of Indian life describing either incarnations — animal or human — of the future Buddha, or episodes of his last earthly life. In these narrative, or sometimes

> decorative works the sculptures grew progressively more skilled; at Bharhut (second century BCE to the middle of the first century CE) they invented an iconography in which the Buddha was represented only by a symbol.

The reliefs carved in the early rock-cut Jaina caves at Udayagiri–Khaṇḍagiri were influenced by the *stūpa* art of Bharhut–Sāñcī tradition. So also were the early ivory carvers of western India. The *yakṣī* figures of ivory found at western Indian sites like Bhokardan and Ṭer and abroad at Pompei in Italy belong to the genre of sculpture first defined by the alluring divine female forms, like the *yakṣī*s on the brackets of the gateway of Sāñcī *stūpa*.

Stone Pillars

The erection of carved stone pillars was a feature of the pre-Mauryan period. The Emperor Aśoka has clearly stated in one of his pillar-edicts (Topra Pillar text, Delhi) that he has got his edicts engraved on pillars erected by himself and on those existing from before (Sircar 1998: 59-62). The Aśokan pillars were erected at major crossroads as well as sacred places in front of *stūpa*s and inscribed with the famous edicts of the Emperor that were promulgated as part of his policy of *dharmaghoṣa* initiated after the tragic Kaliṅga War (Plate 1). The sophistication and beauty of the highly polished pillars was enhanced by fixing on it with tenon a decorative capital showing finely modelled animal figures sometimes further topped by *dharmacakra*s. The lion capital of the Aśokan pillar from Sārnāth is an exquisite example of Mauryan art. The capital, which has been adopted as the state emblem of modern India, comprises four crouching lions set out back to back and facing the four cardinal directions. A similar capital was fixed on top of the pillar erected by Aśoka in front of the *stūpa* at Sāñcī. Other pillar capitals comprise a bull atop the Aśokan pillar at Rampurva (Uttar Pradesh) and an elephant atop the pillar at Sankisa.

Terracottas

Terracotta figures of fine workmanship have been found in the Haṛappan sites. However, the art of terracotta came into its own in the Mauryan period, when some exquisite human figures were made by applique at Mathurā, Buxar and Patna. Some of these terracottas are of secular nature and dated to the fourth–third century BCE. In the succeeding Śuṅga period (second–first century BCE) we find moulded terracotta plaques depicting intricately jewelled female figures in frontal posture and scenes of everyday life, including Bacchanalian revelry. In this period we also find hints of religious iconography, such as the terracotta figures from lower Bengal depicting Gajalakṣmī, Indra and Gaṇeśa. The little clay carts remind us of the ancient Sanskrit play *Mṛcchakaṭikam.* In the Kuṣāṇa period (first–third century CE), the terracottas are mostly three-dimensional. A perusal of the Allahabad Museum collection showed much portraiture, with busts of what seem to be noblemen resident at the ancient Gangetic cities of Kauśāmbī, Bhītā, Jhūsī, etc. Also produced in this period are busts of the Buddha, *bodhisattva*s and Brāhmanical images. The bust of Śiva discovered at Śṛṅgaverapura near Allahabad is a prime example of religious themes in the terracotta art of northern India. In the Gupta period (fourth–sixth century CE), the terracotta art reaches its climax. Large images of Brāhmanical deities, often life-size ones, like the images of Gaṅgā and Yamunā from Ahicchatra, become popular.

Sculptural Art on Stone

The mainstream iconographic forms first appeared on the rectangular copper coins of King Agathocles found in the Ai Khanum hoard dated to 176 BCE. These coins depicted the Vaiṣṇavite deities Kṛṣṇa and Balarāma. We then come upon classical Brāhmanical, Buddhist and Jaina iconography in the stone art of Mathurā and Gandhāra and later in the great art centres of Amarāvatī, Nāgārjunakoṇḍa and Sārnāth (*Map* 3). However, it has to be understood that what we call the mainstream iconography (images of Viṣṇu, Buddha, Jaina *tīrthaṁkara*s) were inspired by earlier anthropomorphic forms of deities worshipped since times immemorial. For example, the image of the Buddha was conceived on the basis of the large *yakṣa* figures in stone that were worshipped in the Mathurā region (*fig.* 4), although S.P. Gupta has recently opined that it may also have been modelled on the terracotta Śiva image of the pre-Kuṣāṇa period. The *yakṣa*s and their female counterparts, the *yakṣī*s, were semi-divinities in human

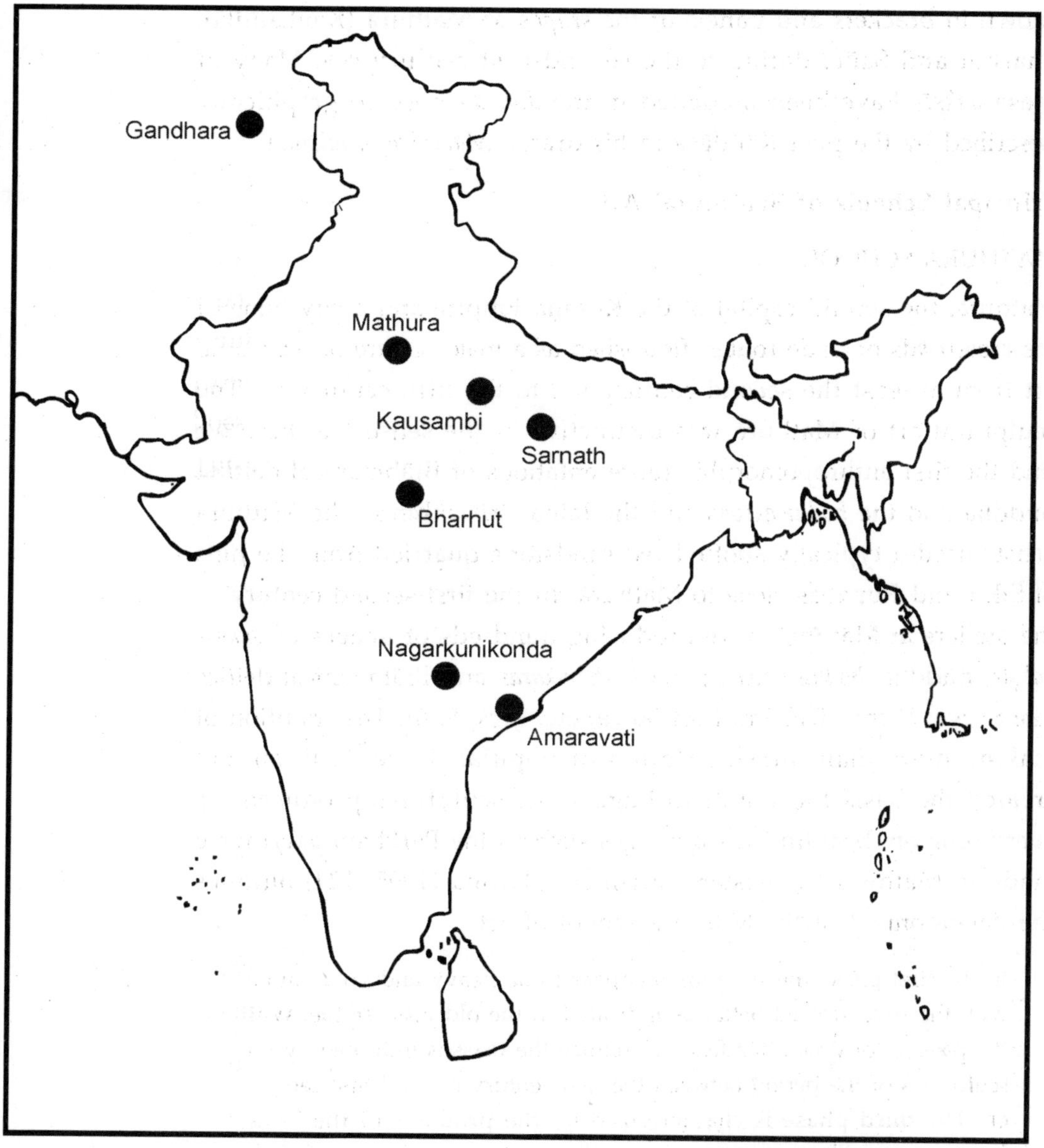

Map 3: Location of major schools of sculptural art in ancient India

form that were revered by common people before the advent of the human representations of gods and goddesses by the great schools of sculptural art at Mathurā and Gandhāra. Some of the *yakṣīs* are shown in brackets and panels of the *stūpas* at Mathurā (Kaṅkālīṭīlā), Bharhut and Sāñcī dating to the second-first century BCE. Many of these *yakṣīs* have been modelled in the *dohada* pose so graphically described by the poet Kālidāsa in his drama *Mālavikāgnimitram*.

Principal Schools of Sculptural Art

MATHURA SCHOOL

Mathurā, the second capital of the Kuṣāṇa Empire and a city lying at the crossroads of trade routes, flourished as a major centre of sculptural art from at least the second century BCE to the fifth century CE. The sculptural art of Mathurā was distinctive in the sense that here we find the first anthropomorphic representations of Brāhmanical deities, Buddha and the *bodhisattvas* and the Jaina *tīrthaṁkaras*. The Mathurā artists used a typically spotted red sandstone quarried from the hills of Sikri and Rupabas close to Mathurā. In the first-second century CE the ateliers at Mathurā were producing hundreds of images of *yakṣa-yakṣīs*, Buddha, *bodhisattvas*, Jaina *tīrthaṁkaras* and Brāhmanical deities like Sūrya, Viṣṇu, Kubera, Kārttikeya, etc. (*figs.* 5, 6). The tradition of making more than life-size statues of popular deities (*yakṣas*) had created the basis for a shift to huge stone sculptures produced for every religion. Beautiful *yakṣa* images such as the Parkham *yakṣa* were made in Mathurā by master craftsmen. Sharma (1995: 124) outlines the development of the Mathurā school of art:

> In the first phase the sculptures appear to be heavy and voluminous with the front treated better as indicated in the old *yakṣa* statue. With the passage of time a tendency to reduce the mass is indicated by the sculptures of the period between the first century BCE and first century CE. The third phase is characterized by the products of the Śaka-Kuṣāṇa age. These are mundane, sensuous, graceful and full of movement. A good deal of foreign traits are amalgamated with the indigenous trends. The fourth phase of development towards sublimation is indicated by the specimens of the Kuṣāṇa-Gupta period. The fifth phase represents the classical culmination of the Gupta period when sculptural art reached its zenith.

Besides the religious themes, the sculptural art of Mathurā was also focused on "secular" images. Williams (1989: 330) describes the eclectic quality of this art school:

> The amount of sculpture produced in Mathurā was large, whether confined to one or one-and-a-half centuries. In either case, moreover, it was cosmopolitan, including elements derived from the Kuṣāṇas' own Iranian traditions as well as from Gandhāra. This sculpture reflects the prosperity of the city and its critical role within a network of international trade. The speed of stylistic change is more rapid than in most other periods in early Indian art. Certainly, this was a period when new religious solutions were worked out, leading to dramatic acceptance of stone images of the Buddha and of *tīrthaṁkaras*, as well as to the burgeoning of new Hindu iconographic types.

The beginning of the so-called "Kuṣāṇa Art of Mathurā" certainly goes back to the first century BCE on the basis of stratigraphic evidence from excavated sites like Soṅkh, Mathurā and Śr̥ṅgaverapura in the Gangetic basin. In particular, the Kuṣāṇa artworks that are called "dynastic art" include images of Kuṣāṇa kings and courtiers, the most impressive examples being the large-size statues of Wima Khadphises and Kaniṣka from Mat near Vr̥ndāvan.

GĀNDHĀRA SCHOOL

The Gāndhāra school of art emerged in the north-west part of India during the BCE-CE transition. The artists used a grey-blue schist stone quarried from the hills south of the Hindu-Kush range. Principally it was an art devoted to Buddhism, to the life of the Buddha and his previous incarnations as *bodhisattvas* (*fig.* 7). According to Hallade (1968: 75), "The art of Gandhāra, developing as it was in the monasteries, is of an essentially religious character. Consecrated to Buddhism, it perpetuated the ideals of an earlier art of India which dates from the time of the second century BCE and was still evolving until the middle of the first century CE. There are various theories about the foundation and rise of Gāndhāran Art. Some scholars like Foucher say it was influenced by Greek art and according to others like Mortimer Wheeler the impact of Roman art is visible. The Roman influence on Gāndhāran art is evident in certain examples. One is the statue of a goddess identified as Roma, the patron deity of the city of Rome in the early centuries CE. The Indian themes, as well as styles in dress, coiffure, etc. make the art of Gandhāra truly syncretic. Some of the bas-reliefs show the various dresses and hence suggest incorporation of various elements. There are scenes from Buddha's life in which we find men and women in Greek attire. Other scenes show a group of men in Indian dress, the *dhotī*. Still another frieze depicts bearded men in flowing tunics and soft trousers typical of Kuṣāṇa wear. The Parthian and Sassanian influences are also seen in the execution of scenes."

Comparisons have been made between the centres of sculptural art at Gandhāra and Mathurā which were largely contemporaneous, flourishing during the Kuṣāṇa period. Both the schools of art saw incipient creation of sculptures in the last centuries BCE and the climax of art activity in the period of the Kuṣāṇas, from first-third century CE and production of high quality images up to the mid-first millennium CE. Whereas Gandhāra was influenced solely by Buddhism and hence has an austere character, the art of Mathurā celebrated all creeds and beliefs. One of the contentious issues between the two art schools has centred around where the Buddha image was first created. It is clear that the Buddha image appeared almost together at Gandhāra and Mathurā in the BCE–CE transition, with the probability of its conception at Mathurā at least 50 years before Gandhāra. The Buddha figures in the two schools were differently modelled. The Gāndhāra Buddha has some Hellenistic features such as curly hair, sharp facial features, often with incorporation of moustache as well as pleated garment resembling the folds of the Roman toga. The Mathurā Buddha had a typical snail-curl hair style, Indic facial features drawn from the earlier tradition of image making in Central India, thin cloth covering only one shoulder and often depicted in *abhaya-mudrā*. Over a period of time, each school borrowed from the other. The borrowings are most conspicuous in the Buddha images. The Mathurā school assimilated the Gāndhāra drapery covering both shoulders; wavy hair; Scythian dress; round pillars with acanthus leaf on capitals, etc. The Gāndhāra school assimilated: curly hair; lotus seat; drapery covering one shoulder only; *abhaya* pose; monks wearing *dhotī*; Maitreya as ascetic wearing scared thread, etc. (Asthana and Jha 1999).

The spread of the Gāndhāra art style to the Indian coastlands is reflected in the early sculptural art on the western coast of India, specifically in Buddha heads found in the Maldives and terracotta figures in lower Bengal.

ART OF ANDHRA

The predominantly Buddhist art of Andhra developed at Amarāvatī and Nāgārjunakoṇḍa in the lower Kṛṣṇā Valley. The Amarāvatī *stūpa*, with a pillar in its front, was built in the third century BCE and continuously renovated till the third century CE. The *stūpa* at Amarāvatī was the hub of early Buddhist art and architecture on the south-eastern coast of India. The Amarāvatī *stūpa* was embellished with sculptures in generally low relief (Knox 1992). These depicted the great *stūpa* itself, narrative scenes from the life of Buddha, the Jātaka tales, symbolisms signifying the Buddha (such as the *buddhapāda*) and figures of *yakṣa*s and *yakṣī*s (*figs.* 8, 9). Amarāvatī inspired the art and architecture of Nāgārjunakoṇḍa, a riverine valley upstream of Amarāvatī. Excavations at Nāgārjunakoṇḍa have brought to light Buddhist chapels and Brāhmanical temple complexes built along the river Kṛṣṇā. Nāgārjunakoṇḍa flourished in the third–fourth century CE, the period of Ikṣvāku rule. According to Sharma (1995: 228-29) the appearance of the Buddha figure at Amarāvatī in the second half of the second century CE was a direct borrowing from Mathurā (*fig.* 32). Van Lohuizen was of the opinion that the snail-shell curls and uncovered feet, typical of Mathurā Buddha image, were imitated in the sculptural art of Amarāvatī. However it is sometimes felt that much of what seems to be of Graeco-Roman derivation at Amarāvatī–Nāgārjunakoṇḍa was directly transmitted from the western world because of the overseas trade of the Kṛṣṇā Valley.

SĀRNĀTH SCHOOL

The remains of the ancient site of Sārnāth lie on the outskirts of modern Varanasi. This was the holy spot where Buddha preached his sermon to his first five disciples. There was no art worth the name at Sārnāth during the Kuṣāṇa period, except a large image of the Buddha. The art school of Sārnāth sprung into prominence in the fifth century CE. The Gupta period art of Sārnāth was derived from the Mathurā school. A life-size standing image of the Buddha, made in the Kuṣāṇa period in the typical red Mathurā sandstone, has been discovered at Sārnāth. This shows that there was contact between Mathurā and Sārnāth in the early centuries CE. The Kuṣāṇa period image of the Buddha may have become a model for the Gupta period images of the Buddha produced at Sārnāth. Interestingly, a standing Buddha image found at Mathurā was an import from Sārnāth. The standing image of the Buddha created in Sārnāth is characterized by slenderness. The Buddha is depicted draped in a transparent gossamer cloth and his limbs are slender (*fig.* 10). The Buddha image also appeared at the same time as Sārnāth at Ajantā in western India. The Buddha image of Ajantā was more thickset than the Sārnāth statues. One of the famous images of Buddha from Sārnāth is the seated figure of the master on a lotus seat and in *dharmacakra-pravartana-mudrā* (*fig.* 11). According to Craven (1986: 113),

> The justly renowned Gupta sculptural style appears to have grown out of the Kuṣāṇa style which survived at Mathurā. By the end of the fourth century or the beginning of the fifth a distinctive icon had been created.

The brief review of the main centres of sculpture art and architecture is necessary to understand the spread of "mainstream" art to the Indian coastlands and also discern the local elements that permeated into classical idioms in the littoral regions.

3

Routes of Transmission

SEVERAL of the great art centres, including Mathurā and Gandhāra, lay at or near the crossroads of trade routes and epitomize the connection between art and trade (*Map* 4). These schools of art were unique and innovative as well as syncretic. The influences of the art schools penetrated in different ways into the Indian coastlands. The route from northern India to the southern coastlands is defined by *stūpa* sites such as Bharhut, Sāñcī, Pauni, Sannathi and Amarāvatī (*Map* 1). The *stūpa* site of Amarāvatī is located in the estuary of the river Kṛṣṇā, at the edge of the Bay of Bengal, and became over time an epicentre for spread of sculptural art to South-East Asia. To the west, the influence of the art of Mathurā can be seen in the terracotta figurines excavated close to the Saurāṣṭra coast. In the east, a red stone *bodhisattva* figure from Candraketugaṛh in lower Bengal indicates the import of a Mathurā work of art in the eastern coastlands. The process of transmission was slow and marked by absorption of the great art styles into the local art idioms. For instance, we find a slow acceptance of the Mathurā school of art in the mid-Gangetic Valley. From the site of Kauśāmbī near Allahabad there has been discovered a red stone image of the Buddha dated to the second regnal year of the Kuṣāṇa king Kaniṣka. An imitation of the same in the local buff sandstone has been discovered from Bhītā. This shows that the Buddha figure was being copied in the Kauśāmbī area. So while tracking the process of transmission of the art styles to the coastlands, we have to also focus on the "intermediate" areas through which the classical art permeated. In this section, I shall attempt to trace the spread of the styles of the main schools of sculptural art along the major trade routes of Early Historic India.

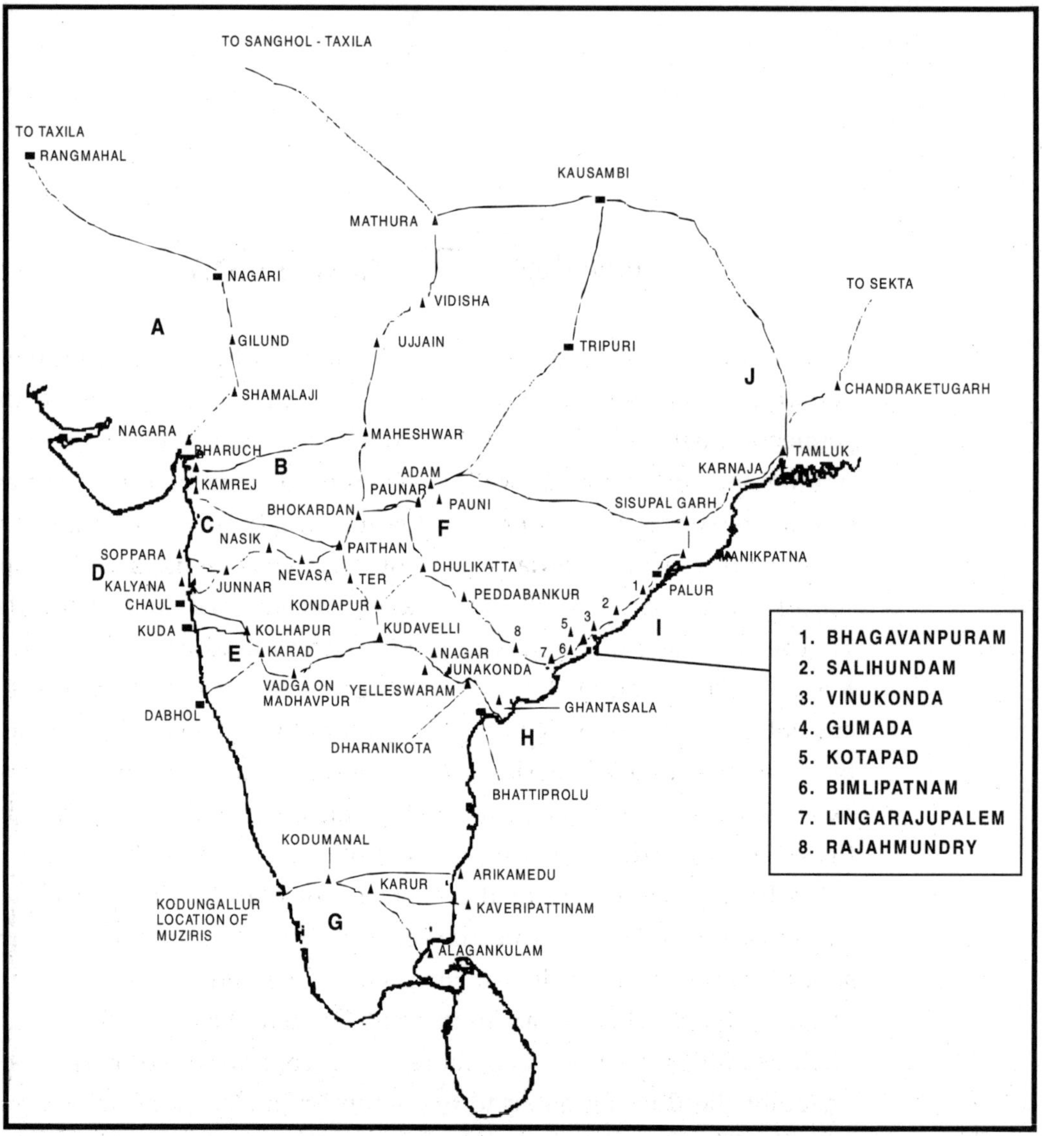

Map 4: Map showing the major trade routes in Early Historic India

The genesis of trade routes lay in the Late Haṛappan migrations and interchange between the Chalcolithic communities of peninsular India. The long distance trade routes had become fully active during the BCE–CE transition. We find a whole-scale transfer of pottery styles, architectural styles (*stūpa*, rock-cut caves), sculptural art styles, ivory crafting, brick size standards and bead crafting techniques from the Gangetic zone to the western, eastern and southern parts of India in the last centuries BCE. However, certain aspects of material culture, like the fine Red Polished Ware and the bead crafting methods developed faster in western India and began to be transmitted to the interiors. Together with the impact of external trade, especially the Roman contact in the early centuries CE, there was a quickening of urbanism and industry in Early Historic India. Interconnections of trade and cultural interactivity happened both ways between the hinterlands and the coastlands. In the discussion below, I have indicated the main trade routes alphabetically (*Map* 4). The routes under review cover much of the Indian mainland. I have defined the routes from the coastlands to the interiors excepting those routes which are totally inland. However, the locus of analysis runs counter to the delineation of the routes, tracing the spread of art styles from the interiors to the coast.

Route A: Western Coast–Rajasthan–Punjab–Northern Pakistan

One of the important trade routes connecting trade-ports on the Gulf of Khambaṭ with resource-areas in Gujarat and further north is plotted as Route A in *Map* 5. This route is visualized as starting from the coastal settlement of Nagara at the head of the Gulf of Khambaṭ and leading up to passes in the Aravalli ranges immediately north of the fortified Early Historic settlement at Śāmalājī. The efficacy of this route for coastal/sea trade is made clear by the excavators of Śāmalājī. To quote from the Śāmalājī excavation report:

> The river Meshvo probably helped the traditional traders, who moved along its banks, and reached the interior from ports of the Arabian Sea. This route entered hilly track from Śāmalājī, so this industrial habitation might have acted as an intermediate station for these traders, and this function probably led to further development of this town. — Mehta and Patel 1967:51

Mediterranean amphorae pieces have been found at the inland trading station of Śāmalājī as well at Devnimorī, an Early Historic Buddhist *stūpa*-site situated a few kilometres from the former. North of Śāmalājī, the land route from the Gujarat coast must have touched major Early Historic settlements in southern Rajasthan. A major crossroad in the

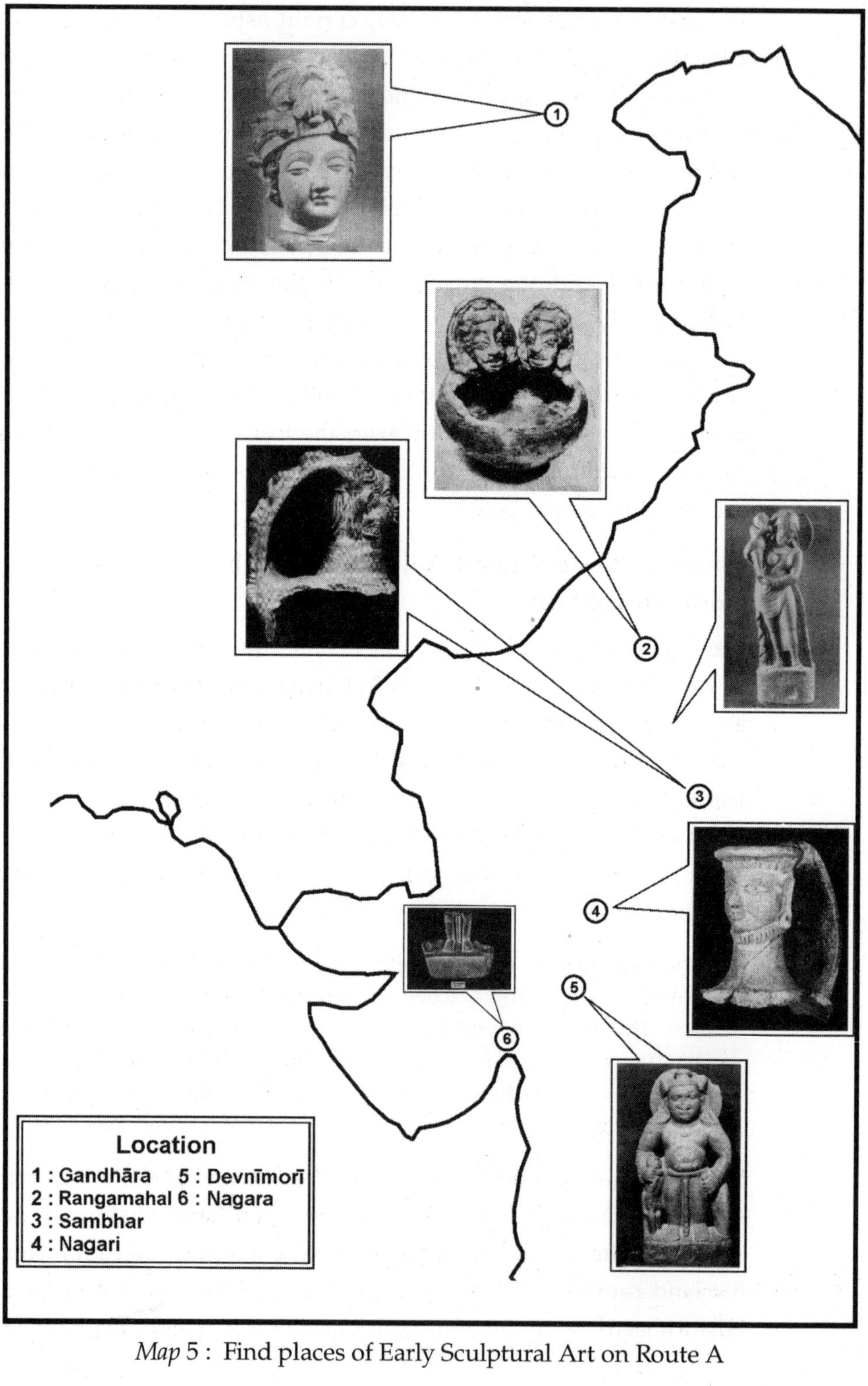

Map 5 : Find places of Early Sculptural Art on Route A

Cittorgaṛh area is represented by the sites of Giluṇḍ and Nāgarī. Nāgarī, in particular, seems to have dominated the passage to Gujarat (*Map* 5). Branching out from Giluṇḍ and Nāgarī the route cut north-west across Rajasthan, passing through the Early Historic settlements around Sambhar and thence to the Raṅgamahal Culture area in the Bikaner District of the state. The Raṅgamahal Culture, flourished in the early mid-first millennium CE in western Rajasthan, midway between the Gujarat coastlands and northern Pakistan. Excavations at Raṅgamahal by a Swedish expedition have brought to light Red Polished Ware "sprinklers" of the type excavated in western India and chalk originating from the Kāṭhiāwāṛ region of Gujarat (Rydh 1959: 147-49, 189-95). The ceramics and other material from Raṅgamahal also show affinity with finds from Taxila in the north-west (Rydh 1959: 155-56). In fact, the archaeological evidence suggests that this land route connected the ports of Gujarat with Gandhāra–Bactria through southern and western Rajasthan in Early Historic times.

Elements of the art of Gandhāra penetrated into the littoral state of Gujarat through this route. A unique clay pot from Raṅgamahal has the busts of two human figures on its lid. The conception of the facial features resembles images made in Gandhāra region in the fourth-fifth century CE (*Map* 5: 2). A statue of Skandamātā from Tanesara-Mahādeva shows Hellenistic quality in the folded drapery and facial features reminiscent of the late phase of the art of Gandhāra (*Map* 5, between 2-3). Some of the terracotta figures from central and southern Rajasthan show a Hellenistic influence which may have come from the Parthian–Sassanian regions of West Asia. This influence is manifested in the moulded figures on handles of terracotta vases, such as the figure of lady from Sambhar and another from Nagar (*Map*. 5: 3, 4). The *stūpa* at Devnimorī near the Arāvallī passes in northern Gujarat also shows the influence of late Gāndhāra art (fifth century CE). According to the excavators, the panels at Devnimorī resembled the late period of the Buddhist art of Gandhāra. To quote:

> This phase is dated by the hoard of 38 coins of the later Kṣatrapa ruler, the latest coin in the series belongs to Svami Rudrasena III,

> ascribable to CE 351. Stylistically also the images and the decorative elements show great affinity to the later Gāndhāra Art
> — *Indian Archaeology — A Review*, 1961-62: 12-13

A number of *gaṇa* figures from Devnimorī, sculpted in green schist and dated to the second-third century CE, seem to be made by local sculptors who incorporated elements from the art of Gandhāra and Mathurā (*Map*. 5: 5). Closer to the Gujarat coast, the influence of Gāndhāran art is seen in the festoons and *mālavāhaka* decorations on rock-cut pillars in the Buddhist cave at Jūnāgaṛh near the Saurāṣṭra coast (discussion in Chapter 4).

Route B: Bharuch–Ujjain–Vidiśā–Mathurā

Another line of communication, beginning at the great port of Bhṛgukaccha/Barygaza (modern Bharuch) (Plate 2), charts its way upstream to Maheśvar on the Narmadā and then turns north towards Ujjain. The Ujjain–Bharuch stretch is mentioned in the *Periplus* (49) as the conduit for a range of northern (Gangetic) goods reaching the coast. As Route B in *Map* 6 shows, the route starting at Bharuch is plotted through Maheśvar–Ujjain–Vidiśā–Mathurā. Maheśvar, in particular, seems to have been a major inland crossroad. Maheśvar, or ancient Mahiṣmatī also received men and goods on the way to northern India from ports of the Western Deccan. A stone plaque of Gaṇeśa dated to fifth-sixth century CE found at Maheśvar indicates art influences from the Gangetic zone (Sankalia et al., 1958: 242-43). This was the trade route along which the art of the Mathurā school permeated to the western coastlands, particularly Saurāṣṭra. While assessing the spread of art styles along Route B, it is to be noted that besides Mathurā, the route also ran through the traditional art centres of Central India like Vidiśā and Sāñcī. This was the place where the old Buddhist *stūpa* art of Bharhut was refined. The ivory carvers of Vidiśā must have been involved in creating the exquisite *yakṣī* figures at the *stūpa* of Sāñcī. These influences were transmitted into the western Deccan where beautiful ivory figurines have been discovered at the sites of Bhokardan and Ṭer (*Map* 7). At Ujjain, a sandstone head of a lioness resembling Graeco-Roman lioness figures is indicative of foreign influences in art (*IAR* 1968-69: 66). Ujjain is mentioned in

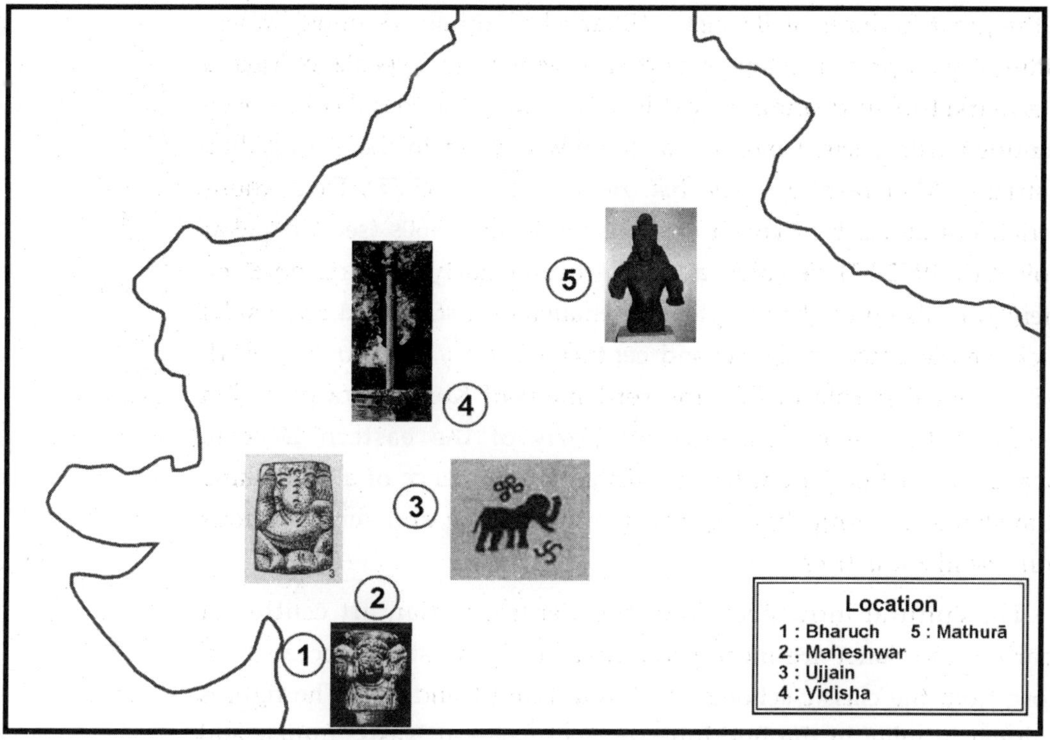

Map 6 : Find places of Early Sculptural Art on Route B

the Greek sea guide, the *Periplus Maris Erythraei* as a seat of royal power, presumably of the Kṣatrapa kings. Ujjain was a hub of ancient Indo-Roman sea trade and a major inland exchange centre mediating between the powerful Kuṣāṇa centres in the north like Mathurā and the ports on the western coast like Bharuch and Kamrej.

Route C: Western Coast–Western Deccan (Trans Axis)

A major overland channel for overseas trade passing through Paiṭhan was the trans-peninsular route described in the *Periplus* (51). The *Periplus* states that Paiṭhan was twenty days journey from the port of Barygaza/Bharuch and a further ten days journey eastward from Paiṭhan lay the market-town of Tagara/Ṭer. This trans-peninsular route is plotted as Route C in *Map* 7. The extension of this route into the eastern Deccan is plotted as Route G in (*Map* 9). The points of Route C are represented by the sites of Bharuch–Kamrej–Paiṭhan–Ṭer–Koṇḍapura. The *Periplus* (49) vividly details the imports and exports of the great harbour of Barygaza/Bharuch. Paiṭhan, as noted, was a centre of semi-precious stone export. The *Periplus* (51) speaks of Tagara as a market-town dealing in textiles. Tagara of the *Periplus* has been identified with ancient mounds at the town of Ṭer in the Osmanabad District of Maharashtra (*Ency. Ind. Arch.*, vol. II: 435-37). Excavations carried out at Ṭer by two different teams in the 1960s (see Chapekar 1969; *IAR* 1972-73) revealed a single-culture Early Historic horizon. There was also brought to light the remains of a *stūpa* and an apsidal brick temple dated to the second century CE (*Ency. Ind. Arch.*, vol. II: 435-37). Further east of Ṭer, the settlement of Koṇḍapura provided access to the resource-areas and ports of the eastern Deccan. Excavations at Koṇḍapura have revealed the existence of a flourishing Sātavāhana township having iron manufacturing and semi-precious stone bead industries.

The cultural influences from the Central Indian art centres of Bharhut and Sāñcī are more prominent in the western Deccan than those from the classic schools of Mathurā and Gandhāra. The figures sculpted in relief in the Buddhist rock-cut caves at Nasik, Junnār and Kārle are inspired by the Buddhist *stūpa* art of Central India. The typical trefoil headdress of male figures and the females in the *mithuna* compositions are related to the "Śuṅga" art of northern India. Interestingly, the art of Amarāvatī, that emerged in the estuary of the river Kṛṣṇā as a result of Buddhist ideas migrating east, was transmitted back to the western Deccan. A *stūpa* discovered at Ṭer shows the influence of the art of Amarāvatī (*fig.* 12). According to the report in *Indian Archaeology — A Review 1961-62*:

> Sri M.N. Deshpande discovered at Ṭer a *stūpa* mound together with several brick structures in the neighbouring fields, indicating the existence of a large Buddhist establishment. He also brought to light five sculptured limestone slabs from the fields in the vicinity of the *stūpa* mounds and from the debris near the Maruti temple at Panwadi, a small village to the north, on the other side of the town of Ṭer. The sculptures belonging to *circa* second century CE, presuppose the existence of a *stūpa* decorated *with limestone slabs in the Andhra fashion.* The find suggests the influence of the Amarāvatī school in the Deccan.
>
> — p. 102

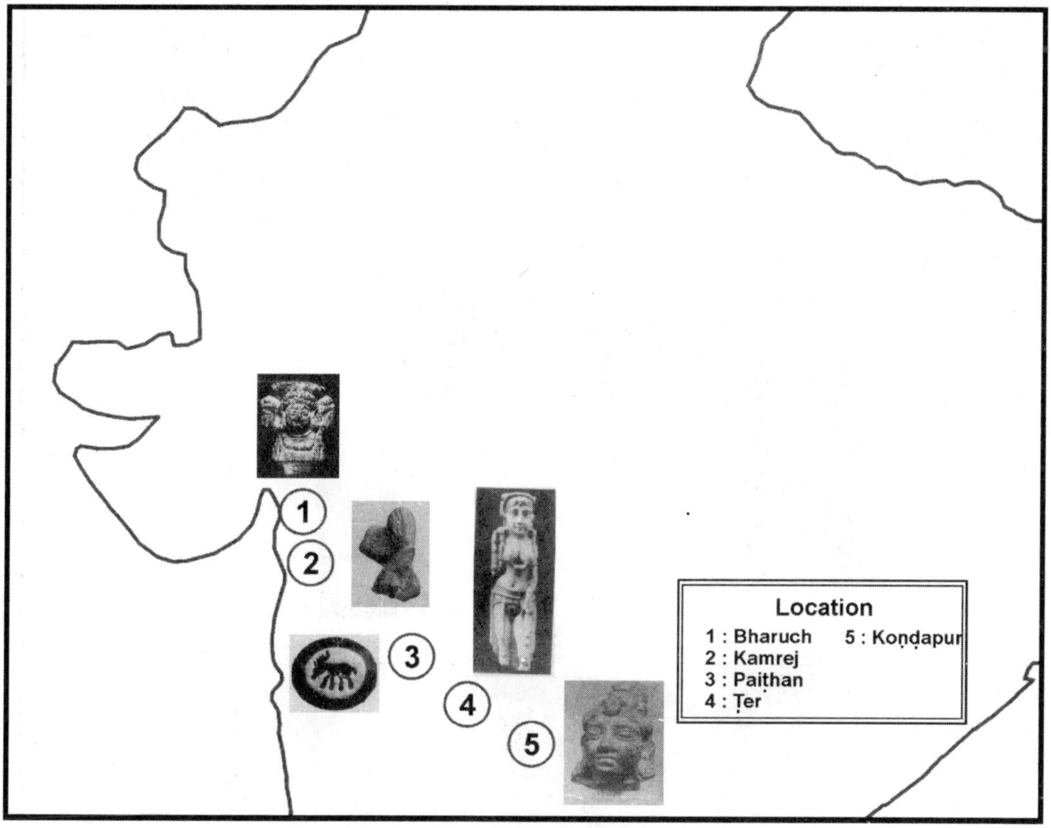

Map 7 : Find places of Early Sculptural Art on Route C

By the early centuries CE, the trans-peninsular routes across the western Deccan manifested cross-cutting influences of art from northern, central and southern India.

Route D: Western Coast–Western Deccan (Straight Axis)

This land-route connected Paiṭhan with the flourishing harbours of Kalyāṇa/Kalliena and Sūrapāraka through the crucial Nānāghāṭ pass (Barrett 1957: 1). An inscription discovered on a rock-cut cave at Kanheri records an endowment of a *kuṭi* (temple) and *kodhi* (hall) excavated in *Rājataleka Paiṭhanapatha* or the royal road to Paiṭhan (Lüders' List No. 988 in *Epigraphia Indica,* vol. X, 1909-10). This linked also to the smaller routes in the southern Koṅkaṇ connecting the *Periplus* harbours of Semylla/Chaul, Mandagora/Kuḍa and Palaepatmae/Palshet with inland trade centres like Nasik, Kolhapur

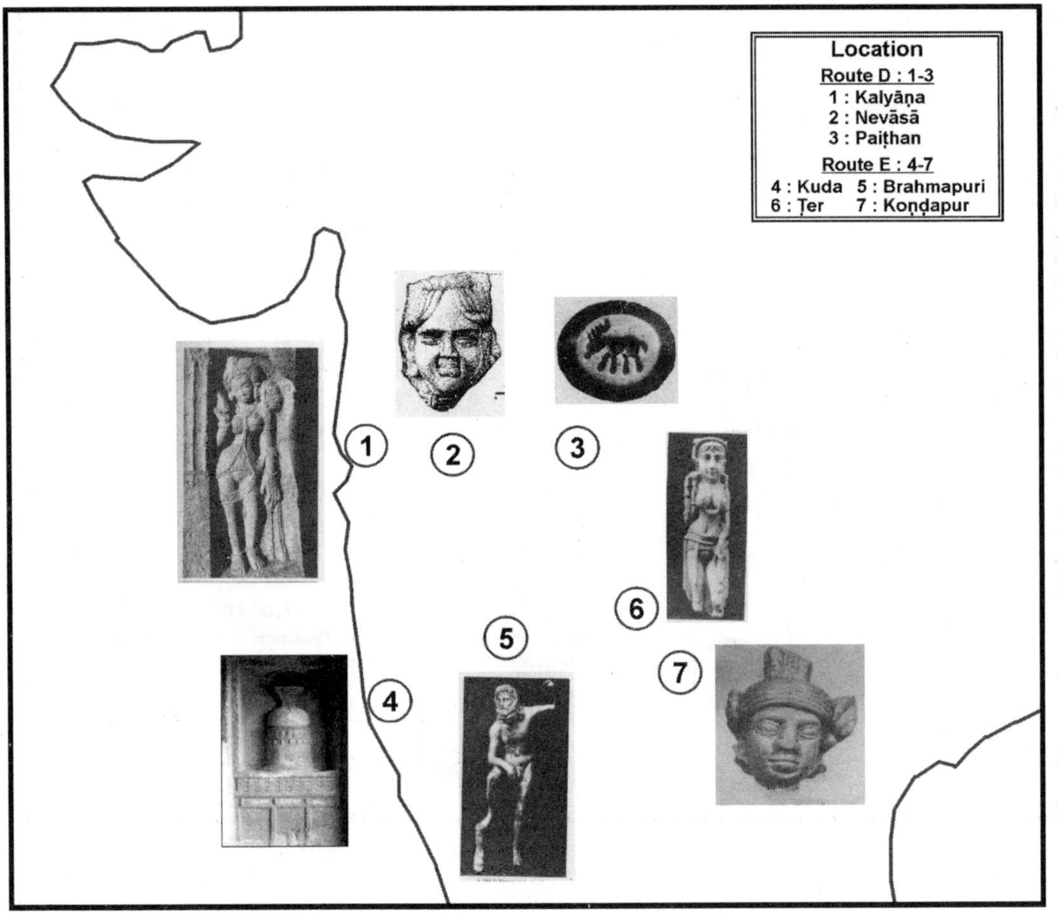

Map 8 : Find places of Early Sculptural Art on Route D and Route E.

and Karaḍ. The linkages are marked out by Buddhist cave groups (*Map.* 8).

This route also cut through the western Deccan, connecting the ports on the Koṅkaṇ to the large inland centres at Junnar, Nevāsā and Paiṭhan (*Map* 8). Here, the focus is on the terracotta and kaolin art of Nevāsā, the inland settlement on the Pratiṣṭhanpatha which was involved in trade with the Roman world (*Map* 8). The art objects in question are a set of terracotta and kaolin busts showing Hellenistic influence. In particular, the "smiling boy" head from Nevāsā has been related to similar statuary from Taxila. In my opinion, the sculptural art of Nevāsā owes much to the intense and enduring Roman contact with the settlement (Gupta 1998a: 86-102). The infusion of Hellenism witnessed at Nevāsā is also manifest in other sites along the trans-peninsular route like Bhokardan, Ṭer and Koṇḍapura (*fig.* 21).

Route E : Brahmapurī–Ṭer–Koṇḍapura

The *Periplus* (section 51) mentions that goods were brought up to Barygaza from coastal areas beyond Tagara. The extension of the trans-peninsular route passing through Koṇḍapura to the estuarine areas of the Kṛṣṇā and Godāvarī indicates acquisition of trade-goods from the east coast. Concomitantly, the commodities from the "coast" may have also been those sent from the littoral tracts of the western and southern Deccan. In this regard Route E in *Map* 8 shows the links between Early Historic ports on the Koṅkaṇ and inland settlements in southern Deccan such as Brahmapurī, Karaḍ and Vaḍgāon Mādhavapura. Brahmapurī, in particular, has yielded a rich hoard of bronze objects of Mediterranean origin. These objects include the bronze figure of the Greek sea god Poseidon (*fig.* 13). Another interesting find along this route is a syncretic image of Lakṣmī-Pārvatī dated to the early centuries CE. This is a unique image, the first of its kind in South Asia. The image was discovered during excavations at Siddhapura conducted by the Deccan College, Pune (Shinde et al. 2004: 117).

Route F : Kauśāmbī–Tripurī–Pauni–Sannathi

This land route came down from Kauśāmbī through Tripurī and connected to the major Early Historic settlements in Vidarbha (Route F in *Map* 4). In the Vidarbha region, the crossroad is represented by the large settlement of Adam (*Map* 4). It is posited here that Adam happened to be a major inland centre of trade (like Ṭer, Paiṭhan, Ujjain), offering access for goods from ports of Kalyāṇa/Soppārā/Chaul to traders from ancient cities like Tripurī and Kauśāmbī. This route passed through the famous *stūpa* site of Pauni. Excavations at Pauni reveal that the sculptural friezes were directly inspired by the Buddhist art of Bharhut and Sāñcī. It appears that the elaborately built *stūpa* complex of the Maurya–Śuṅga period deteriorated with the passage of time, though attempts at repairs to the railing, etc.

were made in the early centuries of the Christian Era (Deo and Joshi 1972: 29). The *stūpa* is associated with Hīnayāna Buddhism from fourth–third century BCE to second–third century CE. The route from Pauni cut westwards into the Deccan and another branch veered to the south, linking up with the *stūpa* site of Sannathi and further on to Nāgārjunakoṇḍa and Amarāvatī.

Route G: From Gāndhāra–Mathurā to Lower Bengal (Map 9)

The trans-Gangetic route goes from Mathurā through Kauśāmbī to Patna and Campā up to Lower Bengal. It is through this route that the art styles of Mathurā and Gandhāra penetrated into the eastern coast of India. That the influence of these art schools was transmitted to the coast is evidenced in an image from Mathurā found in lower Bengal and also a range of terracotta images showing influence of Scythian art of north-west India (discussed in Eastern Coastlands). Presumably, the art influences must have been transmitted along this arterial trade route. One of the major centres of this route was the ancient city of Kauśāmbī, capital of the *mahājanapada* of Vatsa, which first figures in recorded history in the period of the Epics. The *Mahābhārata* informs that the city was founded by King Kuśāmba and according to the Purāṇas King Nicakṣu, a descendent of the Pāṇḍavas, came to live here after Hastināpura was washed away by the Gaṅgā. The stone sculpture from the Kauśāmbī–Vatsa region can be placed on stylistic grounds to the main historical periods of the Gangetic Valley: Maurya, Śuṅga, Kuṣāṇa, Gupta and post-Gupta. In chronological terms they represent a continuity in sculptural art tradition from the third century BCE to the twelfth century CE. There are credible reasons to assert that the art of the Kauśāmbī region was particular and individualistic enough to be distinguished from powerful contemporaenous art centres at Mathurā and Sārnāth (Tripathi 2003). For instance, we notice a clear correlation between the stone and terracotta sculptures of Kauśāmbī. The low relief mould-made and richly adorned terracotta figures are reflected in the sculptural friezes executed in sandstone. The similarity can be witnessed in the near replication of a displayed terracotta Gajalakṣmī

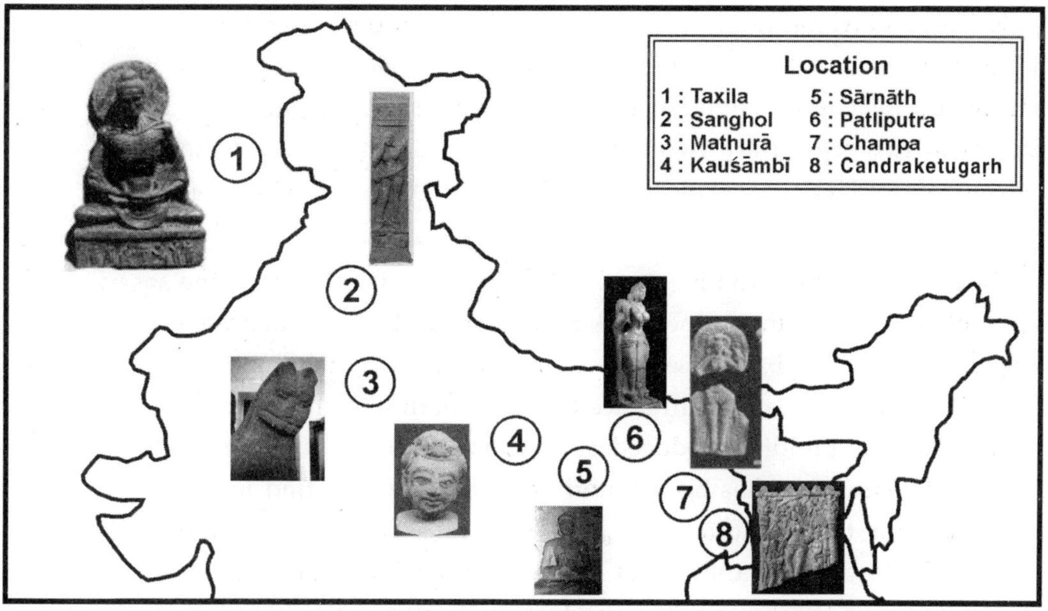

Map 9 : Find places of Early Sculptural Art on Route G

figure upon an exhibited Śuṅga period stone panel. The stone carvers of Kauśāmbī evolved a mature tradition, imbibing outside influences and subtly stamping their genius on artworks produced in their ateliers. With the emergence of a full-blown, three-dimensional portrait sculpture at Mathurā in the Kuṣāṇa period (first–third century CE) many enterprising sculptors at Kauśāmbī took to carving in high relief. The city also imported fine sculptures for sale as well as to serve as models for artisans. A displayed red-stone Buddha figure from Mathurā found at Kauśāmbī is a beautiful example of such imports. A terracotta image of a headless figure — probably Buddha — betrays the influence of the Gāndhāra school of art in the folded drapery (Plate 4). The best of the clay art of the Gangetic valley is to be found at Kauśāmbī: richly adorned figures of Śuṅga times and the rounded freestanding images, toycarts and game pieces of the Kuṣāṇa–Gupta periods. Thematically distinct from the stone sculptures, the terracottas of Kauśāmbī depict secular subjects as much as the religious. The secular themes can be seen in the special Kauśāmbī plaques showing scenes of hunting, chariot racing and baccanalian revelry. One picture brings before us a dramatic moment in the history of Kauśāmbī where the city's King Udayana abducts his beloved Vāsavadattā, daughter of the Lord of Avantī. The religious element in Kauśāmbī terracottas is manifested in iconic images of gods and goddesses. Of particular interest in this regard are two large images of Gajalakṣmī and the Buddhist deity Hārīti excavated from the Ghoṣitārāma monastery at Kauśāmbī.

Further east, the Sārnāth School of Art reached its climax in the fifth century CE. Sārnāth, on the outskirts of Varanasi, lay on the trans-Gangetic route to the Bay of Bengal. As discussed above, the Buddhist art of Sārnāth was heavily influenced by the Mathurā school of art. An image of the Buddha produced at Mathurā in the Kuṣāṇa period (first-third century CE) has been found at Sārnāth. As we find in the Kauśāmbī area, the Mathurā image at Sārnāth must have inspired the local artists to develop the world famous school of art at Sārnāth. Patna or ancient Pāṭaliputra was the former capital of the Mauryan dynasty (fifth–third century BCE) and was also the stronghold of the Gupta dynasty between the fourth-sixth century CE. Pāṭaliputra was an important settlement on the trans-Gangetic route. However, there are few stone sculptures reported from Bihar sites in the Kuṣāṇa period. There are many Gupta and post-Gupta sculptures created indigenously at Bodh-Gayā, Nālandā-Rājgīr and Patna (Asher 1980: 3-34).

Taking an overview of the spread of art styles across the Gangetic Valley, it is clear that the classical idioms and iconographic forms developed at Mathurā penetrated slowly eastwards into the Gangetic Valley. The discovery of a stone image of Buddha from Mathurā at Candraketugaṛh in Bengal (*fig.* 14) completes the picture of solitary imports from Mathurā in the middle and lower Gangetic Valley. Therefore, no independent schools of art rose along the trans-Gangetic route between the fourth–second century BCE (the period of Mauryan art) and fifth century CE (the rise of the Sārnāth school). However, there was a rich tradition of terracotta art in the Gangetic Valley in the BCE–CE transition. In particular, the moulded terracottas of the Gangetic Valley are distributed right up to the Bengal coast. Some of the prominent female divinities, such as the *pañcacūḍa* goddess, were sculpted in terracotta and have been found as far apart as Kauśāmbī near Allahabad and Tamluk in lower Bengal (Plate: 5).

Summary

The brief review of the major trade routes of Early Historic India and the artistic activity along these routes reveals that the transmissions of classical idioms along the routes was marked by experimentation and syncretic expressions. These aspects are evident in the art styles of the Raṅgamahal culture of the early centuries CE of western Rajasthan and in the imitation of Mathurā sculptures in the mid-Gaṅgā valley. Chronologically, the transmission of art from the interiors to the coastlands can be grouped under the following: the spread of rock-cut cave excavations; the spread of *stūpa* architecture; and lastly, the spread of the classic sculptural art of Mathurā, Gandhāra and Sārnāth. The earliest rock-cut caves have been discovered in northern India. These are represented by the Barābar-Nāgārjunī cave group in the hills near Bodh-Gayā. The Lomas Ṛṣi cave is, in all likelihood, dated to the 2nd century BCE (Gupta 1980: 215-220). The rock-cut sanctuaries began to be carved by the Buddhists, Jainas and also those of the Brāhmanical religions in the eastern and western coasts in the BCE–CE transition. The former are represented by the Udayagiri-Khaṇḍagiri cave groups in Orissa and the sea-facing Buddhist caves on the northern Andhra coast. The early western cave group is the one at Bhaja, cut into the western ghats in the second-first century BCE. The *stūpa* building activity begins at Sāñcī, Bodh-Gayā, Vaiśālī and Bharhut in the third-second century BCE. We can trace the spread of *stūpa*s westwards and southwards in the BCE–CE transition. On the western flank the following line of activity is clear: Bharhut–Sāñcī–Pauni–Ṭer. In the southern flank the following line of activity is observed: Bharhut–Sāñcī–Pauni–Sannathi–Amarāvatī. The influence of the Bharhut relief art on the growth of the free-standing sculptural art of Mathurā is fully acknowledged. The spread of the sculptural art of Mathurā and Gandhāra was therefore the last stage in the spread of art idioms from the interiors to the coastlands.

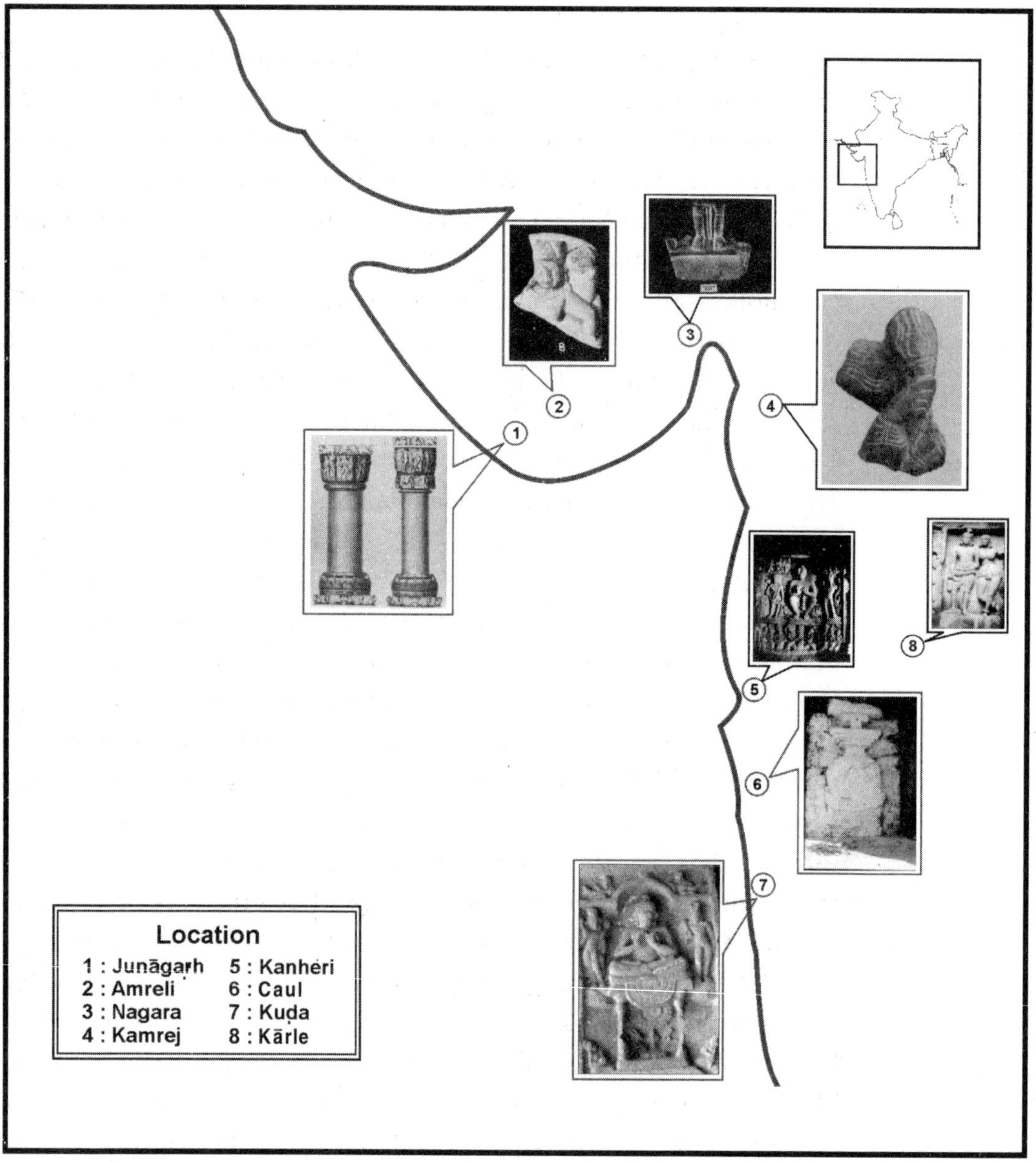

Map 10 : Find places of Early Sculptural Art on the Western Coast

4

The Western Coastland

THE first Iron Age sites appeared on the western coastlands nearly a millennium after the demise of the Harappans. The earliest levels of the Iron Age sites like Bharuch, Nagal and Prabhāsa Paṭan show the principal pottery to be the Black and Red Ware. Not long after, we find the appearance of the Gangetic Northern Black Polished Ware in these coastal sites, signalling the expansion of the Gangetic polities to the coastlands. In the BCE–CE transition (around 50 BCE), we find the rock-cut cave carving activity at its most intense in the Western Ghats overlooking the Koṅkaṇ coast (Bhaja, Bedsā, Kārle) and on the Koṅkaṇ coast itself (Kuḍa, Chaul, Kanheri). Among the earliest sculptural depictions in the early rock-cut caves are the so-called Indra and Sūrya figures at Bhaja, executed in the second century BCE. The figures were inspired by low relief sculpture of the last centuries BCE carved on the railings of Buddhist *stūpa*s at Bharhut and Sāñcī. The sculptural art of the early Buddhist rock-cut caves of coastal western India is also manifested in the figures of *dampati, mithuna*s and *yakṣa*s. Some of the finest secular art is seen in the sculpted figures of humans and animals atop the capitals of rock-cut pillars in the caves of Kārle, Bedsā, Nasik, Junnār and other sites.

The Kārle Cave, created in the first century BCE, represents the high point of rock-cut architecture on western Indian littoral (*Map* 10). Many of its features are to be found in other contemporaenous Buddhist rock-cut sanctuaries in the western Deccan (Nasik, Junnār) and the Koṅkaṇ coast (Kanheri, Chaul, Kuḍa). The main *caityagṛha* at Kārle was hewn out of a hillside in the first century BCE and the work continued into the first century CE (Plates 6, 7). The *caityagṛha* of the Buddhist rock-cut caves at Kārle has the entrance path flanked by rock-cut colonnades. The *stūpa* is situated at the end of the apsidal *caitya* hall. The *stūpa* is complete with the *aṇḍa* (drum), *harmikā* and *chatarī*. A number of donative inscriptions are carved in Brāhmī on the rock-cut pillars in the Kārle *caitya*. Some of these donative inscriptions contain the names of *yavana* donors, indicating that Westerners had also taken to the Buddhist faith as they had done in the Gandhāra region (Plate 8). There *yavana*s must have included some traders from the Roman world. According to Cimino (1994: 71-72):

> In Cave 17 of Nasik, it is specified that the *yavana* Indrāgnidatta, resident of Daṁtamitrī, together with father and son, had commissioned the excavation of a *caitya* and three cisterns. Near Junnār, in four inscriptions found on Shiveni Hill, *yavana*s are equally mentioned as donors of two cisterns and of a refactory in the first location, and for the façade of a *caitya*, in the second. More numerous are the inscriptions at Kārle, where 17 donors offer the pilasters of the great *caitya*, of which 7 are said to be *yavana*s.

The numerous inscriptions of the *yavana*s at Kārle bring us to the question of Roman influence in the internal architecture of the *caitya* cave, a case put forward by a body of scholarship (Fergusson and Burgess, Coomaraswamy). Fergusson (in Fergusson and Burgess: 233) advances the following argument in favour of western features in the layout of the Kārle cave,

> The building resembles to a great extent an early Christian church in its arrangements, consisting of a nave and side aisles, terminating in an apse or semi-dome, around which the aisle is carried.

How do these features compare with other rock-cut sanctuaries, both inland and on the coast? The rock-cut caves at Bhaja and Bedsā, situated close to Kārle, can be taken as examples for comparison. We find the layout of Bhaja similar to that of Kārle: a horse-shoe shaped entrance, a line of columns (without embellishments) and the *stūpa* at the end of the apsidal-shaped cave. The fact that Bhaja is about 150 years older than Kārle, having being carved around the second century BCE points to a common tradition going back into time. It is a cave which seems to hark back to the tradition of early caves like Lomas Ṛṣi in northern India. The cave architecture that began at Bhaja, Pītalkhora and even Ajantā (early phase) matures at Kārle. The cave entrance at

Bhaja assiduously imitates wooden architecture whereas the horse-shoe shaped entrance to Kārle is bereft of this quality (Plate 7). There is a progression in sculptural and architectural tradition that resulted in the mature expressions at Kārle. The point is that just the fact that there is "a naïve and side aisles, terminating in an apse or semi-dome" at Kārle is not enough to qualify the cave as an Indian version of a Roman basilica. The coincidence is of course there, and may have been noticed by the *yavana* donors, as it was by Fergusson.

The sculptural elements in the Bhaja–Bedsā–Kārla cave group tell their own story of cultural transmission and syncretism. I have referred to the Indra and Sūrya panels carved on either sides of an inner entrance at Bhaja (*fig*. 15). These carvings in low relief are dated to the second century BCE and comprise the earliest sculptural features in the western cave group. The Bhaja panels exhibit a vital aesthetic that seems to be missing in Bharhut and Sāñcī, the centres of Buddhist narrative art to which the former relate. According to Coomaraswamy (1972: 26-27), one panel shows Indra sitting on a moving elephant which can be identified as Airāvata (*fig*. 16). The trunk of the divine elephant is raised, holding an uprooted tree, and the mouth open, suggesting that the pachyderm is trumpeting as it moves. Indra is shown in full regalia, with a decorative headdress, long garland and bracelets. He is chaperoned by an attendant holding sceptres. Indra has a goad in his hand with which he is controlling Airāvata. The legs of the divine beast are rather longish, with the hind legs longer than the front, giving a hint of an upward climb. Airāvata seems to be charging upwards through the melee and confusion of the world. One of the front legs of the elephant is placed over a tree in full bloom and as noted above, another tree is held aloft after being uprooted. Numerous human figures, finely sculpted, are shown in various postures. The entire conception is suffused with rhythm and energy.

The other panel depicting the Sun-God Sūrya (Coomaraswamy 1972: 27) is again carved with force and vision. Sūrya is shown riding a horse-drawn chariot with his two attendants (*fig*. 17). The face of Sūrya looks resolute and regal and the attendants deferentially blow the fly whisks. Two spoked wheels of the chariot are partially visible. There are four steeds with head plumes, as if in readiness to gallop. The inaction of the steeds can be attributed to the fact that the entire chariot seems to be borne across the heavens by a huge *yakṣa* or monkey-like figure reminding us of Hanumān. Though both the friezes are in low relief, yet the unknown artist (or artists) have imbued the carvings with a sense of depth and dimension. Though the Indra-Sūrya panels are intrinsically connected to the narrative art of Bharhut and Sāñcī, Anand Coomaraswamy placed them on a different plane when he said:

> These are not personal deities conceived in the manner of Hindu theism, but powers personified only in the way they are personified in the Vedic hymns. Both reliefs are a creation of a wild and fertile, not to say an uncanny, imagination. . . . None of the mystery appears in the orderly reliefs of Bharhut and Sāñcī, and only some trace of it in the far less accomplished art of the Orissa caves.
>
> — Coomaraswamy 1972: 27

However, not all scholars are convinced that the Bhaja panels depict the Vedic Gods Indra and Sūrya. In a recent study, Ajit Kumar (2003-04: 83-89) identifies the Indra panel as a sculptural rendering of the Buddhist *Kulavaka Jātaka* and the Sūrya panel as a depiction of King Prasenajit's visit to the Buddha as narrated in the *Majjhima Nikāya*. In any case the Bhaja panels can be taken as a unique feature of the sculptural art of the western Indian littoral, artistically related to the narrative art of the great *stūpa*s of Central India (Bharhut, Sāñcī), yet very different in spirit and composition. The Bhaja reliefs, representing the earliest example of sculptural art in the Western Ghat–Koṅkaṇ area, are also a tribute to the adventurous spirit of the mendicants, traders, caravaneers and travellers who were opening the land routes to the Arabian sea through the hilly tracts of the Western Ghats. Another early relief is carved at the entrance of a Buddhist cave at Junnār, within 100 km of Bhaja and located close to the Nānāghāṭ pass providing access to the ports on the Koṅkaṇ. The carving shows a Gajalakṣmī conception: the figure of the female divinity in frontal posture and profiles of elephants on either side with their trunks uplifted, signifying the spraying of water. Yakṣīs are shown dancing at the sides of the elephants, their upraised hands held together and inclined towards the central figure of the deity (*fig.* 18). The relief has been dated to the second century BCE, making it contemporaneous to the Bhaja-Bedsā panels. The Gajalakṣmī panel at Junnār can be compared with a similar relief at the Jaina cave group at Udayagiri-Khaṇḍagiri in Orissa (*fig.* 52). The Gajalakṣmī was a favourite goddess of all religions indigenous to India.

A category of sculptures in the early Buddhist rock-cut caves of western India which have escaped critical attention are the animal and human figures carved atop pillars. At Bhaja we find crude carvings of half human–half bull figures atop plain rock-cut pillars, similar to the ones on pillar capitals from Pāṭaliputra now housed in the Patna Museum. At Bedsā, a capital is surmounted by animals (elephant, horse, bullock and sphinx). The rock-cut pillars making up the colonnade at the *caitya* at Kārle have carved atop the capitals men and women in decorative headgear sitting on crouching elephants and horses (*fig.* 19). The human figures on the brackets seem to represent lay worshippers. The men wear trefoil headdresses and earrings, a typical feature of Śuṅga–Sātavāhana art. We find similar figures in rock-cut caves such as Junnār and Nasik in the Western Ghats overlooking the Koṅkaṇ coast. The lion capital on a high pillar outside the Kārle cave is an imposing example of Sātavāhana art (Plate 9). Four lions are sculpted back-to-back, resembling the lions carved on the south gate of the Sāñcī Stūpa. The sculpted animal figures can be imputed a date in the first century CE, considering that the Kārle cave was excavated in the latter half of the first century BCE. As a body of sculpture, the animal sculptures at Bedsā, Kārle and other rock-cut caves of western India can only be compared with the animal figures carved atop pillars in the Mauryan period. While the animal carvings in the western Indian cave group do not match the natural dynamism of the Mauryan figures such as the Sārnāth lion capital or the polished bull atop the Rāmapūrvā pillar, nevertheless the animals on the cave pillars are conceived with a sense of freedom. The crouching lions and the horses at Kārle seem to be part of a joyous occasion, the humans sitting on the animals seeming like lay worshippers looking down at the laity in the cave below.

Another important sculptural feature at Kārle is a couple carved in bold relief at the entrance of the main *caitya* cave during the first century BCE. The couple, commonly identified in Indian art as a *mithuna* or amorous couple, exudes strength, youthfulness and style (Plate 10). The physiognomy of both the man and the woman is robust. The man wears a trefoil headdress typical of Śuṅga–Sātavāhana art. His upper body is uncovered, showing muscular chests and arms and a narrow waistline. The loin cloth is worn with thick twirls of the garment. He holds the end of the lower garment in his left hand. The woman is sculpted in a fashion that brings out her voluptuousness. The face exudes calm and a certain nobility. Her full breasts are uncovered and taut and the waist narrow. The hips are broad, the legs long and muscular. A thin cloth covers her hips. The female figure is stylistically close to the damsels depicted in the toilet scenes in the panels from Mathurā. This is particularly noticed in the posture of the lady in the *mithuna* composition, her left leg kept straight on the ground and the right leg akimbo and resting on her toes (see also *yakṣī* figure in Plate 11). The ladies in the Mathurā panels and some of the Mathurā-produced panels from Saṅghol display the same posture. While the *mithuna* couple fall squarely in the art tradition of the Sātavāhanas, the influence of the Mathurā school is also evident.

Following the Kārle group in the Western Ghats, the next group of rock-cut caves which need to be discussed are those which directly overlook the creeks and rivers on the Koṅkaṇ coast. The major sea facing caves, lying in north-south orientation, are Kanheri and Kondivte near Mumbai, Chaul at the entrance of the Rohā creek and Kuḍa at the head of the Jañjīrā creek. Like the Kārle group, all these caves were cut by Hīnayāna Buddhists between the first century BCE and the first century CE. All the Koṅkaṇ caves are simpler in conception and decoration. First of all, most of the Koṅkaṇ caves are *vihāra* caves, sanctuaries for monks to stay in recluse. The following description of the cave cells at Kanheri could fit the other Koṅkaṇ caves:

> . . . great majority of the excavations consist of a single small room, usually with a little verandah in front, supported by two plain square or octagonal shafts, and stone beds in the cells. Their style is certainly

> primitive, and some of these monks' abodes may date from before the Christian Era. — Fergusson and Burgess 1880/1988: 349

The caves at Kanheri have been cut into a hill on the island of Salsette at the head of Mumbai harbour. There are about 109 caves. The *caitya* cave at Kanheri has been conceived like Kārle, with remains of pillars on both sides of the central hall and the *stūpa* at the apsidal end of the cave. The screen in front of the *caitya* cave at Kanheri showing small *yakṣa*-like figures below circular decorations is similar to the one at Kārle.

At Chaul, the ancient port on the western coast situated about 50 km south of Mumbai, a *stūpa* is found carved in bold relief in the interior wall of a Buddhist rock-cut cave. In fact, it is the presence of the *stūpa* in relief that identifies the cave as Buddhist. The absence of any image of the Buddha shows that these caves were excavated by those professing the Hīnayāna form of Buddhism. The *stūpa* on the wall surface is complete, showing the drum (*aṇḍa*), the *harmikā* and the *chatarī* (Plate 12). The caves at Chaul were executed, in all likelihood, in the last century BCE. The white wash on the *stūpa* has been done by the local Koḷ community which has converted the caves into a temple of Hiṅgalāja Mātā, a local deity.

Some 50 km further south of Chaul, we come to the town of Murud near the Arabian Sea. A deep creek cuts into the hilly tracts of the Koṅkaṇ, going about 20 km into the land (Plate 13). The fortress of Jañjīrā, built in the eighteenth century by Abysinnians, lies at the mouth of the creek. At the head of the Jañjīrā creek are Buddhist rock-cut caves. The Buddhist rock-cut caves of Kuḍa are visible as a narrow dark slit along the escarpment (Plate 14). The Kuḍa caves overlook the northern end of the Murud-Jañjīrā creek. The beachhead below the caves has yielded fragments of Early Historic pottery. The beachhead at Kuḍa has been identified with the port of Maṇḍagora mentioned in the Greek sea guide, the *Periplus Maris Erythraei* dated to the first century CE (Gupta 1998). A *stūpa* has been carved as a pilaster at the entrance of one of the Hīnayāna rock-cut cave sanctuary at Kuḍa (Plate 15). In another cave, a *stūpa* has been carved in the round (Plate 16). The *stūpa* has a decorative band in the middle of the drum (*aṇḍa*), a *harmikā* and the *chatarī*. It can be dated to the first-second century CE. The *stūpa* is carved within a high niche and rests upon a podium decorated with cross-bands. The decoration seems to imitate a wooden fencing (Plate 17).

An interesting facet of the Koṅkaṇ caves are the sculpted images of Buddha made at a later date by Mahāyānists. At Kuḍa there is an image of the Buddha sitting in *dharmacakra-pravartana* pose. The sculpture has been carved in a niche inside a rock-cut cave at Kuḍa (Plate 18). The snail-curl decoration of the hair, the prominent *uṣṇīṣa* and the meditating posture immediately recall the well-known Buddha figure from Sārnāth preaching the sermon (fig. 11). Though the decorated nimbus is missing, the flying *gandharva*s are an influence of the Sārnāth school. The Buddha figure was carved long after the Hīnayānists excavated the caves. The Buddha figure can be imputed a date of the late fifth or early sixth century (see Fergusson and Burgess 1880/1988: 208). Similarly at Kanheri there are Buddha images and also of Avalokiteśvara dating to the sixth century (*fig*. 20). The appearance of Buddha images in the seafacing caves at Kanheri, Kondivte and Kuḍa indicates the intensity with which the Mahāyānist creed spread to the western coast. As I have discussed in the chapter on the Eastern Coastlands, the same process of Mahāyāna ascendancy was happening in Orissa around the sixth century.

In a sense, the sculptural elements like pillar capitals, *mithuna* images and Buddha figures in the rock-cut caves of western Deccan and the Koṅkaṇ were secondary to the monumental conceptions like the *stūpa*s and the pillars created inside the *caitya*s. I shall return to art in rock-cut caves later. At the moment it would be appropriate to focus on free standing sculpture in the round in terracotta and stone. Much of the discussion centres around Early Historic sites on or near the coast of Gujarat, further north of the rock-cut caves which are situated in Maharashtra state. Undoubtedly, the major influences on the early art of the western Indian littoral are from Mathurā, Gandhāra and even Amarāvatī. However, we can also discern a uniquely local element in the execution of religious and secular figures. Besides the amalgamation of elements from "outside" (Mathurā, Gandhāra,

Amarāvatī), the regional styles are also evident in the Early Historic sculptures of western India. For the sake of convenience, we can call the regional idioms the Sātavāhana and Kṣatrapa styles, after the dominant political dynasties of western Deccan and the Gujarat regions. There is also another extraneous element, that of Graeco-Roman art that was transmitted along the sea route from Egypt. We see this manifestation in the terracotta art of western India, specifically in the kaolin sculptures produced in the western Deccan (*fig.* 21). The influence of Scythian elements is also observed in western India, such as the terracotta head of a warrior (?) with conical cap found at Ṭer (*fig.* 22).

One of the striking features in the coastal art of western India is an influx of terracotta plaques that faithfully copy the Kuṣāṇa and Gupta art of Mathurā. In this regard a unique discovery is that of a fragmentary terracotta plaque from the site of Amreli (Saurāṣṭra) resembling the large stone statue of King Kaniṣka kept in the Mathura Museum (*fig.* 23). A lower part of a standing human figure excavated at the Early Historic site of Amreli in Saurāṣṭra seems to have been inspired by the royal statue of the Kuṣāṇa king Kaniṣka discovered at the *devakula* (sanctuary) at Mat near Mathurā. According to Rao (1966: 97), the terracotta figure "closely resembles the standing stone figure of Kaniṣka from Mathurā . . . in gait and dress it is comparable with the sculptures of the Kuṣāṇa kings in their long skirts and scarfs." The terracotta figure shows parts of the Kuṣāṇa long skirt and the end of the scarf, both features similar to the large stone image of Kaniṣka in the Mathura Museum. The left foot, little obscured, is splayed out at a right angle and seems to be in a boot. Again, these features are observed in the stone statue of Kaniṣka. The fragmentary terracotta figure has been dated to the second century CE on stratigraphic grounds (Rao 1966: 97; *fig.* 23). The imitation of Kuṣāṇa figures produced in Mathurā seems to have been quite popular in the Kṣatrapa dominated territories of western India. Apart from the religious iconographic forms inspired by the Mathurā school of art, we find a number of examples in the secular themes. For instance, a terracotta figure from Jūnāgaṛh is shown wearing a long coat reminiscent of Kuṣāṇa dress (Sounder Rajan 1985: Plate 5).

Amreli is located in the littoral region of Saurāṣṭra and is directly accessible from the coast. In his report on the excavations at Amreli, S.R. Rao makes incisive observations on the nature of the emergent sculptural art of the western Indian littoral:

> Examples of three main schools of art are repeated in terracottas. . . . Firstly the Graeco-Roman art is represented by a plaque with a bearded figure. The second group represents the Kuṣāṇa art of Mathurā school, and the third one the Gupta art. There are a few terracottas which reveal the influence of the Amarāvatī school also. It may however be added here that the art-in-the-round is not represented by any figure, human or divine, except one. Most of them are plaques taken from a single mould and without any applique decoration. Amreli has not yielded any example of early Śuṅga art. The plaques of the Kuṣāṇa period are in high relief with refined forms, well regulated contours and gradation of planes. The female figures are neither coiffured nor wear elaborate dress and jewellery. New ethnic types are also found here indicating a racial influx of the early Kṣatrapa period. — Rao 1966: 96

The emergence of distinct Kṣatrapa features in the art of western India is specifically observed in the Viṣṇu images of the first–second century CE found in different places in coastal Gujarat. A fragmetary image of Viṣṇu on a stone plaque was excavated at the Early Historic port-site of Kamrej on the banks of the river Tāpī (Plate 19). The execution of the Viṣṇu image in low relief on a plaque is a tradition that is borrowed from terracotta art. The Viṣṇu image has been described in detail by Gupta et al. (2004: 68):

> A plaque of fine grained buff sandstone with carvings on both surfaces. The front shows a human figure with four hands, most of them are now broken. The image has been carved in frontal posture. It is standing in *sthānaka* pose. The right hand is held in *abhaya-mudrā* while the left hand is akimbo. The chest is bare but bearing an *ekāvalī* or single string necklace. It has a *yajñopavīta*. The deity is clad in *dhotī* held in position with a *mekhalā*. The right third hand is broken and the *āyudha* cannot be identified. The back of the plaque shows the back of the deity in low relief with features deeply engraved.

The figure is dated to the first-second century CE on stratigraphic considerations.

The Viṣṇu figures from Gujarat show an indigenous style at variance from the typical iconography of Kuṣāṇa–Gupta Viṣṇu images of the Mathurā school. One of these is a stone plaque depicting the God Viṣṇu in frontal posture (*fig.* 24). The sculpture was excavated from the Kṣatrapa levels in Amreli (Rao 1966: Plate XXX, 8). The fragmentary plaque shows partially the bust and torso of Viṣṇu as well as his left arms. The figure can be identified as Viṣṇu because he holds a *cakra* (wheel) in his upper left hand. The facial features are not so finely formed. A single pearl necklace adorns his neck and the headdress is like a flat hat rather than the high *kirīṭa* that distinguishes the Viṣṇu figures of the Mathurā school of art (*fig.* 6). The incised lines on the arm of the God indicates the drapery. This is a specific feature of the Mathurā art. However, the headdress of Viṣṇu can be considered a specific feature of the Kṣatrapa art style, at variance with Mathurā, and deriving more from Scythian idioms. The Viṣṇu figure from Amreli has been imputed a date of third century CE on stratigraphic grounds (Rao 1966: 95). A unique figure of a four-armed Viṣṇu in terracotta from Karvan, obtained from a layer ascribable to the fourth century CE, shows a *kirīṭa* strongly resembling an Iranian or Central Asian cap. A similar one in yellow schist though badly weathered was also recovered from the same layer (IAR 1974-75: 16). There is no doubt that Viṣṇu images conceived in the Kṣatrapa domains borrowed from the art of Mathurā but also had an indigenous stamp which can be called the "Kṣatrapa style."

The absorption of classical idioms in the local genre was also expressed in new images of goddesses. A stone plaque showing a goddess with four arms was excavated from Amreli. The goddess is shown with a spear in the upper right hand. Other features are not clear. Interestingly, her headdress is the *uṣṇīṣa* type similar to those decorating the female figures in the Kārle caves (*fig.* 25; see Rao 1966: 94; Plate XXV, 9). The figure is dated to the first-second century CE on stratigraphic grounds. Another stone plaque excavated from Amreli shows a female divinity holding a *vajra* (thunderbolt) and *khaḍga* (spear) and wearing a headdress resembling the flat topped Scythian type headdress found on the head of the Viṣṇu figure from Amreli. She is possibly a representation of Vaiṣṇavī (*fig*. 26; see Rao 1966: 98-99). The figure is dated to the first-second century CE on stratigraphic grounds. The syncretic art that grew in Gujarat was the result of cross-mingling of art idioms. The regional Kṣatrapa style can therefore be discerned from the small terracotta images and itinerant sculptures in stone that seem similar to the Kuṣāṇa art yet unique to the Gujarat region (*fig*. 27).

To return to rock-cut sculpture. The sculptural freizes in the rock-cut caves at Jūnāgaṛh near the coast of Saurāṣṭra reveal a syncretic art that flourished in the early centuries CE incorporating elements of the art of the Sātavāhana, Mathurā and Gāndhāra school as well as specific motifs borrowed from the Scythian and Graeco-Roman art. In particular, the figures of ladies in the capital of the pillar in the Buddhist caves of Uperkoṭ at Jūnāgaṛh are interesting (*Map* 10; *fig*. 28). Their robust bodies with rounded torsos, strong but slender arms and legs recall the physiognomy of the Mathurā sculptures as well as the stylization of the Andhra art. The figure of the ladies in the capital are carved "almost in the round" and therefore show an attempt at full sculptural art. The combination of low relief and three-dimensionality in the same pillar shows that the artisans at work in the Uperkoṭ cave complex were not following any one dominant art style but were engaged in experimentation. One unique motif is seen in the crouching lions in a frieze at the top of the pillar indicative of a Scythian influence. Such lions are also present in the art of Gandhāra where they have been borrowed from the Scythian art styles of Central Asia. Undoubtedly, the caves being located in the heart of the Śaka dominion (Kṣatrapa–Kardamaka dynasties) the Śaka art motifs were naturally to be incorporated. The garland bearers at the base of the pillar are ubiquitous in the art of Gandhāra and Mathurā (influenced by Gandhāra).

However, what strikes me as unique is that the garland-bearers (*mālāvahakas*) are holding creepers of acanthus leaves. The acanthus leaf motif appears in the art of Gandhāra and the art of Mathurā, as part of a decorative matrix. However, the Uperkoṭ representation shows the acanthus leaves prominently and in exquisite detail. In

Gāndhāra sculptures, the garland-bearers are shown under the weight of thick, rounded python like flower garlands. In his architectural description of the Jūnāgaṛh caves, Sounder Rajan (1985: 43) describes the acanthus scroll thus:

> The lowest part portrays a delightful representation of the *mālāvahaka*s or garland-bearers, typical of Buddhist decorative element from Gandhāra and Andhra, and is further highlighted by the garland itself bearing an imaginative scroll of acanthus leaf having vertical loops at the corner.

In my opinion, the acanthus leaf creeper at the base of the Uperkoṭ pillar is an art idiom that was directly introduced from the west because of maritime trade links with the Roman empire. As we know, the acanthus leaf is typically employed in Roman art and constitutes the basic decorative feature of the Corinthian capital. The caves are situated on the crucial land route to the Early Historic harbour at Prabhāsa Paṭan which has yeilded a late Roman amphora. From the caves themselves, a clay bullae inspired by Roman coins, shows the face of a Kṣatrapa ruler. The entire composition of the Uperkoṭ pillar is unique and can be termed an example of what can be called the Kṣatrapa style. Sounder Rajan (1985: 43) brings out the intermingling art idioms: "the pillars are strongly suggestive of the heydey of Sātavāhana art as galvanized by exotic elements of the Scythian and Graeco-Roman contacts and would be easily datable to the second century CE."

To recapitulate, the execution of the figure of Kaniṣka in clay, the Viṣṇu images in stone and clay as well as the carvings in the Jūnāgaṛh cave show how the impact of the Mathurā school of art was absorbed at the regional level. These images must have been made by artists who had actually visited Mathurā and Gandhāra and observed the images first-hand and reproduced them in far Saurāṣṭra. The elements of Gāndhāra art are observed in the "flying *gandharva*" figures in a goldsmiths die of fine sandstone from Amreli (Rao 1966: 93-94). There is also the need to look closely at the Buddhist art of the *stūpa* of Devnimorī, the *stūpa* site on the land route from Raṅgamahal (Rajasthan) to the Gulf of Khambaṭ. According to the excavators, the panels at Devnimorī resembled the late period of the Buddhist art of Gandhāra. To quote:

> This phase is dated by the hoard of 38 coins of the later Kṣatrapa ruler, the latest coin in the series belongs to Svami Rudrasena III, ascribable to CE 351. Stylistically also the images and the decorative elements show great affinity to the later Gāndhāra art
>
> — *IAR* 1961-62: 12-13

A *gaṇa* figure in green schist recovered from Devnimorī again reveals the mingling of local styles with classical elements (*fig.* 29). The *gaṇa* sits on a throne in frontal posture which can be easily related to some of the statues of the great Kuṣāṇas, in particular the image of Wima Khadphises found at Mathurā. The *gaṇa* grasps a human figure in his right hand, the significance of the act being not clear. On the whole, the *gaṇa* figure is an example of cultural absorption and syncretism.

The direct impact of Graeco-Roman art in the growth of early sculptural art in the western Indian littoral is also a matter of discussion. For instance, the Hellenistic quality of a bearded terracotta figure holding a horn of plenty from Amreli cannot be denied (Rao 1966: 97). Another instance of overseas influence on the indigenous art of the Indian coast is seen in the terracotta and kaolin busts found at some Early Historic sites of western Deccan. In particular, the site of Nevāsā has yielded these busts in some profusion, the well-known of these being the "smiling boy" figure. These figures in kaolin also occur on other sites like Ṭer and Koṇḍapura, situated on the route from the port of Bhr̥ghukaccha to the eastern Deccan (*fig.* 21). The excavators have compared the Nevāsā terracottas to Hellenistic figures found at Taxila in north-west Pakistan. However, Nevāsā has yielded evidence of direct contact with the Roman world in the form of Mediterranean amphora fragments. The amphorae have been found in succeeding Early Historic Period V which has also yielded the unique double moulded terracotta "smiling boy" figure. A scientific study of the amphora fragments from Nevāsā revealed most of them to be products of Naples in Italy (Gupta et al. 2001: 7-18). The evidence as a whole points to the absorption of Graeco-Roman art idioms directly by artisans in western India. This syncretism came about due to the trade contact between Nevāsā and the western world. There is no evidence for the transmission of the Gāndhāra style so deep inland. Instead, the Hellenistic terracotta and kaolin figures from Nevāsā can be viewed in the same framework as the direct infusion of certain Roman elements in the art of Nāgārjunakoṇḍa in southern India and Jūnāgaṛh in Saurāṣṭra. Interestingly, some of the fine red glazed terracotta figures excavated from Early Historic levels in north India were fired in the same fashion as the fine Red Polished Ware (RPW), a pottery that appeared in western India under the influence of the Roman sigillata wares (Plates 22, 23). The RPW was a transmission from the coastlands to the interiors. Therefore some of the RPW from the site of Kauśāmbī in the Gangetic Valley is inferior to that from Nevasa in western India, the latter site being in the vicinity of the Koṅkaṇ coast (Plate 24).

One of the examples of transmissions back from western India to the west is an Indian ivory figurine discovered at Pompei in Italy from levels dated to first century CE. (Plate 20). The ivory figurine from Pompei is very similar to the ivory figurines from Ṭer and Bhokardan in the western Deccan. These sites were involved in trade with the Roman world. The Pompei ivory, together with those from Ṭer and Bhokardan, constitutes the finest expression of Sātavāhana period art of western India. The ivory carvers of western India belonged to the greater tradition of sculptors who created the beautiful *yakṣī*s on the brackets of the Sāñcī *stūpa*. The bronze figurine of a *yakṣī* at Khoṛ Rorī, Oman also belongs to the rich tradition of sculptural art that flourished in western India in the BCE-CE transition (see Chapter 7).

Summary

The overview of Early Historic sculptural art on the western coastlands shows that the creative spirit of the "periphery" was no less than the cultural efflorescence in the great art centres in the interiors. The rock-cut *caitya*s and *vihāra*s in the Western Ghats and the Koṅkaṇ display a surprisingly vast range of sculptural art: finely carved *stūpa*s with elongated drums, sensuous figures in relief, animal forms atop pillar capitals and intricate screens. Further north on the coast of

Gujarat we find classical idioms of the art of Mathurā and Gandhāra mingling with local art styles and even imported Central Asian modes that led to the development of the "Kṣatrapa style." While strains of the art of Gandhāra, particularly the late phase, did permeate into western India through Rajasthan, the intense sea trade between western coast of India and the Roman world directly brought western cultural elements into the sculptural art of the region. However, there is a need for caution while we attempt to untangle the source of Hellenism in Indian art. As discussed, the comparison of the Kārle *caitya* cave with Roman tomb architecture, though valid on the surface, does not justify a western inspiration for Kārle which seems to be firmly rooted in the tradition of Indian rock-cut architecture going back to Bhaja and Lomas Ṛṣi. The development of religious iconography is most popularly expressed in the images of Viṣṇu and the Buddha in terracotta in the Saurāṣṭra region. It is also to be noted that the worship of Śiva was popular on the western coast since early times. Inscriptions of the early centuries CE in the Kuḍa caves include names like Śivadatta, etc. which suggest the worship of Śiva. While the image of the Buddha was mostly found in the Gujarat region, the strong Hīnayāna creed kept the Buddha image out of the Maharashtra region till the fifth–sixth century CE. There seems to have been a wave of Mahāyāna Buddhism and infusion of Brāhmanical deities into western India after the fifth century CE. Note for example the appearance of the Buddha figure on the sea facing caves of Kanheri and Kuḍa in the sixth–seventh century CE. This is also the case with Sūrya shrines which are seen in Saurāṣṭra in sixth–seventh century CE. The Lakulīśa figure on a brick at Karvan in Baroda, looking uncannily like a seated Buddha image (Plate 21), brings to mind Debala Mitra's observation of a similar development in Orissa, where Lakulīśa images were being produced in the likeness of Buddha as the rivalry between these religious denominations intensified.

5

The Southern Coastland

THE area under review comprises the coast of Karnataka (specifically the coastal districts of Uttara and Dakshin Kannada), the coast of Kerala, the offshore islands of Lakshadweep, the littoral districts of the state of Tamil Nadu, the Union Territory of Pondicherry abutting the Bay of Bengal and the coast of Andhra Pradesh comprising the estauries of the rivers Kṛṣṇā and Godāvarī and ending in the hilly tracts of the Eastern Ghats in the northern part of the state bordering Orissa. This is broadly the region that was accessible through the Dakṣiṇāpatha, the great southern route mentioned in the *Arthaśāstra*. The Greek sea guide of the first century CE, the *Periplus Maris Erythraei* refers to the region of Dachinabades, the Greek corruption of Dakṣiṇāpatha (modern Deccan). The *Periplus* also refers to the coastal regions of Dachinabades/Dakṣiṇāpatha. The term in the sea guide, Limyrike or Damirica refers to the coastal areas of southern India, broadly the Karnataka and Kerala coasts. Taken together the terms Dachinabades and Limyrike broadly allude to the southern zone of the Indian subcontinent comprising the Indian states of Karnataka–Kerala abutting the Arabian Sea and Tamil Nadu–Andhra Pradesh along the Bay of Bengal.

It is most appropriate to begin the discussion with the earliest centre of coastal art in the southern coastland, one which emerged in the lower Kṛṣṇā Valley in Andhra Pradesh as early as the third–second century BCE. This was the art of Amarāvatī, a Buddhist *stūpa* site in the vicinity of the ancient port-site of Dharaṇīkoṭa (*Map* 11). The art of Amarāvatī later inspired the art of Nāgārjunakoṇḍa, the site of the royal capital of the Ikṣvāku dynasty built along the banks of the Kṛṣṇa, largely in the fourth century CE. The mainly Buddhist art of Amarāvatī

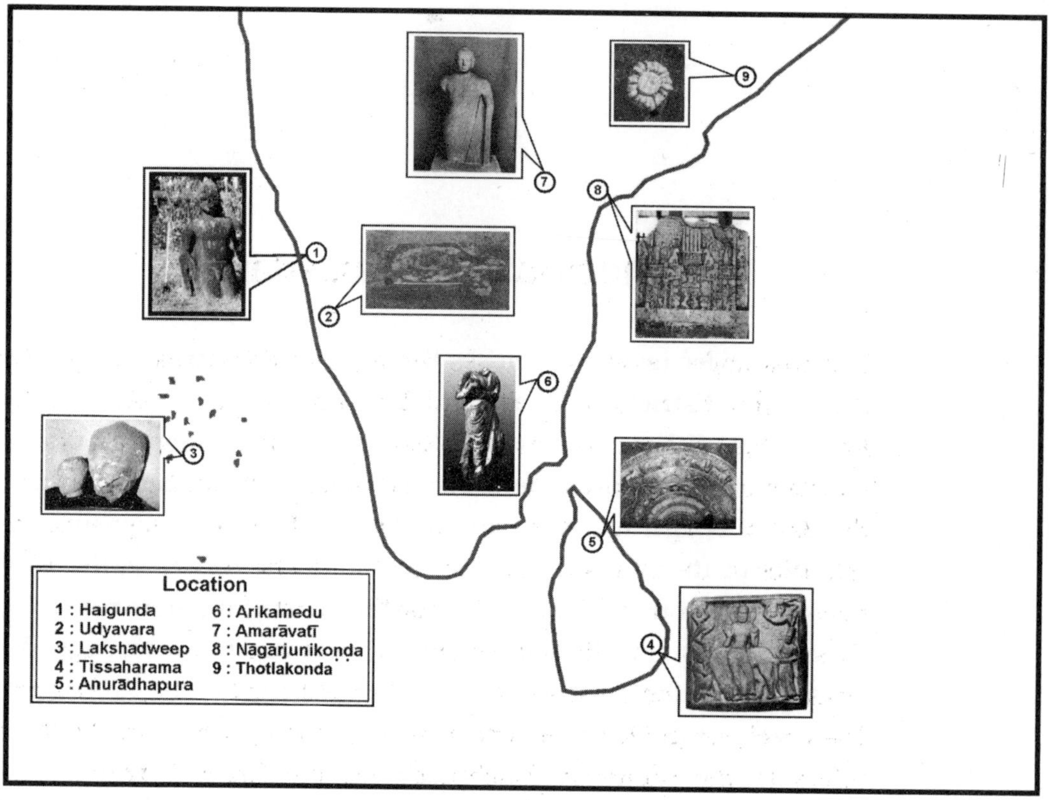

Map 11: Find places of Early Sculptural Art on the Southern Coast of India & Sri Lanka

and Nāgārjunakoṇḍa spread its influence into the Godāvarī estuary to the north and the Tamil coast to the south. It is also on the Andhra littoral that we find the earliest iconic representation of Śiva, in the form of the *puruṣa* carved on the *śivaliṅgam* dated to the second century BCE. The *śivaliṅgam* was discovered in a temple at Guḍimallam in Chitoor district (*fig.* 34). The estuary of the river Kṛṣṇā, where the *stūpa* complex of Amarāvatī is located, was also a major point for the spread of sculptural art to South-East Asia. North of the river Godāvarī (which demarcates the southern zone), a number of Buddhist monastic complexes have come to light at Thotlakoṇḍa, Bavikoṇḍa, Salihundam and Kaliṅgapaṭnam. Many of these monastic complexes, besides being located in free standing structures, are also rock-cut sanctuaries, as at Salihundam. Most of the *vihāra*, *stūpa* and *caitya* areas reveal the worship of Buddha in aniconic form. On the Arabian Sea littoral, specifically on the Karnataka coast, we find sculptures from the Early Historic period. In particular, the great *yakṣa* figure at Haiguṇḍa island in the estuary of the river Śarāvatī, is an imposing example of early sculptural art in the southern coastlands. Also, the discovery of the Buddha heads of the early-mid centuries CE from Lakshadweep and Maldives shows that early sculptural art had well and truly penetrated into the Indian coastlands. Let us examine these finds in detail.

The Kṛṣṇā Basin: The Art of Amarāvatī and Nāgārjunakoṇḍa

The Buddhist *stūpa* at Amarāvatī started to be built in the third century BCE and the rebuilding activity at the *stūpa* continued till the second century CE. The earliest sculptural representations at Amarāvatī were visible from the third century BCE together with Aśokan inscriptions on a pillar of local stone. According to Prasad (1980: 29),

> There is now tangible evidence to establish the early beginnings of the formative phase of Andhra art. Amarāvatī, Kesarapalli, Chandravaram, Dhūlikaṭṭa, etc. provide the nuances of the Andhra style. The *triratna* in bold relief on a granite upright and an outline of the *stūpa* and *vṛkṣa-caitya* on an inscribed crossbar datable to the third century BCE from Amarāvatī . . . reveal hesitant handling of different planes in the depiction of *stūpa*-complex. From this stage, the earliest phase of Amarāvatī art emerges in second century BCE as evidenced in the limestone stele and *yakṣī* figures.

It is emphasized that the art of Amarāvatī was not confined to the *stūpa* at Amarāvatī but, as Prasad points out, various other centres of Buddhism which flourished in the last centuries BCE. Inscriptional evidence suggests that the *stūpa* at Dhūlikaṭṭa in coastal Andhra was built in the second century BCE. Sculptural representations on the *stūpa* include the five hooded Mucalinda *nāga* and the *bodhi* tree. Influence of the art of Bharhut is manifested in stylized lotuses and other floral ornamentation (*figs.* 30, 31; *Indian Archaeology — A Review*, 1983-84: 2-3). Other *stūpa*s dating from the second century BCE in the Kṛṣṇā estuary are Jaggayyapeṭa, Kesarapalli and Guḍivaḍa (*Map* 1).

The early phases of all these *stūpas* show sculptural art in relief and the Buddha represented in aniconic mode. However, the Buddha image was introduced into the art of Amarāvatī in the first century CE itself. According to Anamika Rai of the University of Allahabad (personal communication) small figures of the Buddha are found carved in relief among other symbolisms. At this stage the Buddha figure was still not significant but by the second century CE we find creation of free standing three-dimensional images of the Buddha. The Buddha images showed the influence of both the Mathurā and Gandhāra schools of art (*fig.* 32). The snail-curl hairdo was a typical idiom from Mathurā. Many of the Buddha figures, especially those from the *stūpa* site of Golī, showed a preference for covering both the shoulders with the *saṁghāṭi* or robe. This feature indicated the influence of Gāndhāra art. The prominence of the Buddha image at Amarāvatī came about due to a change in religious thinking espoused by the *caityakas*, a sect of the Mahāsāṁghikas. However, even as the Buddha image came into vogue in the lower Kṛṣṇā Valley, the symbolic representations of the Buddha continued to be popular. Buddha continued to be "represented by the symbols like lotus springing from a vase, lion crowned pillar, throne or footprints under a tree, wheel crowned pillar, *stūpa* and the pillar of fire" (Prasad 1980: 43).

In the late phase of Amarāvatī, the third–fourth century CE, the sculptors at adjacent Nāgārjunakoṇḍa had started their work to build the Buddhist complexes and Brāhmanical temples on the banks of the Kṛṣṇā. Therefore there is an intrinsic linkage between the late art of Amarāvatī and Nāgārjunakoṇḍa in the fourth century CE. Many principal deities were made by sculptors at Nāgārjunakoṇḍa. Besides the collosal figures of the Buddha we have remains of large statues of Kārttikeya and the Buddhist fertility deity called Hārīti. The large Hārīti image from the temple at Nāgārjunakoṇḍa reminds of the terracotta image of the sitting Hārīti excavated from the monastery complex of Ghoṣitārāma at Kauśāmbī. The Buddha images at Nāgārjunakoṇḍa were related to, yet different from, their Amarāvatī counterparts (*fig.* 33). The Buddha figures from Nāgārjunakoṇḍa seemed to be more monumental and with heavier physiognomy than the Amarāvatī examples. In conception, the Buddha figures of Nāgārjunakoṇḍa were closer to the Mathurā idiom where the heavy physiognomy was coming into vogue in the third–fifth century CE.

The Brāhmanical sculptural remains from Nāgārjunakoṇḍa are no less interesting. More than a dozen temples were found along the citadel and on the bank of the river Kṛṣṇā; majority of them dedicated to Śiva and Kārttikeya. These temples can be dated to the third–fourth century CE. A standing figure of Kārttikeya in the *samabhaṅga* pose (dated third–fourth century CE) is a unique find of its kind (*Indian Archaeology — A Review*, 1956-57: 35). At Yelleswaram, opposite Nāgārjunakoṇḍa on the Kṛṣṇā

> 5 miniature votive shrines (were) found very close to the temple complex. These shrines have a low *adhiṣṭhāna*, a flat *kapota* and a *vimāna* of 2 steps surmounted by a semi-circular *śikhara*. One of the shrines contained an inscription, the characters of which are similar to those of the Viṣṇukuṇḍin period, datable to *circa* fourth century CE.
>
> — *Indian Archaeology — A Review*, 1964-65: 4

Undoubtedly, the most noteworthy discovery of early sculpture on the Andhra littoral is the *śivaliṅgam* with the image of a standing *puruṣa*, in fact Śiva himself, discovered at Guḍimallam, in the Chittoor District of Andhra Pradesh. The *śivaliṅgam* has been dated to the second century BCE, the earliest example of the emerging iconography of Śiva. The *śivaliṅgam* is kept within the Paraśurāmeśvaraswāmī shrine at Guḍimallam (*fig*. 34). Anand Coomraswamy describes the *śivaliṅgam* thus,

> This is a realistic phallic emblem, five feet in height, with the figure of Śiva carved on its lower side. The deity is two armed, holds as attribute a ram, battle axe and water vessel, and stands firmly on a crouching *yakṣa* of the Bharhut pedestal type. The *yakṣa* is evidently the *apasmāra puruṣa*, the symbol of *malā* or evil, which is exampled by Naṭarāja in the later iconography; can it too have been by this route, and by sea, that the formula reached Japan?
>
> — Coomaraswamy 1972: 39

The shrine was archaeologically investigated by I.K. Sharma of the ASI in the 1970s. Sharma's excavation revealed Iron Age ceramics and early Amarāvatī motifs, indicating the antiquity of the *śivaliṅga*.

The following excerpt from the ASI report clarifies the issue of the early date of the *śivaliṅga*:

> The temple complex itself stands on an extensive but compact mound of the early historical period, yielding Black-and-Red Ware, Russet-coated white-painted Ware and baked bricks. Removal of cut stone slabs of granite for conservation revealed interesting facts about the unique *liṅga*; the earliest and only extant example of its kind in the country. The rectangular *pīṭha,* evidently a later one, found to be in two pieces fitted to the *liṅga* from either ends, was removed and the stumpy dwarf figure and the original *pīṭha* were exposed to view. Certain unique features of the figure are the elephant legs and shrunken body. The *liṅga* shaft is square at the bottom and is fixed into two consecutive rings of the original platform (*pīṭha*), simulating the *yoni,* of brownish sandstone with finely polished surfaces. A square rail, reminiscent of that of the early phases at Mathurā or Amarāvatī was found to run around the *liṅga* set-up.
>
> — *Indian Archaeology — A Review*, 1973-74: 1-2

Another *śivaliṅga* found at Ānandeśvara Temple at Gaṅgāḷabudur in the East Godāvarī district of Andhra Pradesh is much later than the Guḍimallam *liṅga,* dating to the fifth century CE. Made of Dachapalli limestone, it has an *ardhanārīśvara* carved upon it (*Indian Archaeology — A Review*, 1989-90: 1).

To return to the art of Amarāvatī and Nāgārjunakoṇḍa. An important issue associated with the maturation of the art of Andhra is the incorporation of Graeco-Roman themes and styles. In her seminal work, Elizabeth Stone demonstrates how a popular motif of the Roman world, the figure of Venus and Cupid has been skilfully built into the narrative frieze on the Rudrapuruṣadatta Pillar dating between CE 290/300 to 315. She is quite clear that the Roman motifs were imposed upon an already well established tradition of sculptural art at Amarāvatī–Nāgārjunakoṇḍa (unlike at Gandhāra where the Roman influence was intrinsic to the art). A number of indicators, such as the distribution of second century Roman coin hoards, suggest that the lower Kṛṣṇā Valley became a hub of Roman trade in the second century CE. Therefore a distinct Roman element directly entered into the sculptural art of Amarāvatī and Nāgārjunakoṇḍa. In the words of Stone (1994: 78):

> Just when this trade ceased is not clear, but we do know that Roman amphorae as well as Roman coins were found during the Ikṣvāku phase at Nāgārjunakoṇḍa. Objects similar to Begram in Afghanistan have been represented in the art of Amarāvatī while similar comparisons may be seen between Roman objects and Nāgārjunakoṇḍa reliefs. The existence of what appears to be an arena, or perhaps a classical *bouleterion* (a rectangular stepped assembly hall) at Nāgārjunakoṇḍa seems to indicate an Ikṣvāku receptiveness to certain western notions. In terms of sculptural relief, unlike in the art of Gandhāra, this receptiveness was received upon a foundation of Buddhist narrative art which was over four centuries old. Thus, when we see a *mithuna* couple in Roman style dress on a late Amarāvatī drum frieze we are seeing the imposition of a Roman style figure on an already pre-existing Indian concept. In another vein, we wonder if the well-known Scythian type guardian figure, represented on a pillar from Nāgārjunakoṇḍa, is a borrowing from Kuṣāṇa art, or from reality, or from both.

In her work on the epigraphs and architecture of Amarāvatī and eastern Deccan, Anamika Roy compares the sculptural friezes at Amarāvatī and Sannathi. She is struck by the western element in the reliefs at Sannathi, the Buddhist *stūpa* site which lay much inland of Amarāvatī but on the trade routes leading to other Buddhist sites like Pauni, Sāñcī and Bharhut. To quote Roy (1994: 160):

> The sculptures from Sannathi and the sculptural period under discussion belong to the same period and ruling dynasty, but, to some extent differ in style. . . . In Sannathi we detect more Roman influence than in Amarāvatī. From the mass of sculptures from Amarāvatī we find only one lady in foreign dress, holding a chalice and a couple of women in foreign hairstyle and costumes on drum slabs. On a slab from Sannathi the female attendants are depicted with a Roman hairstyle. Their facial features have a foreign appearance. Their armlets and ear ornaments are different to those of Amarāvatī. On one of the broken slabs we find the inscribed names Yavanikā and Saṁghamitrā.

Shoshin Kuwayama, in his article *A Hidden Import from Imperial Rome Manifest in Stūpas,* endeavours to prove that the "wheel shaped" layout of *stūpa*s in the subcontinent, especially those "around the mouths of the Kṛṣnā and Godāvarī rivers," may have been an architectural borrowing from the Roman world (*fig.* 35). In his own words:

> There are striking structural similarities between the circular tombs of stone or brick built in Imperial Rome and its provinces, and the *stūpa*s of large scale in the South Asian subcontinent: concentric circles of walls; a thick, outermost wall (hence, a high drum); and a wheel-like plan comprising a hub with spokes.
>
> — Kuwayama 1997: 162

According to Kuwuyama, the fact that all the wheel-shape planning of the Indian *stūpa*s is done in the early centuries CE, concordant with the time when such architecture was also introduced in the Roman world, the transmission of this architectural feature to the subcontinent happened in course of the flourishing sea trade between the Roman Empire and Early Historic India. However, the concept of a direct western infusion of art and architectural idioms is not shared by all scholars. Kuwayama admits that S.P. Gupta and other scholars consider the wheel shaped plan of the first century CE *stūpa*s in India as deriving from the *dharmacakra* symbolism. In fact, it had started in the third century BCE itself as can be seen in the plan of the Dharmarājika *Stūpa* of Taxila, excavated by John Marshall. Kuwayama's idea of the Roman borrowing of the *stūpa* layout, though interesting, does not demonstrate much except point out similarities in planning in two far-flung civilizations. Like the proposition for a Roman design for the Kārle caves, the postulates of Kuwayama suffer from a space-time gap. Even if we accept his contention that the spoke-like radials introduced in the ground plan of *stūpa*s were purely functional and did not have any religious significance (*dharmacakra*), the likelihood of the concept developing indigenously in India cannot be wished away. Kuwayama labours to show that most of the *stūpa*s in India with wheel-shaped layout cannot be placed before the first century CE. For those which can be dated before, like Amarāvatī, Kuwayama insists that the thick ring wall that held the radials "is not assignable to the earliest *stūpa*" and came up "after the third century BCE and before the second quarter of the second century CE, *most probably of the first to early second century* CE" (Kuwuyama 1997: 130; italics mine). The phrase in italics is obviously his bias for a date later than the time the wheel-shaped ground plan was introduced for circular tombs in Rome.

However, the wheel-shaped plan of the Amarāvatī *stūpa* may have been earlier. Then again, the importance of Bhaṭṭiprolu *stūpa* situated close to Amarāvatī also lies in its wheel-shaped plan. An overview of the *stūpa* ground plans in India, including the *stūpa* at Saṅghol and Taxila, reveals that the wheel-shaped plan and the *āyaka* platforms came into use in the second century BCE (Prasad 1980: 18). In fact, with the hindsight of earlier dates for the *cakra* groundplan in India, Kuwayama's proposition can be turned on its head to propose that the *cakra* design may have been transmitted from India to the western world.

Leaving the *cakra* tradition aside, we cannot also totally block out the possibility of some themes and idioms from the western world having been directly accepted by the artisans in the Kr̥ṣṇā Valley. Coastal Andhra had become a major hub of Roman trade in the second–third centuries CE. This is indicated by the concentration of Roman coin hoards in the region, the highest concentration in India after the Coimbatore region in the deep south of India. The discovery of gold medallions in Nāgārjunakoṇḍa carrying portraits of Ikṣvāku royalty and made in imitation of Roman coins are an example of such transfusions. According to S.P. Gupta (personal communication) the western element in the art of Andhra Pradesh is reflective of influences of the Gandhāra School and also of Mathurā but in their naturalized forms; the garland bearers or *mālāvahaka*s on the Amarāvatī *stūpa* are an example (*fig.* 36). While one cannot have any dispute with this view, I am also inclined to the observations of Stone above. There is no contradiction between the two transmissions, one closely tied with the major art centres of the interiors and the other the creative fallout of long distance trade. On the whole, of course, the art of Amarāvatī and Nāgārjunakoṇḍa had established its own idiom and this style and therefore, as Stone points out (above) that foreign elements were accommodated by a long-established sculptural and architectural tradition going back to the fourth–third century BCE, it is necessary to reiterate that when we speak of the art of Amarāvatī, we allude to a classicism that was pioneered at one particular *stūpa* site which was contemporaenous with (at least from the first century CE) other Buddhist sites in the Kr̥ṣṇā–Godāvarī coastal region. For instance, the Buddhist *stūpa* sites at Ghaṇṭaśāla and Bhaṭṭiprolu are located further downstream of Amarāvatī, while Aḍurru is located on the Godāvarī estuary and Peḍḍagañjam on the coast south of the Kṛṣṇā (*Map* 1). At Guṇṭupalli in West Godāvarī district a number of brick and stone Buddhist *stūpa*s came to light. At the entrance and also inside one of the *stūpa caitya*s sets of limestone statues of the standing Buddha of the early centuries CE, three in each, were found (*Indian Archaaeology — A Review*, 1961-62: 97).

The art of Amarāvatī and Nāgārjunakoṇḍa not only influenced the adjacent coastal regions of the Coromandel but spread along land and sea routes. The influence of Amarāvatī is observed in the Buddhist *stūpa* at Ṭer in the western Deccan (Chapter IV) and in images carved in the Jūnāgaṛh rock-cut caves. The art of Amarāvatī appeared in South-East Asia in the form of Buddha images dated to the third century CE. Human figures carved on a commemorative stone slab discovered in Yemen recall the art of Mathurā and Nāgārjunakoṇḍa (*fig.* 63). A limestone slab found at the Buddhist *stūpa* of Tissamaharama in south-eastern Sri Lanka is an example of the art of Nāgārjunakoṇḍa (*fig.* 66). We shall be touching upon the appearance of the Amarāvatī–Nāgārjunakoṇḍa idioms in various parts of the book. The period between the third century BCE and the third century CE was a period of quick and fast growth and spread of Buddhism by passionate Buddhist monks on the move, fired with the zeal of spreading the *Dhamma* across the world.

Northern Andhra Coast

The northern Andhra coast, bordering Orissa has an unusual terrain. Here, unlike the flat estuarine valleys of the Godāvarī and Kṛṣṇā or the lagoonal environment of the Cilkā lake, the hills of the Eastern Ghats closely overlook the Bay of Bengal. On the face of it, there was little to recommend this area for large-scale settlement. However, the hilly tracts attracted Buddhist mendicants. Here recent excavations have brought to light Buddhist *stūpa* and *vihāra* complexes, in particular the Buddhist sites of Thotlakoṇḍa and Bavikoṇḍa. Lars (2004: 78) provides an overview, "The Buddhist monastery of Thotlakoṇḍa is located 16 km north of the modern city of Visakapatanam in north coastal Andhra Pradesh. Located on a low hill overlooking the Bay of Bengal, it is one of the three monasteries in the immediate area. The closest monastery, Bavikoṇḍa, lies on an adjacent hill less than 2 km from Thotlakoṇḍa. The Andhra Pradesh Department of Archaeology and Museums excavated Thotlakoṇḍa between 1987 and 1991. The excavations revealed several *vihāras*, *caityas*, *stūpas* and other Buddhist remains. The excavators dated occupation of the site between third–second BCE to second–third century CE." At Thotlakoṇḍa and other places on the northern Andhra coast we find the sculptural rendering of Buddhist symbolisms like the *buddhapāda* and stories from Buddha's life. Excavations also brought to light a broken terracotta figurine in *pralambapāda* posture and a miniature figure of Mucalinda *nāga* (*Indian Archaeology — A Review*, 1989-90: 5-8). At Bavikoṇḍa, exquisitely carved *buddhapāda* slabs showing *aṣṭamaṅgala* symbols were found on the southern and northern *āyaka* platforms (Subrahmanyam 1998: 73). Further north of Thotlakoṇḍa/Bavikoṇḍa there are more Buddhist sanctuaries, both free standing and cut into the hills of the Eastern Ghats. One of these is the Hīnayāna monastic complex adjoining the village of Salihundam (District Srikakulam, Andhra Pradesh). This monastery, situated on a hillside, is distinguished by the excavators from the modern village of Salihundam below. The antiquity of the latter is traced by them to the name Salipeṭaka (Emporium of Rice ?) found inscribed on potsherds, conches and stones of the monastery (*Indian Archaeology — A Review* 1953-54: 11-12). The village of Salihundam is situated on the bank of the River Vaṁśadhārā and is merely 5 miles upstream of the ancient seaport of Kaliṅgapaṭnam or *Kalingoe* of Megasthenes (*Map* 12).

Interestingly, a progression of Roman coin find spots have come to light along the coastland north of the Godāvarī delta (*Map* 12). The find places, in northward order, and extending almost up to the border of Orissa are Liṅgarājupalem, Bimlipaṭnam, Koṭapad, Gumada, Vinukoṇḍa, Salihundam and Bhagavanpavam. The area of Bimlipaṭnam includes the Buddhist sites of Bavikoṇḍa and Thotlakoṇḍa. The coin finds include issues of Augustus, Tiberius, Vespasian, Domitian, Hadrian, Antoninus Pius, Marcus Aurelius,

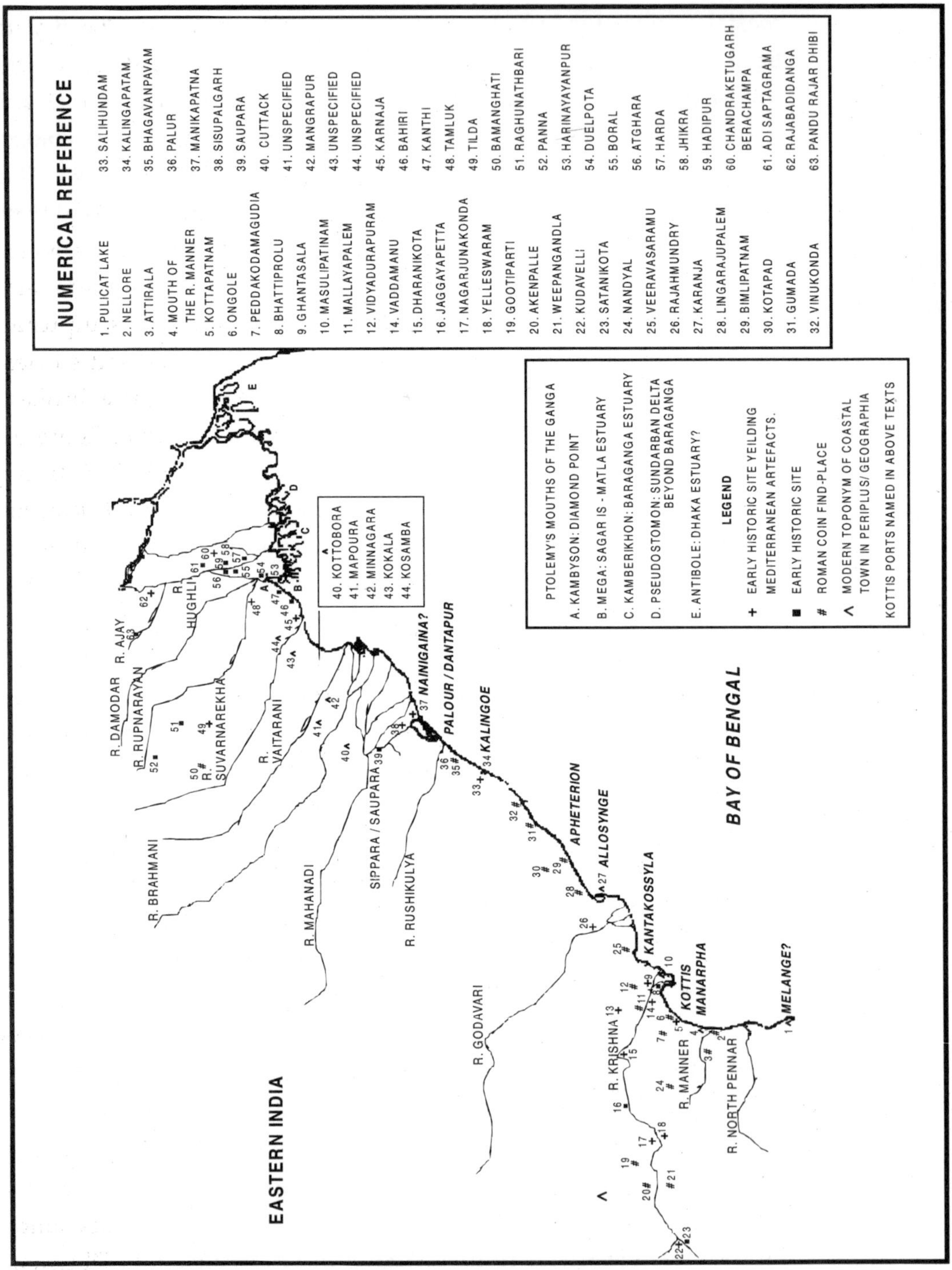

Map 12: Map showing the Roman coin find places on the northern Andhra coast

Commodus, Caracalla and Septimus Severus; covering the full Imperial Roman period from first–third century CE. Interestingly, imitations in gold of the issues of Augustus, Tiberius, and Septimus Severus were also recovered (for details of finds see Turner 1989: 46-87). Why were so many Roman coins and their imitations found in this desolate stretch of coast marked by hills of the Eastern Ghats and reclusive Buddhist *vihāra*s? I believe the regular distribution of Roman coins north of the Godāvarī is related to the last coastal point in *Maisolos* listed in the *Geographia* of Ptolemy (dated second century CE): the *apheterion* or point of departure for ships bound for Chryse (Burma/South-East Asia). Interestingly, Yule (in McCrindle/Shastri 1927: 68-69) provides a later historical parallel for Ptolemy's *apheterion* by citing the tradition of ships choosing Bimlipaṭnam near river Baroua as the embarkment point for sailing to Burma in the eighteenth century (*Map* 12). Roman and Sātavāhana coins recovered from Bimlipaṭnam and other sites of the northern Andhra coast mentioned above suggest Roman trade contact with this area, most possibly by sea. The Roman coins at Liṅgarājupalem (one an imitation of an Augustan issue) were washed up on the beach, perhaps from an ancient shipwreck somewhere off the northern Andhra coast. The conspicuous spread of Roman coins north and south of Bimlipaṭnam show that the *apheterion* existed, and departure of ships from it to further shores involved Roman trading interests as well.

Therefore, the hilly tracts of the Eastern Ghats were not so desolate as they seemed. The influence of the art of Amarāvatī and the Jaina and Hīnayāna Buddhist rock-cut art of Orissa converged in the hilly coastland north of the Godāvarī basin. The connection between religion, art and trade cannot be more conspicuous. The rock-cut sanctuaries and free standing *vihāra-stūpa* sites overlooking a crucial staging area of sea trade on the Bay of Bengal coast parallels in every way similar processes at work in the Western Ghats overlooking the Koṅkaṇ Coast, expressed in the early rock-cut caves at Bhaja and Kondivte. In Guṇṭupalli in northern Andhra Pradesh, not far from the Eastern Ghats, there is an important group of Buddhist caves, including *vihāra*s and *stūpa*s. According to Coomaraswamy (1972: 38-

39) these caves are curiously like the early caves at Junnār in western India and recall the Lomas Ṛṣi cave in Bihar.

Southern Andhra–Tamil Coast

South of the river Kṛṣṇā, the core area of the art of Amarāvatī–Nāgārjunakoṇḍa, the main *stūpa* sites near the coast are at Peḍḍagañjam and Candravaram (*Maps* 11, 12). The Peḍḍagañjam *stūpa* is similar to that of Ghaṇṭaśāla. The Candravaram *stūpa* is situated near the mouth of the river Manara. The Manara flows between the rivers Kṛṣṇā and the north Pennar. The Department of Archaeology, Government of Andhra Pradesh undertook excavation at Candavaram in the early 1970s. The site was found to contain many *stūpas*, *vihāras* and beautifully carved sculptures showing *dharmacakra* and *Jātaka* tales carved in Amarāvatī idiom. Large limestone slabs on the body of the brick *stūpa* were found carved in low relief. The themes on the stone slabs relate to the aniconic worship of the Buddha (*vajrāsana* worship) and Jātaka tales (Murthy 1997-98: 106-108). An inscription in Brāhmī characters of the second century CE suggests the date of the site. Since the image of Buddha is absent, the art is affiliated to the first phase of the art of Amarāvatī (*Indian Archaeology — A Review*, 1972-73: 3). However, it must be borne in mind that even when the Buddha image was born, Buddha's aniconic representation never ceased.

The *stūpa* sites on the southern Andhra coast seem to have come up in the context of trade. The *Geographia* of Ptolemy (second century CE) lists two trade ports, Kottis and Manarpha lying north of the Pennar but south of the estuary of the Maisolos or river Kṛṣṇā. McCrindle (in Sastri 1927: 65-67) does not give an exact location for Koṭṭis, holding that the settlement "lay not very far" north of the mouth of the river Manara. The toponym for ancient Koṭṭis suggests itself in the settlement of Koṭṭapaṭnam which lies on the seaboard between the Pennar and Kṛṣṇā rivers (*Map* 12). Prospections carried out at Koṭṭapaṭnam, a sea-facing village (in Vakaḍu maṇḍala of Nellore district, Andhra Pradesh) by Rao (1994a: 829-31) has brought to light extensive pottery deposition of the Early Historic period on a sandy beach-head along a creek. Rao has also discovered an artificial channel (1.25 km long, 200 m wide) which he suggests as a docking area for merchant vessels. Among ceramics recovered from Koṭṭapaṭnam by Rao are the fine Rouletted Ware type which Wheeler et al. (1946, 45-49) first discovered at Arikameḍu. Rao also retrieved a variety of stamped/impressed pottery decorated with combinations of linear and geometric designs. Rao finds parallels for this decorated pottery from Koṭṭapaṭnam in South-East Asian and southern Chinese ceramic types of the BCE/CE changeover. Rao (1994b) also reports finds of Roman glassware pieces from Koṭṭapaṭnam. The place name similarity between Koṭṭis/Koṭṭapaṭnam, evidence for harbour facilities at the site and the artefactual remains indicating maritime trade contact with South-East Asia and the Western World present a strong archaeological context for this site to be the Koṭṭis of the *Geographia*. The location of Koṭṭis/Koṭṭapaṭnam is close to that of Peḍḍagañjam. Similarly, the *stūpa* of Candravaram is in proximity to the estuary of the river Manara, the location proposed here for Manarpha, Ptolemy's other port between the Kr̥ṣṇā and the Pennar (McCrindle in Shastri 1927: 65-67).

The next major site showing influence of the art of Amarāvatī is situated at Kāverīpaṭṭinam, the site of a major Early Historic port at the mouth of the river Kāverī in Tamil Nadu. In this regard, the following observations of the excavators S.R. Rao and K.V. Raman are crucial:

> An outstanding discovery was Buddhist vihara consisting of 5 square rooms and a common verandah laid bare in a locality called Pallavaneśvaram. The walls were originally decorated with moulded bricks and stucco ornamentation. Traces of a few layers of painting have also been noticed on the stucco pieces recovered in the excavation. A small bronze figurine of the Buddha in *dhyāna* pose and a broken terracotta figurine of a goddess were found in one of the cells. In a subsidiary structure, of probably a later phase, a slab of limestone bearing the *buddhapāda* and sacred symbols such as the *pūrṇaghaṭa, svastika* and *śrīvatsa* were found in disturbed condition. The material used and the decorative style show an unmistakable affinity with the Buddhist art of the Andhra country as seen in Amarāvatī and Nāgārjunakoṇḍa. The available evidence suggests that the main building belonged to the fourth-fifth century AD with reconstruction made in a later phase.
>
> — *Indian Archaeology — A Review*, 1964-65: 24-25

A *stūpa* like structure also came to light during the excavations at Kāñcīpuram, the famous temple town in Tamil Nadu. The structure was found at the lowest level, Period IB (*Indian Archaeology — A Review*, 1972-73: 55). Far from the coast, but on the trans-peninsular route that connects the Kerala and Tamil seaboard, a terracotta bust of a bearded man, having the countenance of a warrior, came to light at Eroḍe in Tamil Nadu (*fig.* 37). It is in the possesion of the Kalaimagal Meenakshisundram Archaeological Learning and Research Centre, Eroḍe. The soldier wears a spiked helmet. The eyes are round and fierce. The man has a curving moustache and a sharp clipped beard. The long ears mark him as an important person, going by similar anatomical feature on the Buddha figures. The moustache and the beard show a Hellenistic impact. This moustache is similar to that found on a number of Buddha figures produced at Gandhāra. However, this Hellenistic element on this figure may or may not have been direct even if we assume that the bust is a representation of a Westerner or Yavana. There are numerous references to Yavana (Roman?, perhaps Westerners in general), guards in the Tamil Saṅgam literature of the early centuries CE. The intense sea trade between the southern kingdoms of the Coḷas, Pāṇḍyas and Ceras with the Roman empire brought the Westerners to India. Many of them were employed as guards by local rulers. The terracotta bust was found on the ancient route that connected the Coromandal to the Malabar coast. Though it is a surface find, a tentative date of first-second century CE is proposed.

Few sculptures of stone have been found on the Coromandal coast before the fifth century CE. The terracotta art is more conspicuous, as evident in the finding of figurines in the early levels at Kāverīpaṭṭinam and Kāñcīpuram. A terracotta human head from Kāñcīpuram, dated to the early centuries CE, shows the hair piled into a *jaṭā* (*fig.* 38). There is a fine execution of the nose and eyes. Another example of a clay sculpture of quality is a standing figure found at Arikameḍu (*fig.* 39). The head is broken off but the posture and the long flowing dress showing Hellenistic influence suggests it to be a lady. The sculpture is indicative of life at the port of Arikameḍu, visited regularly by traders from the Roman world (*Plate* 25). The lack of sculptural art on the Tamil coast is no reflection on other aesthetic expressions, such as the sophisticated glass and stone beadcrafting industries at Arikameḍu and Koḍumanal, the urn burials at Aḍichallanur with fine copper objets d'art, the sacrophagi from coastal "megalithic" sites like Souttekeny and the orthostats and anthropomorphic figures in stone from megalithic sites.

Kerala–Lakshadweep

Surprisingly, the coastland of Kerala is almost bereft of sculptural art in the period of our review. The only exception is the Buddha heads of Gupta style found at the island of Lakshadweep off the Kerala coast (*Map* 11). The island group of Maldives, south of the Lakshadweep chain, also has a strong pre-Islamic tradition rooted in Buddhism and all these cultural transmissions to the Lakshadweep and the Maldives must have occurred through the Kerala coast. Two Buddha heads have been discovered in Androth Island in the Lakshadweep chain off the coast of Kerala (Plate 26). These are made of the local coral rocks and coral paste. The facial features are worn off due to weathering of the sea. Yet in the larger of the two busts one can discern a long angular face, the long ears and the snail-curl hair typical of the Buddha statues of the Gupta period from Mathurā and Sārnāth. Tripati (1999: 833) has bracketed the busts between CE 400–500. According to Tripati (1999: 834), Buddha heads made out of the local coral rock have also been uncovered from mounds on the Minicoy Islands. Some of these Buddha heads have sockets for attachment to torsos. The creation of Buddha images inspired by the classic style of north India in the Gupta period and the use of local stone to make these images reveals that classical art styles from northern India had reached the south-western coast of India, most likely through trade. The Buddha head from Maldives is also part of the distribution of Gupta style Buddha images in the Lakshadweep, Minicoy, Maldives chain.

The Karnataka Coast

The Kanārā has been little known in history and archaeology. The

Kanārā Coast, divided into two administrative sub-regions by the present Uttara Kannada and Dakshin Kannada districts of the state of Karnataka, stretches for about 320 km from the Karwar Peninsula in the north to the Malabar coast (or the river Netravali) (*Map* 13). The coastal dunes near the sea give way in the interiors to small alluvial plains with coconut fringed lagoons. The low lying coast is overlooked by the hilly edge of the Deccan plateau known as the Western Ghats. The Ghāṭs are heavily forested and rise some 2500-3000 ft above sea level. The Ghāṭs are also the sources of rivers flowing into the Kanārā, such as the Śarāvatī and the Netravali. East of the Ghāṭs are the scrub lands of the Central Deccan plateau, through which flow the rivers Tuṅgabhadrā and the Kāverī. The creeks and rivers of the Kanārā are more easily accessible from the sea than from the interior plateau because of the barrier presented by the Western Ghats. The sheer elevation of the uplands is indicated by the height of the Gersoppa Falls, at 253 m the highest waterfall in India. Deep water creeks penetrate the coast for many miles at Karwar, Gokarṇa, Basrur and Malpe, offering safe anchorage for watercraft. Of the rivers, the Śarāvatī and the Netravali provide deep and stable water bodies that facilitate transport from the coastal interior right up to the Arabian Sea (*Map* 13).

The Kanārā Coast has not been conspicuous in Indian historical sources. The *Mahābhārata* makes a solitary reference to Gokarṇa, the place of pilgrimage in Uttara Kannada district associated with Paraśurāma (Gururaja Bhatt 1969). The Kanārā coastland can be recognized in place-names mentioned in the following western sources of the early centuries CE: the *Periplus Maris Erythraei* (first century CE), *Geographia* of Ptolemy (second century CE) and the *Papyrus Oxyrhynchus* (second century CE). Section 53 of the *Periplus* provides the first historical account of the Kanārā. It was with the intention of investigating Early Historic ports on the Kanārā that I undertook an exploration of the coast in company of Dr S.K. Aruni of the Indian Council of Historical Research (Bangalore). The details of the exploration have been reported in the *Journal of Indian Ocean Archaeology* (see Gupta and Aruni 2005: 42-54). In this section, my focus is on the sculptural artefacts observed by us first-hand at the coastal sites of

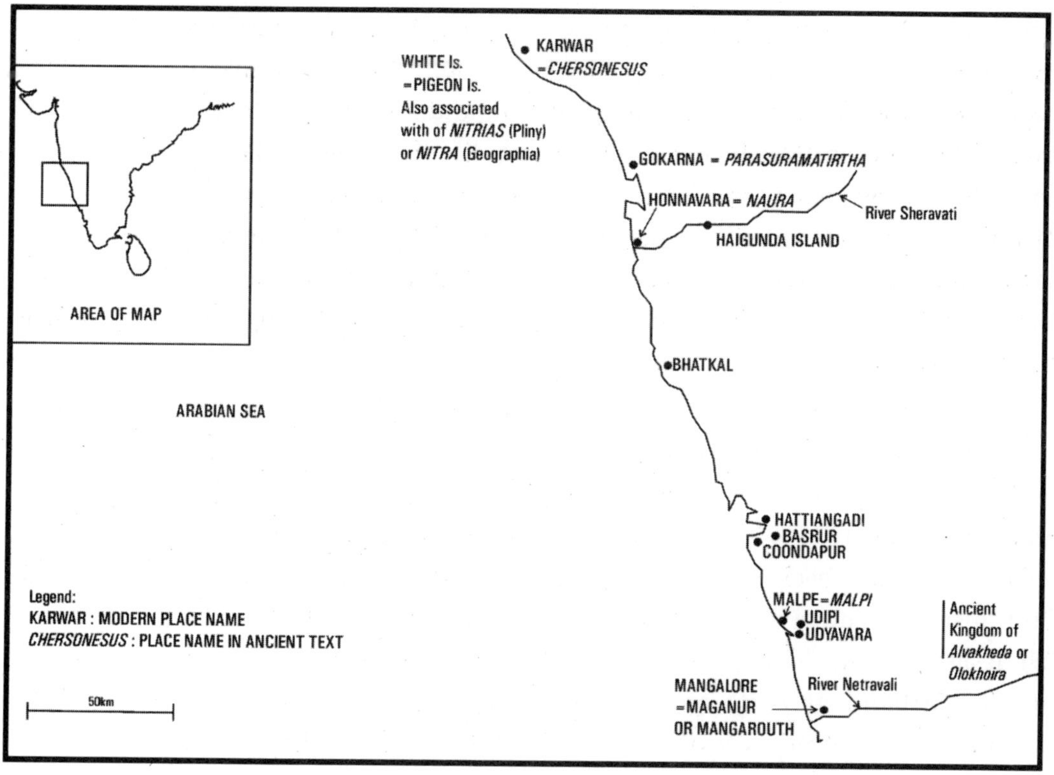

Map 13: Map of Karnataka coast

Haigunḍa (northern Kanārā) (Plate 27) and Malpe Udyavara (southern Kanārā; Plate 35).

The modern town of Honnavara, situated near the mouth of the river Śarāvatī, was where we commenced our field trip in December 2001 (*Map* 13). It was decided to first survey the riverine island of Haigunḍa. This island is situated in the middle of the estuarine channel of the River Śarāvatī, some 20 km east of Honnavara (Plate 27). Haigunḍa seemed prospective because pottery and structures dating to the early centuries of the Christian Era have been reported from here by previous explorers (Poonacha and Vishveshvara 1991: 69; Sundara 1992: 100-01). To reach Haigunḍa we took a bus from Honnavara to Allanki Village on the Honnavara-Siddapur road. The journey was through the lower hills of the Ghāṭs, skirting the river Śarāvatī. From Allanki village the river Śarāvatī was crossed by boat (dugout) to the island of Haigunḍa. Haigunḍa island is about 1 × 1 km in area. The waters of the Śarāvatī split around Haiguṇḍa, forming two arms (Plate 27). The island of Haiguṇḍa is dominated by a hillock on the south-west corner. The village of Haiguṇḍa is situated below this rocky outcrop. Much of the island is cultivated, the landscape characterized by sugar cane fields and palm groves. Three main sites of interest were identified: archaeological deposits on the hilltop, a *yakṣa* statue in a sacred grove and a temple sanctuary with image of Viṣṇu. Besides we observed a number of sculptures (Buddha figures, Viṣṇu and *śivaliṅgas*) scattered in the fields.

The large *yakṣa* statue at Haiguṇḍa, standing tall at 1.69 m, has been dated on stylistical grounds to the second–third century CE and with a preference for the earlier century (Sundara 1990: 39-45; Hegde and Sarvamangala 1997: 75-77). The great *yakṣa*, like a sentinel of this ancient port, has been made in the likeness of the sculptures at the Buddhist rock-cut caves at Kanheri on the Koṅkaṇ coast (Plates 28, 29). It also exhibits "Indianized" Graeco-Roman influence in the setting of the hairband or *paṭṭa* and Scythian features in the jewellery decoration. The similarity of the *yakṣa* to the images of Kārle and Kanheri suggests Haiguṇḍa's connection with Early Historic Koṅkaṇ. The Graeco-Roman style of hair band, albeit indigenized, on the large *yakṣa* hints at western art influences coming with long distance trade. The features of the *yakṣa* have been described in detail by Hegde and Sarvamangala (1997: 76):

> The knotted hair at the top has a single strand of beads tied to it. A hair band or *paṭṭa* closely resembling the Graeco-Roman diadem is tied above the forehead. It consists of a rosette medallion with festoons issuing from its centre and is akin to the similar *paṭṭas* shown as worn by the figures in Kārle and Kanheri. The *yakṣa* of Haiguṇḍa wears an ear-ring *kuṇḍala* type entwining the earlobe. This *kuṇḍala* has a *makara*-shaped terminus. Its animal headed terminus in jewellery may be a Scythian influence. The necklace of *Graiveyaka* type is also noticeable. The armlet resembles a metal band of embossed rosette medallion design. He wears a single hollow grooved bracelet. A waist band tied around the pot belly is knotted on both the sides and its surplus cloth reaches the ground. The right hand of the figure is broken and the left hand holds the folds of the waist band, a typical posture of the early *yakṣa* from north India. The round face

> with protruding lips and wide nose and open eyes have a close resemblance to the figures from Kārle and Kanheri.

The villagers at Haiguṇḍa continue to worship the great *yakṣa* and we had to approach the figure bare footed. Another *yakṣa* figure, similar to the one described above, is in a fragmented state and could not be visited. Two Buddha images and a Viṣṇu figure which we observed in a field just outside the village show familiarity with both the Kuṣāṇa and the Gupta style of art (Plate 30). These sculptures can be properly imputed to the late Kuṣāṇa-Gupta transition in the third–fourth century CE (S.P. Gupta: personal communication). The Buddha and Viṣṇu images on the island indicate contact with central and northern India. The images are described in detail below.

Situated between the two Buddha statues is a buff stone statue of a Brāhmanical God, most likely Viṣṇu (Plate 31). The statue is about 5 ft tall. The lower part of the statue is not fully visible as it is embedded in the ground. Both the arms are broken and therefore the main iconographic attributes are not present. However, the long conical headdress (*kirīṭa*), firmly placed on the head of the God and the wavy coiffure indicate, on stylistic grounds, the period of Kuṣāṇa–Gupta transition. The image shows influences of both periods of northern Indian art. The Kuṣāṇa feature is evident in the robust physiognomy. It does not have the slenderness associated with the Gupta forms. On the other hand the downcast eyes and the aura of an inner divinity anticipates the classic Gupta sculptures. On the body, the crease below the neck shows that the divine figure is draped in a diaphanous body cloth. The lower garment is in form of a *dhotī*. The image is ascribed a date of third–fourth century CE.

Two similar grey stone statues of Buddha, about 5 ft in height, are located in a field on the outskirts of Haiguṇḍa village. One of the Buddha figures has its face weathered but the features can be distinguished in the second statue (Plates 32, 33). The two standing images flank the statue of Viṣṇu. The sculptures are rather crude in conception and cannot be placed in any classic tradition of sculptural art. The faces are heavy and florid and the body cuts quite robust and muscular, with large rolling chests, hands and torso. The snail-curl hair indicates their connection with the classical images of the Buddha from Mathurā and Sārnāth. The bodies of the Buddha statues is uncovered except for a small undergarment. However, the hands seem to hold the edges of the *saṁghāti* and therefore it may be surmised that the Buddha statues are covered with a diaphanous cloth. Since both hands are fragmented, it is not possible to know the *mudrā* adopted by the Buddha figures. It has been suggested that these Buddha figures may be placed in the post-Gupta period because of their rough hewn style. In my opinion the Buddha figures are indigenous in conception, like the Buddha head from Thaddoo island in the Maldives and the Buddha heads from Androth. It would be appropriate to date the standing Buddha images of Haiguṇḍa to the general chronological bracket of the other Buddha figures from the south-west coast of India. I propose a date of fifth–sixth century CE for the two Buddhas.

An image of Viṣṇu in the form of "Janārdana" was found near a modern temple at Haiguṇḍa. It has been placed, on stylistic parameters, in the fifth–sixth century CE (Hegde and Sarvamangala 1997: 77). The sculptural remains at Haiguṇḍa, spread over the period first–fifth century CE, point to the progressive integration of the Kanārā coast to coastal and sea trade networks in this time.

Small statues of Gaṇeśa and *śivaliṅgams* dated to the Kadamba period (fifth century CE) have been reported from Coodnapur in the Uttara Kannada district (*Indian Archaeology — A Review*, 1993-94: 67-68). *Śivaliṅgams* were found in Haigunda also (Plate 34).

Rao and Sundara also report an early Śiva temple at Udyavara (*Indian Archaeology — A Review*, 1968, 69-24). According to Gururaja Bhatt (1969: 23) the "apsidal structure" of the temple can be dated to the early centuries CE. On our visit to the Śiva temple, we found the apsidal shape of the temple faced with new bricks (Plate 36). The remains of a squarish stone which must have been used to hold the deity in the old sanctum lay on the ground in front of the temple. According to S.K. Aruni, the carved stone most likely is of the Early Historic period.

Summary

The southern coastlands had developed a fairly mature tradition of sculptural art in the early centuries CE. As discussed above, the powerful coastal centre of art was Amarāvatī. The classical style that emerged in this *stūpa* site was itself the result of interminglings, of mainstream art from the interiors, the folk art of eastern Andhra (as seen on the panels at Vaḍḍamanu) and elements from the Western world. The northern Andhra coast saw the Hīnayāna traditions flourishing, similar to the Hīnayāna rock-cut caves in the Western Ghats. The recent discoveries of Buddha heads made of coral in the Lakshadweep islands show the spread of sculptural art to the very edge of the Indian peninsula.

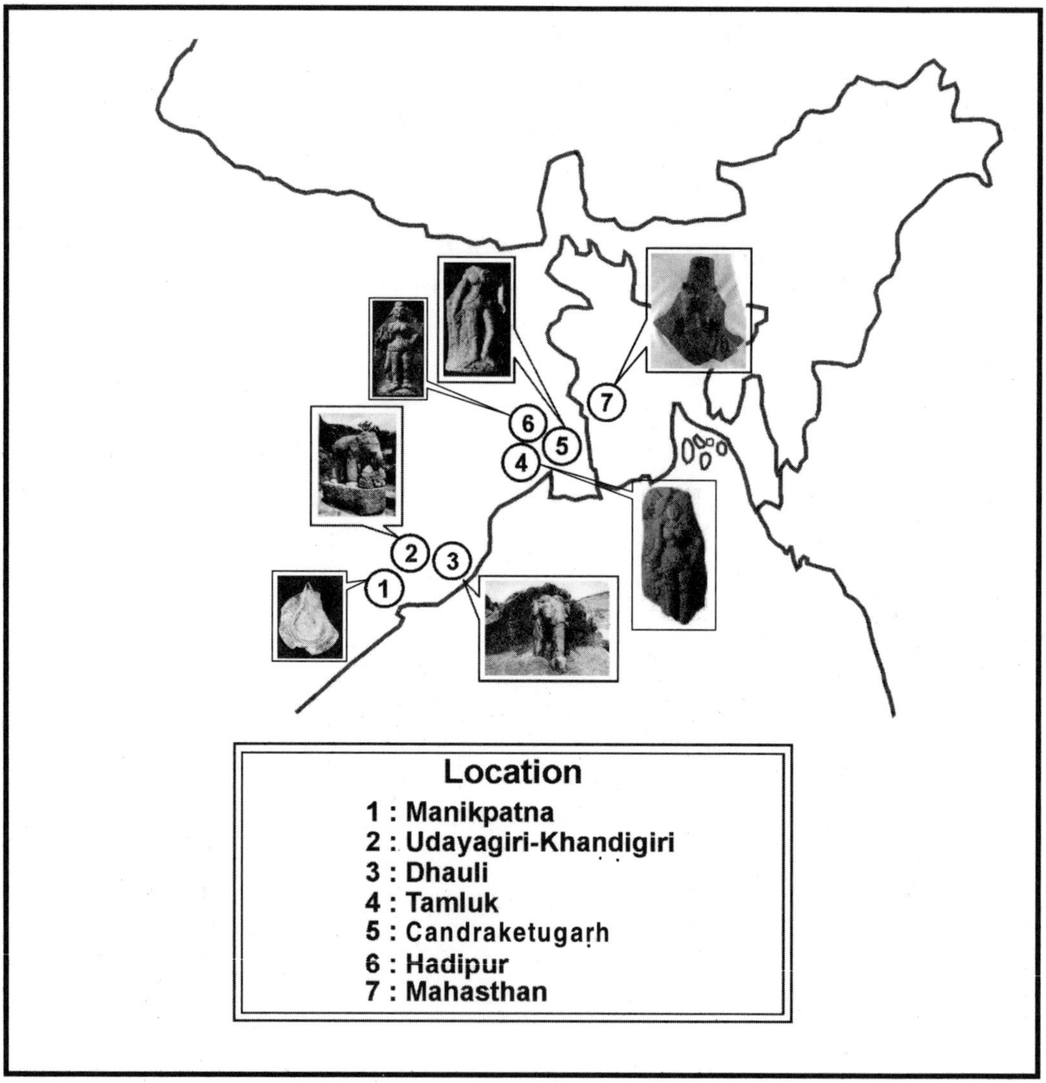

Map 14: Find places of Early Sculptural Art on the Eastern Coast of India & Bangladesh.

6

The Eastern Coastland

THE area under review comprises the coastal regions of the states of West Bengal and Orissa (*Map* 14). The lower Bengal area was firmly integrated with the Gangetic Zone and received regular commercial traffic from the Silk Route crossroads in the north-west of the India. Orissa, on the other hand became more entrenched into the settlement pattern of the Deccan after early Mauryan (third century BCE) linkages with the Gangetic zone became weak. Geographically, Orissa can be differentiated between the hilly tracts — the southern portion of the Chota Nagpur plateau merging into the Eastern Ghats — which make up most of the territory of the state, and the coastal plains which extend south from the river Suvarṇarekhā and range in breadth from 25 to 75 km (Panigrahi 1961: 182; Lahiri 1992: 322). Compared to the uplands, where the Early Historic material culture is characterized by sparse habitations revealing southern Megalithic traits (Pradhan 1991: 12-16) the coastal lowland of Orissa reveals a high urban character manifested in the monumental architecture of the fortified settlement of Śiśupālgaṛh (Lal 1949: 62-105). The southern coast of Orissa borders the hilly tracts of northern Andhra Pradesh where, as we have discussed, a concentration of Buddhist *vihāra*s have come to light. I shall first discuss the evidence from Bengal.

Lower Bengal

It is strange that iconographic forms in stone are almost absent on the Bengal coast till the fifth century CE. Among the solitary finds is a red stone image (second century CE) from Candraketugaṛh of a Buddha or Jaina figure evidently imported from Mathurā (*Indian Archaeology — A Review* 1957-58: Plate LXXXVII; Biswas 1981: 87; *Fig.* 14). However, the terracotta art anticipated the appearance of some of the "main" iconographic forms like Indra, Lakṣmī, Gaṇeśa, Kubera and Sūrya. A male figure sitting atop an elephant has been discovered from Candraketugaṛh, the Early Historic port site in lower Bengal. The figure wears a trefoil turban. The eyes are wide open and the heavy earrings give a look of formality to the figure (*IAR* 1961-62: Plate CI/A; *fig.* 40). The excavator has suggested that the male deity on elephant may be that of Indra on his elephant Airāvata. The figure has been ascribed a date of first century BCE. Indra also appears in the Buddhist tradition as Śakra. That such representations were not isolated is evident from the Indra on elephant carved at the entrance of the Bhaja cave group in Maharashtra (*fig.* 16).

A terracotta figure of an elephant, as an integral part of a terracotta toy cart, has been also discovered from Candraketugaṛh (*fig.* 41). Terracotta toy carts were popular expressions of secular art in the Gangetic region during Early Historic times (Plate 37). The depiction of the elephant figure is unusual. The motive for sculpting the elephant figure may have been to attract children. On the other hand the elephant head may be an early representation of Gaṇeśa, similar to the one in the Udayagiri–Khaṇḍagiri caves in Orissa (*fig.* 42). The object has been dated to the first century BCE (IAR 1961-62: 62-63).

A terracotta figure, about 11 cm in height, has been excavated from the Early Historic port-site of Candraketugaṛh in lower Bengal. The figure sculpted in the round shows a man with a large belly and a heavy face. The terracotta piece is actually a rattle and must have been used as a toy. The figure may denote Kubera, the deity associated with wealth and plenty (*Indian Archaeology — A Review*, 1961-62: Plate CLV/3). Biswas (1981: 85-86) identifies terracotta figures from Candraketugaṛh with Sūrya and the fire god Agni.

Also found from Candraketugaṛh is a clay figure of a female deity holding a lotus stalk. She has been identified as Śrī, the precursor of Lakṣmī (*fig.* 43). This piece is dated to the first century BCE. Biswas (1981: 83) make a detailed observation on the occurrence of such figures in lower Bengal,

> In the domain of the terracotta art of Bengal one of her early forms occurs at Bangarh. She stands on a fully blossomed lotus in a stiff

> *samapāda* posture. Similar figures have been recovered from Candraketugaṛh, Haroā, and Tamluk. Another interesting fragmentary plaque from Haroā of the Śuṅga period visualizes her lower part only. It shows her standing on a pedestal supported by a fully bloomed lotus. Lotus stems are seen on either of her sides. Yet another plaque from Candraketugaṛh stylistically dated to the second–first century BCE gives a complete form of the goddess. Here she stands on a lotus and holds a full bloomed lotus by her hands. The obvious association of all the figurines with lotus establishes their identity as Śrī-Lakṣmī. A terracotta plaque depicting a female figure in frontal pose was excavated at Hadipur, an Early Historic site in lower Bengal. The figurine is mould made and falls squarely in the tradition of Śuṅga period (second–first century BCE). The hairstyle of the female divinity shows long and thick braids. Her lower dress is a *dhotī* with a long vertical fold of the garment. In her right hand she holds a lotus stalk. The lotus emblem identifies her as Lakṣmī. — *Indian Archaeology — A Review*, 1961-62: Plate CI/C

Another female deity found on the Bengal coast is the *pañcacūḍa* figurine showing a female deity with elaborate hairdo. From Candraketugaṛh was found the upper fragment of a moulded terracotta figurine set in a plaque showing a female figure having an elaborate headdress (*fig.* 44). There are thick braids of hair on both sides of the head. Fixed into the braids are five emblems. This female divinity has been identified with the mother-goddess Māyā who brings flood to the river Ganges. A certain *Maia* has also been referred to in the *Papyrus Oxyrhynchus* as the goddess connected to the Ganges (Biswas 1981: 76). The well-known art historian Stella Kramrisch (1939: 99-101) has called the goddess the *apsaras* Pañcacūḍa who emerged in the churning of the Ocean. A terracotta image of the Goddess, dated to the first century BCE, has been found at the port of Tamluk and is now reposited at the Ashmoleon Museum, Oxford. Similar terracotta figures have also been found in the middle Gaṅgā Valley. In Plate 5 we see the *pañcacūḍa* figurine from the Early Historic site of Kauśāmbī near Allahabad. The richly moulded terracotta plaque is typical of the Śuṅga period in northern India and can be ascribed a date of second–first century BCE. The various attributes of the *pañcacūḍa* figure indicate a connection with the coastlands and overseas trade. She seems to have ben a popular deity in the Gangetic Valley in the BCE–CE transition.

The identifications of the terracotta figures above with Brāhmanical deities should be considered to be of a preliminary and tentative nature. Most of these iconographic forms were to emerge in stone at the great centre of sculptural art at Mathurā. However, the similarity of so many terracotta images with gods and goddesses that were to become popular in the early centuries CE is interesting. The terracotta art of lower Bengal in the Early Historic period indicates that divinities had been conceived in human form before their expression in stone sculpture. Interestingly, the terracotta art of lower Bengal kept pace with developments in sculptural art in Mathurā, Gandhāra and Sārnāth. It is to be noted that the Early Historic stratigraphy of lower Bengal sites is congruent with the dynastic periods of the Gangetic Valley. The terracotta art of lower Bengal had matured by the third century BCE and mould made terracotta figures of Maurya style are found in abundance at Mahāsthāngaṛh, Tamluk, Candraketugaṛh and other sites (*Map* 14). The shift from Mauryan to post-Mauryan terracotta style was observed in the stratigraphy of Mahāsthāngaṛh, the large Early Historic settlement in Bangladesh excavated by a Bangladeshi-French team. J.F. Salles, the director of the Mahāsthāngaṛh excavation makes the following observation:

> . . . the most important feature of level 5 is the sudden occurrence of terracotta moulded plaques. The human figurines, which are the most numerous, appear as the earliest finds of this type in the stratigraphy of the Eastern Rampart Area (see their absence in the Early Settlement phase). Their aesthetic and technical variety attests to the existence of different types of fabrics. Their stylistic type, well known in the other sites of the Gangetic Valley, could belong to the Maurya period, or at least follow the Mauryan tradition. The number of finds in levels 6 to 8, especially in level 7, is more than 100; their styles and fabrics being closely affiliated to the typical post-Mauryan ones well known all over Bengal. — Salles 2004: 198

The terracotta art of the post-Mauryan period (the Śuṅga period) was characterized by exquisite moulded figurines. Among some of the most exquisite terracotta images are those collected from

Candraketugaṛh. These are in a variety of poses and most show beautiful coiffure, headdress and jewellery (*fig.* 45). These figurines, which include the *pañcacūḍa* goddess discussed above, were part of the greater tradition of Śuṅga terracotta art in the Gangetic Valley.

> Excavations and surface explorations have yielded terracotta sculptures which can be compared with the best examples of Kuṣāṇa–Gupta period art. For instance, excavations at Tamluk by the University of Calcutta produced some beautiful terracottas of the third–fourth century CE, showing Kuṣāṇa and Gupta influence. Mention may be made of a superb terracotta figurine (only the lower part found) which was characterized by a graceful modelling and transparent drapery of the early Gupta period.
>
> — *Indian Archaeology — A Review*, 1954-55: 20

Two terracottas, one each from Tilda and Tamluk show the treatment recalling the famous Sārnāth Buddha (*fig.* 46; Biswas 1981: 87).

In a seminal article *The Impact of Gandhāra on the Art of Ancient Vanga*, B.N. Mukherjee (1997: 173-88) identifies a range of terracotta sculptures of the Kuṣāṇa–Gupta period (first–fifth century CE) which show Hellenistic and Scythian elements in facial features, vestments and headdress (*fig.* 48). The sculpting of these figures reminds Mukherjee of the sculptural art of Gandhāra and to a lesser extent, of the Mathurā school. Mukherjee makes his point quoting specific examples, as the following excerpt from his articles shows:

> Certain specimens from the territory of ancient Vaṅga bear a stylistic resemblance to classical Gāndhāra art. For an example we can refer to a partly broken female figure in terracotta found during excavation at Tamluk at a level dated to the third or fourth century CE. The extant portion shows the lower part of a shapely figure standing in an easy stance and clad in semi-diaphanous drapery. The limbs beneath the deep folds are treated sensuously. In both these respects the Tamluk figure can be compared with the Gandhāra statue of a woman found at Mathurā.
>
> — Mukherjee 1997: 179

Other figures mentioned by Mukherjee include a terracotta male head with conical headgear from Pāṇḍurājārdhibi in Burdwan and a horse rider wearing a Kuṣāṇa costume from the coastal site at Hadipur (Mukherjee 1997: *figs.* 9 & 10).

In lower Bengal we find the idea of iconography very strong in the terracotta art. The paucity of stone and the availibility of the rich alluvium soil of deltaic Bengal created a magnificent range of artworks in terracotta during the BCE–CE transition. Though there was a paucity of artworks in stone in lower Bengal, a scattering of indigenous stone images in other parts of undivided Bengal suggests that the artists were not ignorant of other media. Frederick Asher (1980) has reviewed the evidence of stone sculptures of the Kuṣāṇa–Gupta period in West Bengal and Bangladesh. Of the less than dozen stone sculptures of the Kuṣāṇa–Gupta Period found in Bengal, the prominent ones are a Viṣṇu figure from Māldā, two Sūrya images from Māldā and a stone Kārttikeya figure from Mahāsthāngaṛh (Asher 1980: 11-23). The Viṣṇu image from Māldā (*fig.* 47), to which Asher attributes a 4th century CE date, has a flat topped *kirita* similar to the Viṣṇu figures from Gujarat (chapter 4). It was only in the eighth–ninth century CE that Brāhmanical and Buddhist iconography was fully expressed in an indigenous stone art. Images of Viṣṇu, Sūrya, Bhairava and Avalokiteśvara were sculpted in black basalt from the Bihar hills. These images were part of the post-Sārnāth tradition of Pāla style (for discovery of Pāla statues in lower Bengal see Chakrabarti and Chattopadhyay 1992: 135-53).

Orissa Coast

While terracotta defines the early sculptural art of lower Bengal, it is the rock-cut sculptural friezes and sculptures which characterise the art tradition on the the Orissa coast in the BCE–CE transition. The great elephant sculpture at Dhauli, made under the patronage of the imperial Mauryans, in all likelihood Aśoka, represents the Indian genius in sculpture in stone in the pre-Christian Era (*fig.* 49). In his work *Roots of Indian Art,* S.P. Gupta describes the huge rock-cut elephant thus:

> It is hailed as the earliest example of Indian lithic art, carved out possibly in the tenth regnal year of Aśoka, long before the pillars were erected. Carved out of live rock, it is shown emerging from the depths of a cave, slowly and majestically, in a most dignified manner. In the boldness of its conception, it goes with the Mauryan royalty; in the gentle feeling it exhibits it goes with the Aśokan message of peace; and finally it stood for the birth of Buddha as the elephant of Māyā's dream. In its monumental proportions, linear rhythm and

> flowing plasticity, it is unsurpassed. No contemporary piece of rock-cut art in western Asia can match it. Truly, with its lowered trunk and quiet look it conveys all that the Buddha stood for.
>
> — Gupta 1980: 85

In fact, no other elephant figure made in Orissa in the last centuries BCE could match the Dhauli elephant in grandeur, style and boldness of conception even though it is not too large a figure. Two examples close in time, a full sculpture of an elephant discovered at the site of Kamaya near Dhauli (Plate 48) and a elephant sculpture outside the Gaṇeśa Gumphā at Udayagiri (*fig.* 50) make for an inadequate comparison with the Dhauli elephant.

A very strong tradition of aniconic worship prevailed on the coast of Orissa and northern Andhra Pradesh in the last centuries BCE. In the Jaina caves at Udayagiri we find sculpted in relief the auspicious symbols like *śrīvatsa, svastika* and others (*fig.* 52). These symbols are shown fenced in and surrounded by worshippers. The detailed sculpting of the *aṣṭamaṅgala* signs at Udayagiri recalls the words of the famous art historian Anand Coomaraswamy who said that the *aṣṭamaṅgala* signs could be regarded as a form of iconography. The Hīnayāna Buddhist complexes on the Andhra coast, in the Godāvarī Valley especially, depict the Buddha in aniconic forms like the *buddhapāda,* the Mucalinda *nāga*, etc. Debala Mitra has commented on the lack of the "mainstream" religious iconographic art in Orissa in the early centuries CE . To quote:

> In the early centuries of the Christian Era also belong a heavy *yakṣa*- and *nāga*-statues, specimens of which are exhibited in the Orissa State Museum. One life-sized pot bellied *nāga* and two *nāgī*-sculptures can be seen under worship in the village of Kapilprasad south of Bhubaneswar. . . .
>
> — Mitra 1978: 9

Mitra further says,

> The history of Bhubaneswar following Kharavela and preceding the rise of the Śailodbhavas in about the seventh century CE is extremely obscure. . . . Though we cannot definitely assign any temple of Bhubaneswar to the Gupta age, which saw the emergence of the characteristics of Indian temple-styles, as there exists no specimen of the initial formative stage, still faltering due to an insufficient

> technique, a few architectural fragments and sculptures — the latter mostly hieratic divinities like Umā-Maheśvara, Kārttikeya, Gaṇeśa and Pārvatī recall the Gupta art idiom . . .. But it is difficult to be certain about their date in view of the persistence in Orissa of the Gupta art idiom even in the post-Gupta period.
>
> — Mitra 1978: 8-10

Debala Mitra has clearly pointed to a gap in development of sculptural art on the Orissa littoral. The art of the Mauryan period, so magnificently manifested in the great elephant of Dhauli, did not transform into religious iconography of the kind that emerged at Mathurā during the BCE–CE transition. As noted, this may have been due to the strong Hīnayāna tradition in Orissa and northern Andhra which militated against the use of images. While we cannot be sure, as Mitra rightly observes, of the Gupta period sculptures of Brāhmanical gods (they may be post-Gupta), the sculptural panels and rock-cut images in the Udayagiri-Khaṇḍagiri cave complex show that the tradition of sculptural art, both religious and secular, did not wither away in the Orissa coastlands after the Mauryas. I have already alluded to the *aṣṭamaṅgala* signs carved in deep relief in the caves. There are other figures, both auspicious and secular, which trace a narrative line, though very thin, from the BCE–CE transition to the fifth–sixth century CE.

Some of the early friezes at Udayagiri-Khaṇḍagiri are interesting. There are no *caitya* halls here as we see on the western coastlands. A sculptural panel above a doorway shows a Gajalakṣmī conception (*fig.* 52). The female divinity is shown in frontal posture and the carving is in deep relief, giving a rounded quality to the images of the goddess and the elephants on either side of her. The panel is dated to the late first century BCE. It can be compared with a Gajalakṣmī panel carved above the entrance of the Buddhist cave at Junnār. The Junnār panel is more simpler in treatment, the carving is in low relief. The Gajalakṣmī panel at the Ananta Gumphā could be related to similar carvings at Sāñcī and Bharhut, a connection that was first made by Fergusson and Burgess (1880/1988: 71-72). The figure may have also been inspired by the terracotta art of the Gangetic Valley. The Gajalakṣmī figure, with her moulded look and voluptuous quality can easily fit into the exquisite set of female divinities created in northern India during the Śuṅga age (second–first century BCE).

The statue of a *dvārapāla*, dated to late first century BCE, depicts a male standing upright (*fig.* 53). Much of the torso and face of the figure is eroded. However, the lower part is clearly visible and we can see the figure clad in a sort of tight kilt and wearing long boots. The taut posture and location at the entrance of the cave (Rānī Gumphā) suggests that the male figure is a guard or *dvārapāla*. The aggressive stance of the figure and its western dress (short kilt and boots) indicates that the sculpture may be that of a Yavana, foreigner from the Graeco-Roman world. The Tamil Saṅgam poems reveal that Roman guards were recruited by south Indian chieftains. *Dvārapāla*s can be considered a separate sub-group in early Indian narrative sculpture. These figures occur in coastal sites, like the *dvārapāla* figure carrying a spear and wearing a Scythian long coat carved on a slab at Nāgārjunakoṇḍa (*fig.* 54) or the imposing *davārapāla* figure depicted in the Buddhist rock-cut cave at Bhaja (*fig.* 55). Most of the *dvārapāla* figures seem to be depicting foreigners and their sculptures occur largely on coastal sites. The *dvārapāla* figure seems to be a reflection of a historical reality on the Indian coastlands. We know of the growing sea trade between Early Historic India and the Western world. This burgeoning trade would have encouraged movement not only of traders but also craftsmen, astrologers, courtesans and soldiers of fortune, looking for patronage and employment. The Yavana figure at the Rānī Gumphā may be the depiction in stone of one such soldier from overseas.

The figure of a *yakṣī* outside the Jayavijaya Cave (No. 5) at the Udayagiri-Khaṇḍagiri complex can rate as one of the finest examples of early sculpture on the Orissa littoral (*fig.* 56). Though much of the figure is eroded, the life size sculpture carved, almost in the round, depicts a lady striking an alluring pose. There is no doubt that the damsel in stone has been inspired by the art of Amarāvatī. The figure has the same plasticity and lissome quality that characterizes the female sculptures on the panels at Amarāvatī *stūpa* in the BCE–CE transition. Also, a bust of a beautiful lady found during clearance near cave 17 should be taken note of (*fig.* 51). Made of local sandstone the image depicts a lady, evidently of noble class, wearing a braided wreath-like headdress. The back profile shows long hair bound in two pleats. The face is exquisitely carved with large eyes, sharp nose and high cheek bones. The lady wears large ring stones in her ears and a heavy necklace from which beaded strings flow down to her breasts. Her countenance strikingly resembles that of the famous Didārgañj *yakṣī* from Patnā.

At the cave-site known as the Gaṇeśa Gumphā there is an elephant bust within a cave and a full figure of an elephant outside the cave (*figs*. 42, 50). The former can be tentatively identified with the elephant-god Gaṇeśa. As discussed, the conception of Gaṇeśa may appear to have emerged in the terracotta art of lower Bengal in the second–first century BCE. The elephant figure outside the cave can be compared with the elephant sculpture found on Kayama Hill near Dhauli (Plate 48). The rock-cut elephant came to light in the excavations at Kayama Hill near Radhanagar (Orissa) carried out by the Orissa Institute of Maritime and South-East Asian Studies, Bhubaneswar (Report in *Frontline*, October 7, 2005). According to the excavators, the elephant (symbolizing Buddha?) was got carved by Tisa, the brother of Emperor Aśoka. The name Tisa is inscribed on a rock-cut bench near the elephant figure. Kayama Hill is close to the archaeological site at Radhanagar. This site has been identified with Toṣalī, the royal capital of Kaliṅga primarily on the basis of a number of inscriptions. However, S.P. Gupta (personal communication) does not believe that the stone elephant from Kayama could belong to the fine Mauryan tradition which produced the elephant sculpture at Dhauli. He considers the Kayama elephant to be a post-Mauryan work. In my opinion, the Kayama elephant figure matches closely with the elephant sculpture outside the Gaṇeśa Gumphā in the Udayagiri–Khaṇḍagiri complex dating to the late first century BCE.

There are later period sculptures and reliefs in the Udayagiri–Khaṇḍagiri complex. One of these shows a hunting scene replete with royal figures, horses, archers etc. (*fig*. 57). According to S.R. Shukla (Allahabad Museum), the panel clearly belongs to the fifth century CE. This is evident from the wavy coiffure of some figures, a style characteristic of Gupta period art. Another panel shows Jain *tīrthaṁkara*s and *devī*s in the Udayagiri–Khaṇḍagiri complex (*fig*. 58). This is again of a date much later than the main carvings in the cave dating to the second–first century BCE. The *tīrthaṁkara* panel can be attributed to the fifth–sixth century CE. As Debala Mitra observes, elements of religious iconography appear in the Orissa littoral during the Gupta period. The image of the Buddha becomes popular after the fifth century CE, indicating a wave of Mahāyāna proselytization in the region. We know the same process was happening on the western coast of India, evident in the sculpting of Buddha images in the seafacing caves at Kanheri, Kondivte and Kuḍa. In fact, the proponents of the Brāhmanical faith seem also to be active in promoting their creed. According to Mitra (1978: 10-11),

> By the fifth century CE the sect (Pāśupata) seems to have established itself in the Bhubaneswar region. The religion it had to combat was Buddhism, which seems to have been the prevailing faith at Bhubaneswar when it came to the scene. This accounts for the great resemblance of the figure of Lakulīśa with that of Buddha; but for the *lakuṭa* (staff) the former would easily be identified with the latter.

Again, there is an uncanny resemblance to similar developments in western India. A figure of Lakulīśa on a moulded brick set in the lower levels of the Śiva temple at Karvan (Baroda) is very similar to the Buddha image (Plate 21).

Summary

We can make a clear distinction between the early sculptural art of lower Bengal and coastal Orissa. The former was dominated by the terracotta medium while in Orissa, after a successful experiment with stone between 300-0 BCE, the art of sculpture is not conspicuous in the early centuries CE. In lower Bengal, the rich terracotta tradition brilliantly displays itself in religious iconography, some of it quite early (hints of the Indra figure) and later in imitation of the art of stone as practised in the upper reaches of the Gaṅgā valley. Influences from the Gandhāra region are also conspicuous in the terracotta art of Bengal. In the precints of the Udayagiri-Khaṇḍagiri caves we find diverse art influences at work; the *dvārapāla* in the likeness of a Yavana, the *yakṣī* at the cave entrance as enchanting as the damsels of Sāñcī and Amarāvatī (*fig.* 56) and the full-bodied elephant image recalling the more exquisite and dramatic one at Dhauli.

7

Spread of Art Overseas

THERE were several ways in which early Indian sculptural art spread overseas. One by actual physical movement of art objects, as evident in the ivory statuette from western India found in Pompei, the Buddha figure in bronze discovered in Sweden or the *yakṣī* figure in bronze found at the ancient port of Khoṛ Rorī in southern Oman. The second mode involved the transfer of idioms and concepts to foreign lands. In this category falls the silver dish from Lampascos (Turkey) having the image of Indirā (?) (as a female figure) upon it (*Map* 15.2). Also, a stone sculpture from the Imperial Roman period shows the bust of a bearded man with a top knot or *uṣṇīṣa,* an auspicious way of tying the hair in ancient India (*Map* 15.10). In fact, there is another mode, involving *wholescale* transfer of classical art styles, as seen in the introduction of Indian sculptural art across South-East Asia in the mid-first millennium CE. I have discussed the "Indianization" phenomenon in the following chapter.

There is no doubt that the movement of Indian art objects and styles took place through the mechanisms of long distance trade. The appearance of the bronze *yakṣī* figure at Khoṛ Rorī must have been due to an itinerant Indian trader or even an Arab or a Greek who had brought the memento back from his Indian sojourn. The same can be said of the exquisite ivory figurine discovered in the excavations at Pompei. The question is whether or how does an exotic object become an influence on local art. In this light we should consider a panel found near Sanaa in Yemen (*Map* 15.8). It is a truly symbolic work which shows two human figures and a lion carved in relief. The human figures are clad in a *dhotī* and the carving is reminiscent of the late art of Amarāvatī and early Nāgārjunakoṇḍa or more likely Mathurā (*fig.*

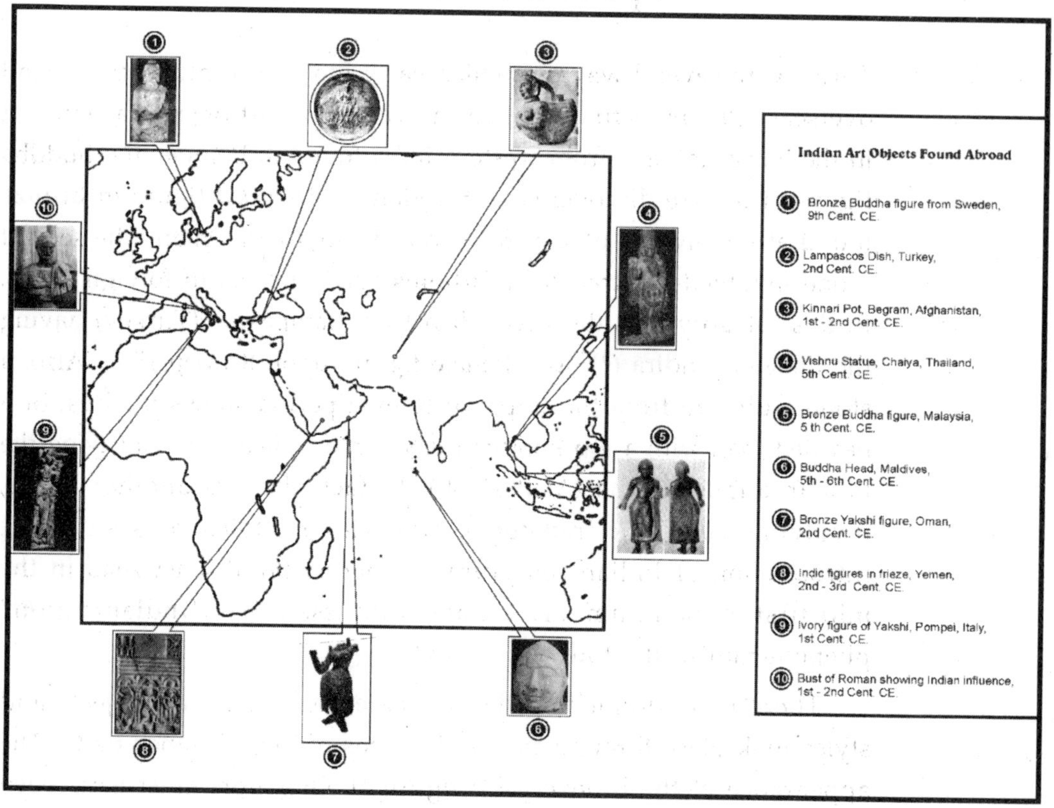

Map 15: Illustrated map showing spread of early Indian sculptural art overseas.

63). The influence of Indian art on this panel would be the outcome of contacts, especially through the medium of trade. Let us take another example, the Lampascos dish. This was discovered in Turkey and shows the central figure of a lady. There is a consensus that the reliefs on the silver dish are related to India. This is because the relief shows the lady surrounded by animals like the tiger and peacock which are typically found in India.

Presented below is a description of some art objects of Indian provenance or inspiration found outside India in the period under study. The findings are disparate, ranging from free-standing sculptures to decorative pots and *buddhapāda* symbols. The countries in which these objects are to be found are truly far flung, from the tropical Indian Ocean island of Maldives to icy Sweden (*Map* 15). The art objects reviewed do not tell the whole story of cultural transmissions abroad. The general focus is on the Indian Ocean world, the littoral regions of eastern Africa, West Asia, South Asia and South-East Asia.

Buddha Head, Coral (?), Thaddoo Island, Maldives, third-fourth century CE

In July 1958, a Maldivian team excavated the archaeological site in Thaddoo Island in Ari Atoll where a figure of the Buddha and a relic casket were found (*Map* 15.6; *fig.* 59). The figure seems to have attributes which can be related to more than one epicentre of art. The Kuṣāṇa element is seen in the open eyes and the robust face-cut. The snail-curl hairdo and the low *uṣṇīṣa* also seem to hark to a later period. Equally interesting is the fine moustache and the hint of a beard. This is suggestive of the Hellenistic elements in the Buddha figures from Gandhāra. A Roman Republican coin of Caius Vibius Pansa minted in Rome in 90 or 89 BCE was found in the relic casket. The worn state of the coin suggests that it was in use for some time before it ended up in the relic casket inside a *stūpa*. The coin also suggests that foreign traders may have been involved in the creation of the Buddha figure. According to Naseema Mohamed (2002: 112), "excavations in other parts of the Maldives show that Buddhism came to be established in the islands by the second century CE. Decorations in coral stones . . .

resemble motifs at Amarāvatī dated to the second century CE." The Buddha has both similarities to and variations from the Buddha heads attributed to the Gupta period at Androth island, Lakshadweep (Plate 26). I would place the Buddha head from Thaddoo island earlier than the Androth Buddhas. The date of the Buddha could be around third-fourth century CE. The Buddha head and the *buddhapāda* are the outcome of intense trade contacts which Early Historic Maldives had with peninsular India and Sri Lanka. The discovery of the Roman coin indicates exchange with Western traders. Maldives must have been an attractive destination for its cowries. As we know, cowrie shells were used as currency in ancient India and were exported through Bengal and north-east India to southern China. Some of the best cowrie beds in the Indian Ocean are located around the Maldives.

Buddhapāda, Stone, Vaḍu Island, Maldives, second-third century CE

One of the earliest indicators of the Buddhist faith in the Maldives is a *buddhapāda* panel (*fig.* 60). In her seminal work on *buddhapāda*s, Anna Maria Quagliotti says,

> The *buddhapāda* was discovered beside a well on Vaḍu Island, Gaaf Atoll . . . What remains of the *buddhapāda* are these three fragments. The footprint is surrounded with a frame consisting of a series of petal motifs. A large *cakra* can be seen on the heel, the part to the end of the heel being surrounded by a *śrīvatsa*-oriented towards the *cakra* and depicted between four *nandyāvarta*s, two on each side, oriented in the same direction. The outer prongs of the *nandyāvarta* turn inwards volute-wise. Between the *cakra* and the toes two rows of symbols can be seen. Taking the footprints in the opposite direction from the observer, they display: upper row, from the outer side to the inner: elephant goad, shell, vase of fertility, fish, sword; lower row: anticlockwise *svastika,* a throne. The phalanges are decorated with clockwise and anticlockwise *svastika*s. It has been dated to the second-third century CE.
>
> — Quagliotti, 1998: 146; *fig.* 68

Statuette of Yakṣī, Bronze, From Khoṛ Rorī, Dhofar, Oman, first-second century CE

A bronze statuette of a dancing *yakṣī* was discovered at the Iron Age port of Khoṛ Rorī (Sumhuram) in the Dhofar region of Oman (*Map*

15.7). The headless statuette shows the *yakṣī*, the *śālabhañjikā* type, striking a typical pose of holding the branch of a tree (*fig*. 61). Though the left hand of the figure is broken at the shoulder, the high angle of the arm suggests the *śālabhañjikā* pose of holding a branch of a tree. The statuette is very similar in style and pose to the *yakṣī* on the bracket of one of the gateways of the Sāñcī *stūpa* (*fig*. 62). The Khoṛ Rorī figure has been attributed a date in the third century CE by Goetz (1963: 187-89). However, the *yakṣī* figure could be easily placed in the first-second century CE. It may be noted that Śuṅga art-motifs have been found in the Persian Art of the fourth century CE for the simple reason that these motifs continued to occur in India through the Kuṣāṇa and Gupta periods (Gupta, 1980: 108-128).

Marble Plaque with Indian Influence, Manakha (Yemen), second–third century CE

A marble plaque found in Manakha (Yemen) is now reposited at Hombrechtikon, in the cantonment of Zurich, Switzerland. Avanzini (1994: 63) describes the plaque thus: "The plaque is only the right part of a composition. In the niches there is an animal turned to the side, a nude man who is dancing and a semi-nude woman. . . . There is a definite Indian influence in the female character and in the composition of the three-arched columns." According to me, the composition is syncretic, showing the fusion of various elements of art. The south Arabian symbols on the upper part of the plaque reveal that this piece was executed in Yemen. Two of the four columns are clearly visible. These are fluted and the capitals show an acanthus leaf design. The impact is Hellenistic. There are three arches above the columns. A horizontal lintel runs just above the arches, dividing the space between the columns from the arches. Three figures are shown below the three arches: a lion in side profile on the right, a nude male in dancing posture in the middle and a lady in frontal posture on the left. In the semicircular spaces between the arches and the lintel we see a man's face above the lion, an object above the dancing man and another human face above the figure of the lady (*fig*. 63).

The stylization of the dancing male and the lady is similar to the *mithuna* couple depicted at Mathurā as well as Nāgārjunakoṇḍa and other Buddhist sites in the Kṛṣṇā Valley. The dancing man in the middle of the Manakha plaque, with his crudely carved physiognomy, flat face, muscular legs and torso can be compared with a *mithuna* panel from the Buddhist site at Vaḍḍamanu in Andhra Pradesh. However, the *mālāvāhaka*s and cupids in the Gāndhāra art also have similar figures. The standing lady, with her upper body uncovered and wearing a *dhotī* with thick fold of cloth falling vertically, but transparent thin muslin-like cloth clinging to the thigh and ankles revealing the warmth and contours of these body parts, is representative of female figures depicted in major art centres of India in the Early Historic period, Kuṣāṇa to be exact, particularly in the art of Mathurā. Also, the human figures above the lintels seem to be onlookers viewing the scenes below. The "onlookers" are a popular feature in narrative sculpture, appearing in the Early Historic art of Bharhut, Mathurā and Amarāvatī. Though the panel shows strong influence of the art of Āndhradeśa, it is to be noted that the panel incorporates other elements. The lion in profile rising on his hind legs could be a borrowing from Persia. The lion motif was transmitted into Indian (Mauryan) art because of interaction with the Achaemenids. The lion motif in the Arabian panel may be a result of south Arabian interaction with the Parthians and Sassanians, the inheritors of the legacy of the Achaemenids. The fluted sides of twin columns and the acanthus leaf capitals of the pillars seem to be inspired by the Graeco-Roman world. But these were fully incorporated in the Gāndhāran art. We have to view the panel as a syncretic piece of art, incorporating Indian, Parthian and Hellenistic elements within a south Arabian conception. This was possible because Yemen had become a major area of international trade in the BCE–CE transition. The Greek sea-guide, the *Periplus Maris Erythraei* refers to ships from Roman Egypt, India and the Persian Gulf calling in at the major south Arabian harbours. The region was lucrative because of the export of the aromatics, frankincense and myrrh. Recent excavations at the ancient south Arabian harbours of Qana and Khoṛ Rorī have brought to light large quantities of Roman, Indian and Persian ceramics. Therefore the common material culture in coastal Yemen reflected the syncretism of the marble plaque from Manakha.

Two dates of second and fourth century CE have been proposed for the marble plaque, on the basis of the palaeography of the south Arabian inscriptions (Avanzini 1994: 57). On the basis of style, and the fact that the dancing male figure and the standing lady below the arches in the frieze show close similarity with the early art of Mathurā, the human figures can be placed in the early centuries CE, which include both the dates.

Statuette of Yakṣī, Ivory, Pompei, Italy, first century CE

A small ivory statuette of a *yakṣī* was discovered in the Roman city of Pompei destroyed by the eruption of Mount Vesuvius in 79 CE (Plate 20; *Map* 15.9). The date of 79 CE provides the *terminus ante quem* to the ivory object. The statuette is about 25 cm tall. The lady is shown standing with her left hand upraised. She seems to be staring into her palm. The right hand is raised and stretched into her back as if she were trying to hold something behind her head. Her face is nicely modelled, with full cheeks, wide eyes and well formed nose and mouth. Her hair is intricately braided and she wears a diadem on her forehead. Her breasts are covered by a thick necklace. There is a girdle on her waist and her legs are covered up to just below her knees with bracelets. Two small female figures are carved along her limbs. These are shown holding up jars. There is now a unanimous opinion that the female figure, which has a hole drilled from the top of her head to the waist, was used as a leg of a wooden table. First identified as such by During-Caspers (1981: 341-53), the concept has found favour in other recent reviews (Cimino 1994: 119-21; Karttunen 1997: 557-62). The statuette from Pompei is similar to ivory statuettes excavated at the sites of Ṭer (Cimino 1994: 120; Plate LIV/3) and Bhokardan (Deo 1974: Plate LVI) in the state of Maharashtra in western India. The ivory-carvers of Vidiśā are also well known from historical sources. What is important to note is that this figurine forms part of a wooden box with ivory inlays and ivory legs. It was a leg.

Kinnarī Pot, Begram, dated first century CE

The *kinnarī* from Begram is part of a Graeco-Roman tradition traced to the "siren" pots made in Egypt, especially at Alexandria (*Map* 15.3).

The Begram *kinnarī* figure is an Indianization of the Alexandrian siren pot. According to R.C. Agrawala (1970: 4-5):

> A glimpse of this particular Greek motif (half woman and half bird pot), is vividly presented in the most outstanding tiny earthern pot from Begram (ancient Kapiśā) in Afghanistan. Now preserved in Kabul Museum as No. 57. 290, this exquisite pot, in bluish green glazed ware, was excavated by Mr J. Hackin more than 30 years ago. . . . The female bust in the Begram pot is modelled in a most artistic manner, she has put on a group of bangles on her fore arms as in the Kuṣāṇa art of Mathurā; the floral band above the head has also been shown in a traditional manner; both the hands have been placed in adoration pose which is completely Indian. Still more important is the depiction of *sapatra-keyūra*s studded with a row of *svastika* motif; the former recalls to our minds the Śuṅga *keyūra*s in the art of Mathurā, Sāñcī, Bharhut, etc. It therefore preserves an interesting early Indian motif. The back portion, of a bird, may be that of a peacock; the bottom of the vase is devoid of any leg, thus suggesting a further improvement upon the Greek designs. Begram lay on the ancient trade route connecting East and West; a number of Roman objects and Indian ivories were also unearthed by Mr Hackin at this site. It is therefore no wonder that the particular potter of Begram came to know of some *siren* pot from the Hellenistic world and designed his own pot thereafter, of course in his own style and highly influenced by Indian art motifs.

A similar *kinnarī* pot was excavated at Ujjain (Agrawala 1970: 7).

Dharmacakra Stambha, Stone, seventh-eighth century CE, Bangkok National Museum

The spoked wheel representing the Buddhist Wheel of the Law (*dharmacakra*) is on display at the Bangkok National Museum (Plate 38). These *cakra*s were made in the Sanskritic kingdom of Dvāravatī in Thailand. The Dvāravatī kingdom flourished in Thailand from the sixth-seventh to the tenth century CE (Brown 1996: XXI). The inspiration for the making of *dharmacakra*s were the decorated *chatarī*s and haloes that covered Gupta period images of Buddha at Mathurā and Sārnāth. According to Brown (1996: XXV-XXVI), the *cakra*s of Dvāravatī "are unusually close to Indian models. In all of the Buddhist world, such three-dimensional stone *dharmacakra*s occur only in two places: in India and in Dvāravatī. Furthermore, the Dvāravatī *cakra*s are covered with designs, the patterns of which have been consistently called Indian, specifically Gupta. . . ." The transmission of the idea of the *dharmacakra stambha* must have taken some time and therefore the evolution of these *cakra*s in South-East Asia falls within the period of our review.

Decorated Pillar, Stone, Dvāravatī Period, Bangkok National Museum

A stone pillar in the Dvāravatī Gallery of the Bangkok National Museum is stylistically similar to Gupta period stone columns in northern India (Plate 39). The pillar is stylistically similar to a sandstone column from Kauśāmbī on display in the Allahabad Museum. The decorative features of the pillar can be divided into three parts. On the top is the base of the capital with a faceted surface. Below that is an *āmalaka* roundel and then the faceted trunk of the column. The pillar was probably part of a shrine. The kingdom of Dvāravatī consciously modelled itself on the classical Gupta period culture of India.

Bodhi Tree on Plaque, Stone, Bangkok National Museum, sixth century CE

The sacred *bodhi* tree is carved in low relief on a circular stone plaque (Plate 40). The symmetrical presentation shows the branches of the tree emerging from the trunk at three levels. At the apex of the tree we see a flower-like motif. *Pīpal* leaves are finely carved in the spaces between the branches. The depiction of the *bodhi* tree in stone shows the popularity of the Buddhist motif in South-East Asia. The *bodhi* tree was a powerful aniconic symbol of the Buddhist faith. The plaque belongs to the beginning of the Dvāravatī Period. It is therefore ascribed a date of sixth century CE.

Buddha Images from Sweden and Norway, ninth-tenth century CE

The discovery of a bronze figure of the Buddha from a Viking burial site of Helgo in Ekero Island in Lake Malaren in Sweden is significant (*Map* 15.1). The statue was discovered in 1954. The Buddha figure in Late Gāndhāran style probabaly entered Sweden through the long distance "amber route" connecting central Asia and Russia to India. The figure could also have reached by the sea route. The Buddha is shown seated on a lotus couch. The *saṁghāti* covers both the shoulders and is pleated in the style of the Gandhāra Buddha figures. The hairstyle is the typical snail-curl coiffure perfected in the Mathurā school. There is a prominent *uṣṇīṣa* and the ears are long with pendulous lobes. The Buddha figure has been attributed a date of eighth-ninth century CE and its provenance lies in Kashmir or the adjoining Swāt region of Pakistan.

The following excerpt from the field report gives the detail of the Buddha statue:

> The face is finely drawn with elbows and mouth inlaid with dark substance: eyes inlaid with turquoise (?) and on the right eye an irregular red colour; caste-mark of gold in the middle of the forehead; the ears have much drawn-down lobes; the hair is ring punched and at the very top a small semi-globular calotte is placed; the neck has two parallel furrows (fat calluses). . . . At the discovery, there was round the neck and round the wrist a leather-strap 0.06 cm W with folded and bent borders. Measures H. 8.4, greatest W (the Throne) 6.4. Site M 34;-12. — Holmqvist 1954-56

More interesting is the discovery of bronze figures in Norway that bear resemblance to a seated Buddha in yogic posture (Plate 41). These have been found as decorative emblems on Viking boats. The body of the so-called Buddha figure is covered with *svastika*s. One of these figures is in the collection of Bergen Museum.

While it would be far fetched to consider that Buddhist ideas had been introduced into Scandinavia via the "Amber route," the possibility cannot be ruled out. The bronze Buddha from Helgo was tied by a leather wrist strap, indicating its use as an amulet by its Viking owner. There were also signs of repair on the Buddha statue from Sweden, pointing to its exotic and perhaps cultural/religious value.

Summary

The relationship between art and trade is intricate. One is driven by thought, religion and aesthetics and the other by the profit motive. However there can be no escaping the fact that great art, especially sculptural art developed in the hubs of long distance trade. Religious precepts and philosophies were part of the movement of early art and therefore the appearance of the Buddha image in Sweden and its impersonation on Viking boats may not be a "freak" event. The Khoṛ Rorī *yakṣī,* for instance, was not an isolated indicator of Indian presence in south Arabia. The range of Early Historic pottery forms excavated at the harbour of Khoṛ Rorī show that the *yakṣī* figure appeared in this port due to intense interactivity between western India and southern Oman. The figure signifies the syncretic spirit, the give and take, the growth of art on the trade hubs in the Indian Ocean coastlands. The examples cited above indicate certain trends in the movement of early sculptural art beyond the Indian coastlands. In the next chapter, I shall further probe the idea of cultural transmissions, absorption and syncretic expressions of art in my review of the Indianization phenomena in ancient South-East Asia.

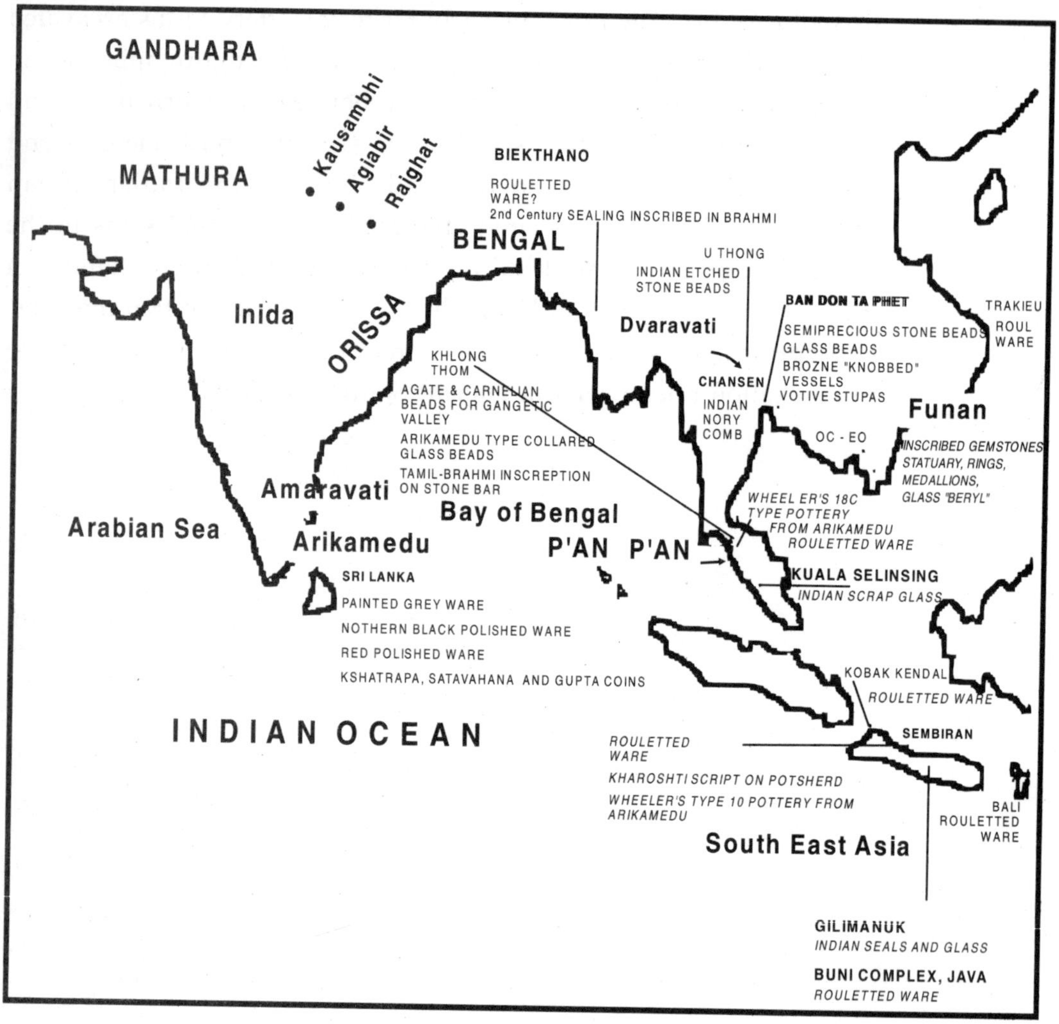

Map 16: Map of the Bay of Bengal Interaction Sphere

8

The Indianization of South-East Asia
A New Perspective

INDIANIZATION is a concept fundamental to the history of contact between India and South-East Asia (*Map* 16). Most studies on the Indianization of South-East Asia are based upon interpretations of the rich art and inscriptions of Indic polities in South-East Asia. Typically, the historical narratives associated with Indianization commence from mid-first millennium CE when sculpture and inscriptions became widespread in South-East Asia. The theoretical connection between art and polity has created a notion that state formation in South-East Asia happened without much precedence and was rapidly effected through enlightened migrants/traders coming from India after CE 500. The previous period has been the preserve of anthropologists and field archaeologists mainly concerned with investigating transitions from early prehistory to the metal ages of South-East Asia. The lack of interface between the archaeological and art historical record has resulted in the idea that Indianization was rapid and late. This notion has persisted since the authoritative writings of Georges Coedès and Ramesh Chandra Majumdar firmly anchored the idea of Indianization in the historical record. I quote from two recent and widely circulated studies on Indianization to substantiate my point.

Robert L. Brown in his important work *The Dvāravatī Wheels of the Law and the Indianization of South-East Asia* says:

> There was, I think, a new intense interaction in the sixth, seventh and eighth centuries based on Indian cultural idioms which brought about *the sudden appearance* of numerous polities mentioned by the Chinese, of the widespread appearance of (mostly Sanskrit) inscriptions in shared South-East Asian scripts, and of the

> remarkably early but interrelated art styles and iconographies.
>
> — 1996: 188; italics mine

Monica Smith, in her paper *Indianization from the Indian Point of View* points out:

> Prior to the fourth century CE, Indian trade activities with South-East Asia appear to have been relatively infrequent, when assessed through the number of items of Indian origin recovered, and the incentives for such trade from the Indian point of view. After the fourth century, the adoption of subcontinental traditions — religious iconography, Sanskrit terminology, coinage and terms identifying leaders — is seen throughout the area of South-East Asia. . . .
>
> — 1999: 1

The "Prior" Record

There can be no doubting that Indic art styles, religious ideas and political precepts spread across South-East Asia after the mid-first millennium CE. Nothing that happened before can compare with the "new intense interaction . . . based on Indian cultural idioms" (Brown 1996: 188) which South-East Asia experienced in the latter part of the first millennium CE. The need is to explain the "Indic surge" adequately; in fact to reach an understanding of the Indianization phenomenon where figurative terms like "sudden appearance" are not required to be employed. For this, it is imperative to search for processes leading up to Indianization in the archaeo-historical record of South-East Asia before CE 500. It is highly unlikely that the rapid and conspicuous spread of Indic traditions post-CE 500 had no prior basis in Indo-South-East Asian interactions before this date.

South-East Asian archaeology prior to this period has principally focused on themes of subsistence, adaptation, migration and chiefdom polities while studies of early Indo-South-East Asian interchange have emphasised trade links (Ray 1991: 357-65; Ardika and Bellwood 1991: 221-32; Gogte 1997: 69-85). There has been little interest in interpreting the prior record in cultural terms, which is what a study of "proto-Indianization" requires. Let us now turn to the archaeological record.

The Sculptures

The earliest Indianized art of South-East Asia is manifested in a corpus of Buddhist and Brāhmanical sculptures which first appear in the material record of South-East Asia before CE 500. These can be traced back to centres of art in northern and southern India (*Map* 16).

Northern Group

One of the earliest Indian inspired images is a stone sculpture of Viṣṇu dated to c. CE 400 recovered from Chaiya, a site on the Thai–Malaysian isthmus and the likely location of the ancient kingdom of P'an P'an (*Map* 15.4; *fig*. 64). The iconography of the Viṣṇu image from Chaiya derives from the Kuṣāṇa–Gupta transitional art of second-third century CE (Dofflemyer 1999: 38-52). The Chaiya Viṣṇu has inspired similar forms in Thailand and southern Vietnam, dated to CE 400-500. In particular I refer to a Viṣṇu image from Nakhon Si Thammarat (Nāgara Śrī Dharmarāja) province in southern Thailand and another from Oc Eo, Vietnam (see Doffelmeyer 1999: *figs*. 3 and 4).

Southern Group

A number of Buddha images, inspired by the art of Amarāvatī, represent the early south Indian related sculptures in South-East Asia. The earliest Amarāvatī type Buddha was found in the village of Pong Tuk in central Thailand. The bronze sculpture, dating between second–fifth century CE, may be an Indian original (le May 1956: 30; *Map* 15.5; *fig*. 65). Similar Buddhist images of the Amarāvatī type have been found in South Sulawesi, in east Java and near Palembang in Sumatra (le May 1956: 31; Sarkar 1970: 126) and on the Malay Peninsula.

The early Indic Viṣṇu and Buddhist figures in South-East Asia, drawing on Indian art styles of the early centuries CE, seem to have inspired a genre of Brāhmanical and Buddhist sculptural art across South-East Asia. This was a dramatic new element in South-East Asian art. According to Brown ". . . much of South-East Asia's earliest Indianized art appears as if full-sprung, with no earlier stages of development — without even a period of copying Indian models" (1996: xxvi). This is a significant statement. Brown goes on to explore the various theories that explain the ways in which Indian sculptural techniques may have been transferred to South-East Asia. However, the sculptures were not just art objects, but religious images with clear, specific meanings. The sculptures could only circulate when these were understood in South-East Asia. The appearance of religious sculptures and their growing popularity in South-East Asia implies prior knowledge of the symbolisms associated with their worship. Logically, such a transfer needed (i) long contacts with the subcontinent and (ii) exposure of South-East Asian communities to the ideological, cultural and religious accoutrements of that contact.

Early Indic Beads: Indicators of Proto-Indianization?

Reporting his excavations at the Iron Age site of Ban Don Ta Phet (BDTP) in Thailand, Glover (1996: 129-158) postulates that certain beads and ritual vessels unearthed at the site articulated Indic religious ideas. The artefacts were dated to the fourth century BCE on the basis of ^{14}C determinations. The beads include several etched agates of likely Indian origin and leaping lion pendants of carnelian. To quote Glover:

> Apart from the etched beads, there is one large, and a small broken fragment of another, carnelian pendant carved in form of a leaping lion which is almost certainly Indian in origin. No precise parallels for these pendants are known and the small lion pendants from Khlong Thom and other locations in southern Thailand are closest, but smaller crouching lion pendants are commonly found in the Buddhist reliquaries of the Gāndhāra civilization . . . .
>
> — Glover 1996: 139

Bronze vessels with a central knob excavated at BDTP also attracted Glover's interest. About these vessels Glover says:

> If we seek a meaning for the base knob and concentric circles then I think this should be seen as the commonly understood *maṇḍala*, a schematic cosmological symbol representing perhaps Mount Meru and the surrounding oceans. . . . They are witness to the adoption, in Thailand, by some groups, of Indian moral, philosophical and political concepts. — Glover 1996: 143

In a sense, Glover's observations emphasizing a religio-cultural element in early Indo-South-East Asian interchange is a major departure from the way Indic artefacts in South-East Asia have been generally interpreted: as indicators of long distance trade or signifiers of status/power among the indigenous communities. Can the exotic beads from BDTP be regarded as markers for early cultural interchange between India and South-East Asia? Can we glimpse in the archaeological record "proto-Indianization" processes which culminate in Indic floruit of the mid-first millennium CE? I believe that exotic stone and glass beads deposited in Iron Age contexts in South-East Asia offer insights into the cultural dimensions of Indo-South-East Asian interchange.

I propose to discuss the bead categories in terms of Indo-South-East Asian linkages. Prior to that I will clarify my position with regard to the debates on the origins of these beads in South-East Asia. The point of emphasis is that the bead categories specified below are found on both sides of the Bay of Bengal in the BCE–CE transition. In my opinion it is unlikely that similar bead categories emerged independently of each other in South and South-East Asia. The common view so far has been that specific stone and glass beads, especially the agates and carnelians, were imported into South-East Asia from India. Recently, the Indian provenances have been questioned in favour of South-East Asian (Smith 1999: 81; Theunissen et al. 2001: 84-105). I shall only stress that Early Historic stone/glass bead categories specified below are strikingly similar in India and South-East Asia and therefore need to be perceived as signifiers of Indo-South-East Asian interchange. As I shall discuss, these stone/glass bead categories seem to derive from older crafting traditions in India. Many "Indic beads" may have been crafted in South-East Asia by Indian craftsmen or local ones trained in Indian techniques. I see no contradiction between transmission of techno-cultural traditions across the Bay of Bengal and indigenous production in either South or South-East Asia.

The Indo-South-East Asian Bead Categories

Following a broad schema (after Basa 1992: 91-104), we can say that the crafting areas for Indic stone bead categories, particularly agate and carnelian, lay in the northern part of India. The glass beads categories — the false "beryls" and the Indo-Pacific beads — were produced in southern India. Below, I have explicated the bead categories in terms of their provenances, chronologies and affinities within the Bay of Bengal Interaction Sphere. My intention is to situate the bead evidence firmly within the Indo-South-East Asian exchange matrix before attempting to understand them as part of the Indianization process. Though I have taken into account a number of sites on both sides of the Bay of Bengal, the focus of my analysis are the beads from Ban Don Ta Phet (BDTP) in Thailand, Kauśāmbī in north India and Arikameḍu in south India. These sites have yielded the most representative of the beads common to Early Historic India and South-East Asia.

Agate Beads

The etched bead tradition is known in India since the Haṛappan Period (third–second millennium BCE; Ghosh 1989: 218). Several imitations in glass of etched agate beads have also been recovered from Early Historic contexts in India (Basa 1992: 91-103), signifying a well established crafting tradition. In a major study of Early Historic stone beads from India and South-East Asia, Bérnice Bellina found that the BDTP etched agates examples were very similar to Indian types (Plate 43). Bellina attributes an Indian origin to these, offering the interpretation that these were "made to order" for South-East Asian consumers (unpublished paper, presented in EURSEAA 2002, Sigtuna, Sweden).

Carnelian Beads

Beads of carnelian proliferate in Iron Age contexts in South and South-East Asia. In particular, the unetched carnelians, comprising spherical and barrel-shaped beads are common finds at Iron Age sites on both sides of the Bay of Bengal. I had the opportunity to study carnelian beads from BDTP at the Institute of Archaeology, University College London (Plate 44). An unpublished list of BDTP beads at the institute showed that out of 153 carnelian beads catalogued, 92 were plain spheres. Plain carnelian spheres and barrels also proliferate in early Iron Age context of north Indian sites. I found the Kauśāmbī bead collection at the Allahabad Museum strikingly similar to the BDTP collection at the Institute of Archaeology, because of the dominant percentage of plain carnelian spheres and barrels. Theunissen et al. (2000: 84-105) have shown through geophysical analysis that most of the carnelians recovered from Iron Age contexts in South-East Asia are indigenously sourced. In the subcontinent, crafting of carnelian goes back to Haṛappan times (Ghosh 1989: vol. I, p. 226). The common carnelian beads have been recovered from early Iron Age levels (early mid-first millennium BCE) of sites situated on the Gangetic trade routes coming down to the Bay of Bengal (Sharma 1969: 103-25; Narain and Singh 1977: 21-54; Gupta 1997: 53). Though the evidence points to an older tradition of carnelian beadmaking in India, the circulation of similar carnelian bead types in India and South-East Asia suggest a shared techno-cultural tradition.

Animal-Shaped Pendants

Animal-shaped pendants have been recovered from Iron Age contexts both in India and South-East Asia with more and greater variety being found in northern India than elsewhere, which might well indicate origins in this region (Plate 42). In particular, animal-shaped beads including lions and tortoises have been found in Buddhist *stūpa*s at Taxila, Piprahwa and Sahet-Mahet (Sharma 1969: 103-125; Glover 1996: 140). The probable ritual significance of these is discussed later.

Glass Beads

Glass beads found at BDTP and other Late Prehistoric/Iron Age sites in Thailand and Peninsular Malaya also reveal strong affinity with Early Historic Indian glass crafting traditions (Basa 1992: 85-102; Basa et al. 1991: 351-65). The exotic glass bead deposition in South-East Asia indicates wider extension of networks emanating from the Bay of Bengal sphere.

Indo-Pacific Beads

A diagnostic glass microbead type — the Indo-Pacific bead — is ubiquitous both in mainland and island South-East Asia. Indo-Pacific beads are of small size (outer diameter range of 6 mm and under), monochromatic and cut from "drawn" glass. The term Indo-Pacific, proposed by Peter Francis (1991: 1-23) is representative of the vast area of distribution of these beads. Francis holds the view that Indo-Pacific beads were first produced at the southern Indian site of Arikameḍu in the fourth–third century BCE and similar production centres emerged in South-East Asia thereafter. This contention is being challenged. Dussubieux and Gratuze (2003: 135-148) make the claim, after analyses of glass from Arikameḍu (India) and Ban Don Ta Phet (Thailand), that the chemical signatures of the bulk of glass finds from two sites was different. However, they do admit that some glass may have been exported from Arikameḍu to South-East Asia. Also, as I have stressed above, the transmission of glass beadmaking techniques did take place either way. We can speak of Indo-Pacific beads as products of a shared techno-cultural tradition in the Bay of Bengal Interaction Sphere.

Glass "Beryls"

The false beryls were known in the ancient Indian and Roman worlds and there are references in the literary traditions of the east and west cautioning buying these false stones. The specimens from BDTP are as much as 4-5 cm in length and 3 cm in breath (Plate 45). Similar specimens proliferate in India, the earliest occurring at the Bhir Mound, Taxila in fourth–third century BCE levels (Basa 1992: 97) and in Kauśāmbī Sub-Period II dated to the third century BCE (Sharma 1969: 116). Evidence for crafting the glass "beryls" has been found at Arikameḍu (Francis 1991: 34).

The brief review of the distribution of stone and glass beads indicates that the specified bead categories were common to Iron Age South Asia and South-East Asia.

From the Aniconic to the Iconic Tradition

From our point of view, the key question is how the beads were "consumed" in South-East Asia. Most of the Indic beads occur as grave goods in South-East Asian contexts. Should we view them purely as signifiers of aesthetics, power and status, or as objects associated with religious precepts and other-worldly ideas? Similarly, how were early

Indic sculptures perceived in South-East Asia? I will try to show how the beads and early sculptures are related and how, in their continuity, the bead-sculpture linkage helps us see Indianization as a gradual cultural process.

Indic beads and bead crafting technologies reached South-East Asia along well defined routes from northern and southern India (*Map* 16). The same conduits also facilitated movement of Indian sculptures and sculptural art styles to South-East Asia. From northern India, the following bead categories transmitted to South-East Asia: agates, carnelians, animal-shaped pendants and triangular/lenticular banded agate pendants. The stone beads, especially the agates and carnelians were produced in western India, principally the Khambaṭ region of Gujarat (Francis 1982). The large Gangetic sites like Kauśāmbī and Rājghāṭ, controlling the trade routes across northern India to ports on the eastern seaboard, had major stone bead crafting industries. In all likelihood, the Indic-style stone beads at Ban Don Ta Phet came via the Gangetic routes. The animal shaped beads from Kauśāmbī and Rājghāṭ are similar to the ones from Iron Age contexts in South-East Asia. The northern group of early Indic sculptures in South-East Asia — the Chaiya Viṣṇu image and the Dvāravatī *cakra*s — were inspired by the Kuṣāṇa–Gupta art styles which flourished along the route of the stone bead transfers. Other examples of early Indic influence include the fine stone statue of Kṛṣṇa lifting Govardhana (Plate 46) and the personification of Garuḍa in stucco (Plate 47). Both images are in the Bangkok National Museum. The Kṛṣṇa image (dated 6th-7th century CE) shows strong affinity wih the Mathurā School. In south India, the coastal site of Arikameḍu was the principal crafting centre for Indo-Pacific beads and the green glass "beryls" (*Map* 16). Though agate and stone beads were produced at Arikameḍu (as well as in neighbouring Sri Lanka), the volume and range of beads produced do not match those of the northern crafting centres. North of Arikameḍu, the great art centre of Amarāvatī was the source of the earliest Buddhist sculptures in South-East Asia (*Map* 16). The Arikameḍu–Amarāvatī axis paralleled the northern Gangetic routes which were linked to ports in Bengal and Orissa.

The bead-sculpture transfer routes in north and south India are associated with developments which help explain why the Indic beads in South-East Asia are "signifiers" of Indianization and why, in spite of the fact that Indo-South-East Asian sea trade was flourishing in the BCE–CE changeover, it was only after CE 500 that Indic sculptural art became common across South-East Asia.

Firstly, in the early centuries CE, major centres of north Indian art flourished in the Upper Gaṅgā and the Upper Indus region, represented respectively by Mathurā and Taxila (*Map* 16). Kauśāmbī in the middle Gaṅgā Valley seems to have been a cosmopolitan trading city, rich in secular terracotta art, production of beads, pendants and intaglios and producing Buddhist and Brāhmanical images inspired by the art of Mathurā (personal communication with Ranjan Shukla, Curator of Sculpture at the Allahabad Museum).

If the Middle Gaṅgā region was poor in free-standing sculptural art, then stone sculpture was virtually non-existent in the Lower Gaṅgā region — Bengal and adjoining Orissa littoral — during the early centuries CE. The Early Historic sites in lower Bengal have yielded terracotta plaques showing secular scenes and figures of mother goddesses but hardly any sculpture with pronounced religious iconography (see entries for Candraketugaṛh, and Tāmralipti in the *Encyclopaedia of Indian Archaeology* vol. II). In this regard, the following observation by Mukherjee (1997: 175) is perceptive:

> . . . recorded discoveries in lower West Bengal of an immense number of terracotta plaques, sculptures in the round and numerous seals, that are datable on the basis of stylistic features, stratification evidence and the palaeographic peculiarities of the seal legends, to the Maurya, post-Maurya, pre-Gupta and Gupta periods (*c.* fourth/third century BCE to sixth century CE). Only a few stone sculptures of ancient Vaṅga in these centuries have been discovered.

In Orissa, a fragmentary *yakṣī* figure in coarse sandstone from the Jaina rock-cut caves at Udayagiri/Khaṇḍagiri (dated first century BCE) has been called "the sole free-standing female figure of the pre-Christian era discovered in this region" (Ghosh 1989: vol. II, pp. 446-47). The Udayagiri/Khaṇḍagiri caves do depict Jaina worshippers and auspicious symbols like *svastika* and *nandipāda* on wall friezes

(Krishnan 1996). However, we find few specimens of religious iconography in stone in the early centuries CE in Orissa. The situation changed during the Gupta period (fifth-seventh century CE) when the great art centre of Sārnāth emerged in the Middle Gaṅgā region. Sārnāth inspired the Indic art of South-East Asia (Coomaraswamy 1972; Krishnan 1996).

The point to emphasize here is that the Bengal-Orissa littoral, constituting the staging area of sea trade with South-East Asia, was strangely bereft of religious iconography in the form of stone sculptures during the early centuries CE. The absence of Buddhist and Brāhmanical images in the Bengal–Orissa region must have had the effect of "holding back" the diffusion of religious iconography from northern India to South-East Asia before the middle of the first millennium CE. In fact, the paucity of sculptures in eastern India during the early centuries CE, and by default in South-East Asia as well, can be partly explained by the aniconic tradition which prevailed in India in the pre-Christian Era. According to Krishnan (1996), the Vedic tradition influenced the mode of worship in India during the pre-Christain Era, the evocation being to formless gods. This is reflected in the depiction of the Buddha in the form of the *buddhapāda* symbol (Quagliotti 1998), the symbolic representation of the Jaina *tīrthaṁkara*s at Udayagiri/Khaṇḍagiri (Krishnan 1996) and the prolific use of auspicious symbols like *svastika, nandipāda*, etc. by all religious denominations (Wayman 1989: 236-46). The first sculptures of the Buddha and those of Brāhmanical deities (Viṣṇu, Śiva, Kubera, etc.) were created at the art centres of Mathurā and Gandhāra at the very turn of the Christian Era (Sharma 1984; Krishnan 1996). At the time the Indic beads were deposited at BDTP (fourth century BCE), the aniconic tradition was dominant in the subcontinent. There were simply no sculptures of the Buddha or Viṣṇu at that time. The virtual absence of religious sculptures in Bengal-Orissa in the early centuries CE suggests that the shift from aniconic to iconic modes of worship was late in coming to the eastern Indian littoral. Buddhist and Brāhmanical sculptures began to proliferate in this region from the mid-first millennium CE, a phenomenon also observed in South-East Asia. At

Amarāvatī on the southern coast of the Bay of Bengal, the Buddha came to be depicted in human form in the second century CE (Knox 1992). The first Buddha images appeared in South-East Asia between second–fifth century CE, directly inspired by the art of Amarāvatī. The first iconic expressions in South-East Asia, seen in the few Amarāvatī-inspired Buddhas and the solitary Mathurā-inspired Chaiya Viṣṇu, can be directly related to shifts in religious practices in India.

In the absence of the iconic tradition or where the iconic forms of worship are in a state of emergence, the use of other tangible symbols of worship gains significance. In this regard, the importance of ritual objects like amulets, beads and pottery, cannot be discounted. The literary and the material records indicate that beads and amulets of gemstones, semiprecious stones and glass did play a major role in religious ceremonies in ancient India. The *Matsya Purāṇa* (Wilson 1983) describes an elaborate Brāhmanical ritual involving offering of pearls, diamonds, cats eyes, sapphires, topazes, corals and lapis lazuli. A frieze in the Sarnath Museum depicts a worshipper approaching a *stūpa* with a garland of beads. On the railings of the Bharhut *stūpa* (second century BCE) displayed in the Allahabad Museum, I noticed a prolific depiction of beads, as items of personal decoration (necklace, girdles) as well as auspicious representation. Two decorated coping stones (A.M. No. 40 and 56) show faceted beads flowing from a lotus stem; an allusion to prosperity like the *kalpavṛkṣa* (wish fulfilling tree) or the *pūrṇaghaṭa* (overflowing vase) symbols (see also Chandra 1966). The association of beads with auspicious symbols is interesting. The use of the *aṣṭamaṅgala*s or the "eight auspicious symbols" has been the most potent form of religious expression in the Buddhist, Brāhmanical and Jaina aniconic tradition. Their significance in early Indian religious practices has been noted by Coomaraswamy: ". . . the importance of these symbols, many of which have remained in use till the present day, lies in the fact that they represent a definite early Indian style, amounting to an explicit iconography" (1972: 45). The *aṣṭamaṅgala* set usually comprised one or more conventional symbols (the *śrīvatsa*, *triratna* and *svastika* being popular) together with associated symbols like the *buddhapāda*s (feet of Buddha), *pūrṇaghaṭa*, conch-shell, *vajra* (lightning), etc. The associated symbols could be drawn from a rich fount of sacred signs, making the *aṣṭamaṅgala* set relevant to myriad cultural contexts (Wayman 1989: 236-46). The beads flowing out from lotus stems on the Bharhut coping stones could well be one of the associated auspicious symbols.

What was the situation in South-East Asia? At Oc Eo in southern Vietnam, the main port of the Funan, *maṅgala*/auspicious signs have been found on tin and gold amulets (Wicks 1999: 14). An ivory comb discovered in Chansen (Thailand) and dated between first-third century CE, has carvings of the *śrīvatsa*, *pūrṇaghaṭa* and conch-shell symbols. According to Glover (1996: 140), the "crouching lion" pendants from BDTP could be symbolic representation of the Buddha as "Śākyasiṁha" or Lord of the Śākya Clan. The crouching lion pendants, alluding to the *śākya* (lion) honorific of the Buddha, are as much auspicious signatures as the *buddapāda*s depicted on the friezes of Bharhut. "Śākya" pendants have also been discovered at Khlong Thom, Tha Chana, Khao Sam Kieu and other sites in southern Thailand (Veraprasert 1987: 323-33; Bronson 1990: 213-30; Glover 1996: 143). The tortoise-shaped bead discovered at Śrīkṣetra (Burma), is another ritual artefact similar to amulets found in Buddhist *stūpa*s in India. Agate beads etched with the auspicious *svastika* sign have been found in Late Prehistoric/Early Historic contexts at Long An (Vietnam) and Khuan Lukpad (Thailand) (Glover and Bellina 2001: 210-11). A recent study shows that the coins of the Indic state of Dvāravatī in Thailand carried auspicious symbols (*pūrṇaghaṭa*, *vajra*, *śrīvatsa*) (Wicks 1999: 12-22). The earliest coins of Dvāravatī are dated to fifth-sixth century CE or a century or two later, suggesting that the auspicious symbols and hence the Indic aniconic symbols were prevalent in the area for some time prior to the release of the coins.

My submission is that the Indic beads in South-East Asia, especially the animal-shaped pendants, were part of a strong aniconic tradition that prevailed in South-East Asia before the introduction of religious iconographic forms in the mid-first millennium CE. The Indic beads in South-East Asia are ubiquitous as grave goods and therefore denote "other-worldly" values. Of course, this is not to say that the beads found in Iron Age graves across South-East Asia were bereft of secular attributes, i.e. as status markers for the deceased. Themes of religion and power often came together in ancient societies. Brown sees the early South-East Asian world as a place where the "spiritual and mundane worlds were a continuum, with the gods the means to this-worldly power and goods" (1996: 199). We can imagine a *śākya* amulet strung together with the more common agates and carnelians, imbuing the whole with religious significance as well as aesthetic charm. The wide use of auspicious symbols in the form of the conventional *maṅgala*s (*śrīvatsa, svastika,* etc.) or associated auspicious signs (*buddhapādas, vajra*) or amulets (śākya beads) in South-East Asia clearly points to the diffusion of aniconic modes of worship from eastern India into former region. As interactive processes across the Bay of Bengal strengthened and South-East Asian communities grew more complex, the material panoply of status initially manifest in beads, amulets and ritual pottery, gradually came to be projected through sculptural art, coinage and architecture.

Indianization: A Reinterpretation

At its core, the Indianization process was marked by absorption of Indic cultural traditions (auspicious symbolisms, religious iconography, political precepts) by the rapidly transforming Iron Age communities of South-East Asia. These borrowings began before the mid-first millennium CE, as indicated by spread of *maṅgala* symbolisms, the arrival of the first Mathurā/Amarāvatī sculptures and references to early Indic kingdoms in South-East Asia (P'an P'an; Funan) in Chinese historical records of the early centuries CE. The Indianization phenomenon requires to be understood in cumulative terms with the mid-first millennium CE recognized as a watershed. The proliferation of Buddhist and Brāhmanical iconographic forms across South-East Asia after CE 500 — the Indic surge — defines this watershed. I reiterate that the sudden appearance of iconic art in South-East Asia could only happen when the indigenous communities of South-East Asia had prior knowledge of the religious ideas underlying Buddhist/Brāhmanical iconography. The auspicious *maṅgala* symbolisms by which Indic religious ideas began to circulate in South-East Asia, facilitated the shift to iconic modes of worship. As I have pointed out, this early phase of Indianization has never been seriously researched. On the other hand, the conspicuous aspect of the Indianization process, epitomized by classical sculpture and royal epigraphical records, became an attractive proposition for Sanskrit scholars and art historians. This body of scholarship equated Indianization with the appearance of Indic sculptural art in South-East Asia, giving rise to the notion that Indianization happened suddenly in the mid-first millennium CE. In this study I have sought to correct the imbalance and reach some conclusions. These conclusions are as follows. Firstly, the point of departure for a holistic understanding of the Indianization process lies in the archaeo-historical record of South-East Asia prior to CE 500. Secondly, the Indianization process in South-East Asia can be demarcated in terms of the shift from aniconic to iconic religious practices in mid-first millennium CE. Thirdly, we can speak of a shared religious tradition in the Bay of Bengal sphere. Developments in eastern India had their resonance in South-East Asia; specifically the shift from aniconic to iconic traditions on both littorals of the Bay of Bengal during the mid-first millennium CE.

9

Conclusion

THE review shows that some of the finest sculptural renderings took place in the Indian coastlands in ancient times. Flinders Petrie in his book *The Arts and Crafts of Ancient Egypt* says, "The art of a country, like the character of the inhabitants, belongs to the nature of the land. The climate, the scenery, the contrasts of each country, all clothe the artistic impulse as diversely as they clothe the people themselves" (Petrie 1909-1996: 1). How does early sculpture find expression in various terrains of the Indian coastlands? In the estuarine areas of lower Bengal, there is a dominance of terracotta art. In contrast, the rocky littoral of Orissa and northern Andhra Pradesh reveal sculptural elements in the rock-cut caves at Udayagiri–Khaṇḍagiri caves in Orissa and the Hīnayāna Bavikoṇḍa–Thotlakoṇḍa complex on the northern Andhra coast. The hilly tracts of the Eastern Ghats presented the right context for carving rock-cut sanctuaries. A similar context prevailed on the west coast. Here, in the hills of the Western Ghats overlooking the Arabian Sea we find the exquisite Buddhist rock-cut caves of Bhaja, Bedsā and Kārle and closer to the sea, the caves at Kanheri, Chaul and Kuḍa. In the deep south, the emergence of the Buddhist *stūpa* architecture and the sculptural art of Amarāvatī and Nāgārjunakoṇḍa along the banks of the river Kr̥ṣṇā was dictated by the narrow estuary hemmed in by hilly outcrops. The sculptors used the white limestone quarried from local outcrops and therefore the panels and medallions from Amarāvatī are referred to as "marbles." The Buddha heads found in the islands of Lakshadweep and the Maldives were made out of the prime marine resource — coral. So we find that geomorpology is an important ingredient in the expressions of early sculptural art on the Indian coastlands.

The classical streams of sculptural art, as well as the early architectural styles (*stūpa*s, rock-cut caves) originated in the interiors. However, it is in the process of spread that particular styles came to be enriched. The epicentre of *stūpa* architecture at Bodh-Gayā and Bharhut was a major influence on Sāñcī and these together contributed to the creation of the art of Amarāvatī. The art of Amarāvatī was both an expression of the accumulated richness of the past as well as the manifestation of its own genius. The Amarāvatī Buddha figures, incorporating influences from the art of Mathurā and Gandhāra, became models for the creation of some South-East Asian Buddha figures. The great *stūpa*s of Bharhut and Sāñcī were built on the trade routes connecting upper India to Ujjain and the western coastlands. The *stūpa* worship also included a number of local cults centred on *yakṣa*s, *yakṣīṇī*s, *nāgā*s and *nāginī*s. Their sculptures adorn the façade of the *stūpa*s.

Before the Common Era most religious art in ancient India was bereft of images of divinities in human form. The emphasis was on worship of particular energies or attributes. The religiosity of the people was marked by acknowledgement of divine energies and fear of the power of the gods. This meant that the gods were seen in abstract terms, as powerful forces far removed from the human condition. In this situation, the closest that the people came to physical objects of worship were certain auspicious symbols like the *svastika*, *śrīvatsa*, etc. Though certain Vedic deities like Indra and Sūrya have been depicted in terracotta art of lower Bengal and in bold relief at the Buddhist caves at Bhaja, these renderings do not seem to be iconic. The well-known art historian Anand Coomaraswamy does admit that a subterranean tendency for anthropomorphism existed in Indian tradition even when Vedic ritualism and abstracted mode of worship was prevalent before the Common Era. In his words:

> It must always be remembered that the Vedas exhibit only a certain aspect of early Indian religion. Behind the pale of Aryan orthodoxy and its tendency to abstract symbolism there lay an extensive and deep-rooted system of popular beliefs and cults and a decided tendency for anthropomorphic representation. These popular beliefs implied an iconography, such as we usually find at Bharhut, of

> *yakṣas* and *nāgas*, *devatās* and *vṛkṣakas*. . . . Gradually all of these found their place in a theistic Hinduism and Buddhism.
>
> — Coomaraswamy 1972: 46

The deep rooted debates within the Brāhmanical, Buddhist and Jaina religious groups converged at one point during the BCE–CE transition; the need to create human forms for the Gods and religious figures like the Buddha, *bodhisattvas* and Jaina *tīrthaṁkaras*. Religious imagery first made its appearance in the Brāhmanical faiths. The figures of the God-King Kṛṣṇa and his brother Balarāma are stamped on a coin of the Indo-Greek king Agathocles dated to the second century BCE. The *śivaliṅgam* from Guḍimallam (Andhra Pradesh), showing the early iconography of Śiva has also been dated to the second century BCE (fig. 34). The creation of images in stone was pioneered at Mathurā in the BCE–CE transition. A similar development in religious art, primarily Buddhist, took shape in the north-west of India at Gandhāra. Other major schools of art which manifested the post-Vedic religious theism were located at Amarāvatī, Nāgārjunakoṇḍa and Sārnāth. Here, images of the Buddha and Brāhmanical deities were created in stone and bronze from the second–fifth century CE. It should be emphasized that the earlier forms of worship also carried on, especially seen in the use of auspicious symbols. This is because of two major reasons. Firstly the aniconic modes of worship were prevalent all over India before the introduction of Brāhmanical, Buddhist and Jaina iconography at Mathurā and Gandhāra. Even after the introduction of mainstream religious iconography, the peripheral areas — which included large parts of the Indian coastlands — remained unaffected and it took some time before religious iconography was introduced. This was particularly the case on the Bengal and Orissa coast when we find that formal iconography of gods appear in stone in a major way after fifth century CE. I have also argued in this review that the reason for the sudden appearance of the statues of the Viṣṇu and Buddha in South-East Asia after fifth century CE was due to this "diffusion" barrier.

There is no doubt that the main schools of sculptural art (Mathurā, Gandhāra, Amarāvatī and Sārnāth), themselves the product of interaction and syncretism, influenced art styles on the Indian coastlands. This is evident in the many specific examples we have discussed, like the "Kṣatrapa" style Viṣṇu images from western India or the Buddha heads from Lakshadweep and Maldives exhibiting local influences with traits of the classical art of Mathurā and Gandhāra. Together with the creation of religious imagery, we find a rich expression of secular themes (portraiture, Bacchanalian scenes, etc.) in stone and terracotta art. The portrait gallery of the Sātavāhanas in the caves of Naneghāṭ comes to mind. Unfortunately, the royal portraits in relief have been eroded, only the labels remain. However, we are reminded of the popularity of portrait art in western India. Was this genre the contribution of the Kuṣāṇas? In the Śaka territories in the present Gujarat state, we find depictions in terracotta of Scythian figures. From the site of Amreli in Saurāṣṭra there has been found a fragmentary terracotta figure imitating a Kuṣāṇa royal statue discovered at Mat near Mathurā (*fig.* 23). From the Uperkoṭ cave group at Jūnāgaṛh in Saurāṣṭra a terracotta portrait seems to be that of a Kṣatrapa royal figure.

Art influences from abroad penetrated through the Indian coastlands. There is a debate on the nature of borrowings. The impact of Graeco-Roman contact on the art and architecture of the Indian coastlands needs to be fully appreciated. The Graeco-Roman influences on the art of Amarāvatī and Nāgārjunakoṇḍa, for instance, has been connected to transmissions from Gandhāra. However, the presence of Roman traders in the Kṛṣṇā estuary makes it more likely that some of the Hellenistic influence was direct and came through the sea trade. The same can be said of the "smiling boy" figure in Nevāsā and the acanthus leaf motifs on the Uperkoṭ pillar. Many *dvārapāla* figures are imbued with western influences in their facial features, dress and posture. The "Yavana" *dvārapāla* at the cave of Udayagiri-Khaṇḍagiri presents one powerful example with his aggressive stance, kilt and long boots (*fig.* 53). Other prominent examples are at Junnār, Pītalkhora and Nāgārjunakoṇḍa. In the deep south, a terracotta bust of a bearded warrior reminds one of the references to the fierce Yavana gaurds in the Tamil Saṅgam poetry of the early centuries CE (*fig.* 37). Imported art, such as the Mediterranean bronzes from Kolhapur and the Atlas figure at Vallabhipura must have inspired the local genius. A cameo from Karvan, set in red and white agate, shows a Greek lady. A number of "Indianized" cameos have come to light in peninsular India, showing figures of ladies and animals.

In the spread of Indian art to overseas locales, the most conspicuous pattern is evident in the distribution and absorption of Indic art in South-East Asia. The transmission of sculptural art from the Indian coastlands to South-East Asia was more prolific than in the western Indian Ocean region. The question that comes to mind is why Indian art did not penetrate into west Asia despite the trade relations with coastal south Arabia and the Persian Gulf being as intense as they were with South-East Asia in the early centuries CE. Was it because of the strong Hellenistic influences upon the art and religion of south Arabia and the Persian Gulf littoral regions? Hellenic influence on the ancient cultures of Yemen (Marib, Saba) is indicated by finds of stone busts of probable Greek origin dating to the last centuries BCE (Lush 1998: 2). The adoption of the Athenian "owl" coins and later the Roman coin standards in the kingdom of Hadhramaut indicate the continuity of western influences upon south Arabia. The Romanization of south Arabian art is seen in the statue of Hadhramaut kings. Therefore, in spite of the presence of Indian traders and even ambassadors (as attested in a Hadhrami epigraph), Indic art and religion did not affect the south Arabians as it did the South-East Asians. However, in South-East Asia we find the best of early Indian sculptural art was transmitted only from the Gupta period, after the sixth century CE. No example of sculptural art of the finest period of the Mathurā and Gāndhāra school, from the first to the third century CE, found its way to South-East Asia. As I have said earlier, there is no simple equation between the commercial logic and aesthetics. However, when these dynamics converged, fresh genre of artworks were created, beautiful artworks that were never seen before. Some of the finest minglings happened in the hubs of long distance trade: the Arabo-Roman statues of Hadhramauti royalty; Buddha images in Graeco-Indian conception at Gandhāra; and Indic styles in South-East Asia. These expressions of syncretic art validate the idea of trade and civilization.

Ultimately this study has convinced me of the "civilizational" view of art. Rather than adopt a purely art historical focus (change of form, perspectives, iconography and other aspects) I have tried to understand the development of art on the Indian coastlands in a more holistic sense, relating renderings in stone and terracotta to their historical and material culture contexts. The classical schools of sculptural art developed in Mathurā, Gandhāra and Sārnāth through cross-cultural influences, combining the indigenous with the foreign. The point is that the styles and idioms of the early schools of sculptural art were essentially syncretic and dynamic and not frozen in time. These classical forms further influenced other local and regional styles and we see the examples on the Indian coastlands. This monograph would serve its purpose if the early sculptural art of India is viewed, not as part of a formal and exclusive domain of culture, but as an expression of creative energy emerging from the clatter and din of life.

Figures and Plates

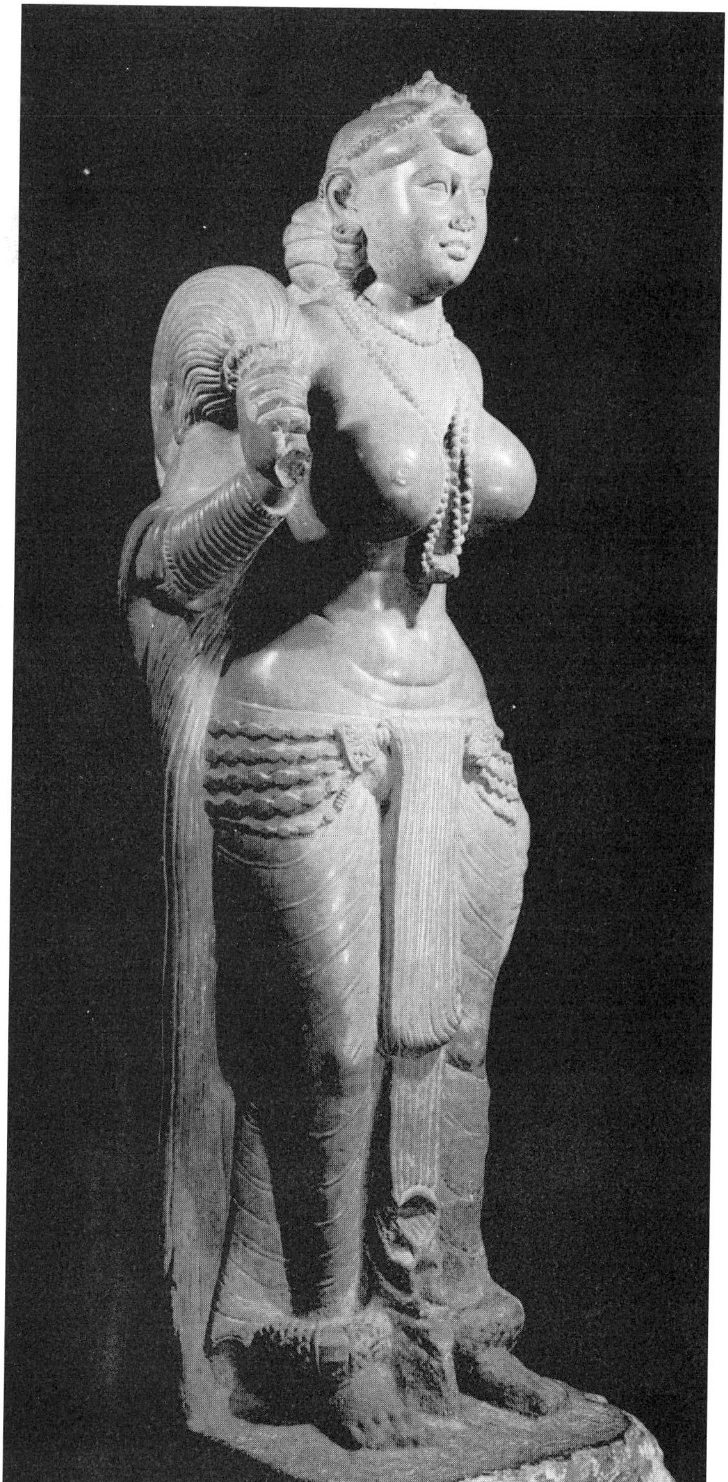

fig. 1: Didārgañj *yakṣī*. Sandstone, 3rd century BCE, Patna Museum.

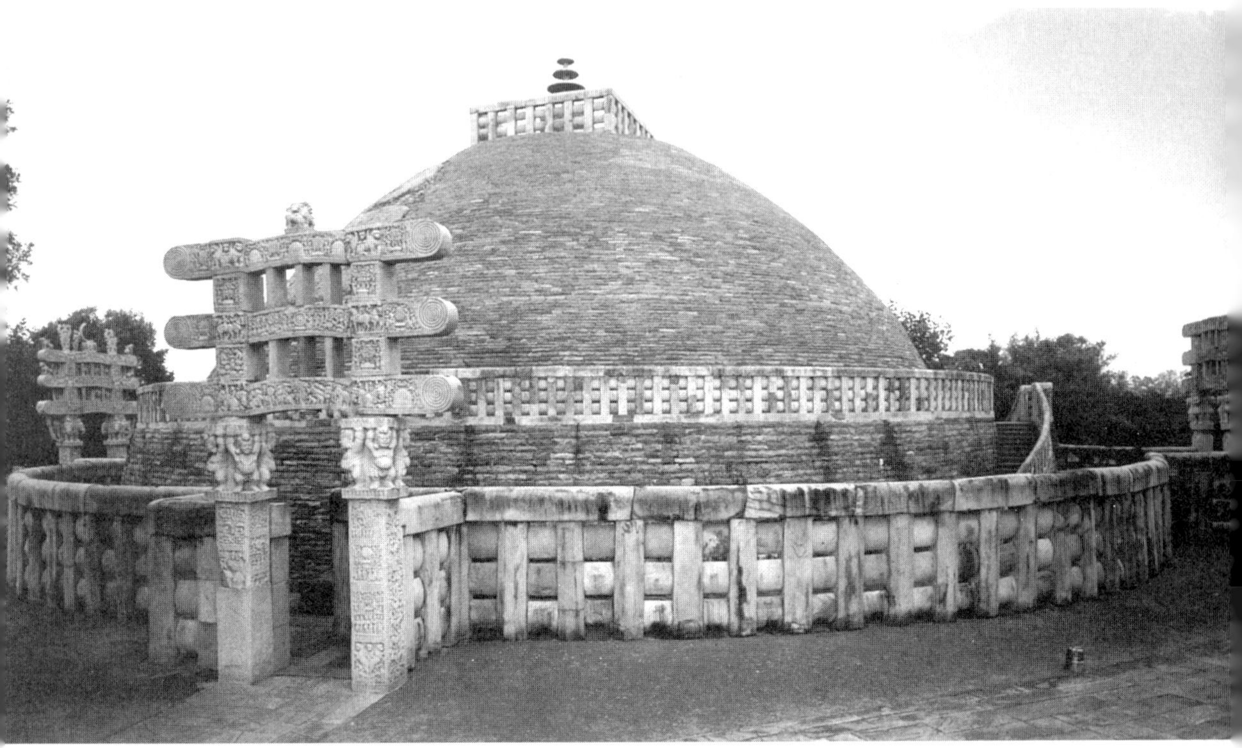

fig. 2: View of Sāñcī Stupa.

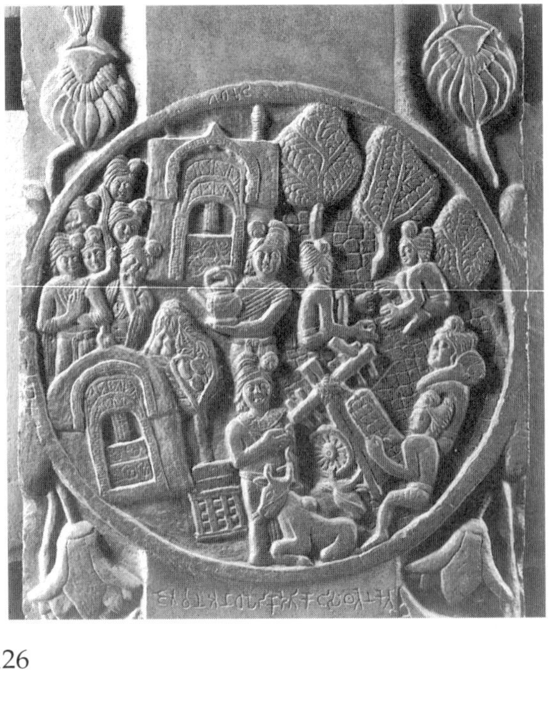

fig. 3: Medallion from Bharhut, 2nd century BCE.

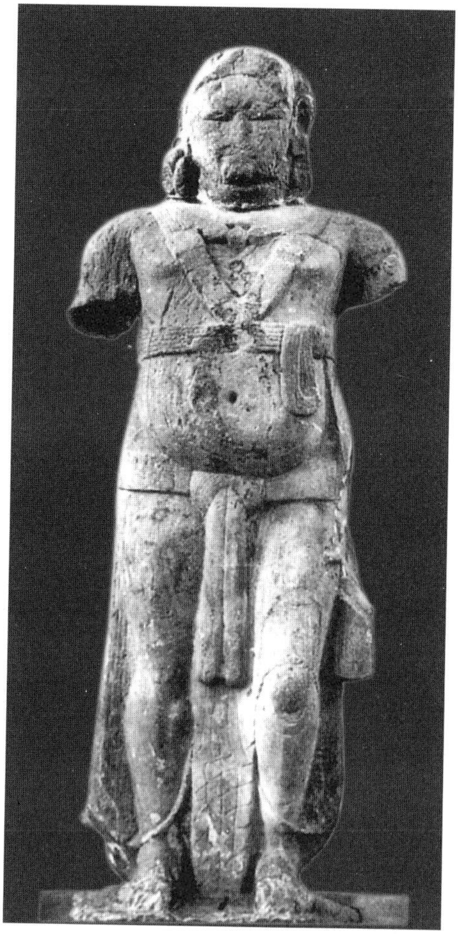

fig. 4: Figure of Parkham *yakṣa*, Mathurā, 2nd century BCE.

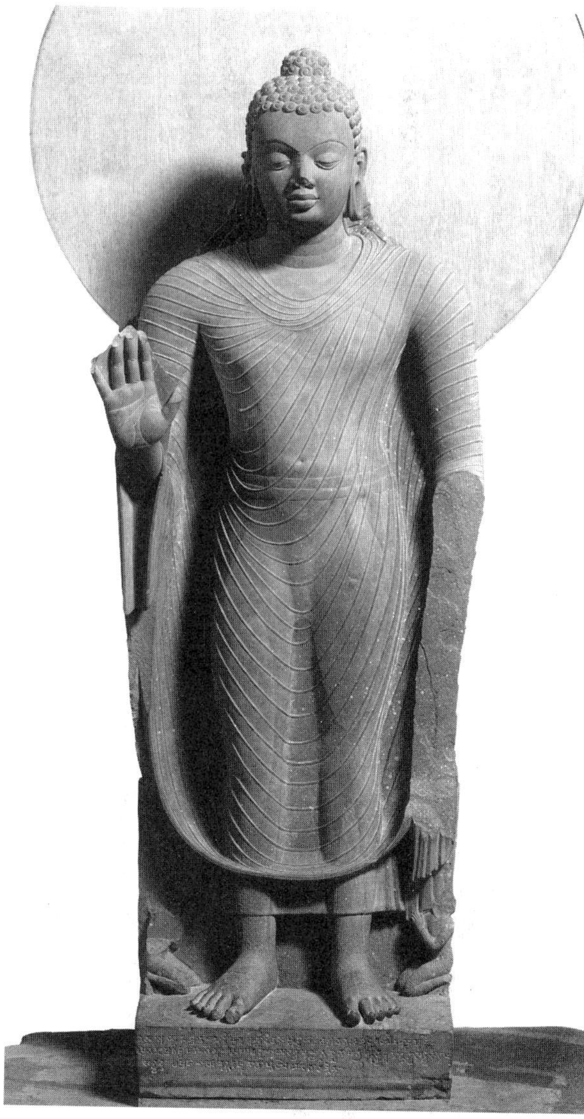

fig. 5: Buddha image of the Mathurā School.

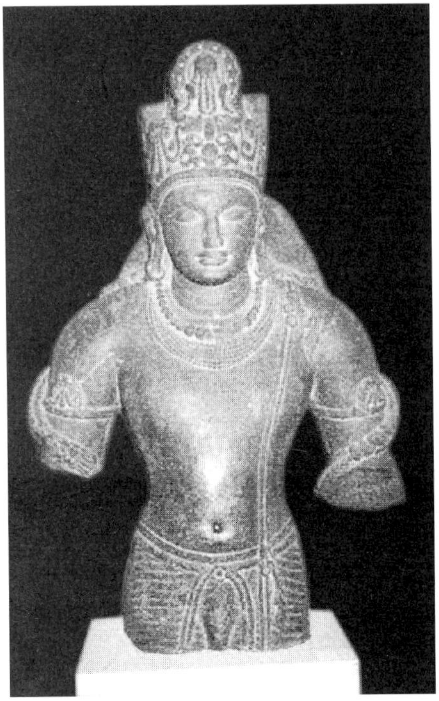

fig. 6: Viṣṇu image of the Mathurā School.

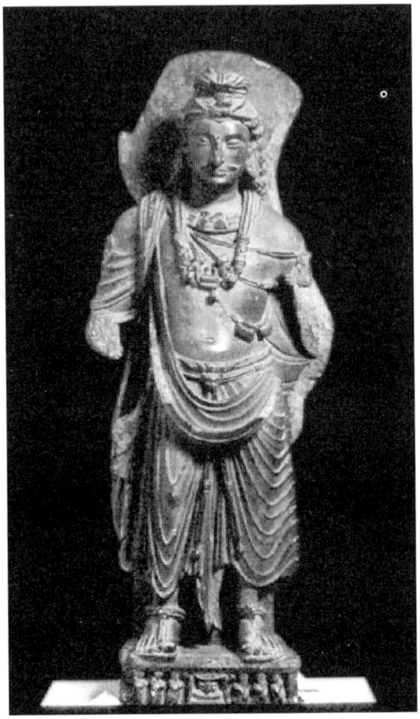

fig. 7: Buddha image of the Gāndhāra School.

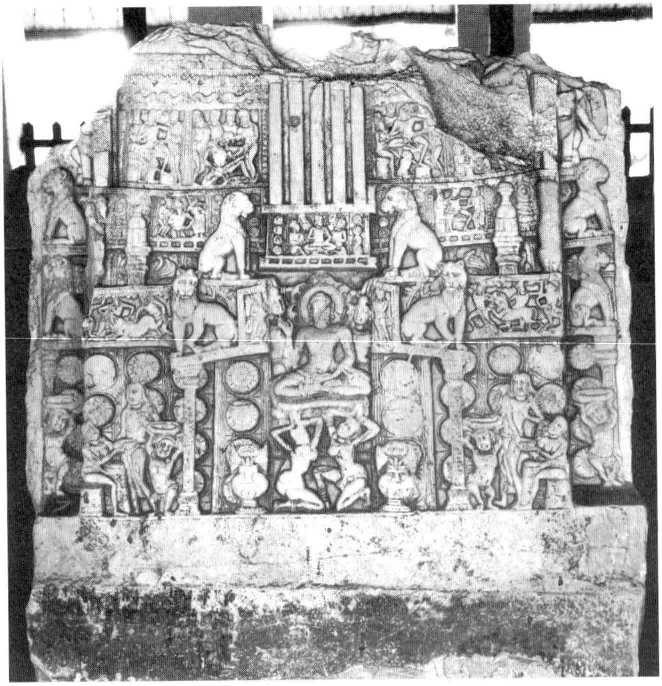

fig. 8: Slab depicting the Amarāvatī Stūpa.

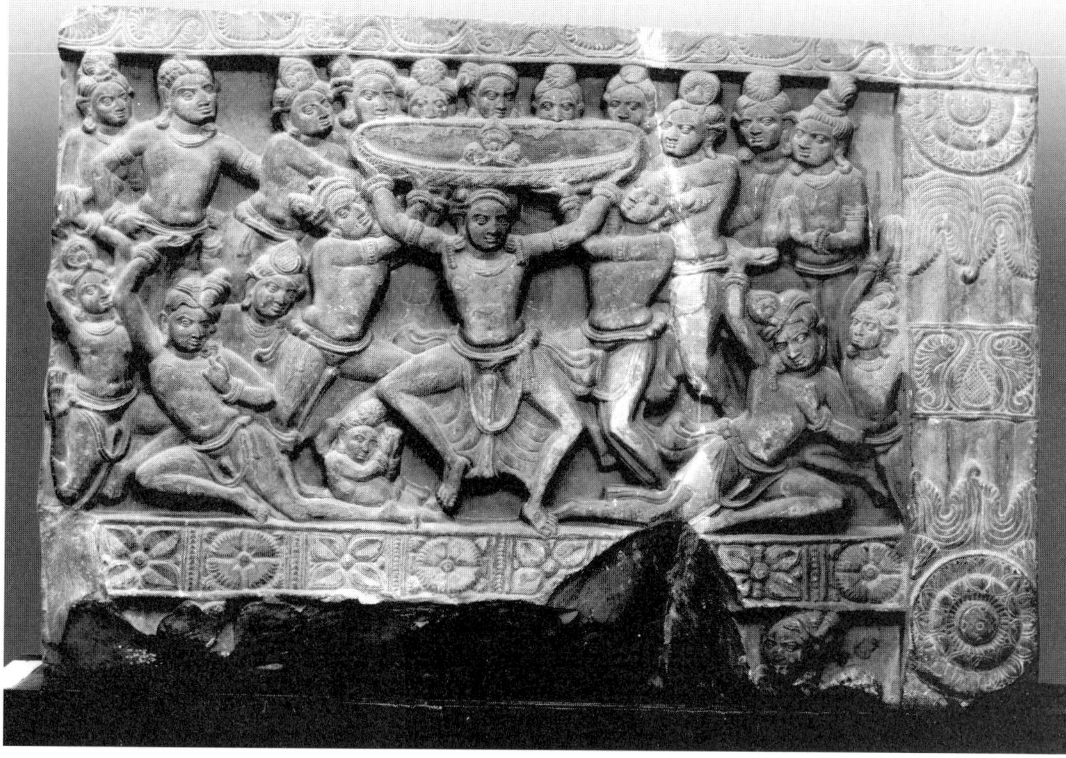

fig. 9: Frieze showing ascent to heaven with turban of Buddha, Amarāvatī, 2nd century CE.

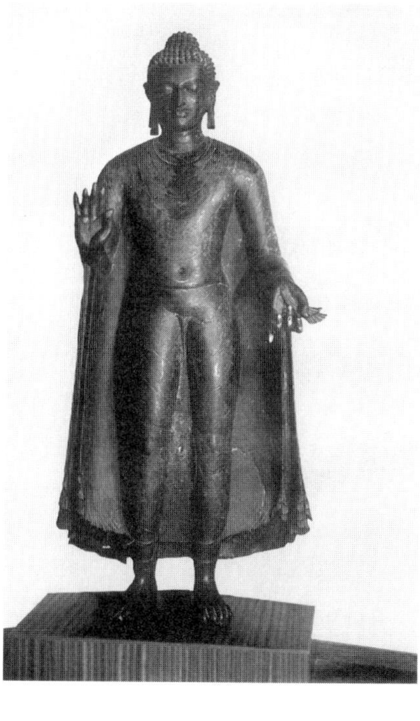

fig. 10: Standing Buddha of the Sārnāth School.

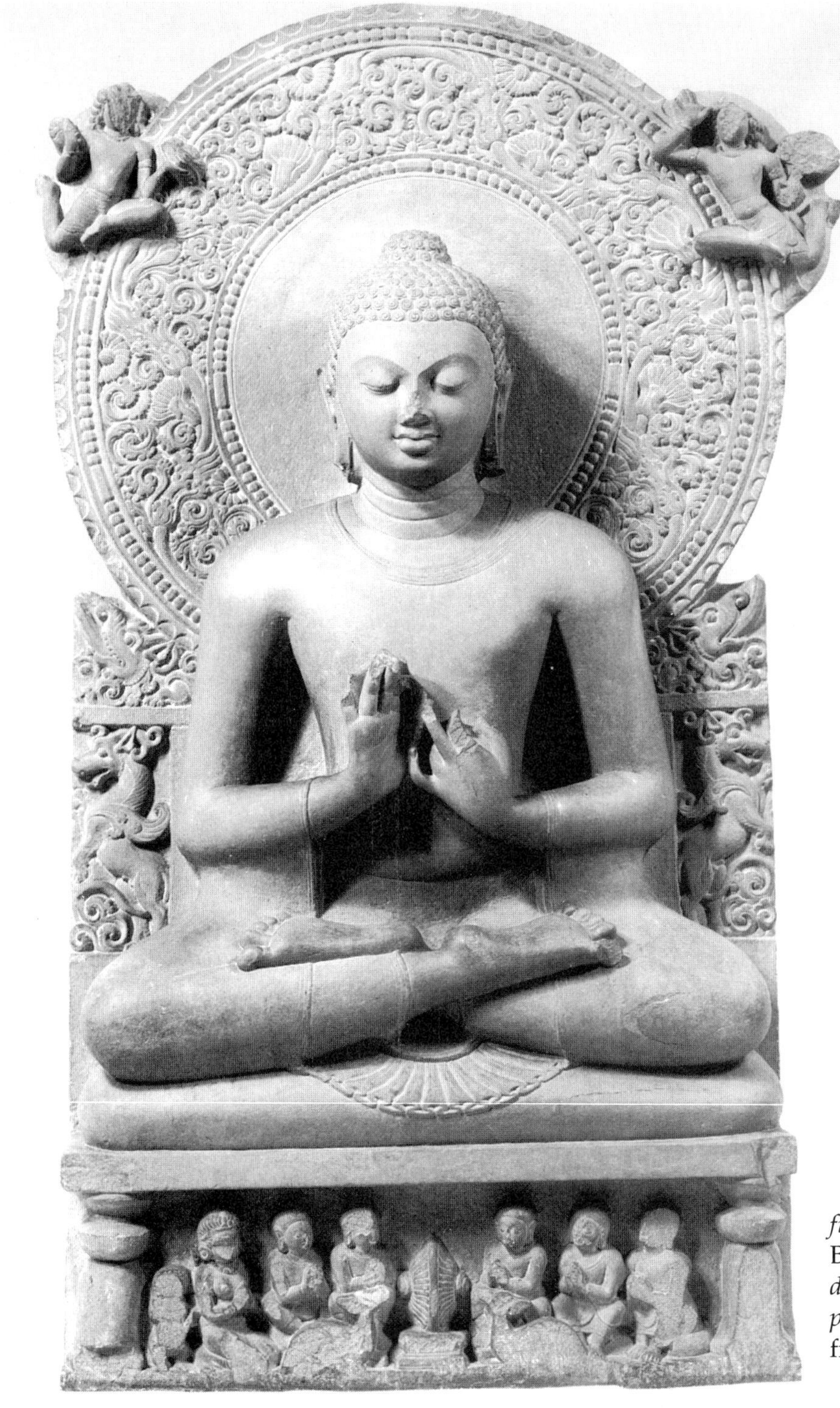

fig. 11: Seated Buddha in *dharmacakra-pravartana* pose from Sārnāth.

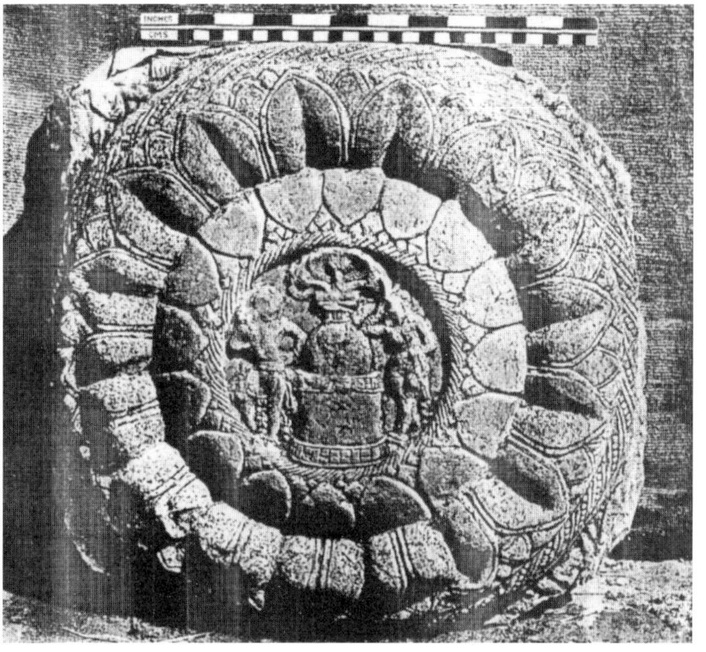

fig. 12: Limestone slab from Ṭer showing Amarāvatī influence.

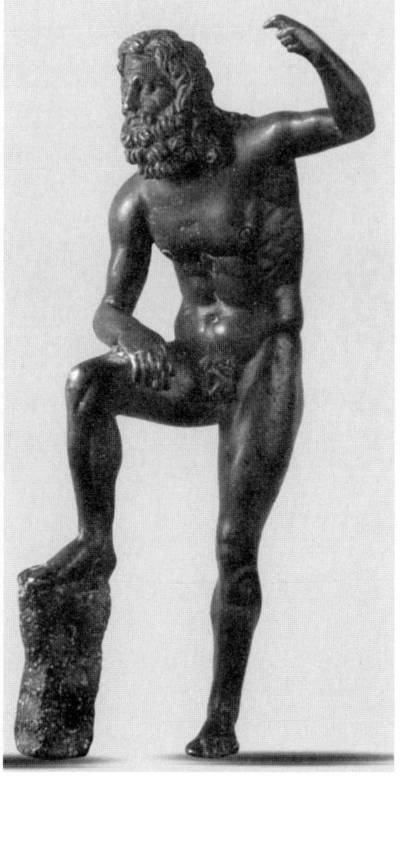

fig. 13: Bronze figure of Poseidon from Brahmapuri.

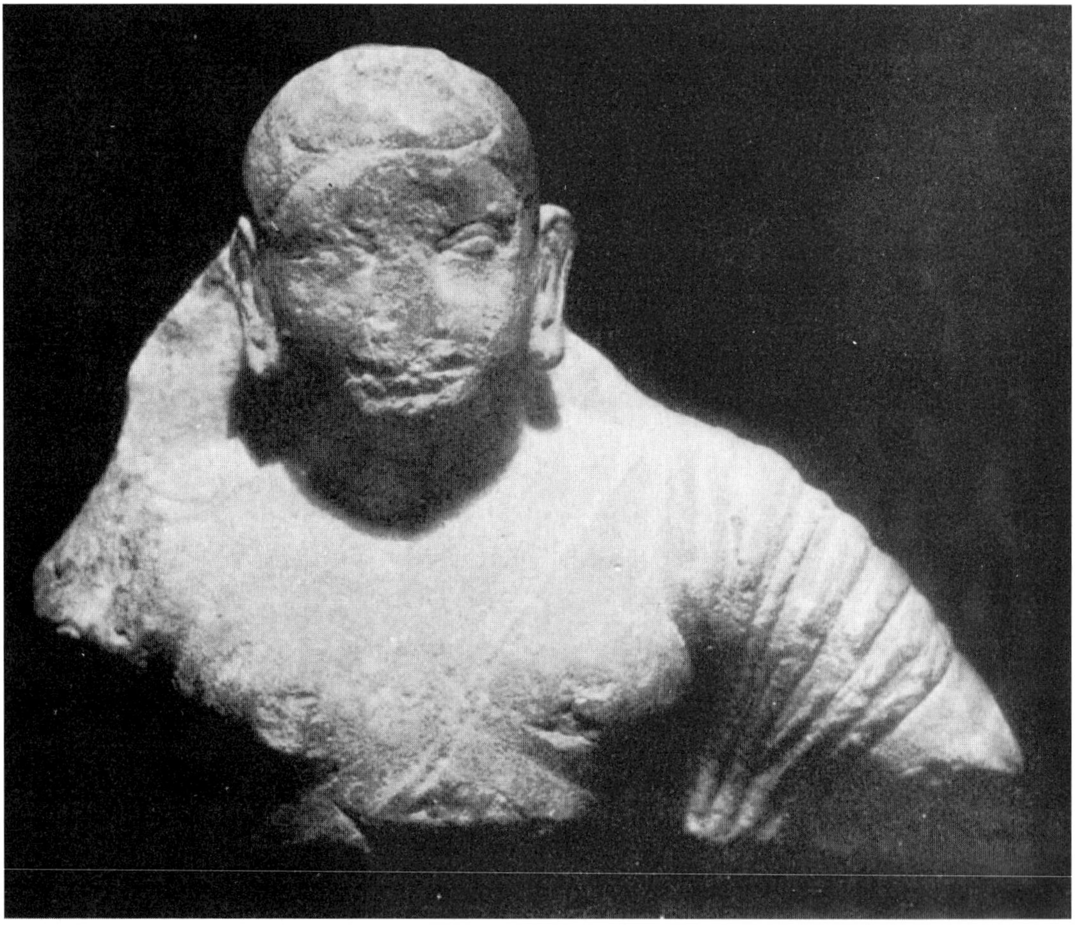

fig. 14: Stone image of Buddha from Candraketugaṛh.

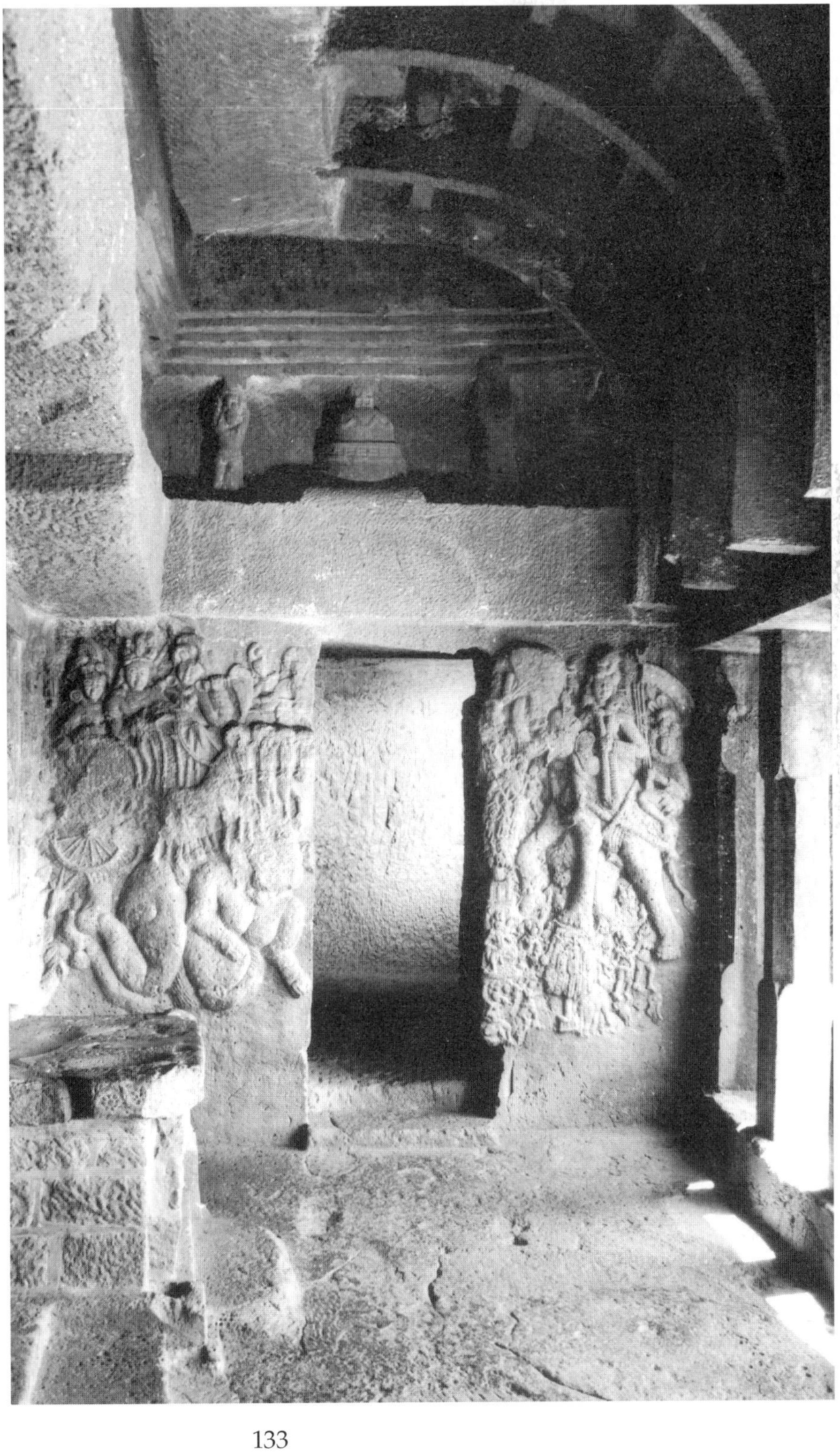

fig. 15: Sūrya–Indra panels, Bhaja Cave, 2nd-1st century BCE.

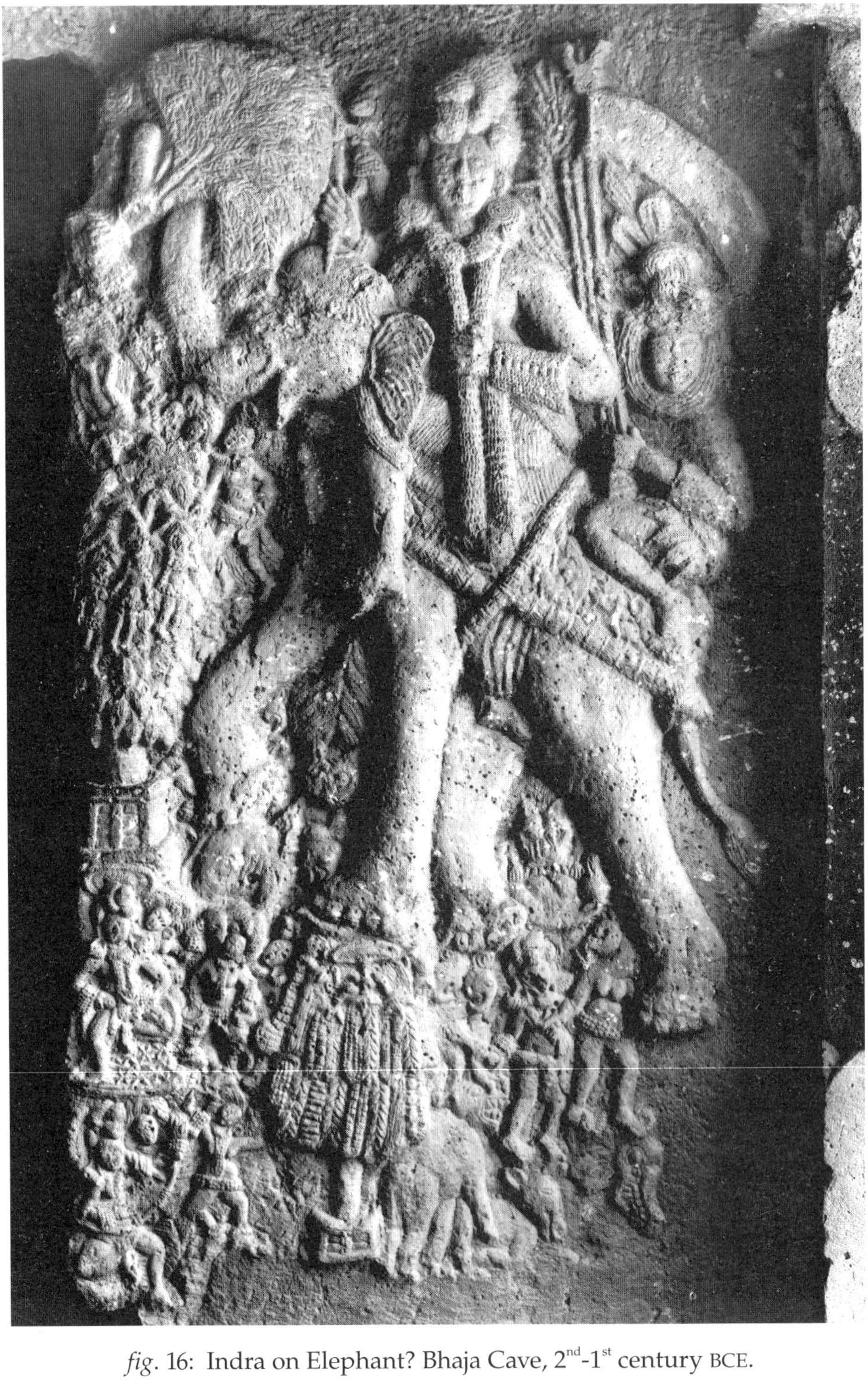

fig. 16: Indra on Elephant? Bhaja Cave, 2nd-1st century BCE.

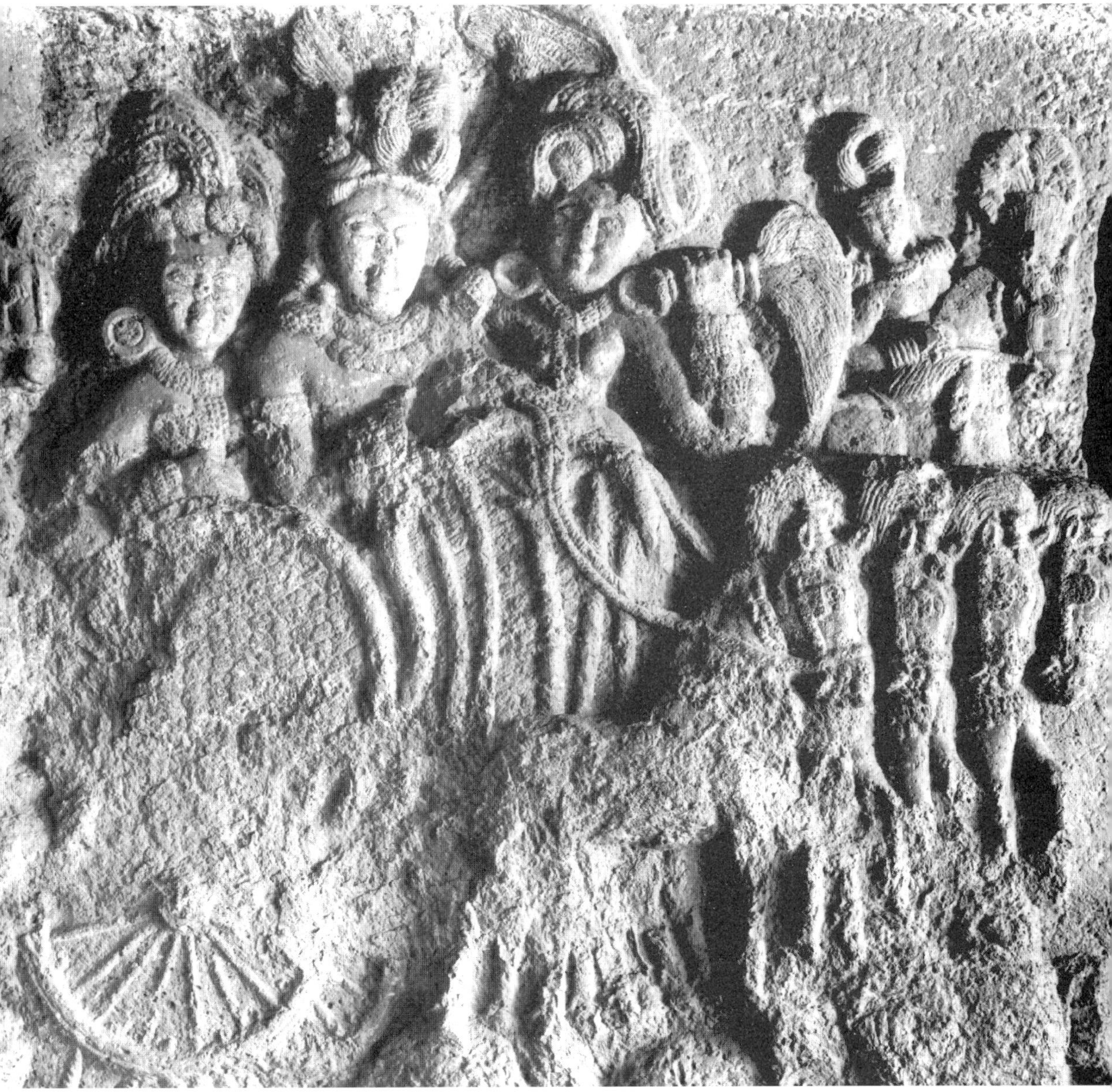

fig. 17: Sūrya on chariot? Bhaja Cave, 2nd-1st century BCE.

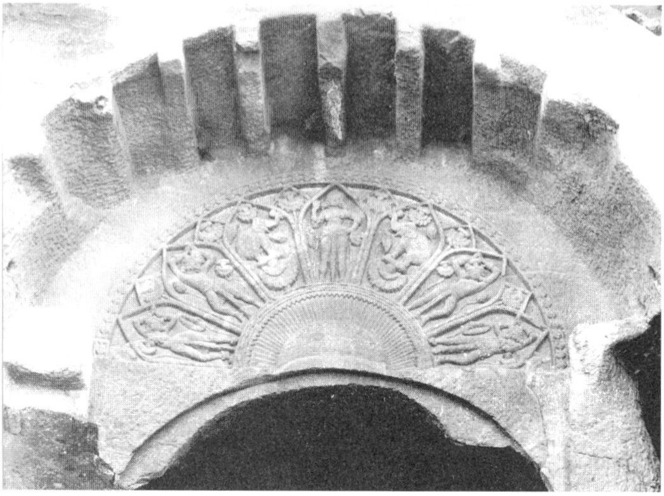

fig. 18: Gajalakṣmī panel at entrance of rock-cut cave at Junnar, 1st century BCE.

fig. 19: Pillar capitals at Kārle showing animals and human figures, 1st century CE.

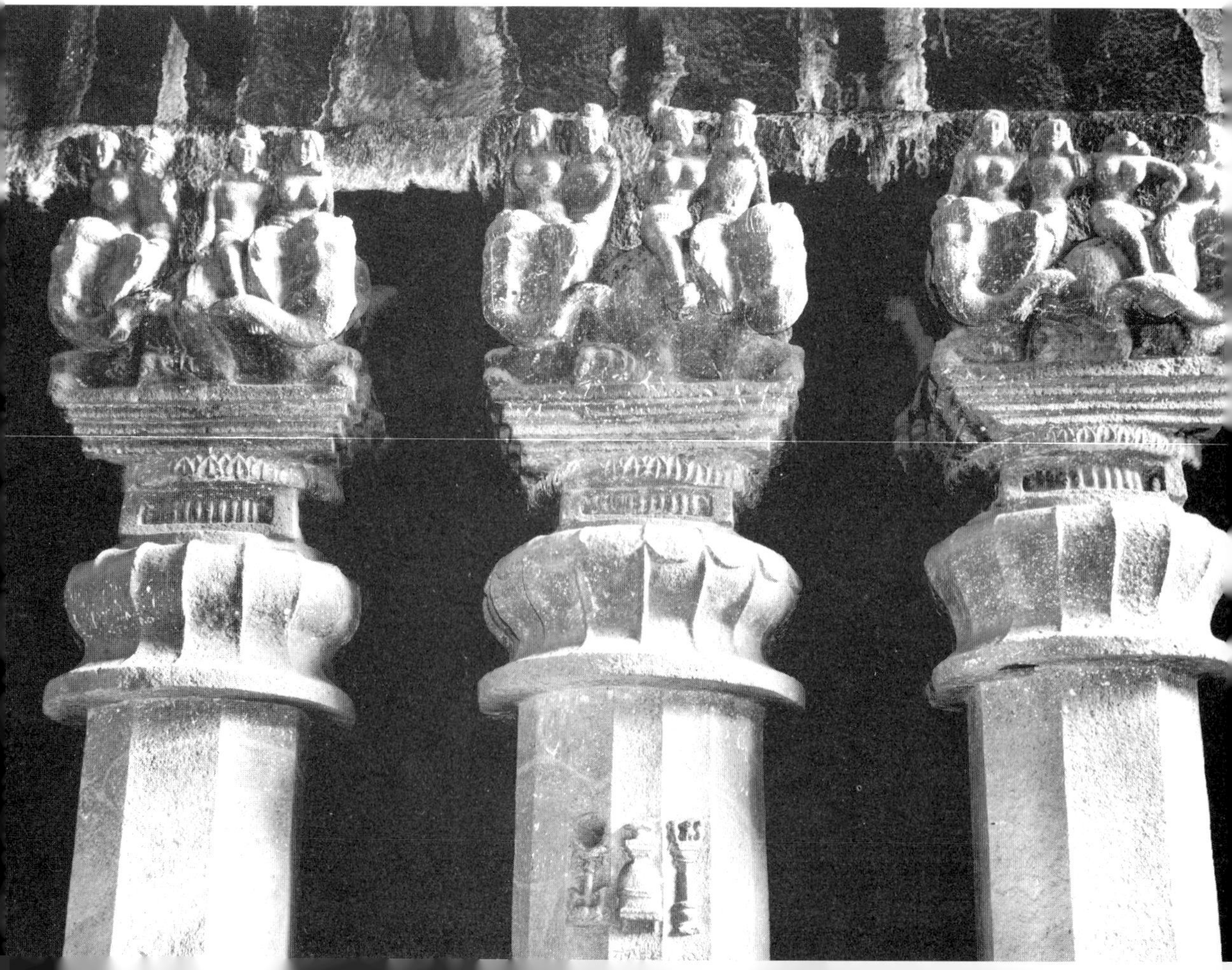

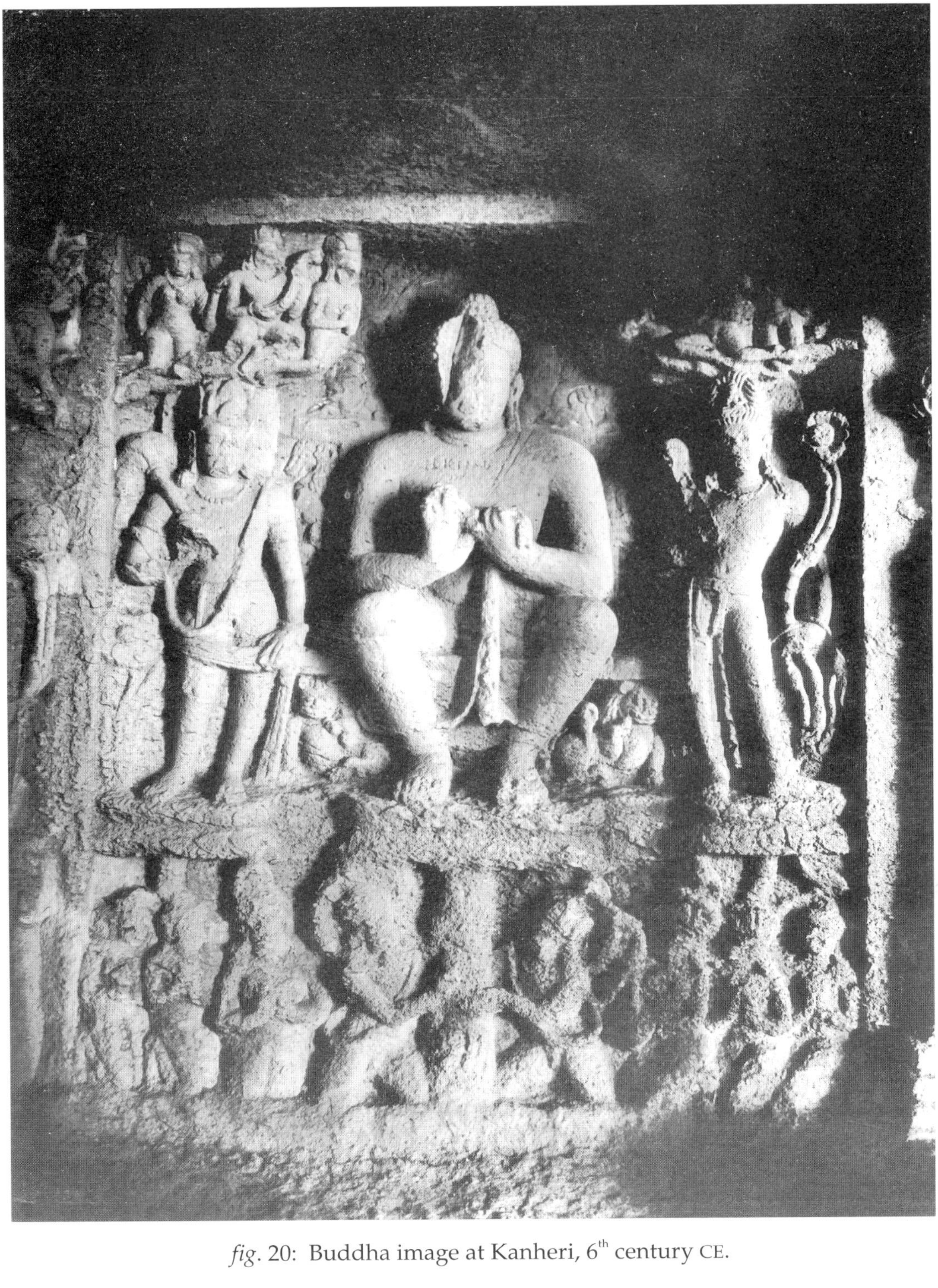

fig. 20: Buddha image at Kanheri, 6th century CE.

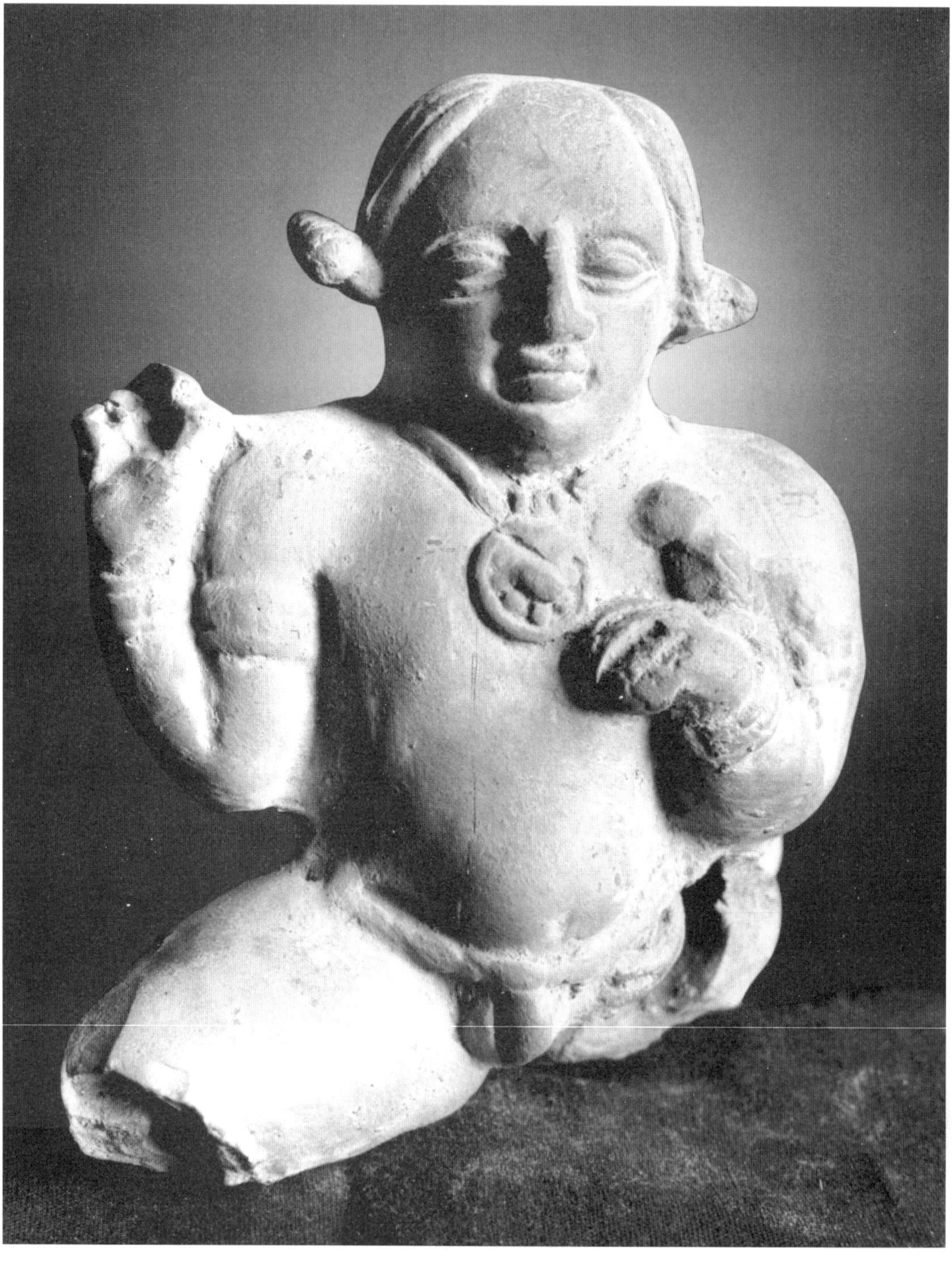

fig. 21: Figure of male in kaolin from Ṭer, 1st century CE.

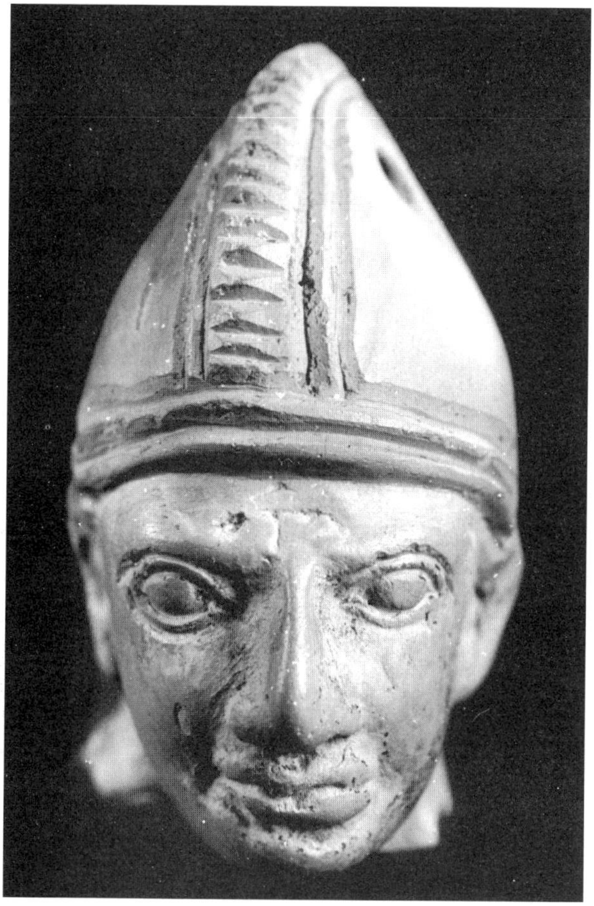

fig. 22: Portrait of Scythian in terracotta, Ṭer, 1st century CE.

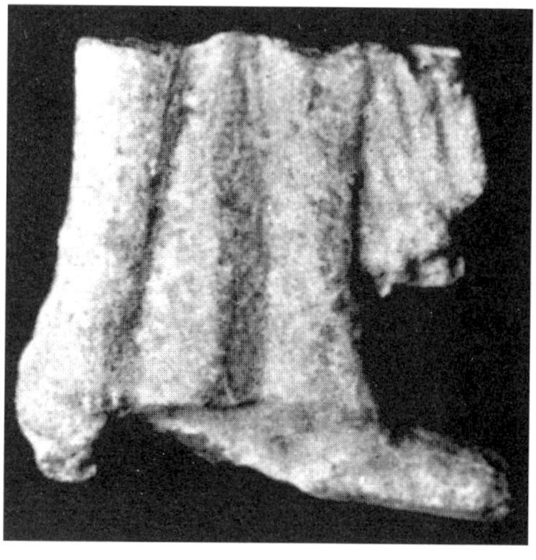

fig. 23: Terracotta imitation of stone image of Kaniṣka in Mathurā, Amreli, Gujarat, 2nd century CE.

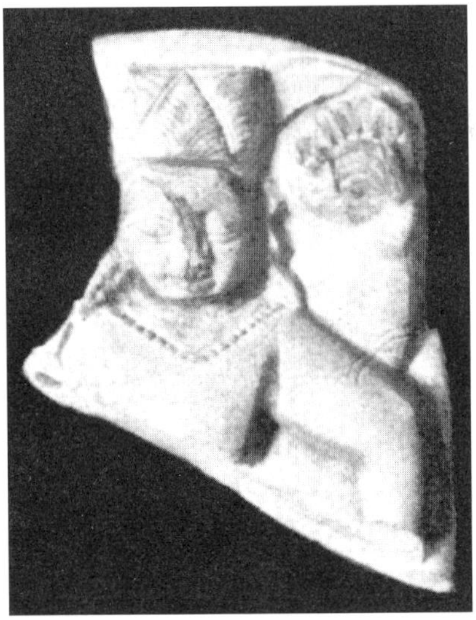

fig. 24: Viṣṇu image from Amreli, Stone, 2nd century CE.

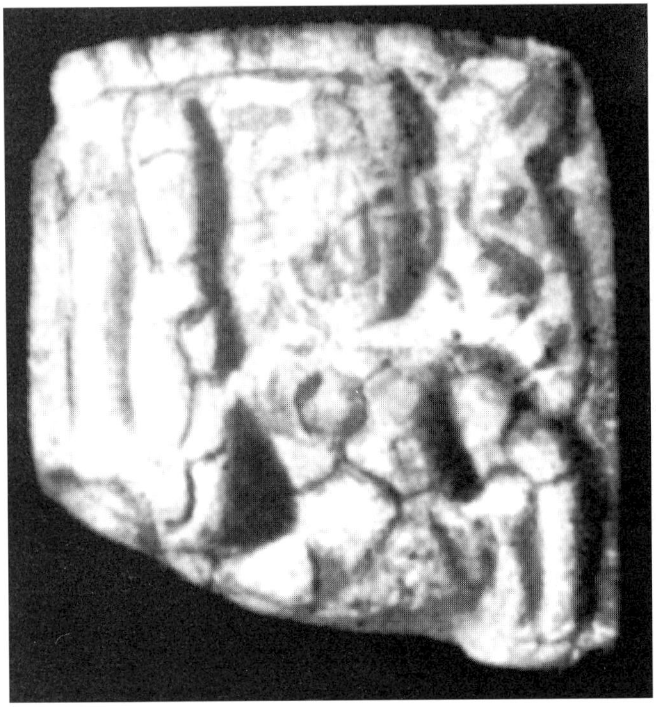

fig. 25: Image of four armed goddess, Stone, Amreli, 1st-2nd century CE.

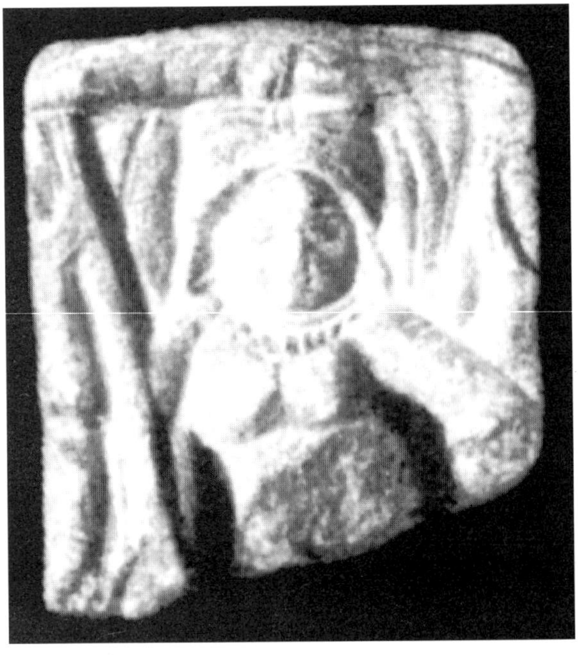

fig. 26: Image of Vaiṣṇavī, Stone, Amreli, 1st-2nd century CE.

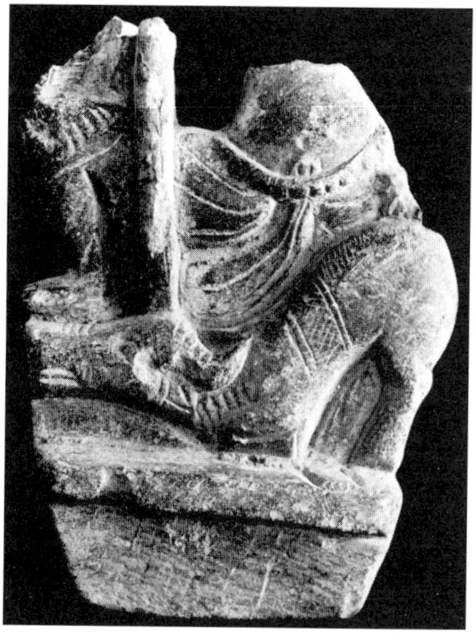

fig. 27: Stone image (fragmentary) of Mahiṣāsuramardinī, stone, Amreli, 5th century CE.

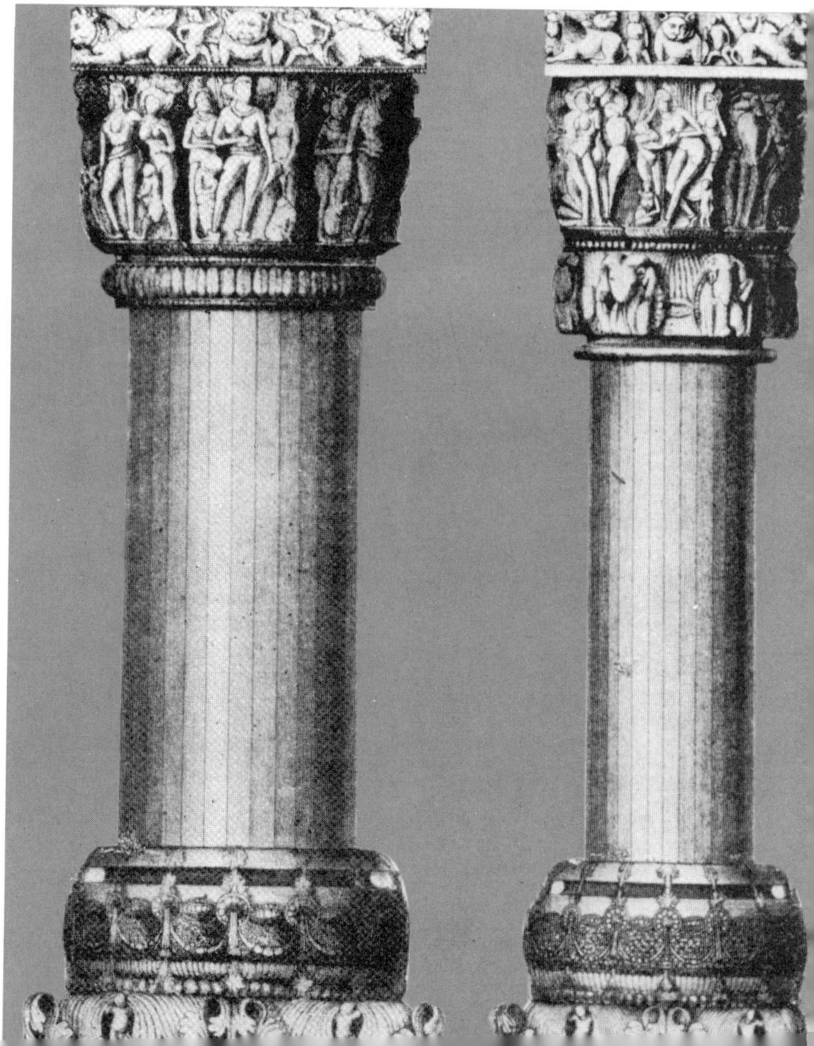

fig. 28: Highly decorated pillars in Junāgaṛh Cave, Gujarat, 2nd century CE?

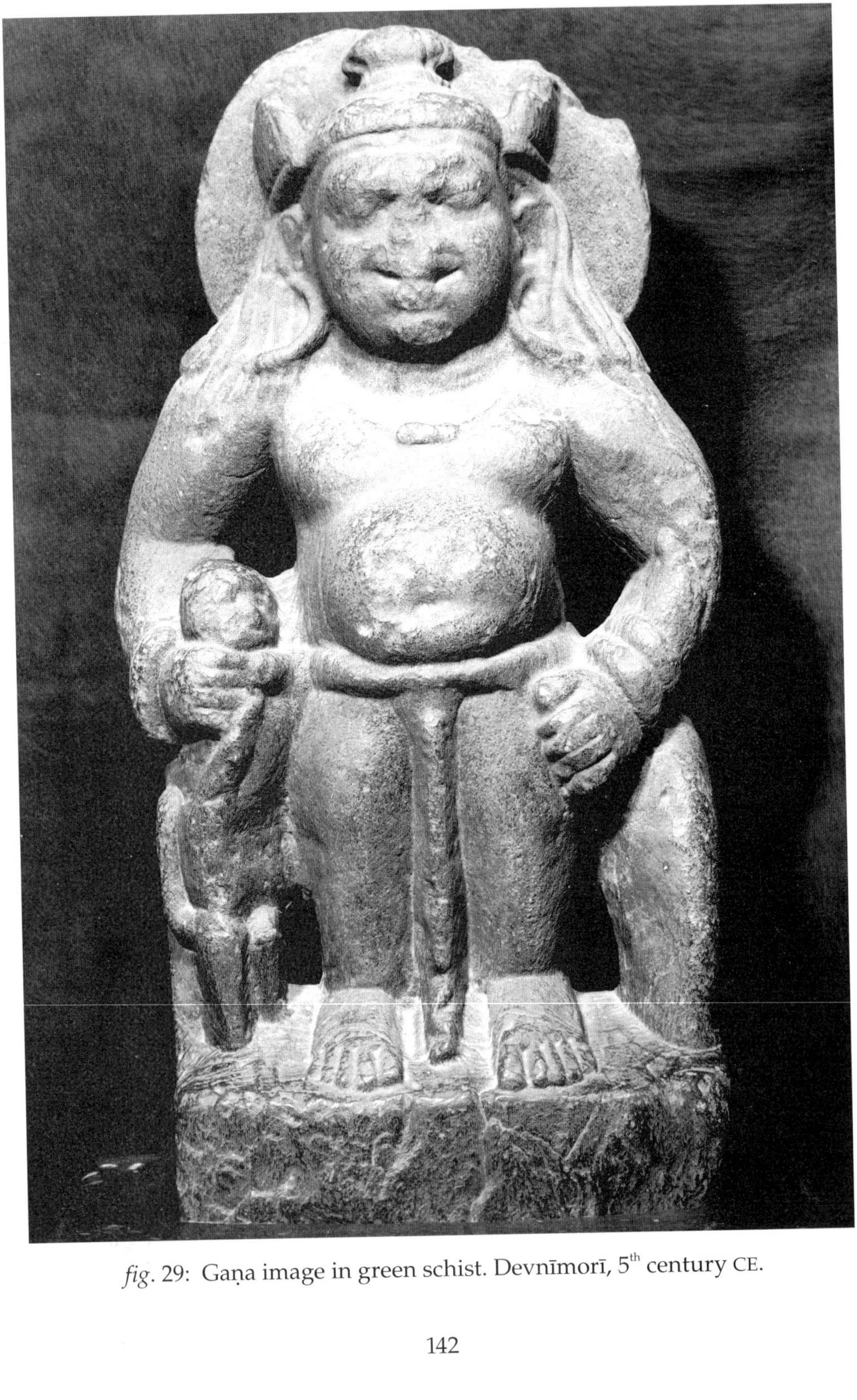

fig. 29: Gaṇa image in green schist. Devnīmorī, 5th century CE.

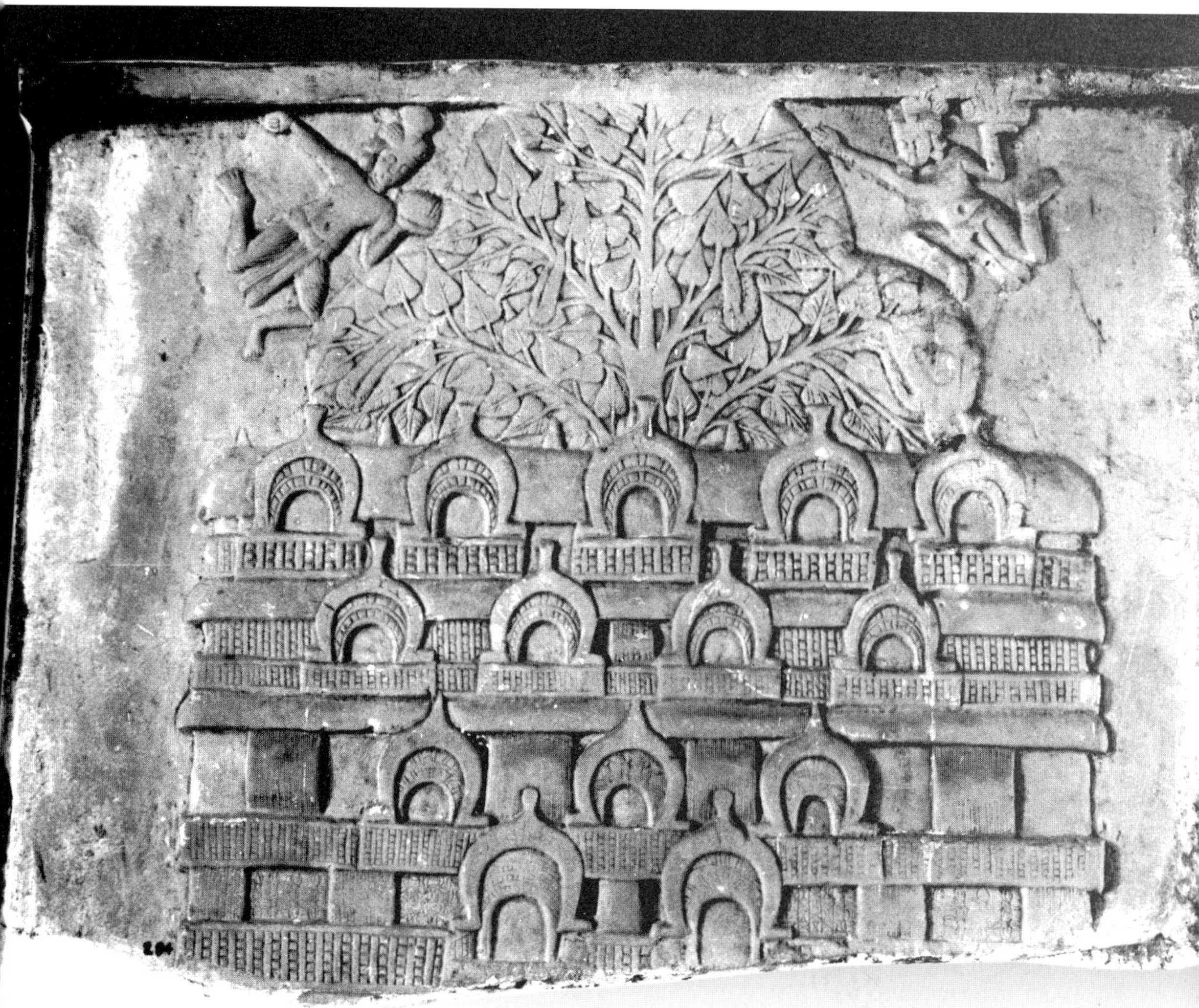

fig. 30: Decorative frieze from Kesanapalli showing Bodhi tree, Limestone, 2nd century BCE?

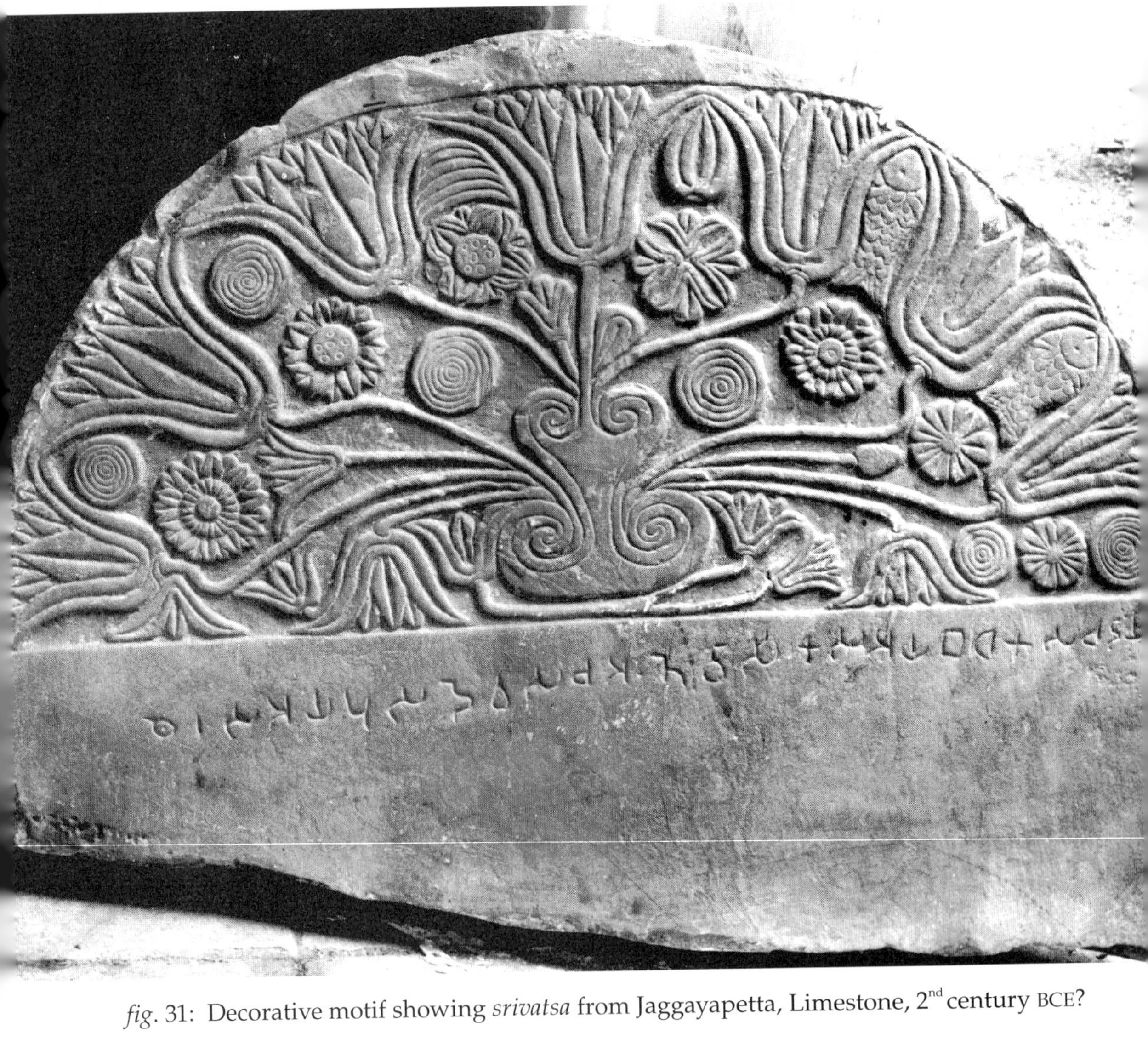

fig. 31: Decorative motif showing *srivatsa* from Jaggayapetta, Limestone, 2nd century BCE?

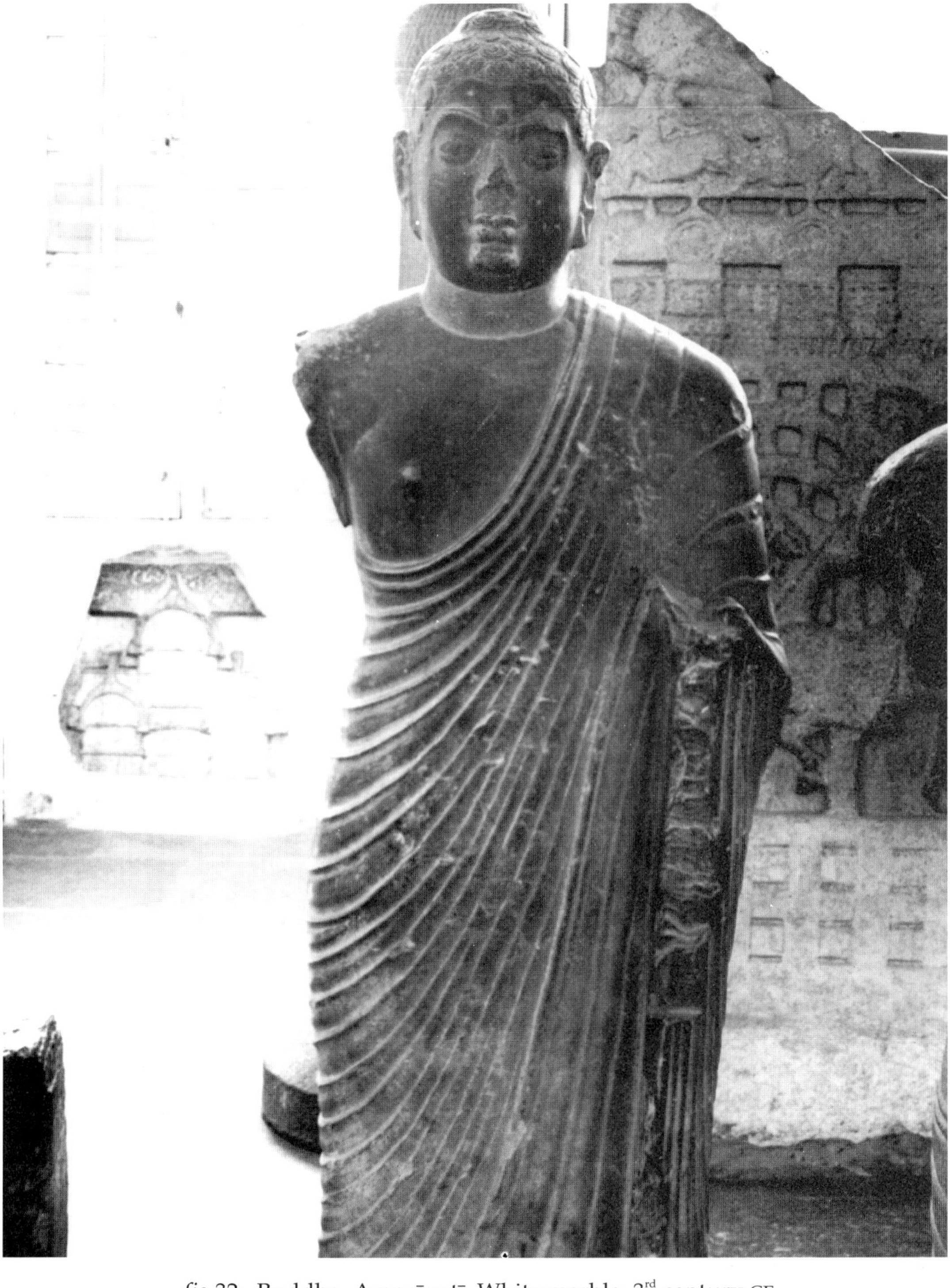

fig 32: Buddha, Amarāvatī, White marble, 3rd century CE.

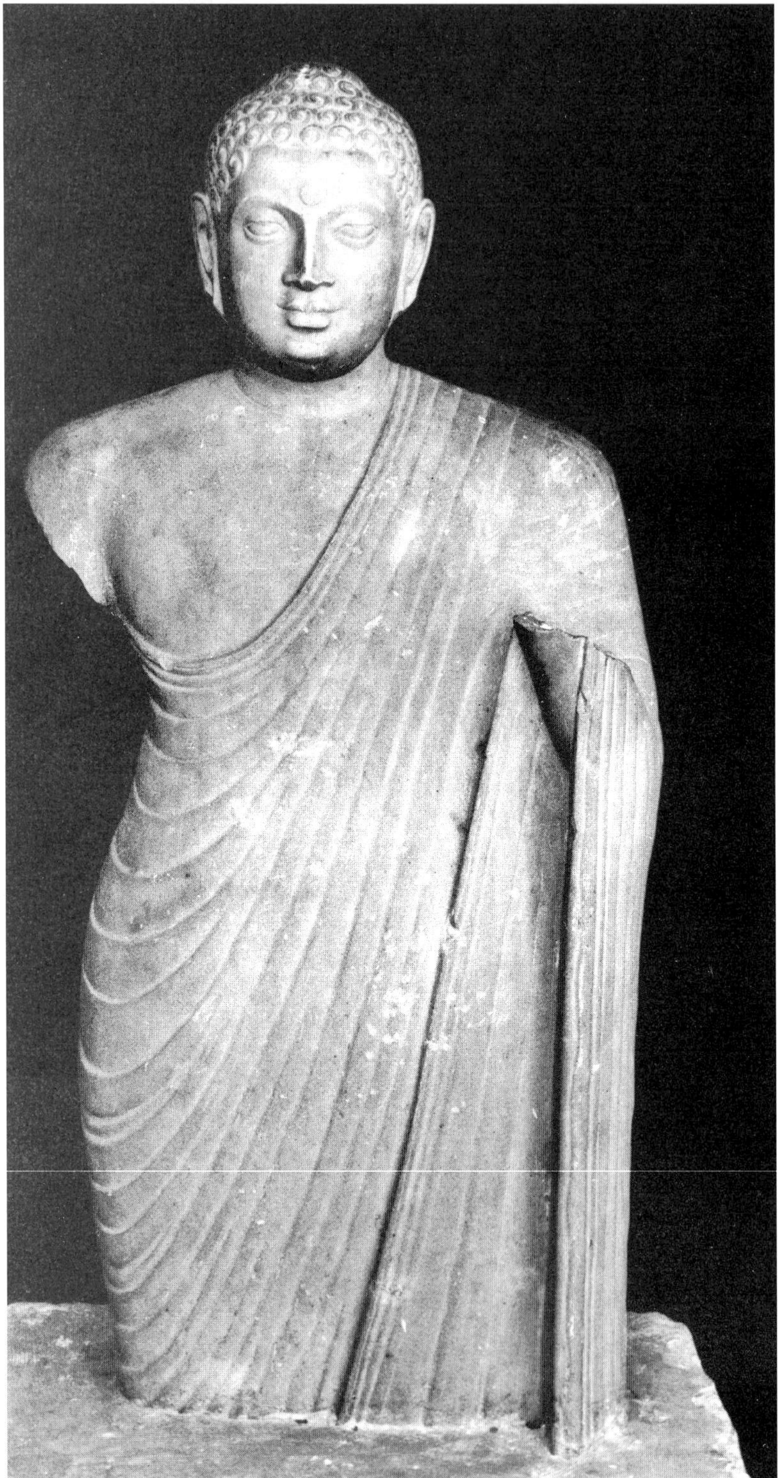

fig. 33: Buddha, Limestone, Nāgārjunakoṇḍa? 2nd-3rd century CE, AP Govt. Museum.

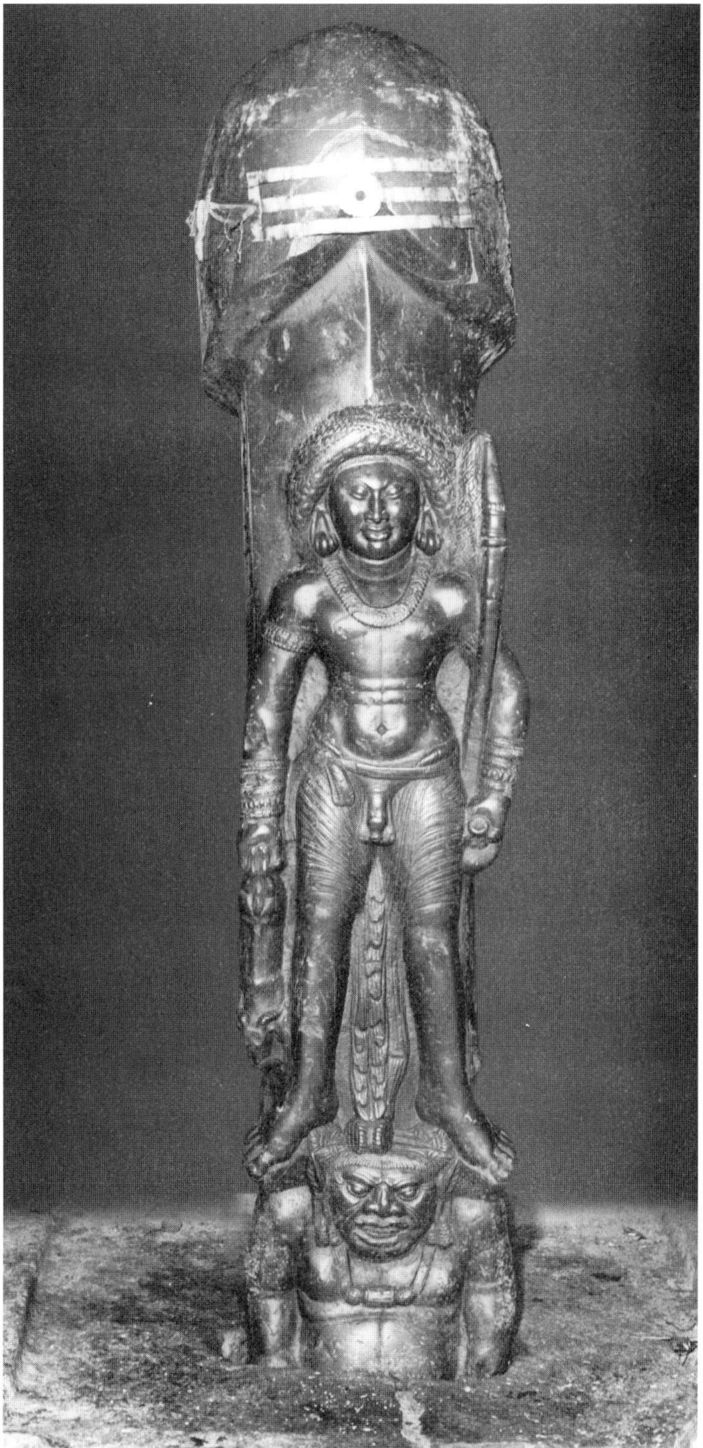

fig. 34: Garbhagṛha, Śivaliṅga, Granite, 2nd century BCE, Parasurāmeśvara Temple, Gudimallam, Chittoor District, Andhra Pradesh.

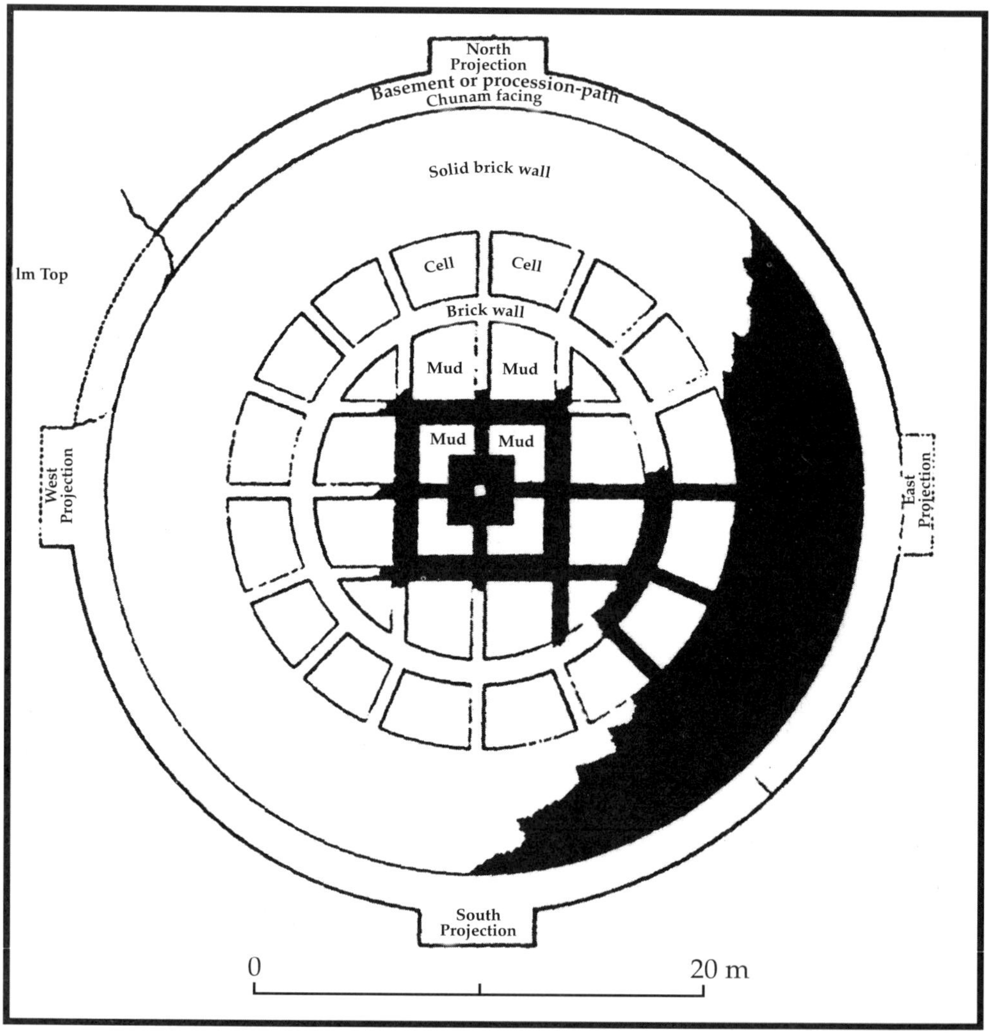

fig. 35: Wheel like plan of *stūpa* from Andhra Pradesh.

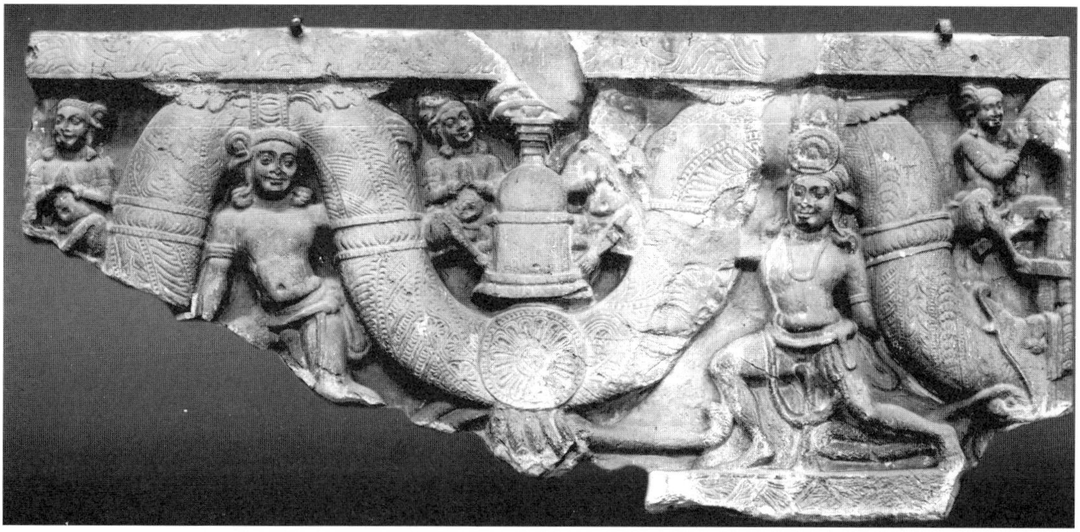

fig. 36: Mālāvāhakas, Limestone, Amarāvatī, 2nd century CE.

fig. 37: Terracotta head of *yavana?* discovered at Erode, Tamil Nadu.

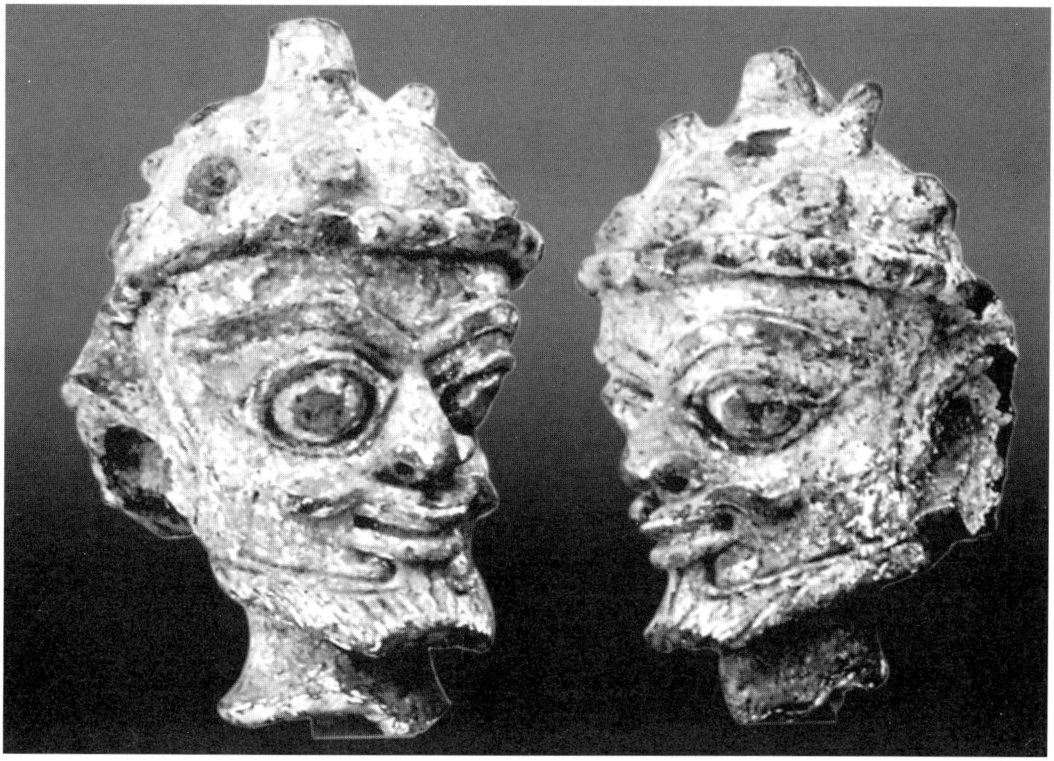

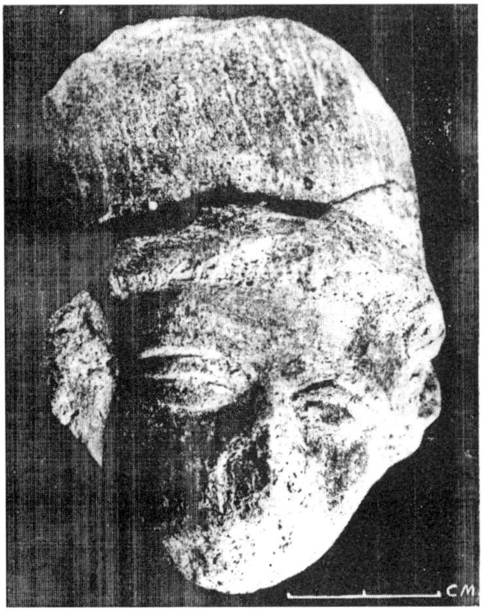

fig. 38: Terracotta head of a lady? from Kañcīpuram, 5th century CE.

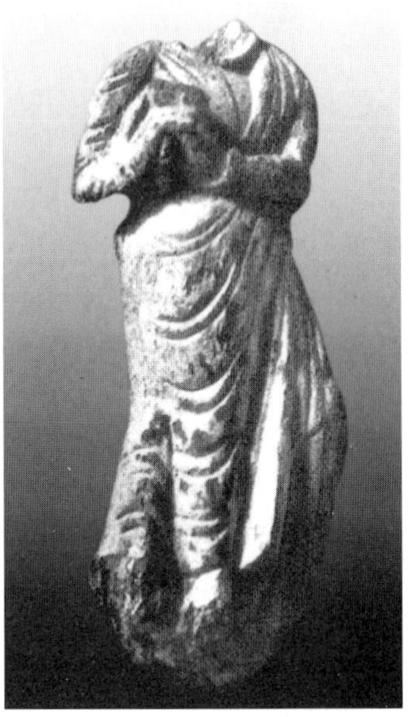

fig. 39: Headless figure from Arikamedu showing Hellenistic/Roman influence.

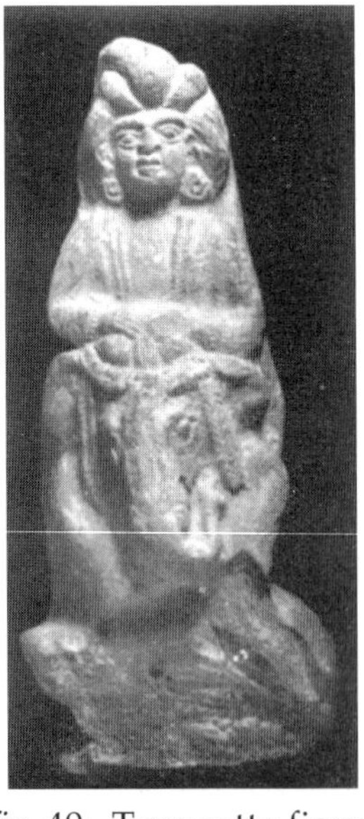

fig. 40: Terracotta figure of Indra on elephant, Candraketugaṛh, 2nd-1st century BCE.

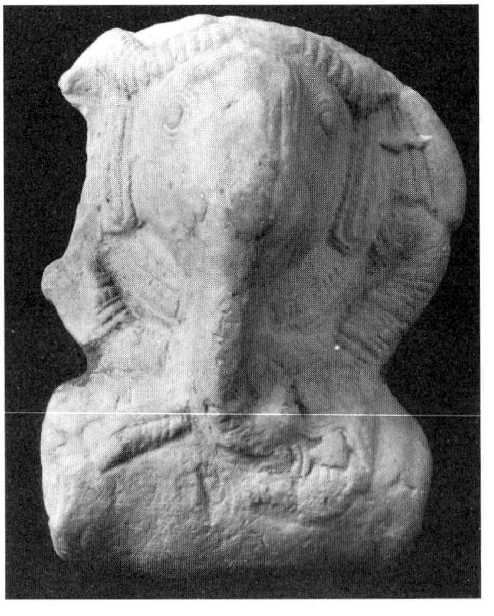

fig. 41: Elephant Toy Cart, terracotta, Mouldmade, 1st century CE, Candraketugaṛh, Burdwan University Museum.

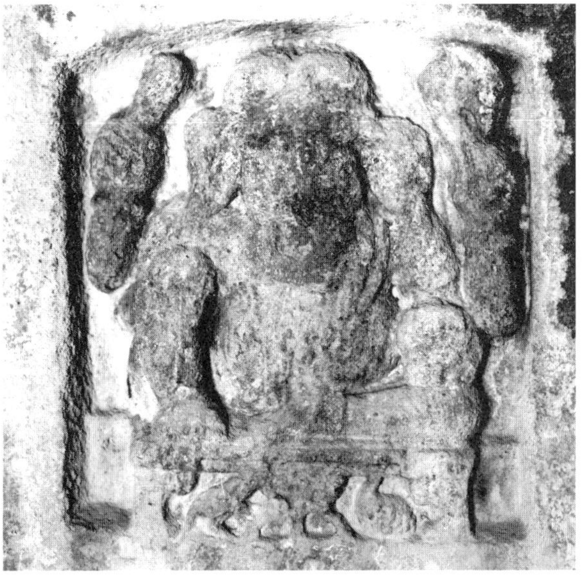

fig. 42: Gaṇeśa sculpture, stone, cave X (Gaṇeśa Gumphā), Verandah, rear wall, Udayagiri–Khaṇḍagiri complex, Puri District. c. 5-25 BCE (?)

fig. 43: Terracotta figure of Lakṣmī, Candraketugaṛh, 1st century BCE.

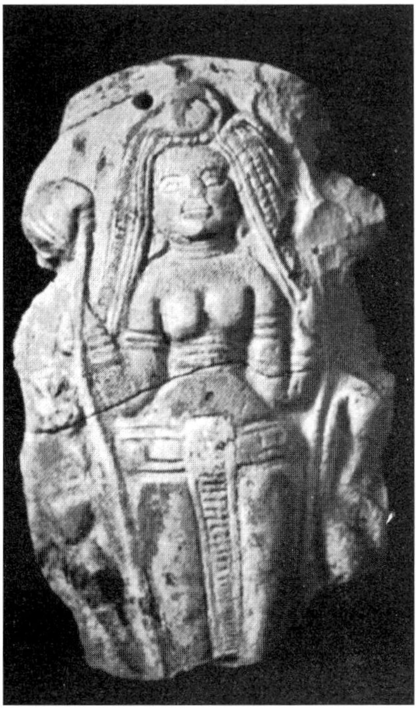

fig. 44: Terracotta figure of a female deity with elaborate headdress, Candraketugaṛh.

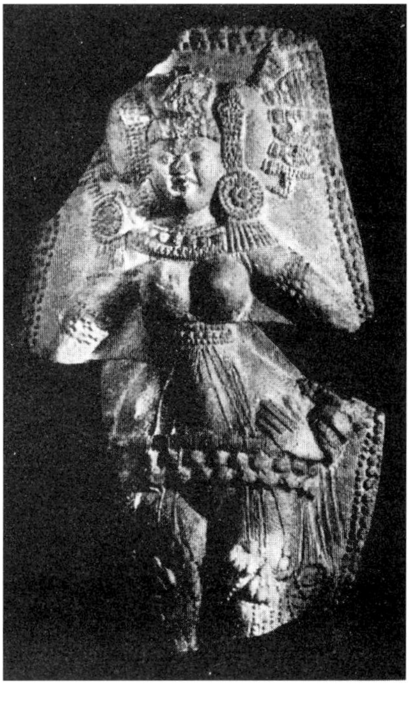

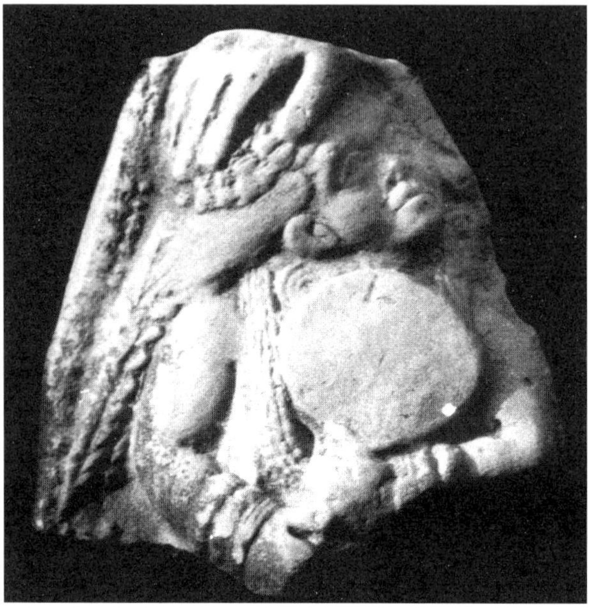

fig. 45: Female Figure with Mirror (part of bigger image), Terracotta, Mouldmade, 1st century BCE, Candraketugaṛh, Burdwan University Museum.

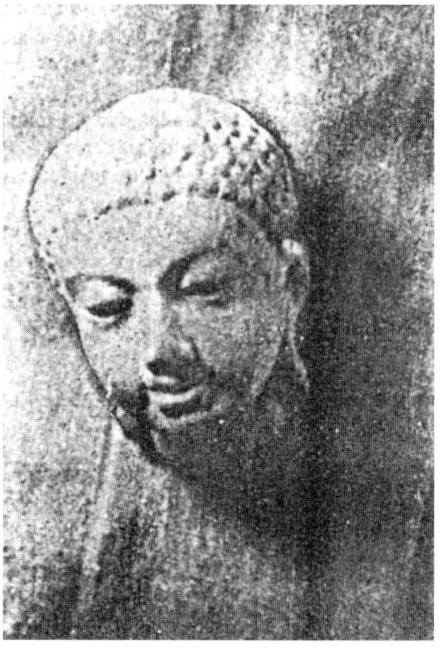

fig. 46: Terracotta head of Buddha from Tilda, 5th century CE.

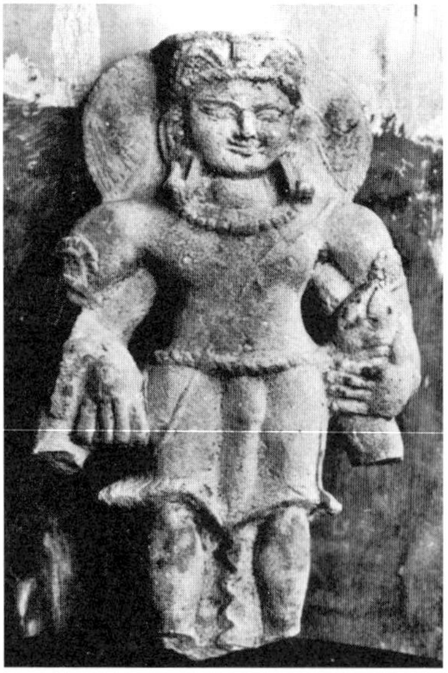

fig. 47: Viṣṇu figure in stone found in Māldā, West Bengal, 4th century CE.

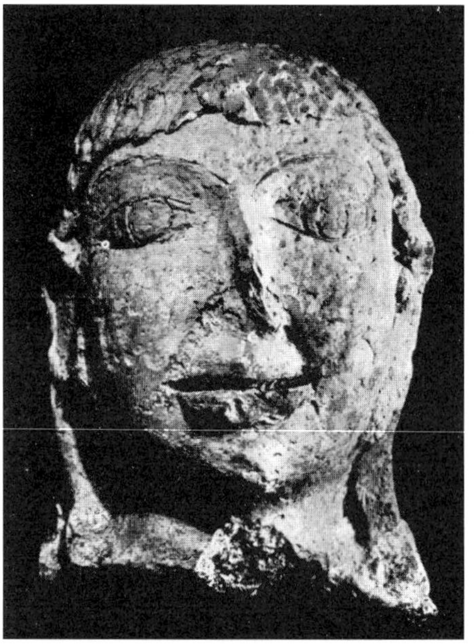

fig. 48: Hellenistic sculpture from Bengal, Terracotta, 1st-2nd century CE.

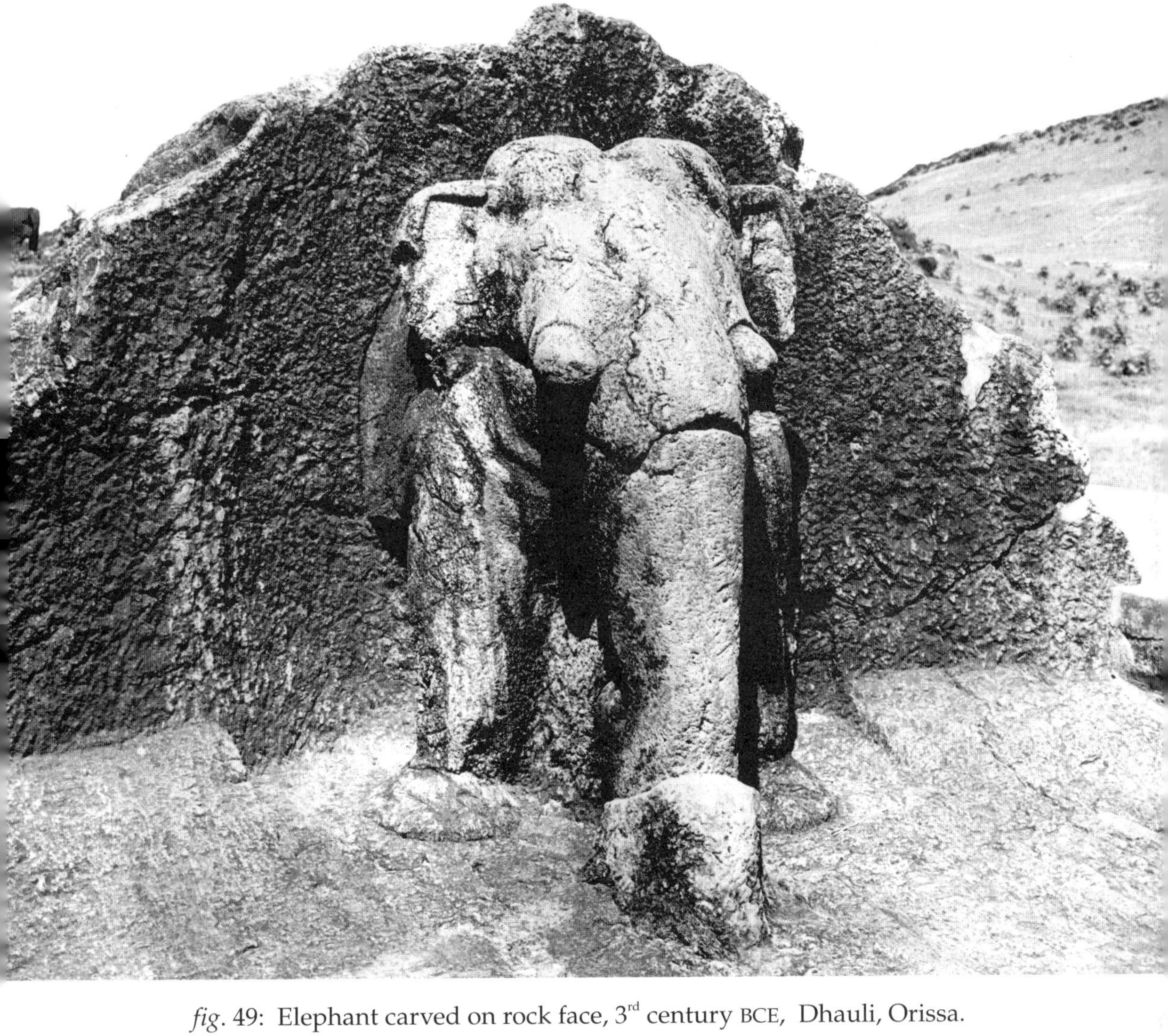

fig. 49: Elephant carved on rock face, 3rd century BCE, Dhauli, Orissa.

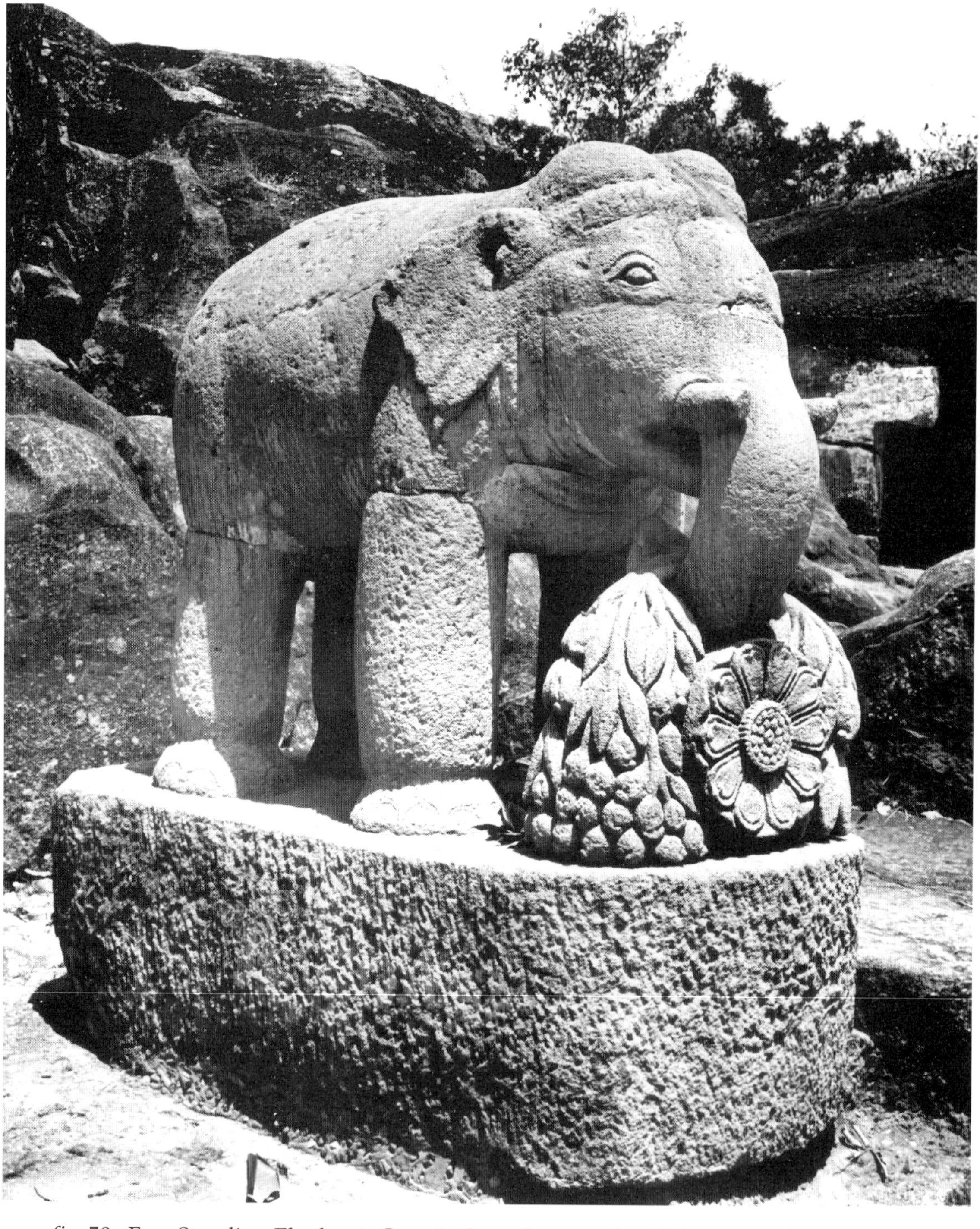

fig. 50: Free Standing Elephant, Gaṇeśa Gumphā, exterior. Udayagiri–Khaṇḍagiri, Puri District, last half of 1st century BCE, sandstone.

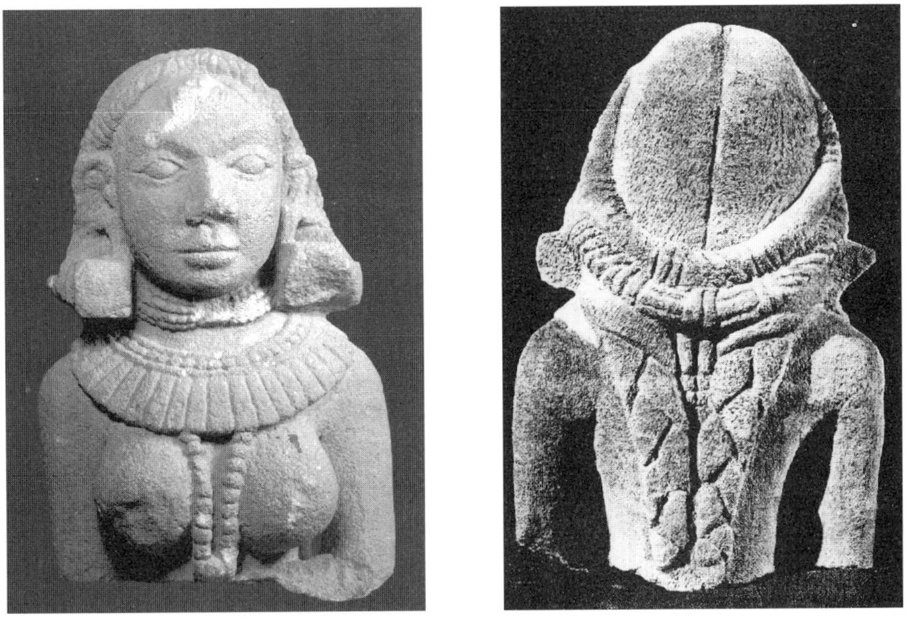

fig. 51: Sandstone bust of *yakṣī* recovered from Udayagiri, 2nd-1st century BCE.

fig. 52: Gajalakṣmī. cave 3 (Ananta Gumphā), Udayagiri-Khaṇḍagiri, 50-25 BCE.

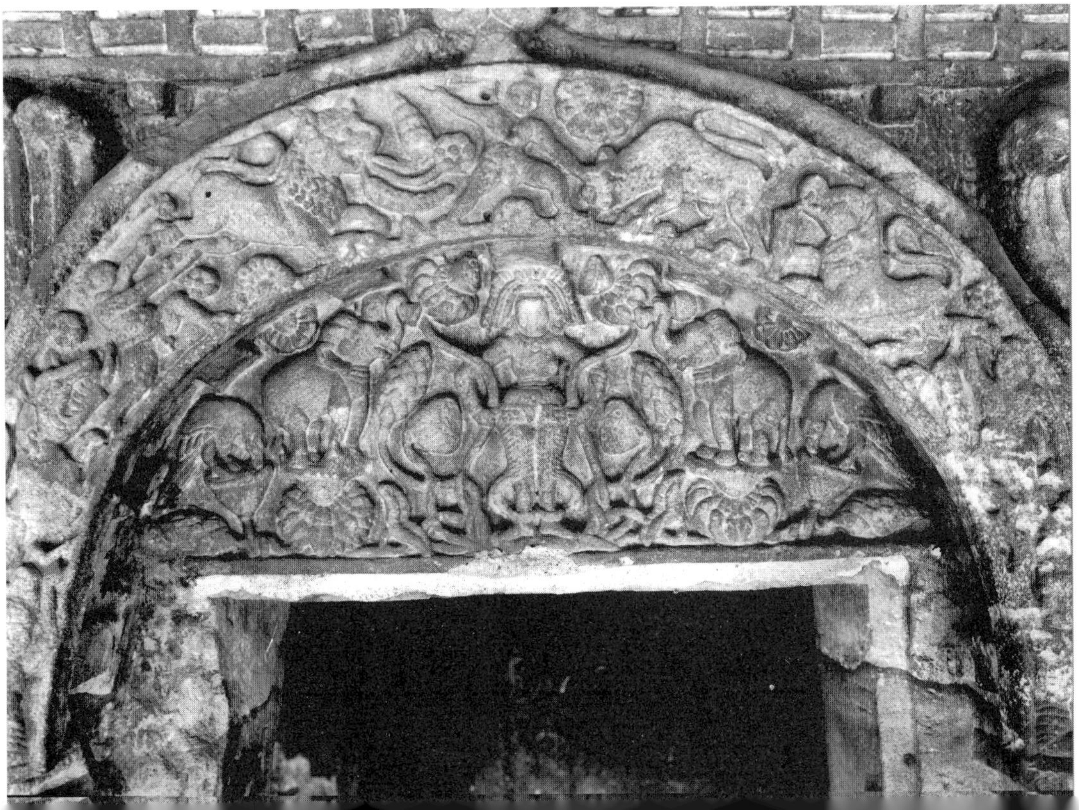

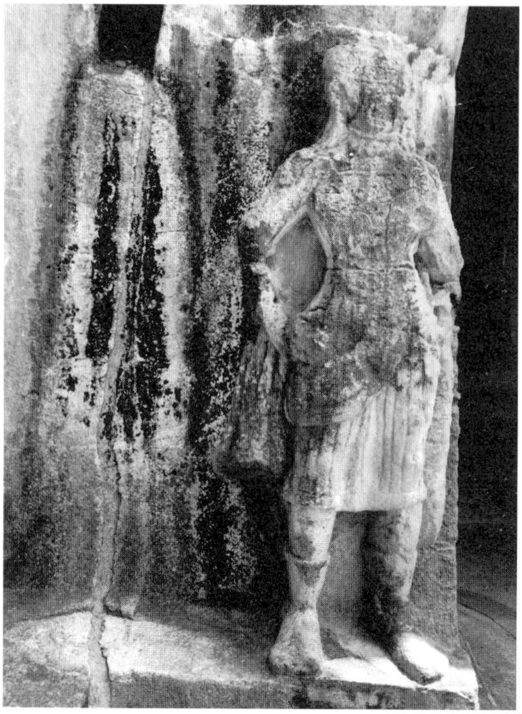

fig. 53: Yavana soldier? cave 1 (Rani Gumpha), Udayagiri–Khaṇḍagiri, sandstone, 50-25 BCE.

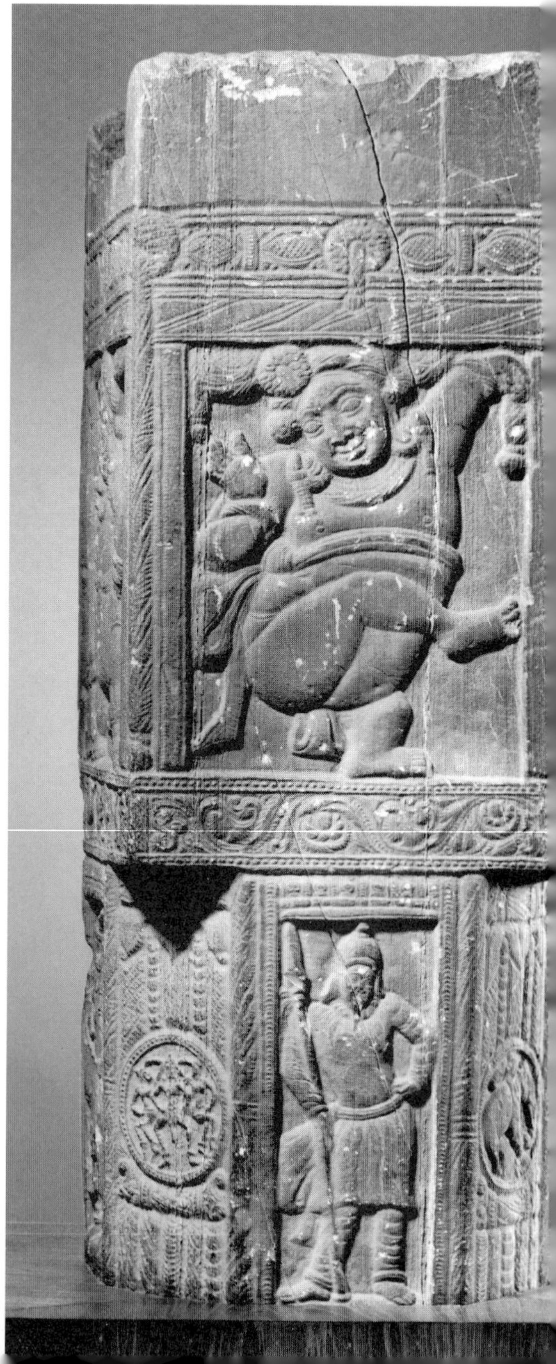

fig. 54: Pillar fragment from palace site, with figure of dwarf *yakṣa* and Scythian soldier, Nāgārjunikoṇḍa, Guntur District, National Museum, 3rd century CE?

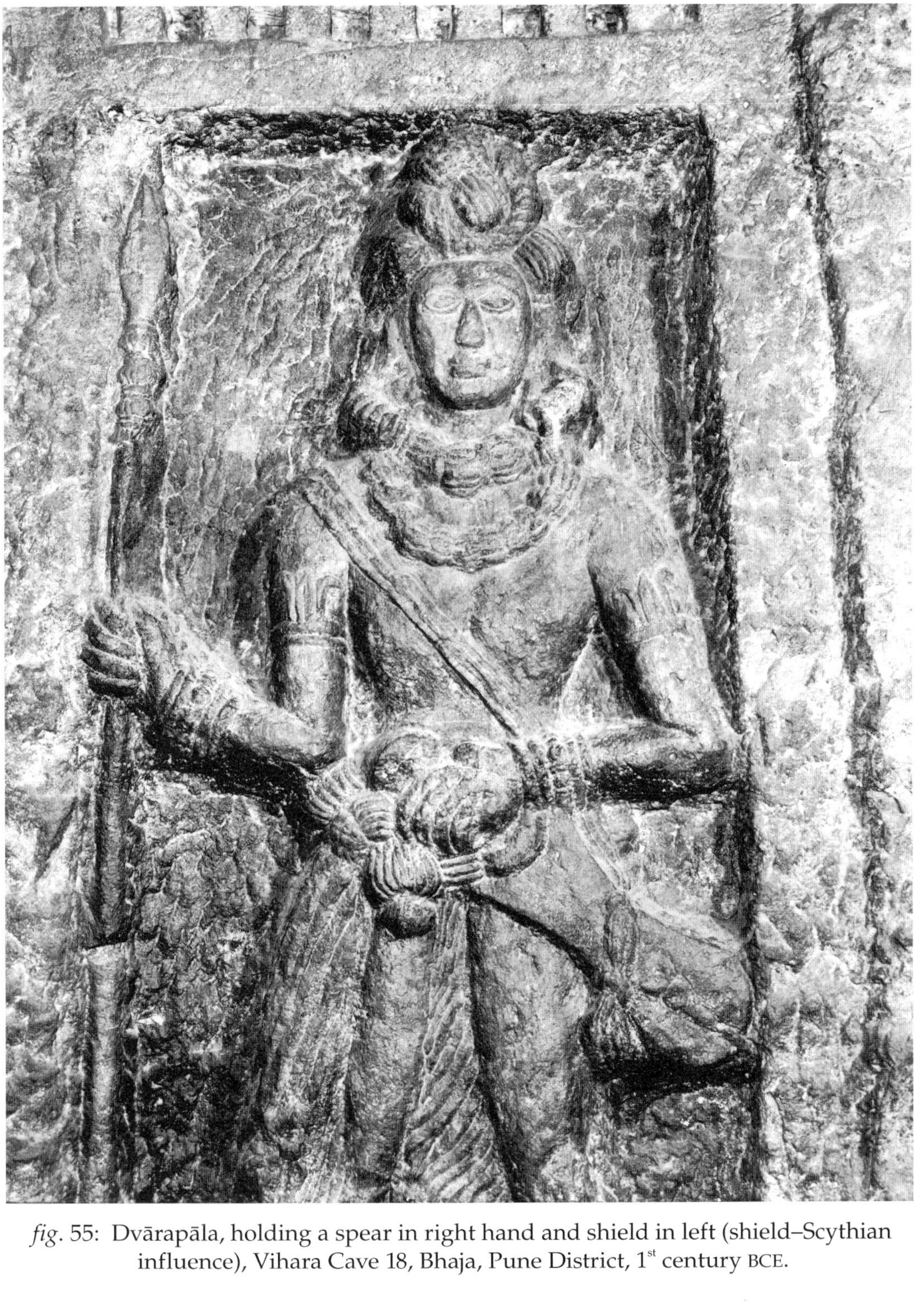

fig. 55: Dvārapāla, holding a spear in right hand and shield in left (shield–Scythian influence), Vihara Cave 18, Bhaja, Pune District, 1st century BCE.

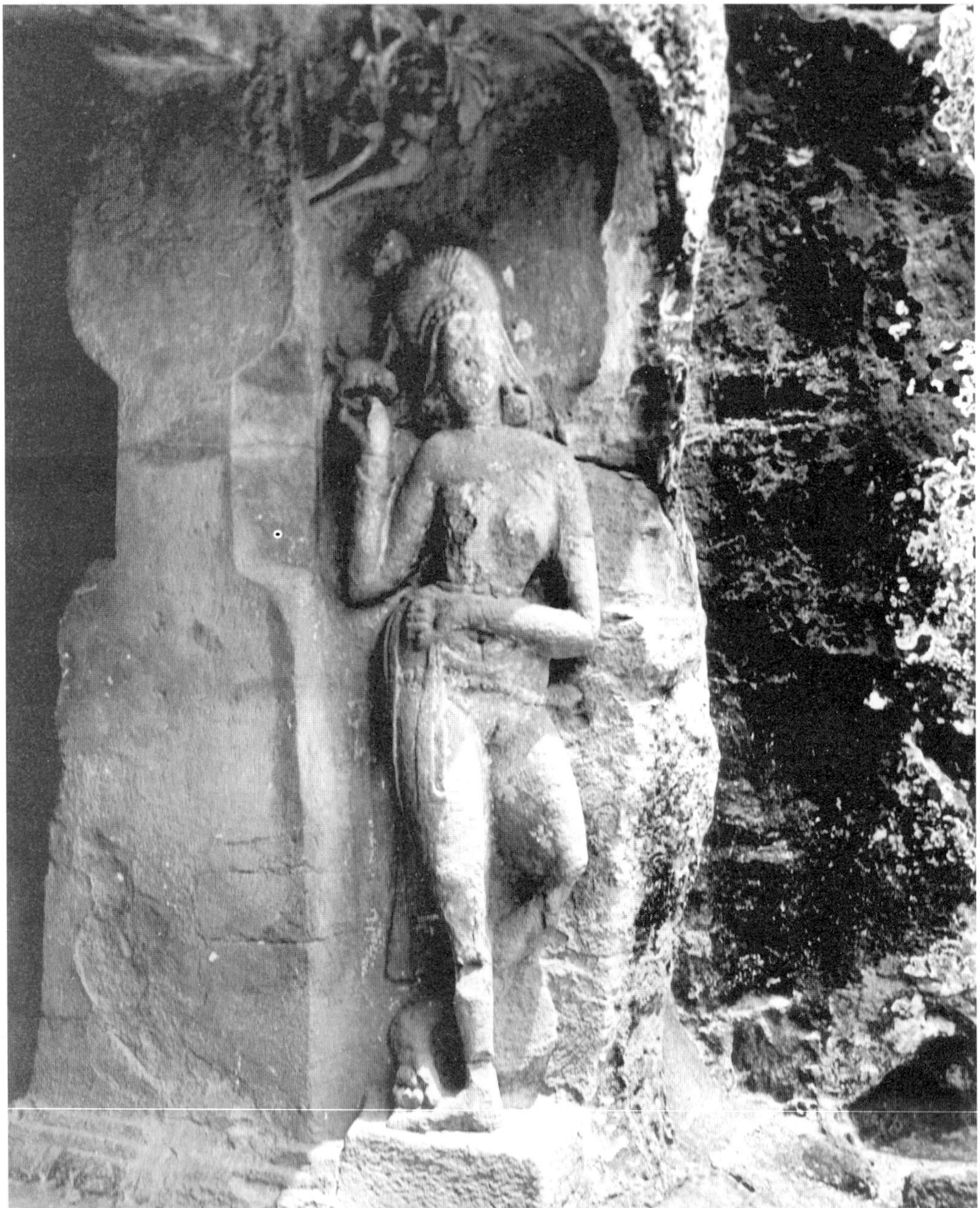

fig. 56: *Yakṣī*, Jayavijaya Cave (no. 5), Udayagiri–Khaṇḍagiri. 1st century BCE, sandstone.

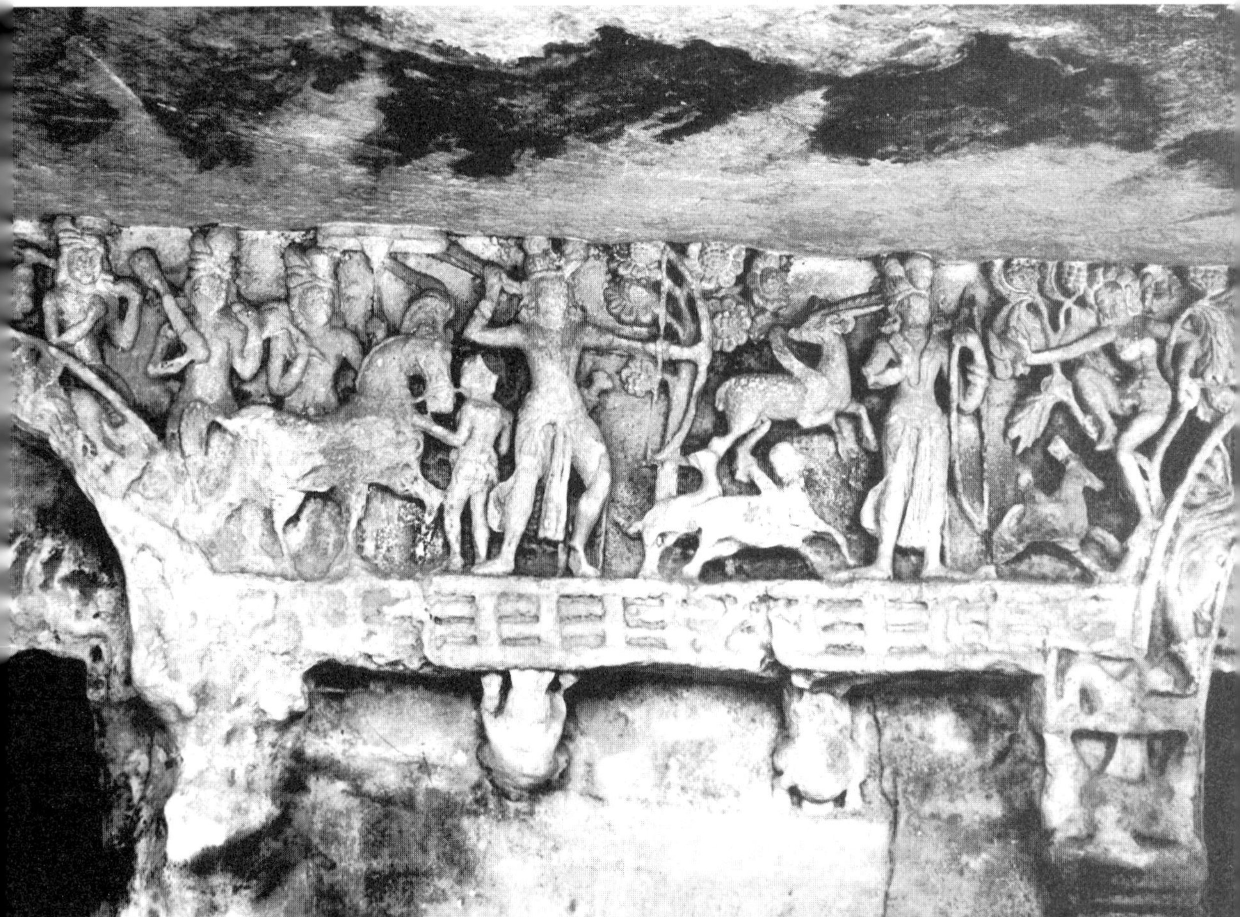

fig. 57: Frieze showing hunting scene, Rani Gumphā no.1, Udayagiri–Khaṇḍagiri, 5th century CE.

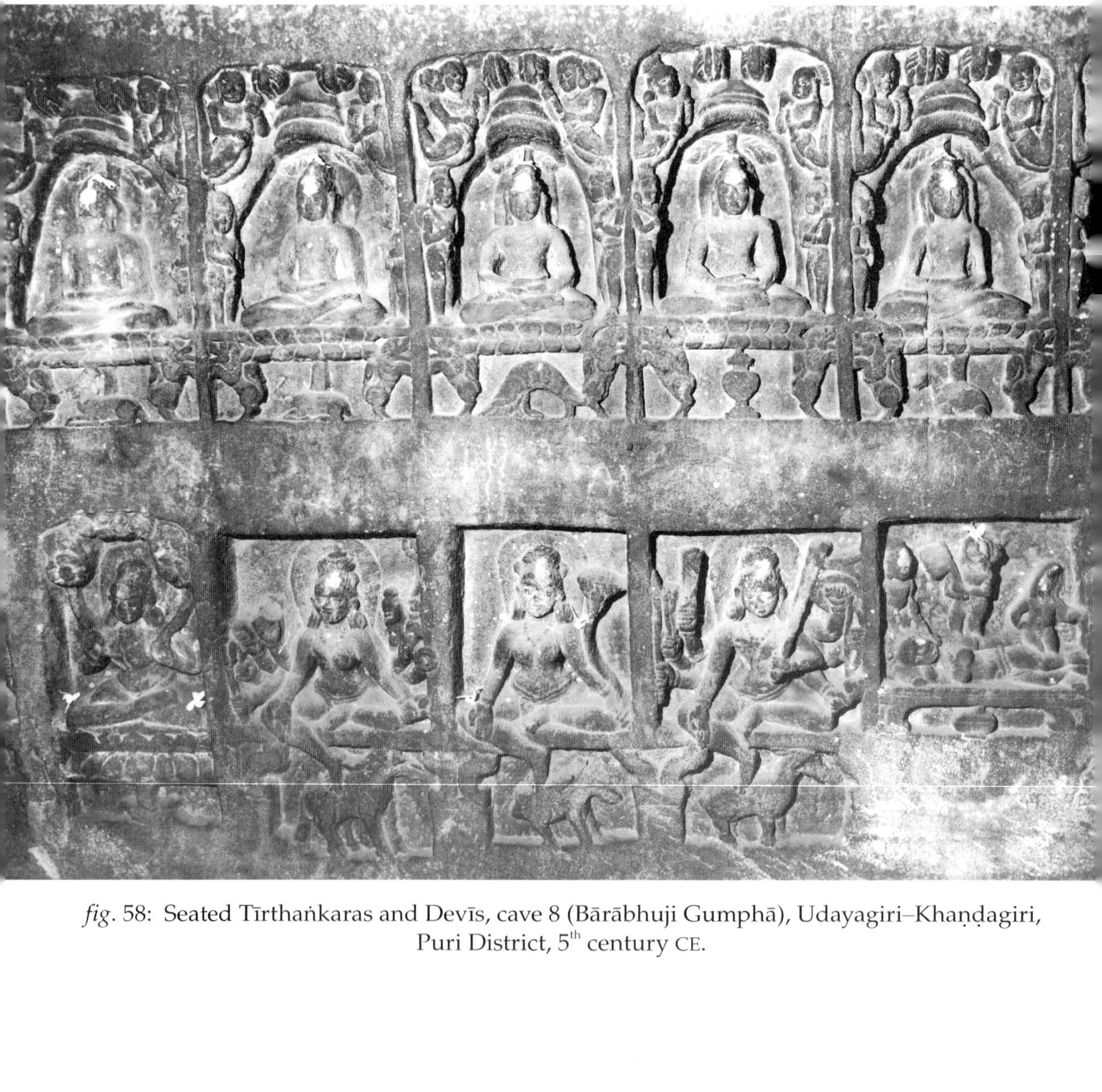

fig. 58: Seated Tīrthaṅkaras and Devīs, cave 8 (Bārābhuji Gumphā), Udayagiri–Khaṇḍagiri, Puri District, 5th century CE.

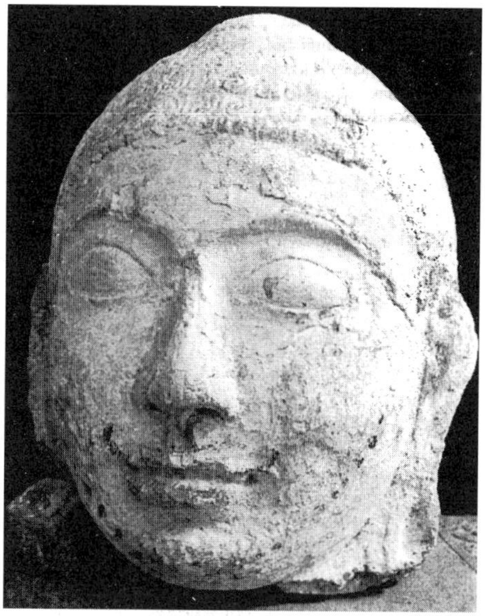

fig. 59: Head of Buddha statue excavated from a *stūpa* in Thoddo Island, Maldives, 3rd-4th century CE.

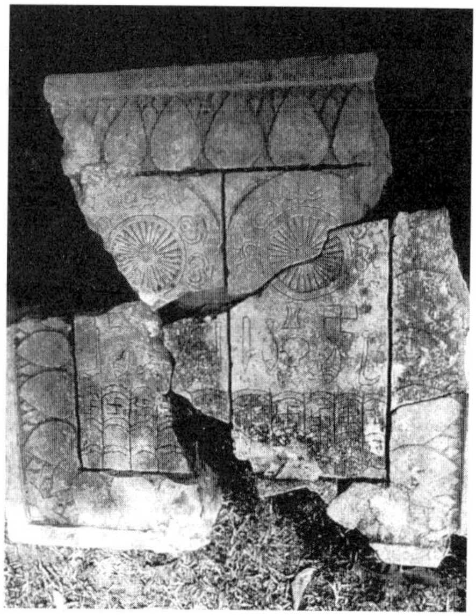

fig. 60: *Buddhapāda* from Vadu Island, Gaaf Atoll (Maldives Islands), 2nd-3rd century CE.

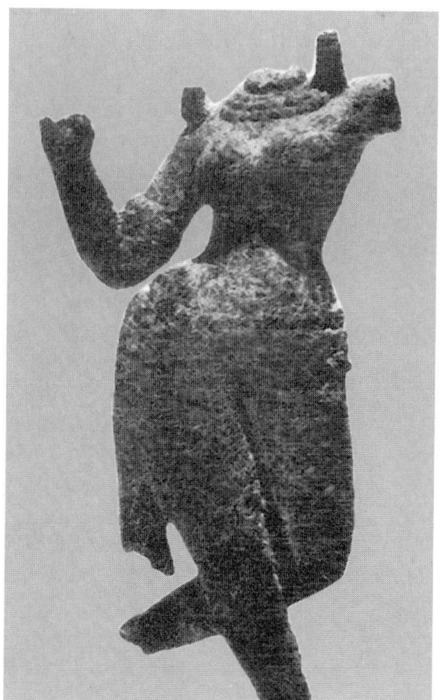

fig. 61: Statuette of *Yakṣī*, bronze, Khor Rorī, Dhofar, Oman, 1st-2nd century CE.

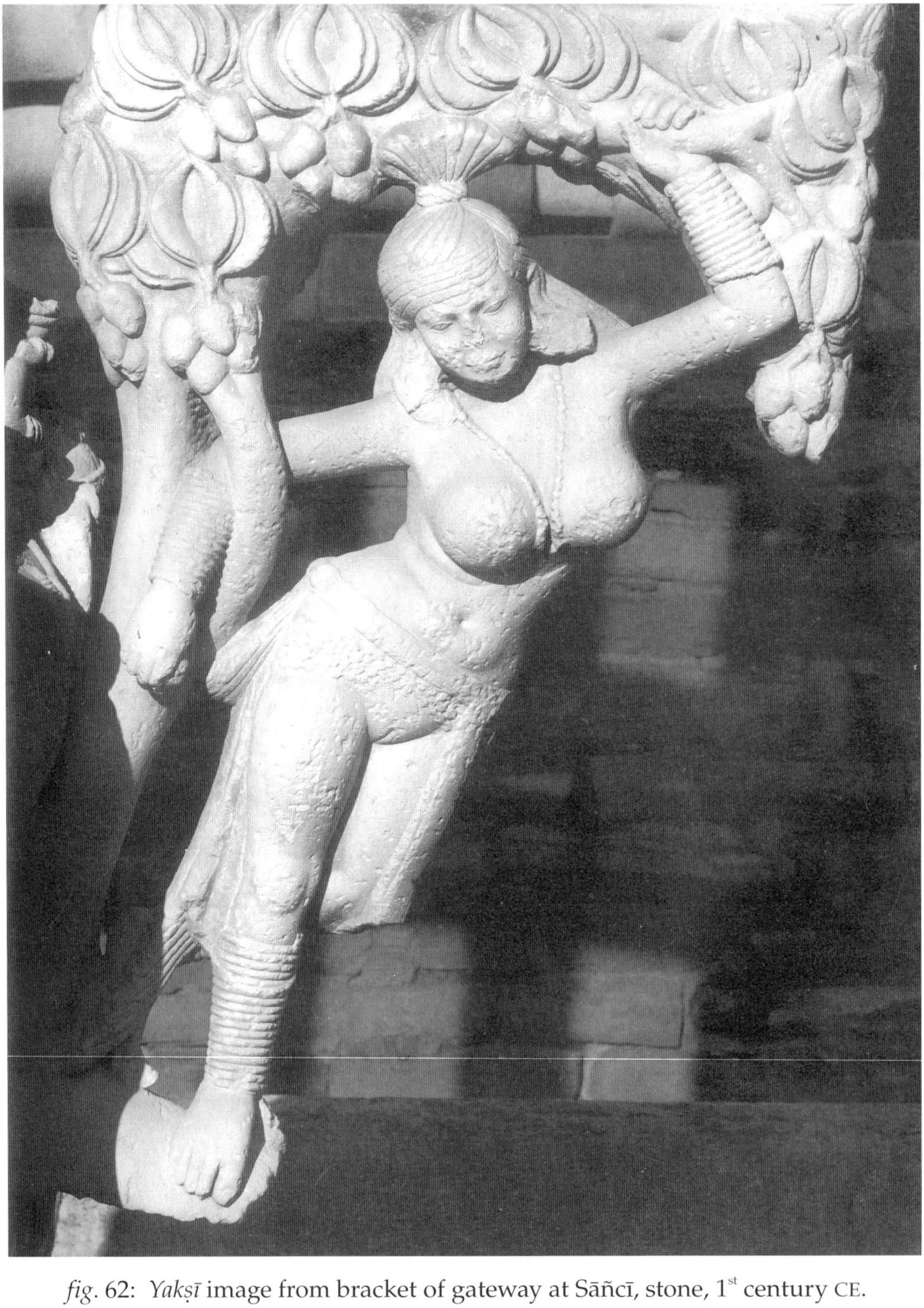

fig. 62: *Yakṣī* image from bracket of gateway at Sāñcī, stone, 1st century CE.

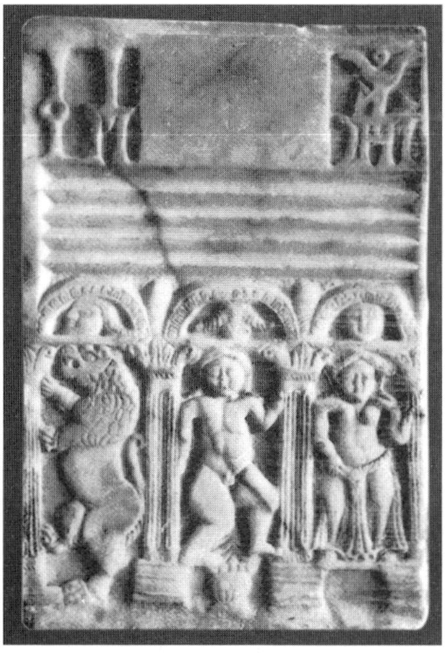

fig. 63: Marble plaque showing Indian influence, Manakha (Yemen), 2nd-3rd century CE.

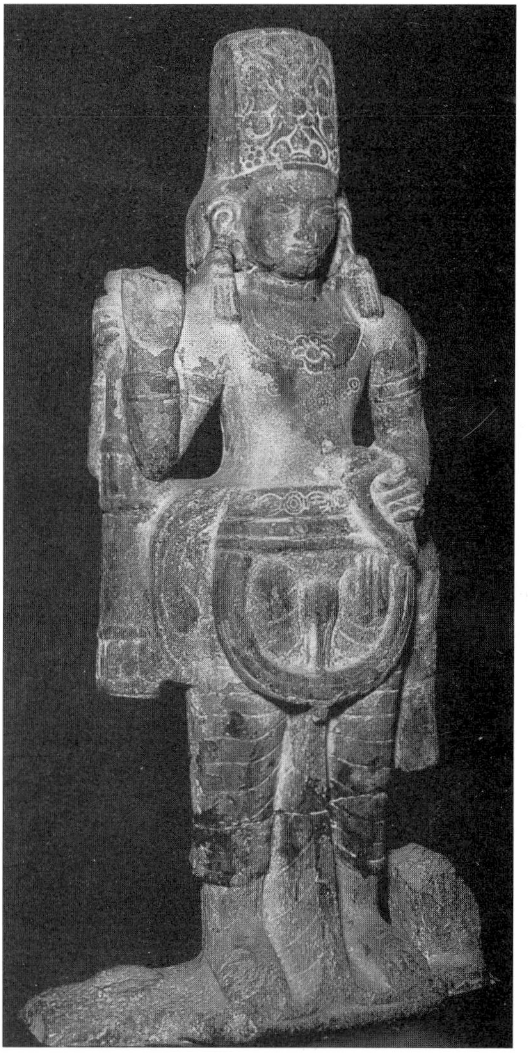

fig. 64: Viṣṇu image from Chaiya, Thailand, stone, 5th-6th century CE.

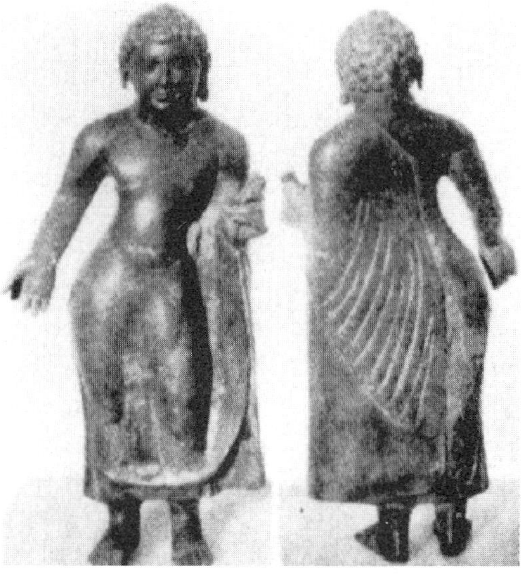

fig. 65: Amarāvatī type Buddha image in bronze from Kedah, Malaysia, 4th-5th century CE.

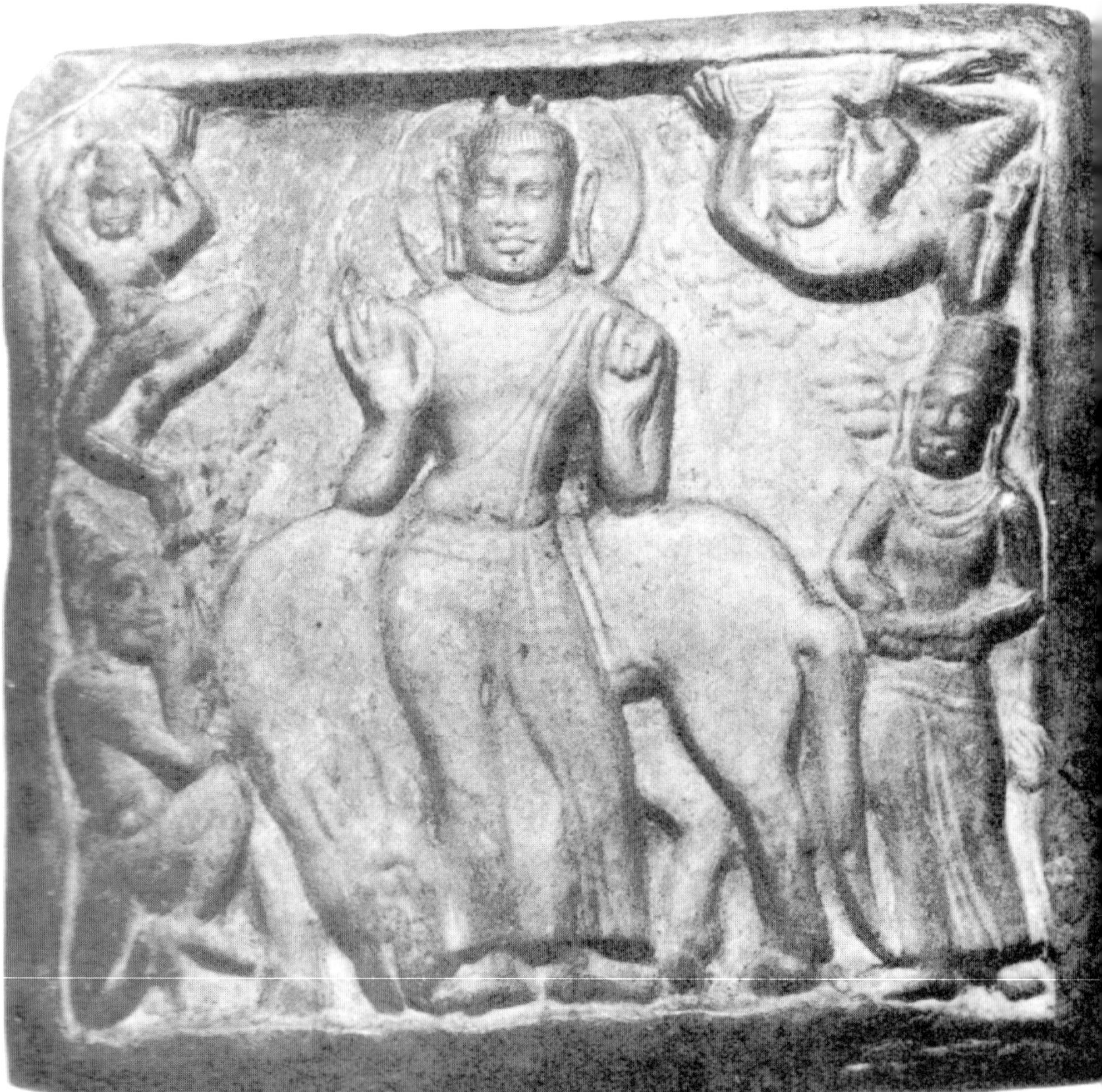

fig. 66: Plaque showing influence of Amarāvatī art found at Tissamaharama, Sri Lanka, 3rd century CE.

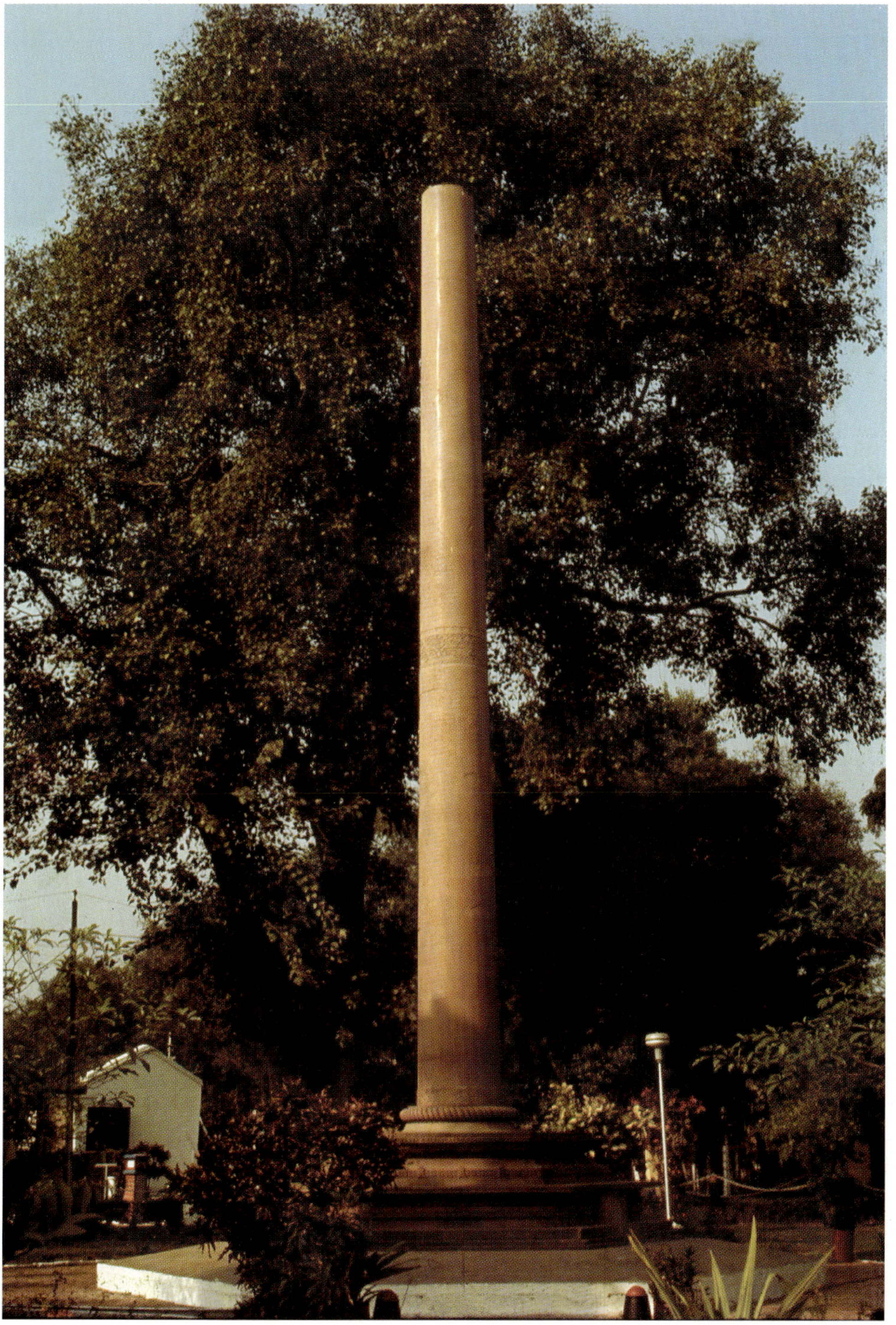

Pl. 1: Aśokan Pillar at Allahabad, 3rd century BCE.

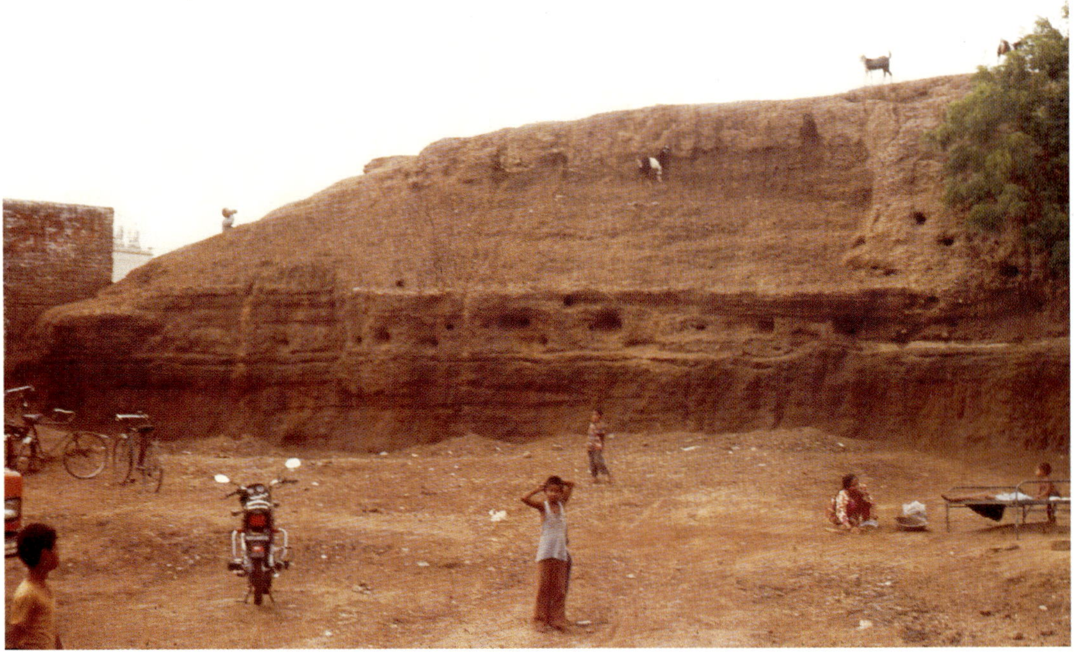

Pl. 2.: Early Historic mound within Bharuch city.

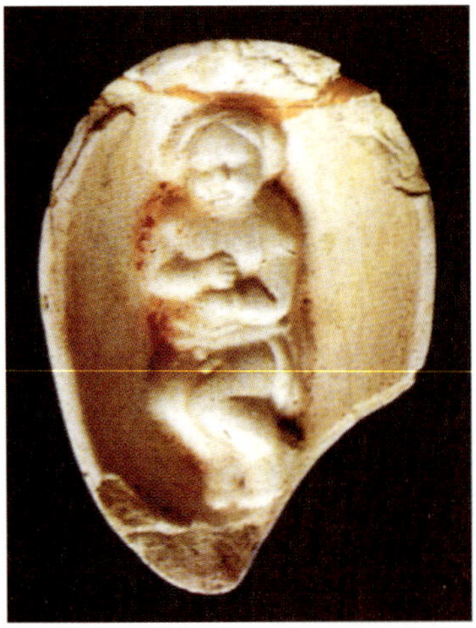

Pl. 3: Figure of Eros from Junnar, Maharashtra. 1st-2nd century CE.

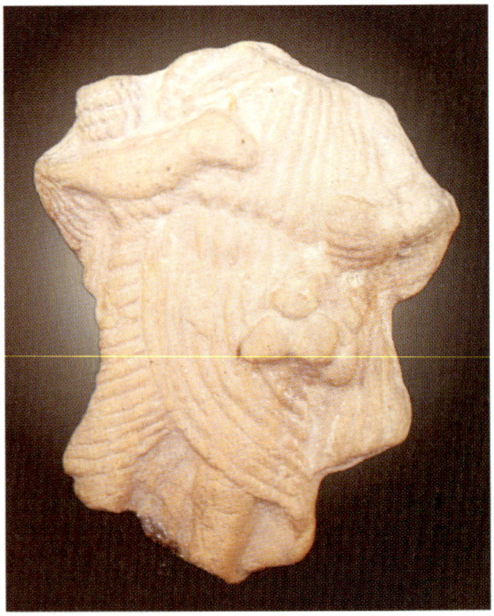

Pl. 4: Headless Buddha (?) image from Kauśāmbī showing Gāndhāra influence.

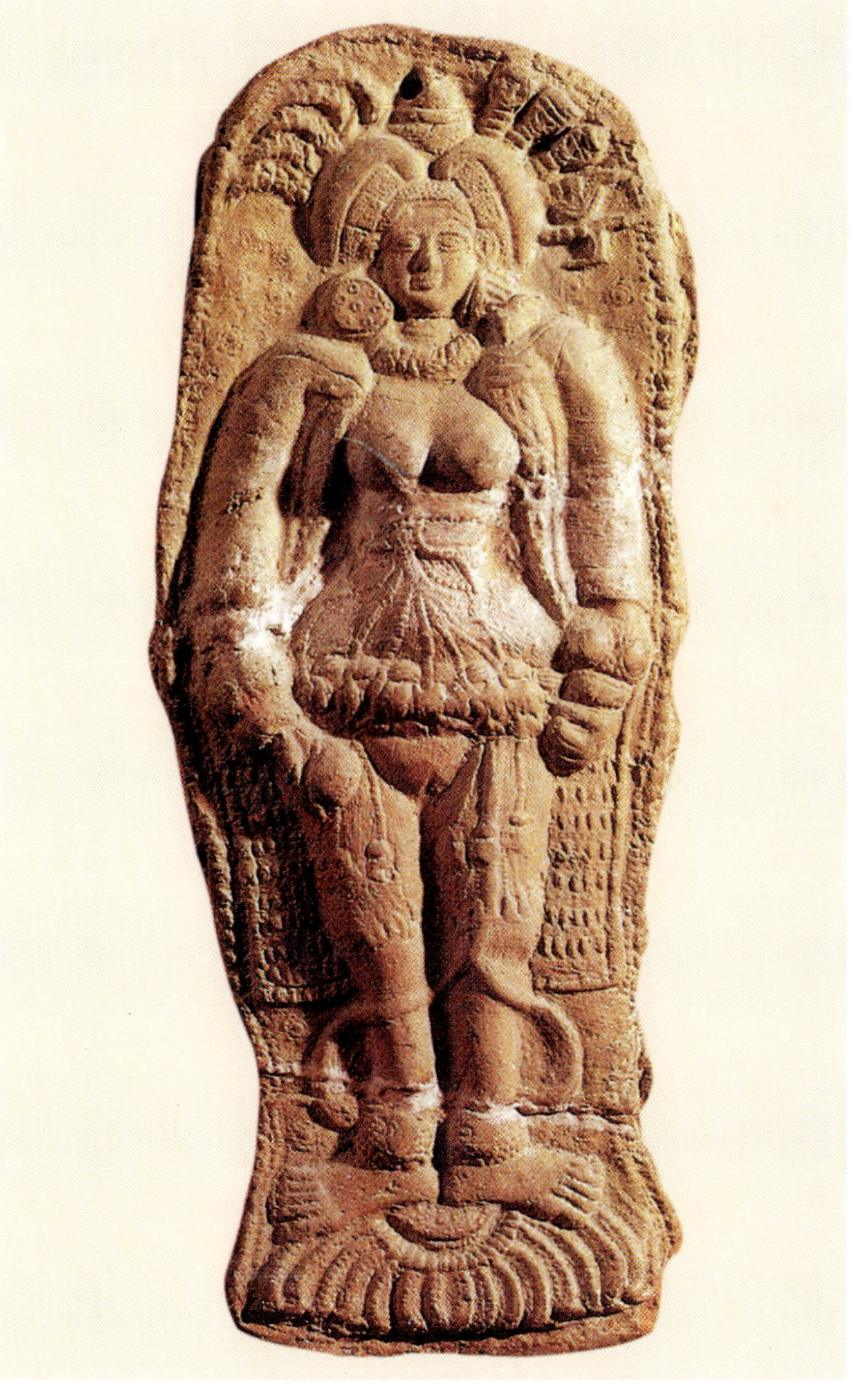

Pl. 5: Pañcajūḍā figurine from Kauśāmbī, terracotta, 1st century BCE.

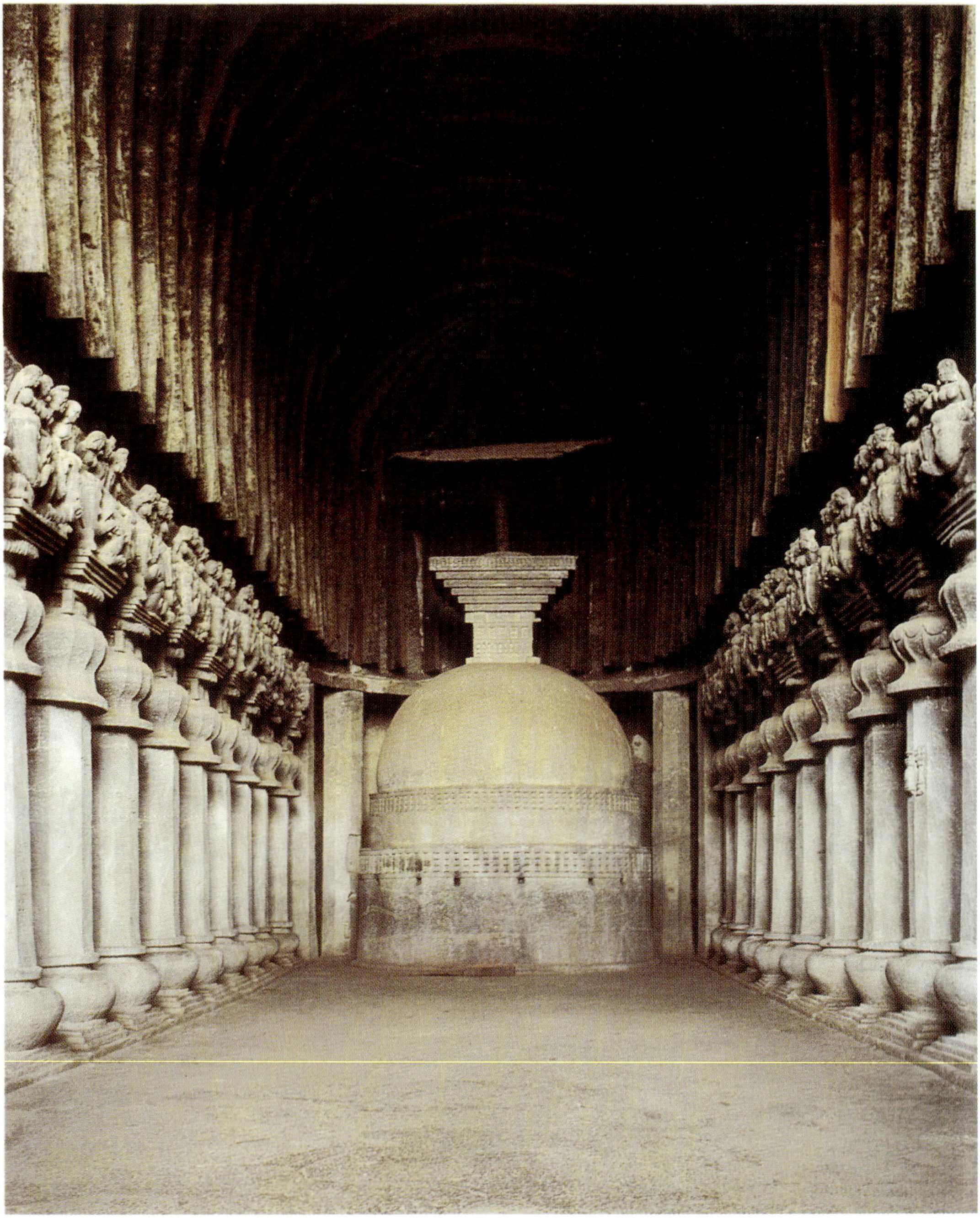

Pl. 6: Caityagṛha at Kārle, 1st century CE.

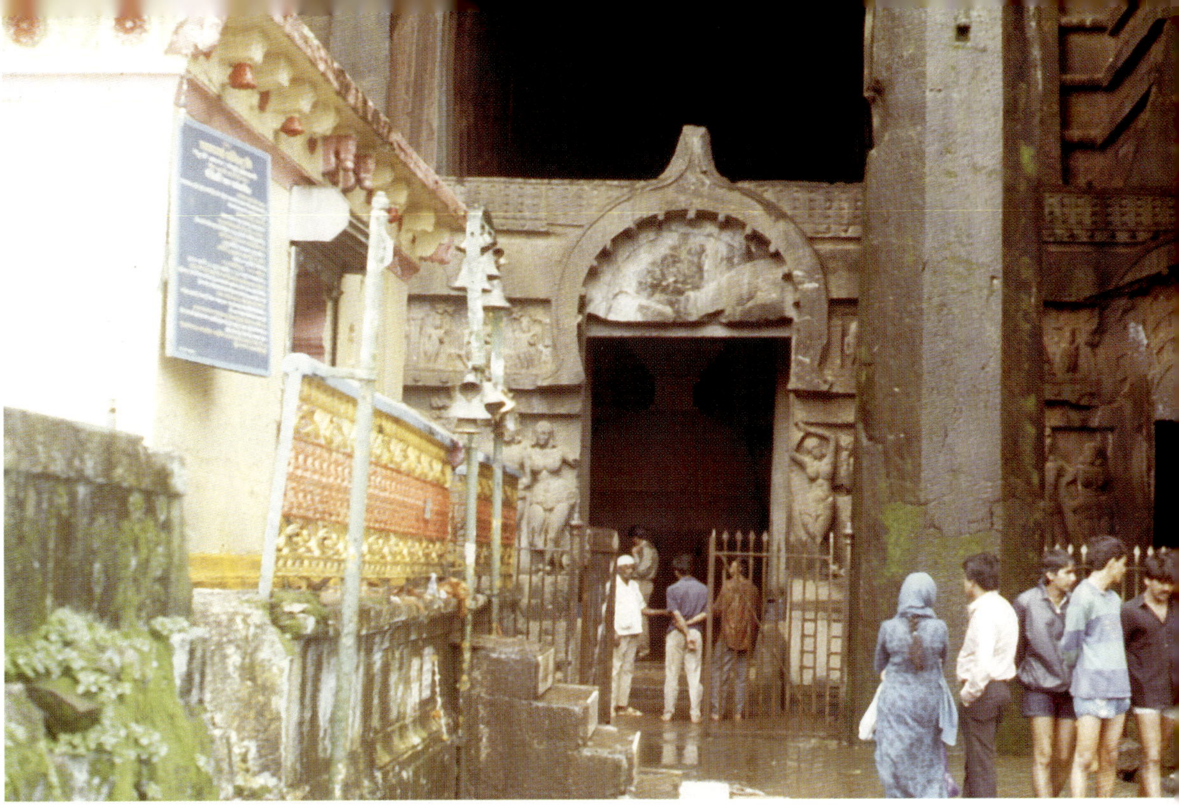

Pl. 7: Horse-shoe entrance of Kārle Cave.

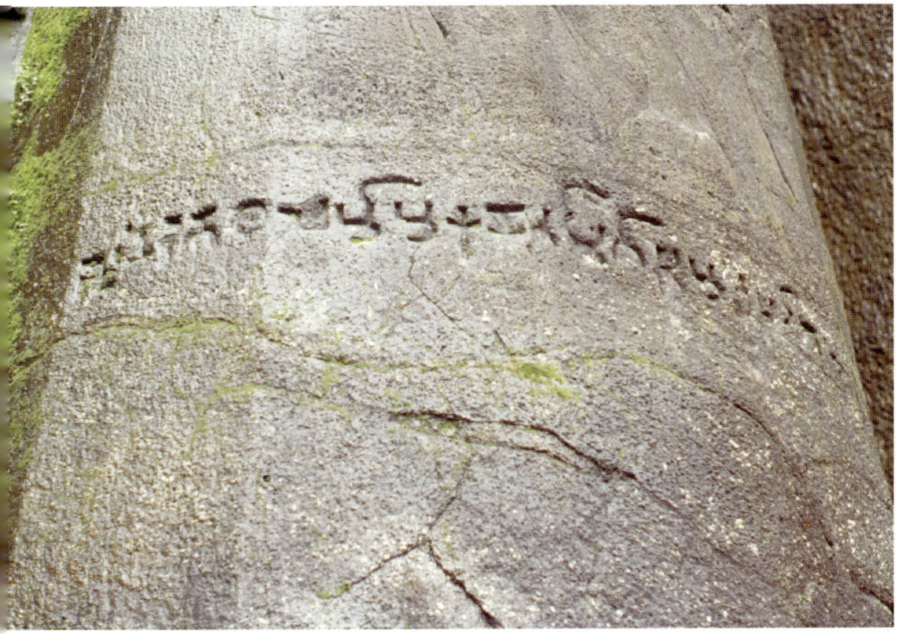

Pl. 8 : Brāhmī inscription mentioning *yavana* donors at Kārle, 1st century CE.

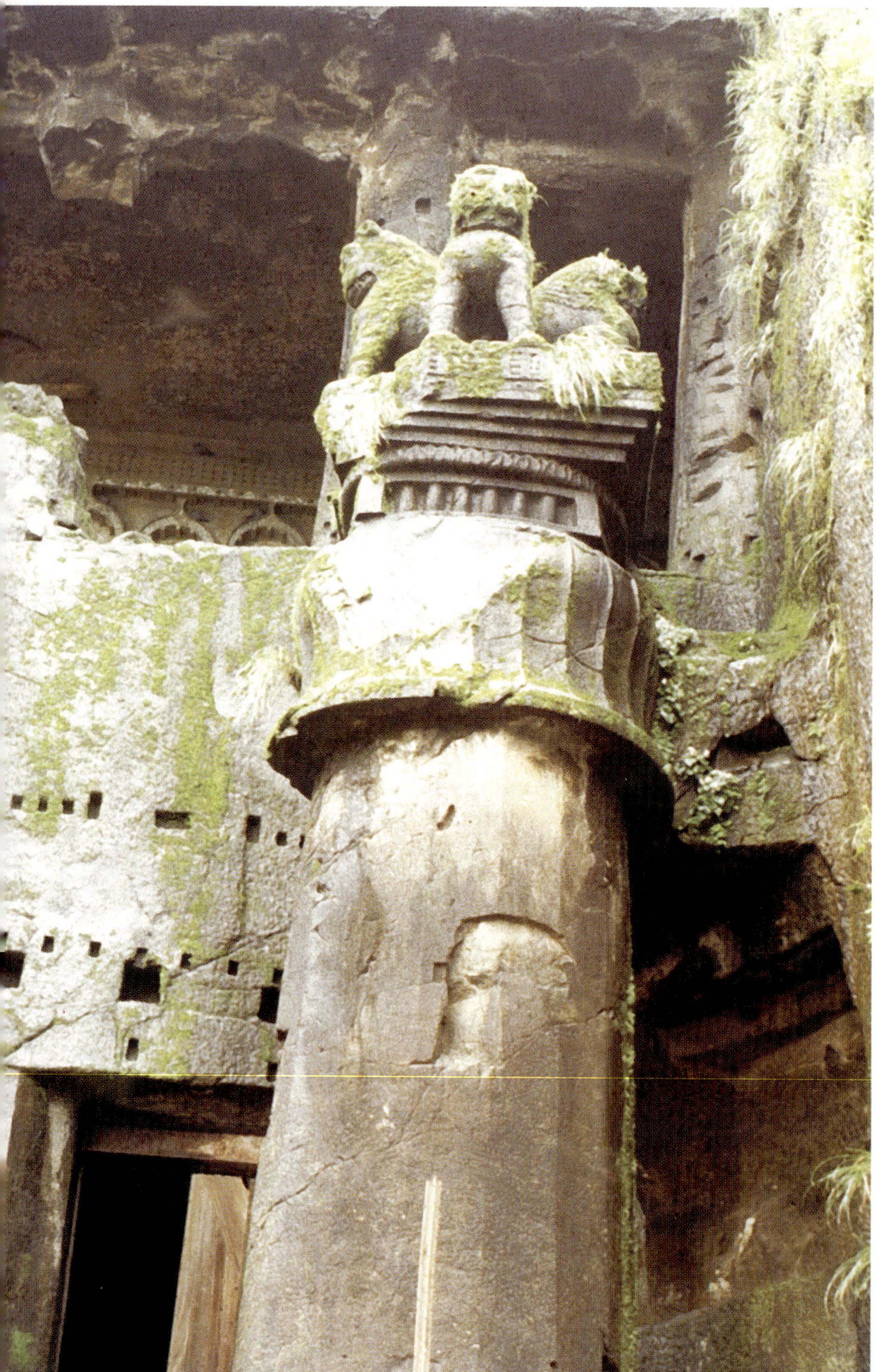

Pl. 9: Pillar surmounted by lion capital at entrance of Kārle cave, 1st-2nd century CE.

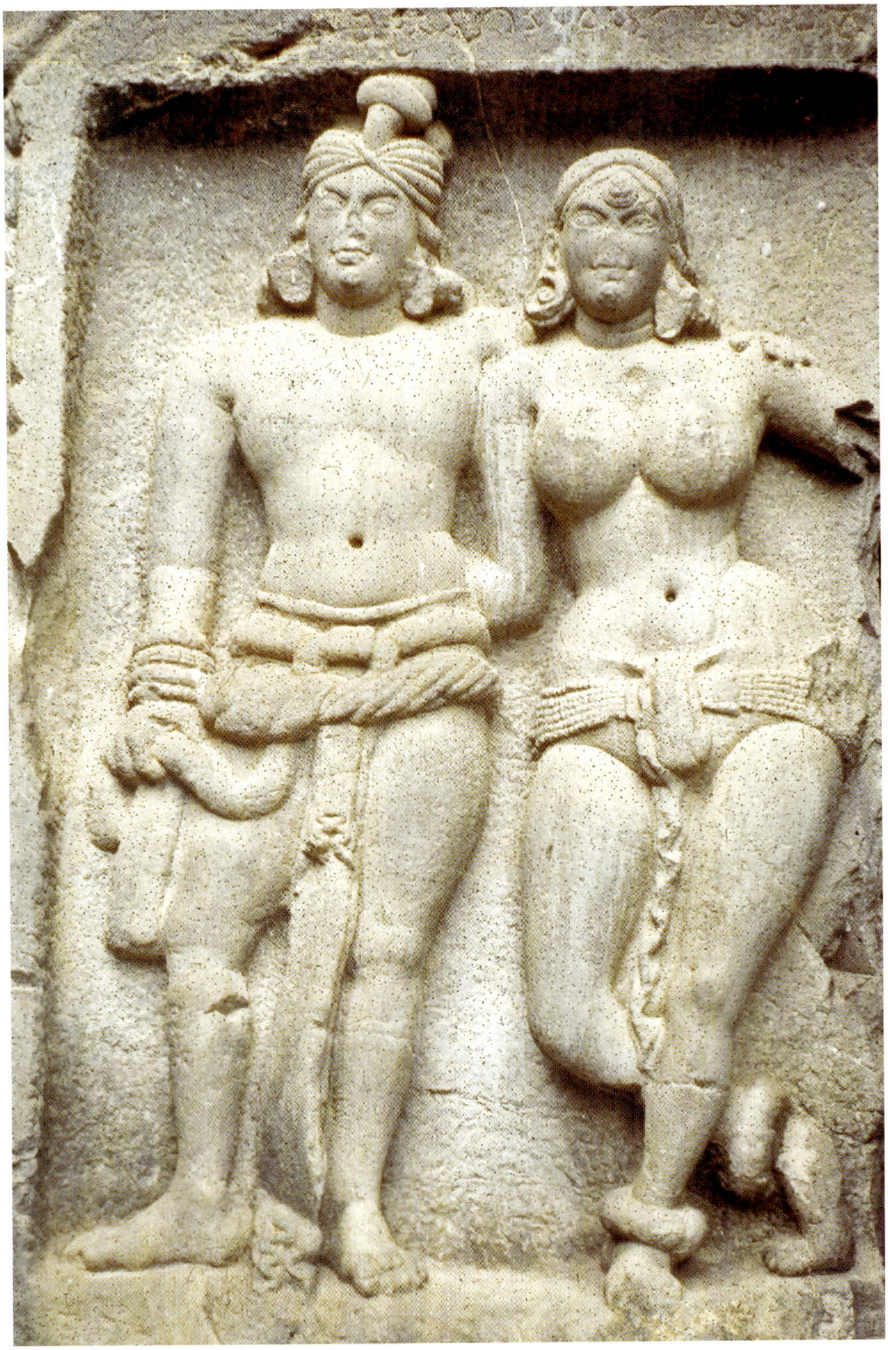

Pl. 10: Mithuna figures, entrance of Kārle caitya cave, 1st century CE.

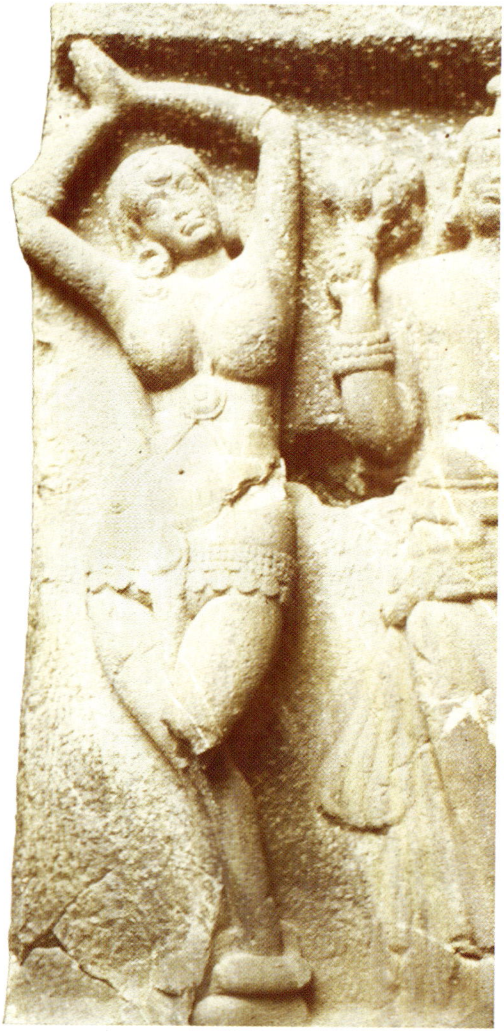

Pl. 11.: *Yakṣī* figure at the entrance of Kārle Cave. 1st-2nd century CE.

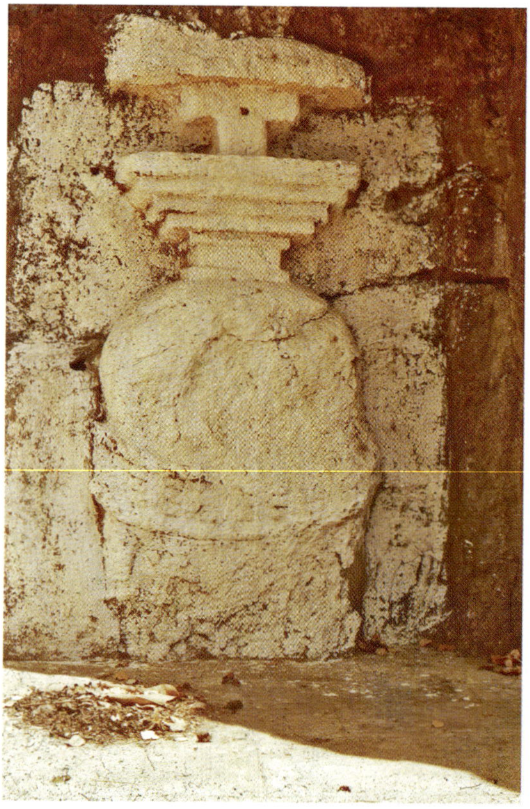

Pl. 12: Stūpa carved in relief inside a rock-cut cave at Caul, 1st century CE.

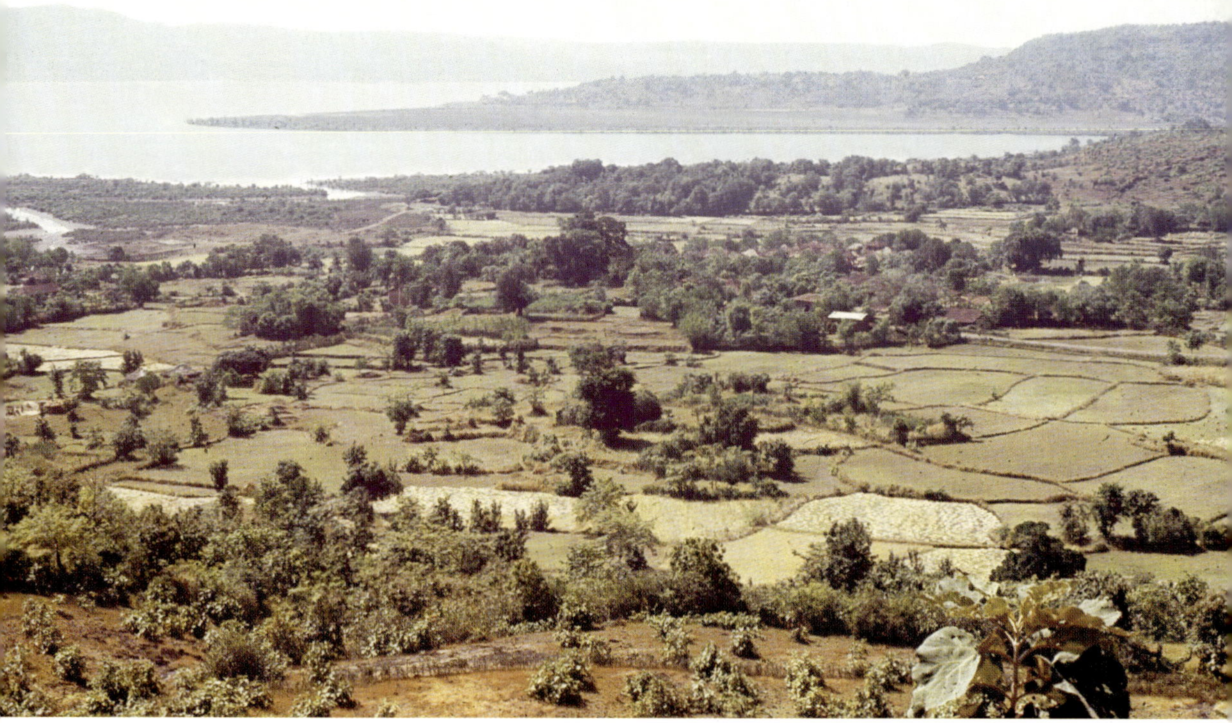

Pl. 13 : Janjira creek viewed from the rock-cut caves at Kuda.

Pl. 14: Buddhist rock-cut caves at Kuda viewed from the beach head.

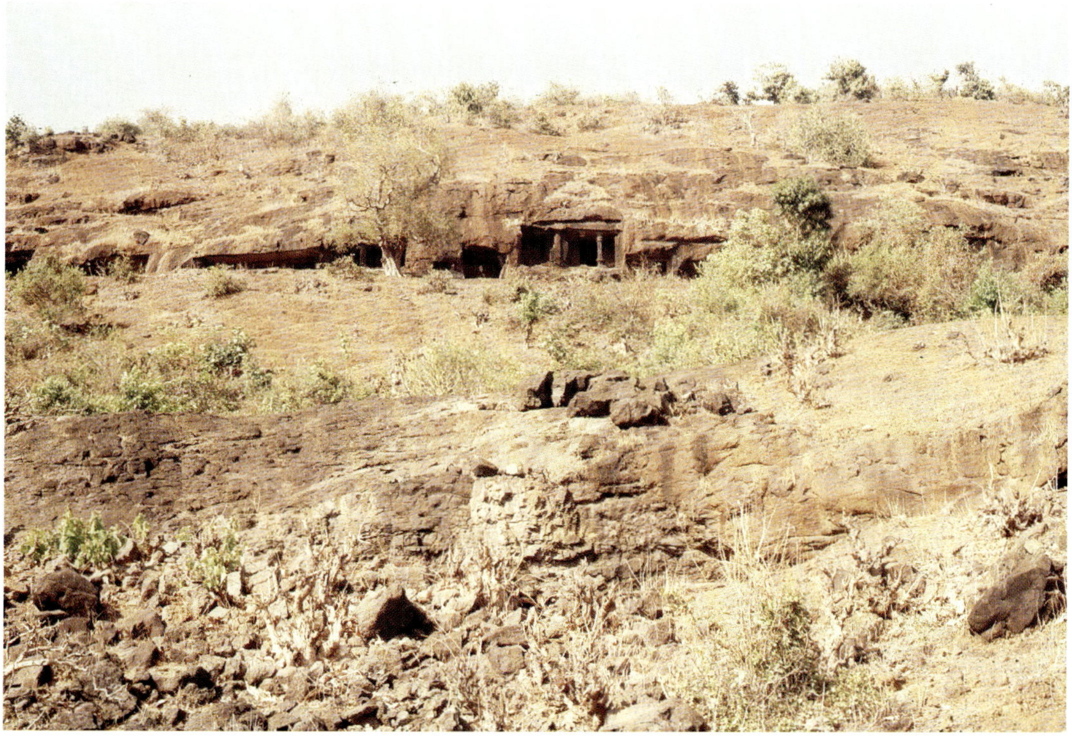

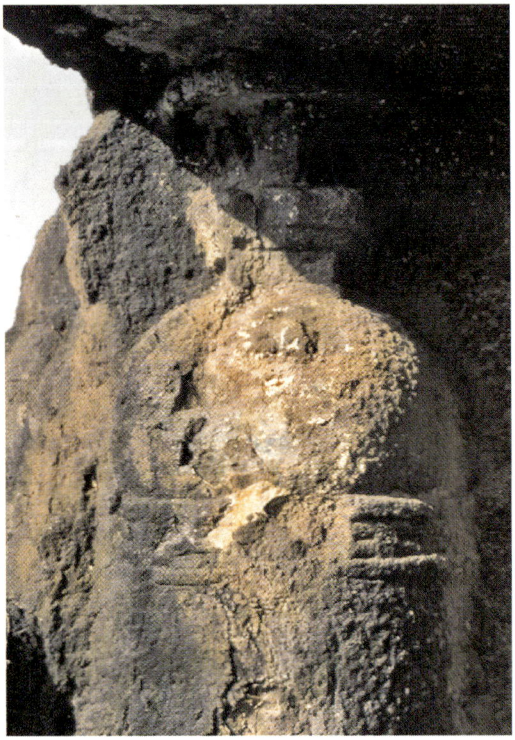

Pl. 15: Stūpa carved in relief inside a rock-cut cave in Kuda, 1st century CE.

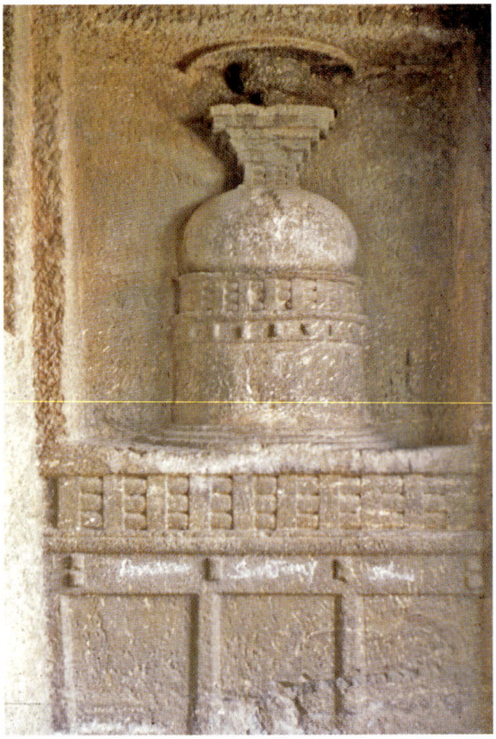

Pl. 16: Stūpa carved in the round inside a rock-cut cave at Kuda, 1st-2nd century CE.

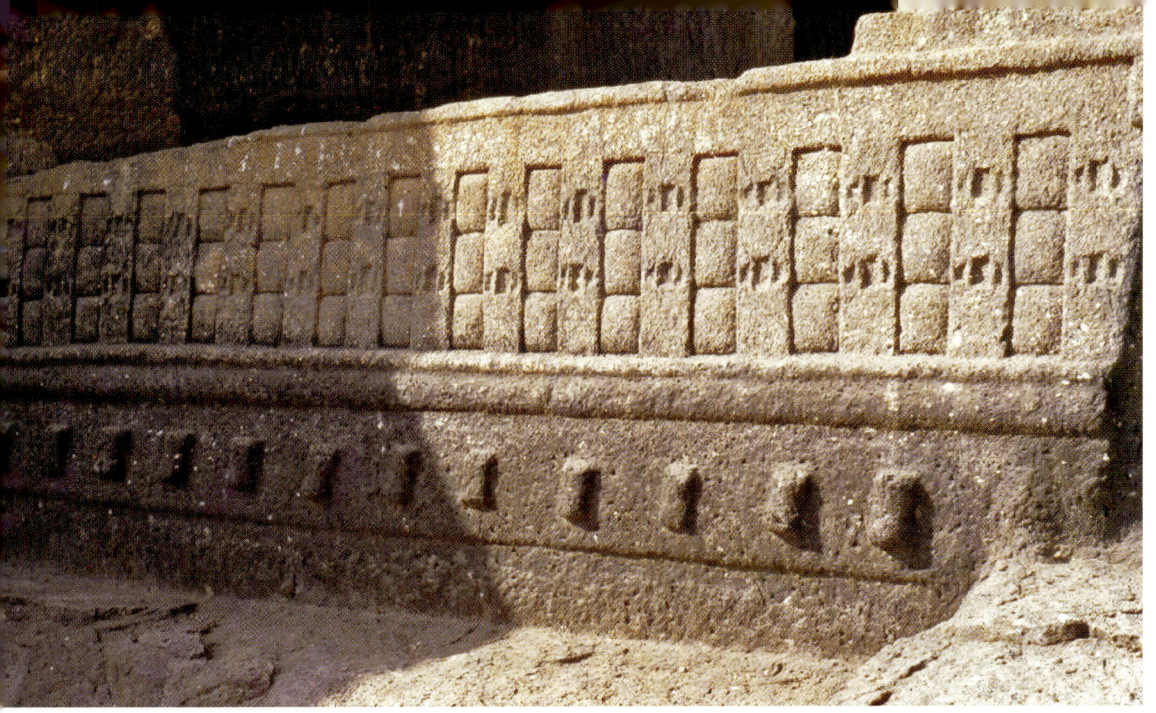

Pl. 17: Decorative balustrade at Kuda imitating wooden architecture, 1st-2nd century CE.

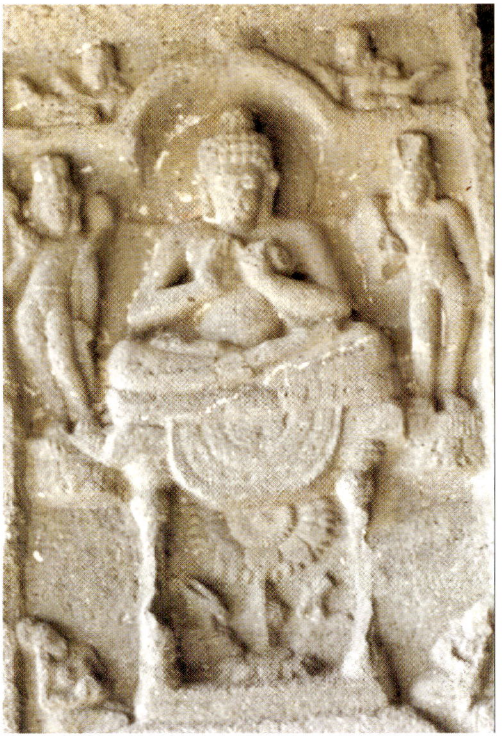

Pl. 18: Buddha image carved inside a rock-cut cave in Kuda, 6th century CE.

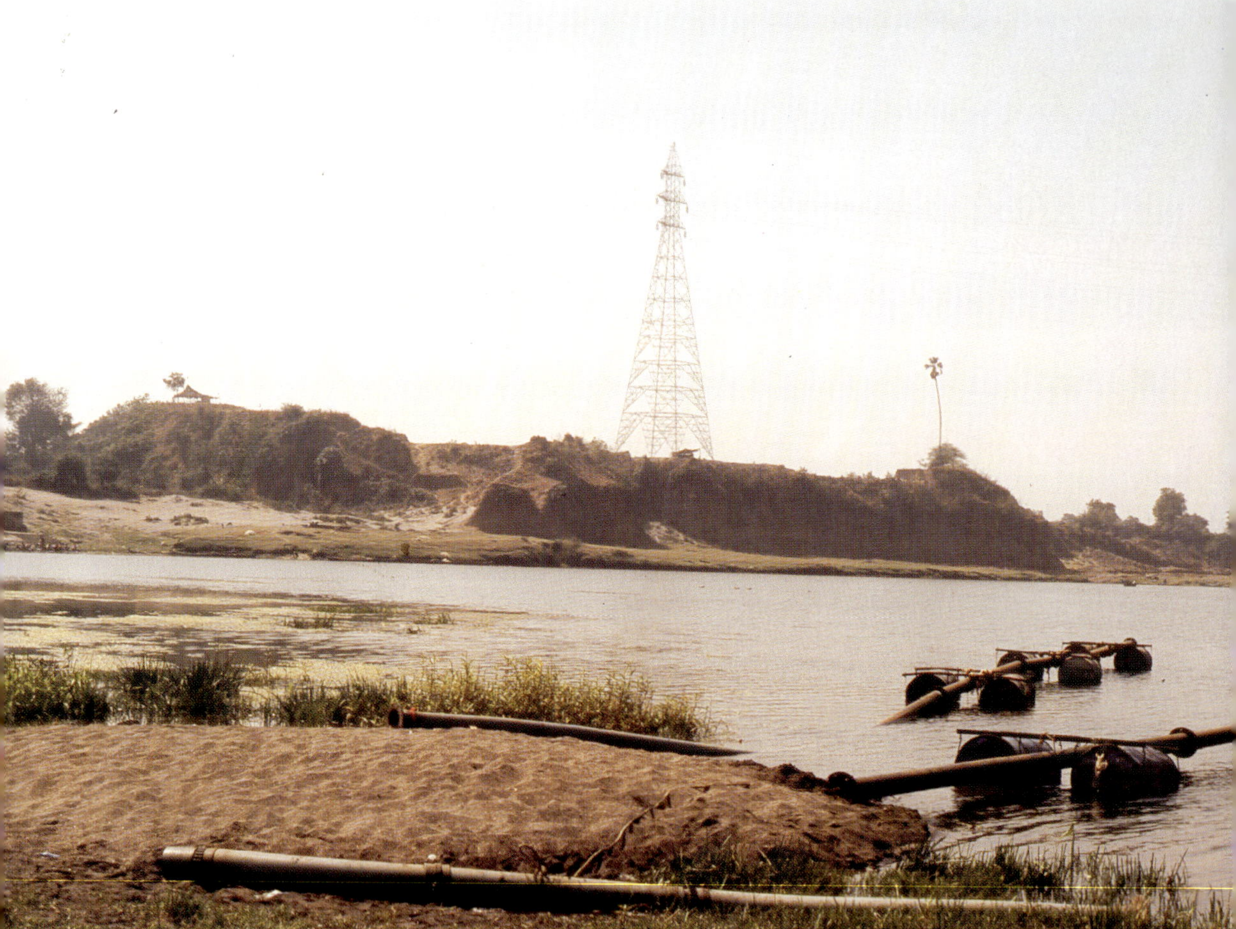

Pl. 19: Site of early historic Kamrej on the banks of the river Tāpti.

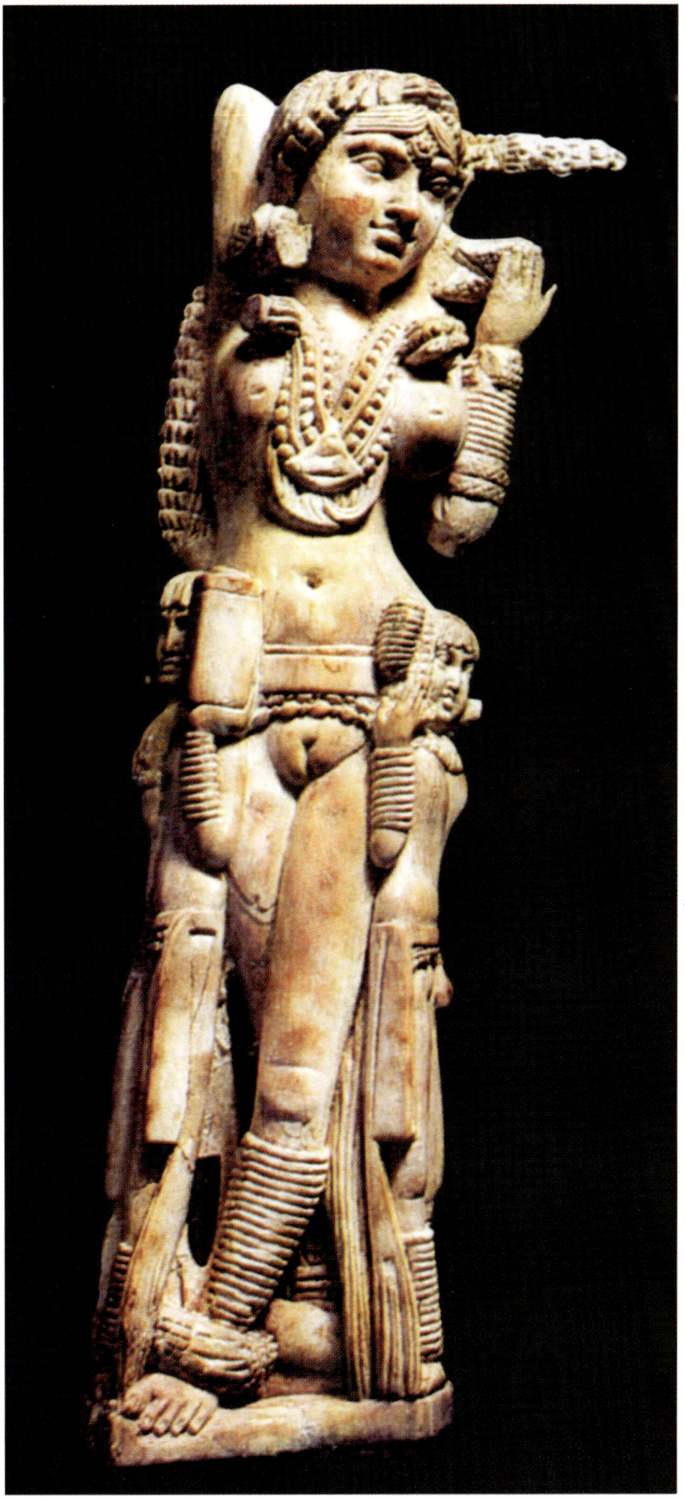

Pl. 20: Ivory figurine of western Indian origin found at Pompei, Italy, 1st century CE.

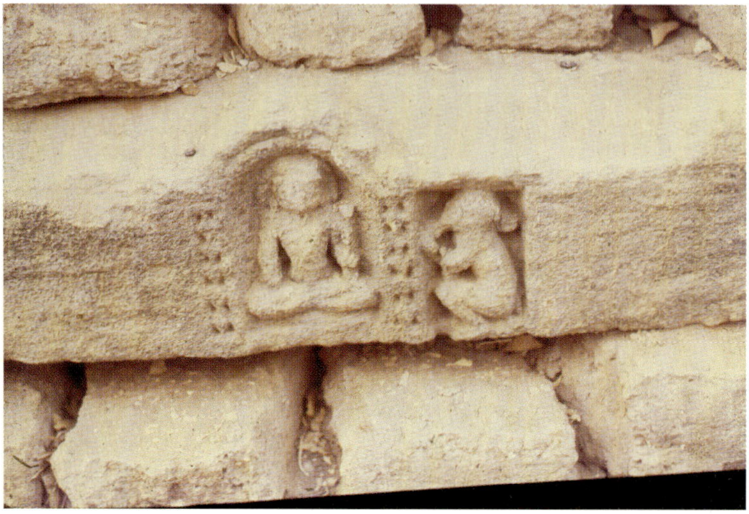

Pl. 21: Lakulīśa image on decorated brick, Karvan, Baroda. 6th-7th century CE.

Pl. 22: Terracotta bust of a nobleman from Kauśāmbī (Uttar Pradesh) having red polish and glaze, 1st-2nd century CE.

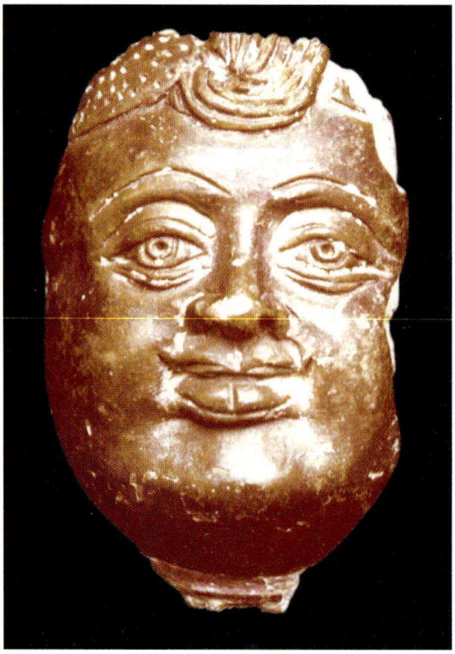

Pl. 23: Terracotta bust of Śiva from Kauśāmbī (Uttar Pradesh) having red slip, 1st-2nd century CE.

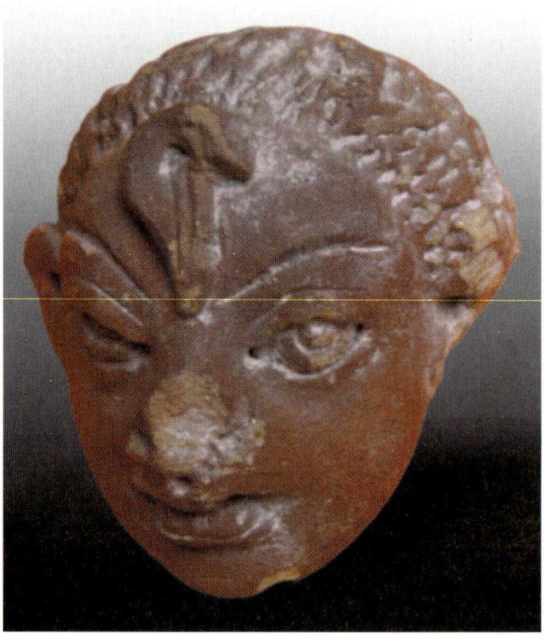

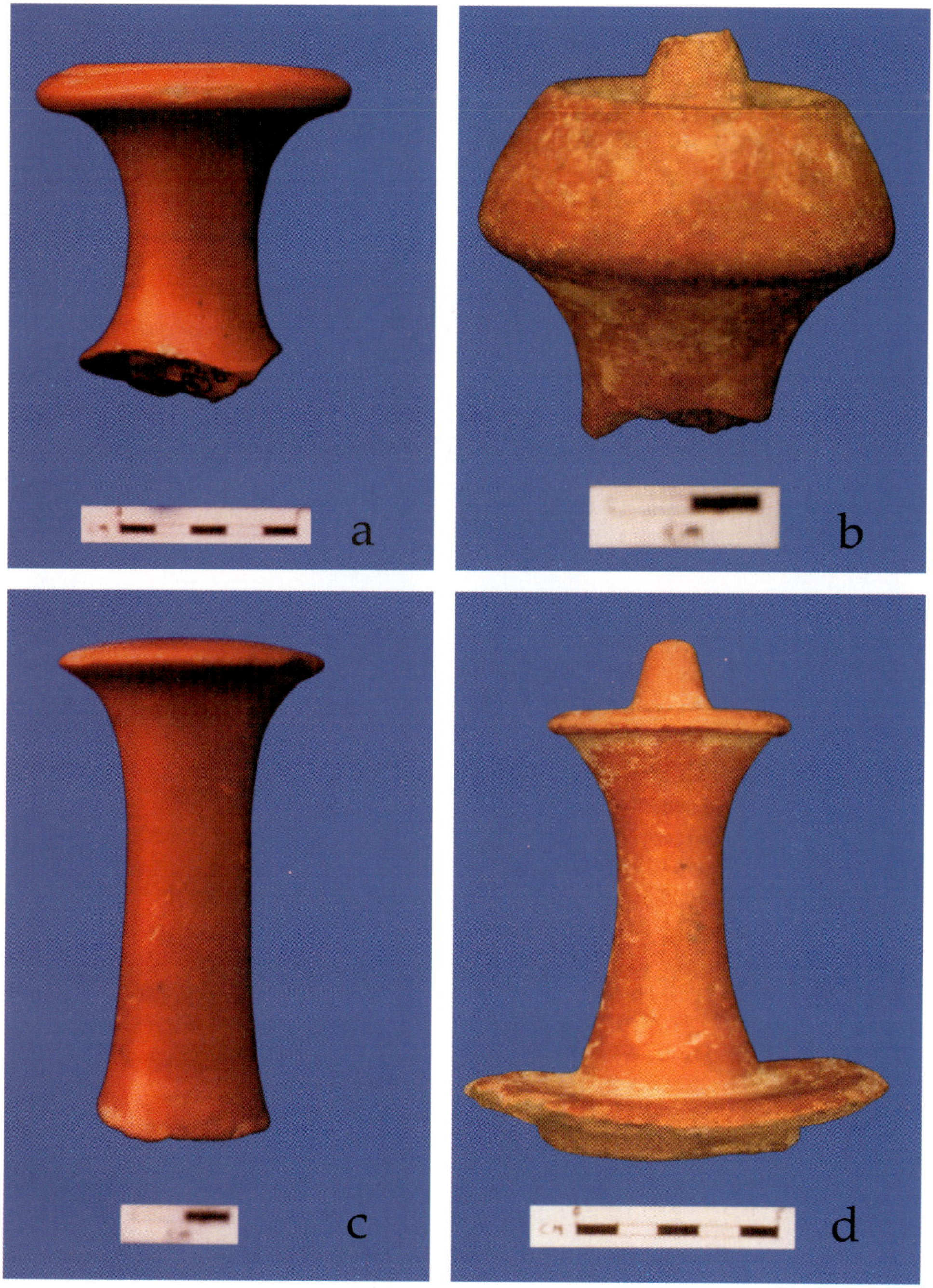

Pl. 24: Fragments of Red Polished Ware vessels from Nevāsā (Maharashtra) and Kauśāmbī (Uttar Pradesh), 1st-2nd century CE.

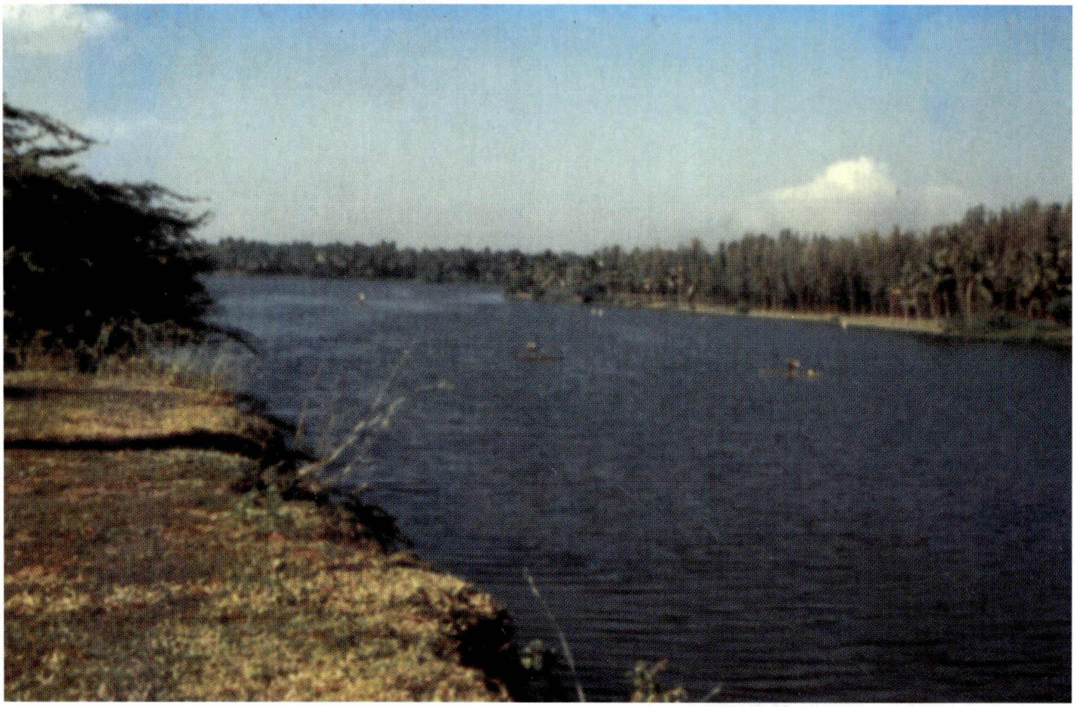

Pl. 25: Early historic site of Arikamedu (Pondicherry) on the banks of the Ariyankuppam river.

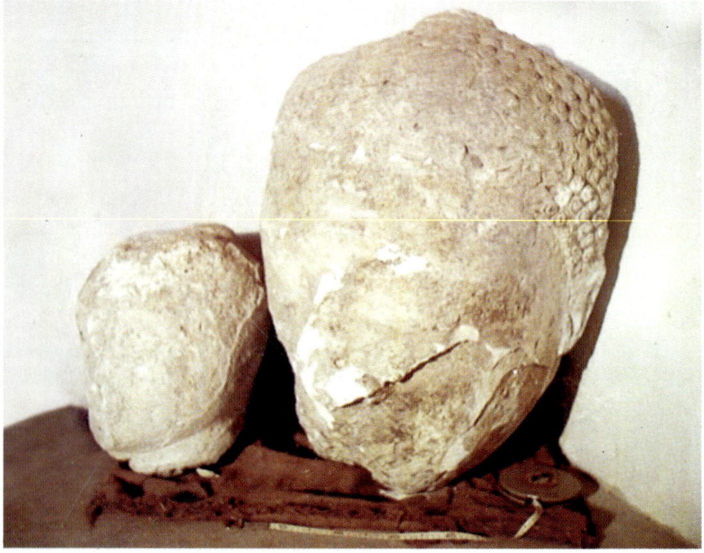

Pl. 26: Buddha-heads from Andhroth Island, Lakshadweep, 5th century CE.

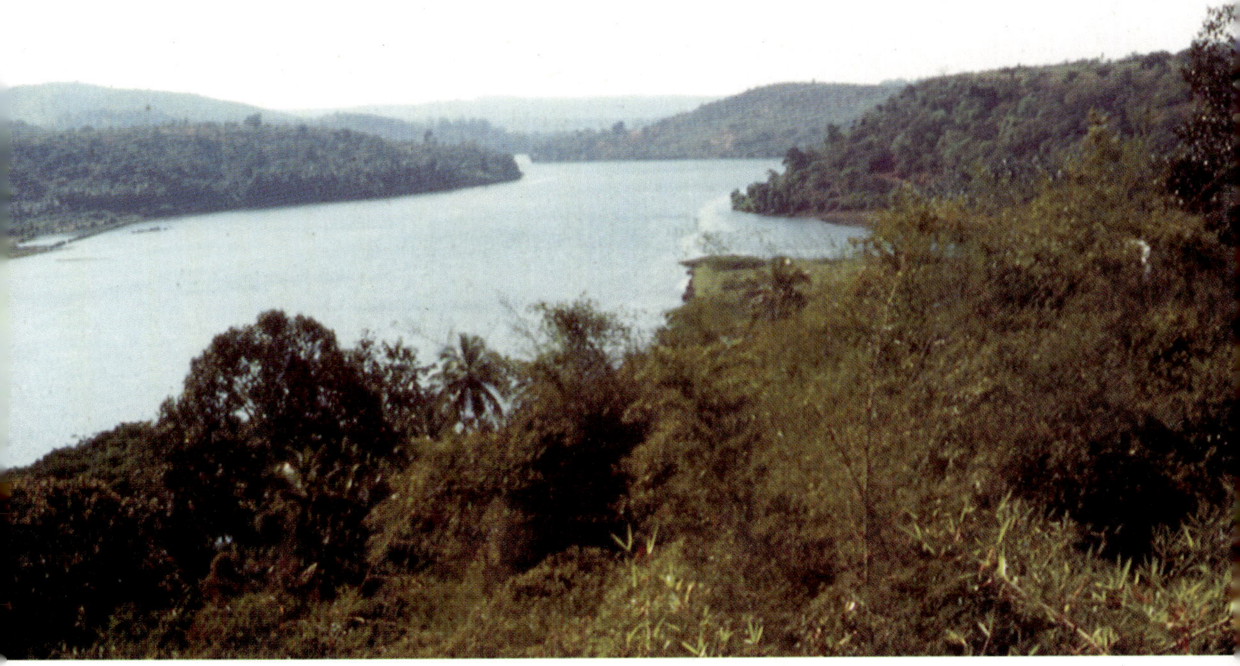

Pl. 27: View of the Śarāvatī river from Haigunda Island.

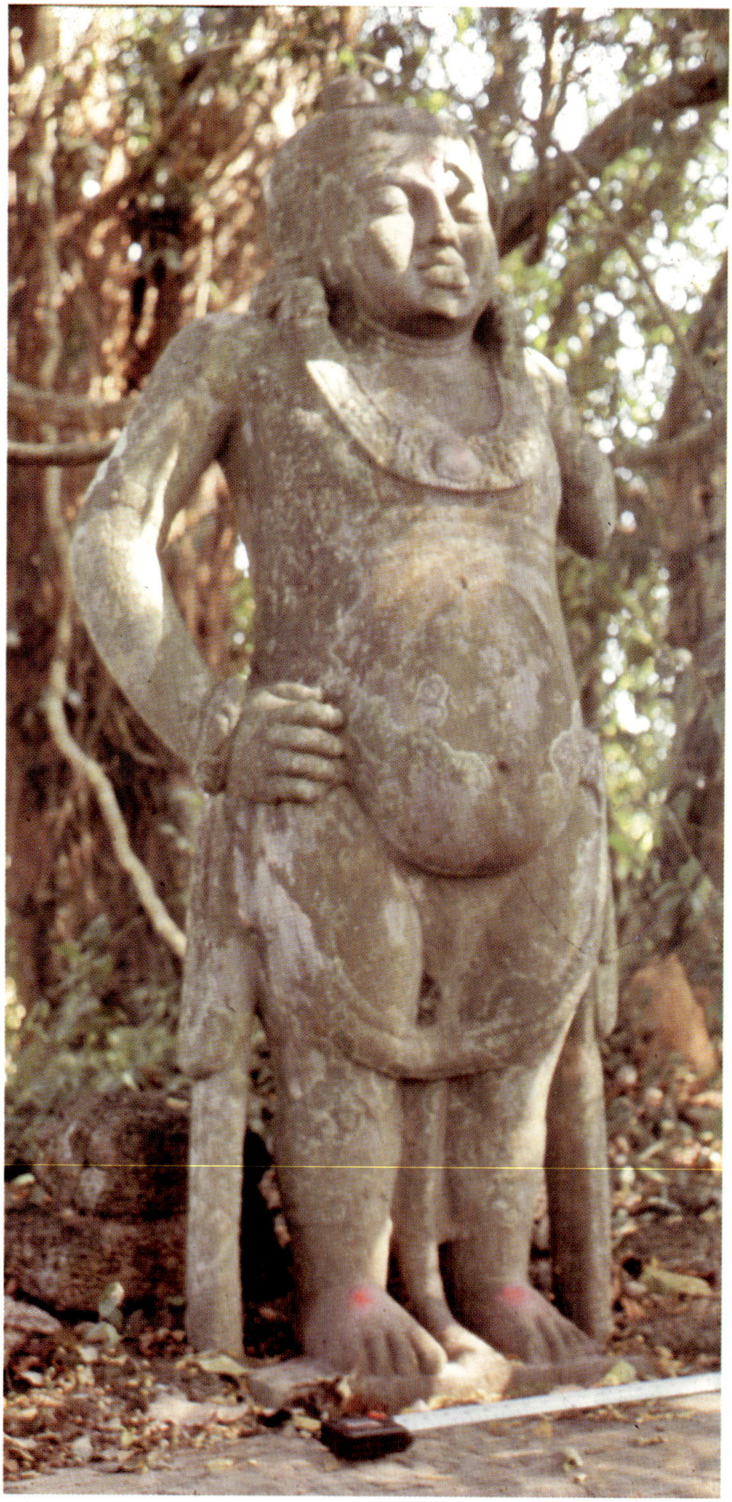

Pl. 28: *Yakṣa* image of stone inside a sacred grove on Haigunda Island, Uttar Kannada Dist., Karnataka, 4th century CE.

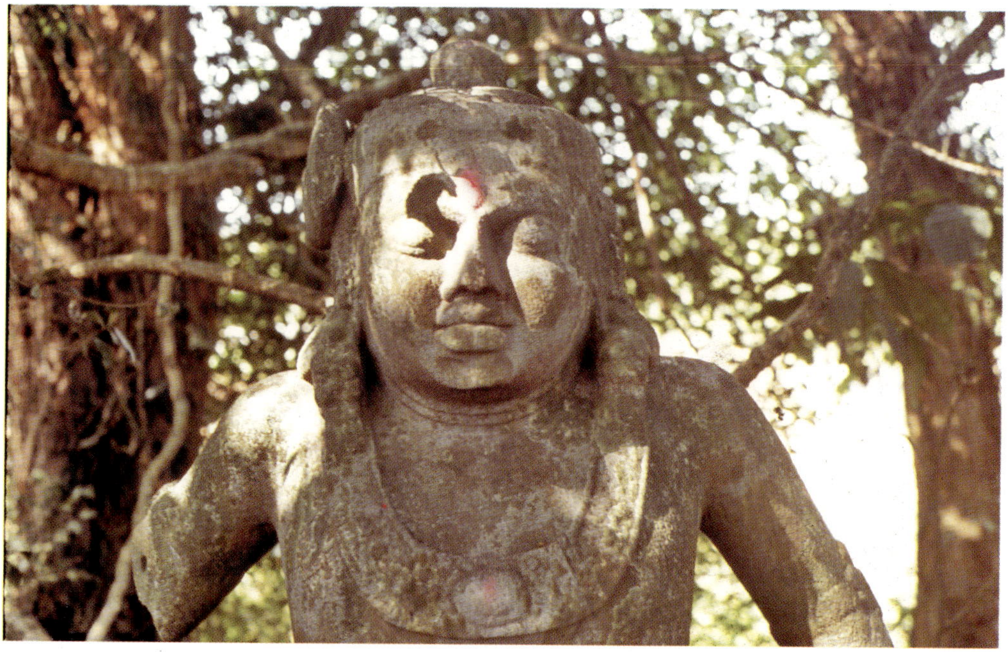

Pl. 29: Close up of *yakṣa* figure on Haigunda Island.

Pl. 30: Viṣṇu image flanked by Buddha figures outside the village of Haigunda.

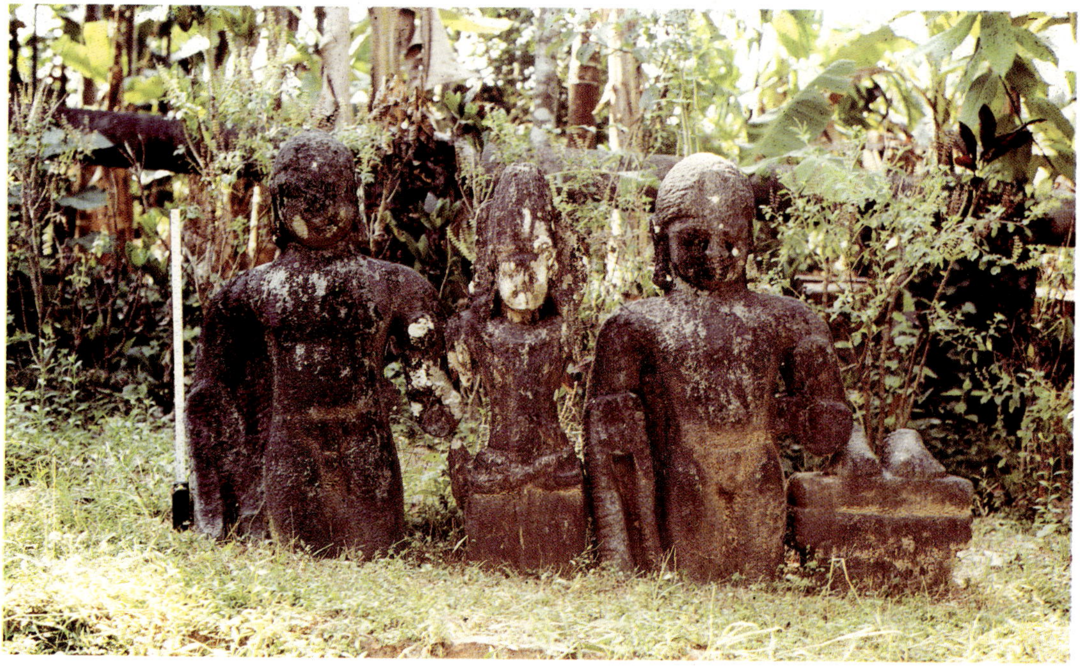

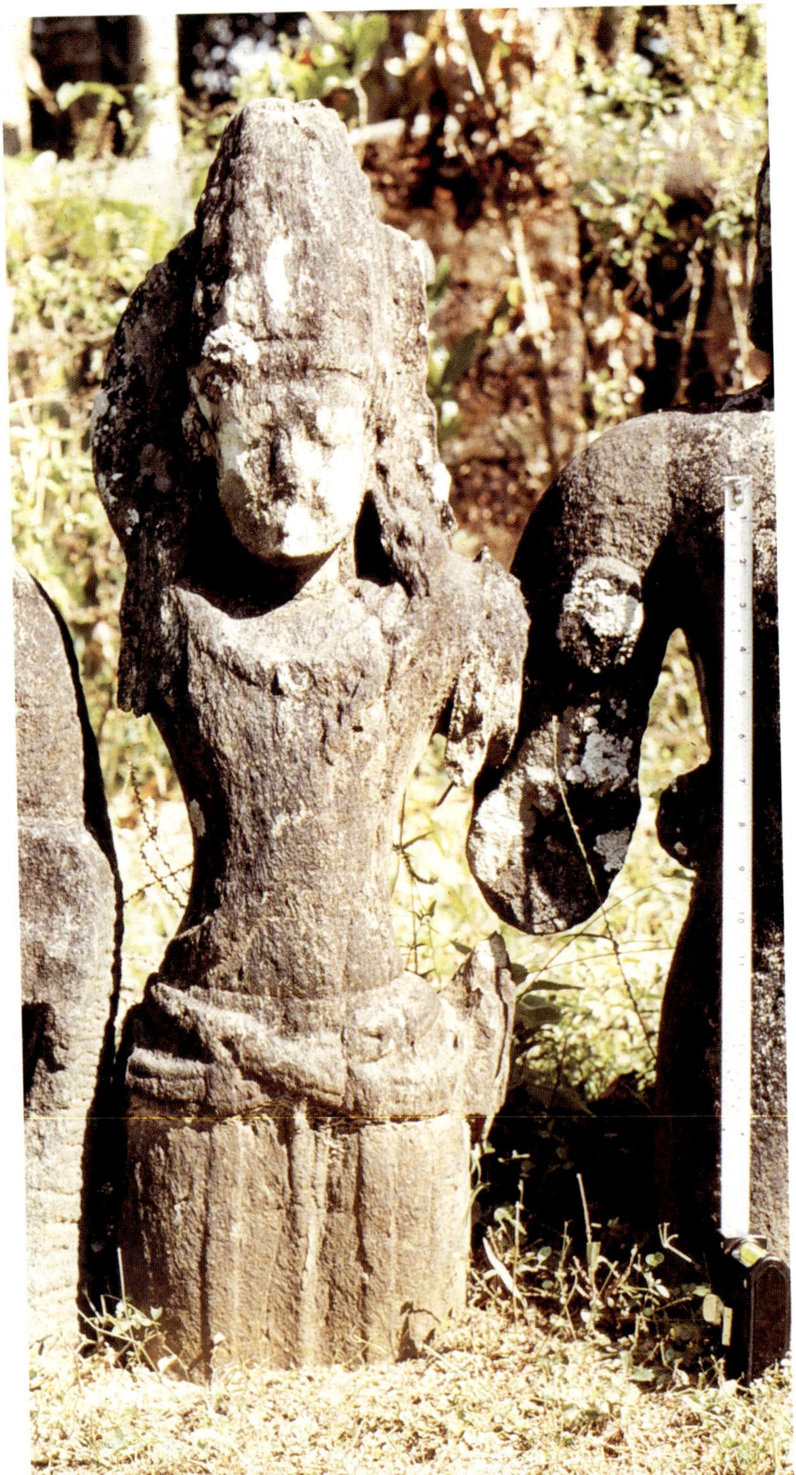

Pl. 31: Stone sculpture of Viṣṇu, Haigunda Island, 3rd-4th century CE.

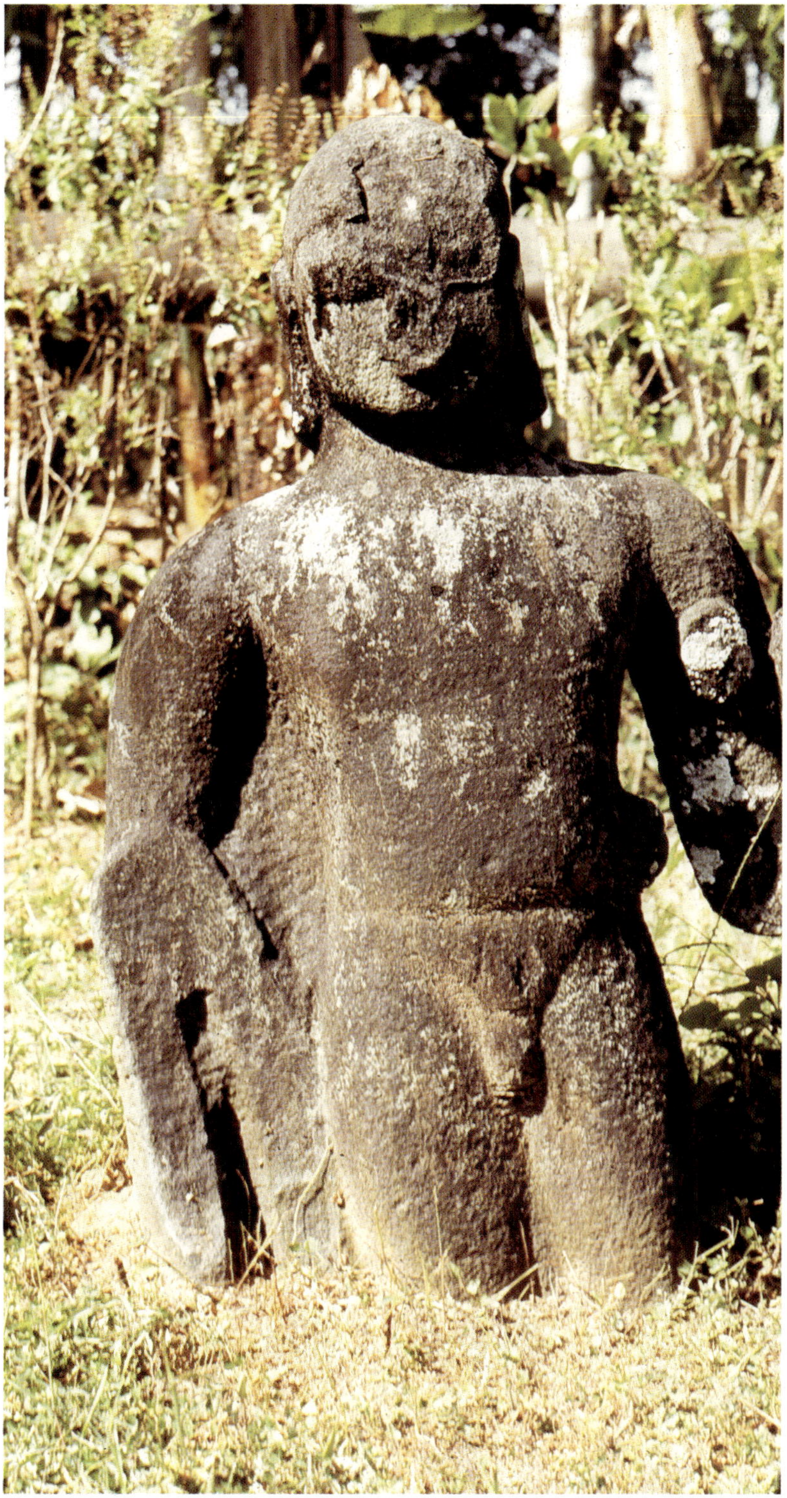

Pl. 32: Buddha image to the left of Viṣṇu figure, Haigunda Island in 5th-6th century CE.

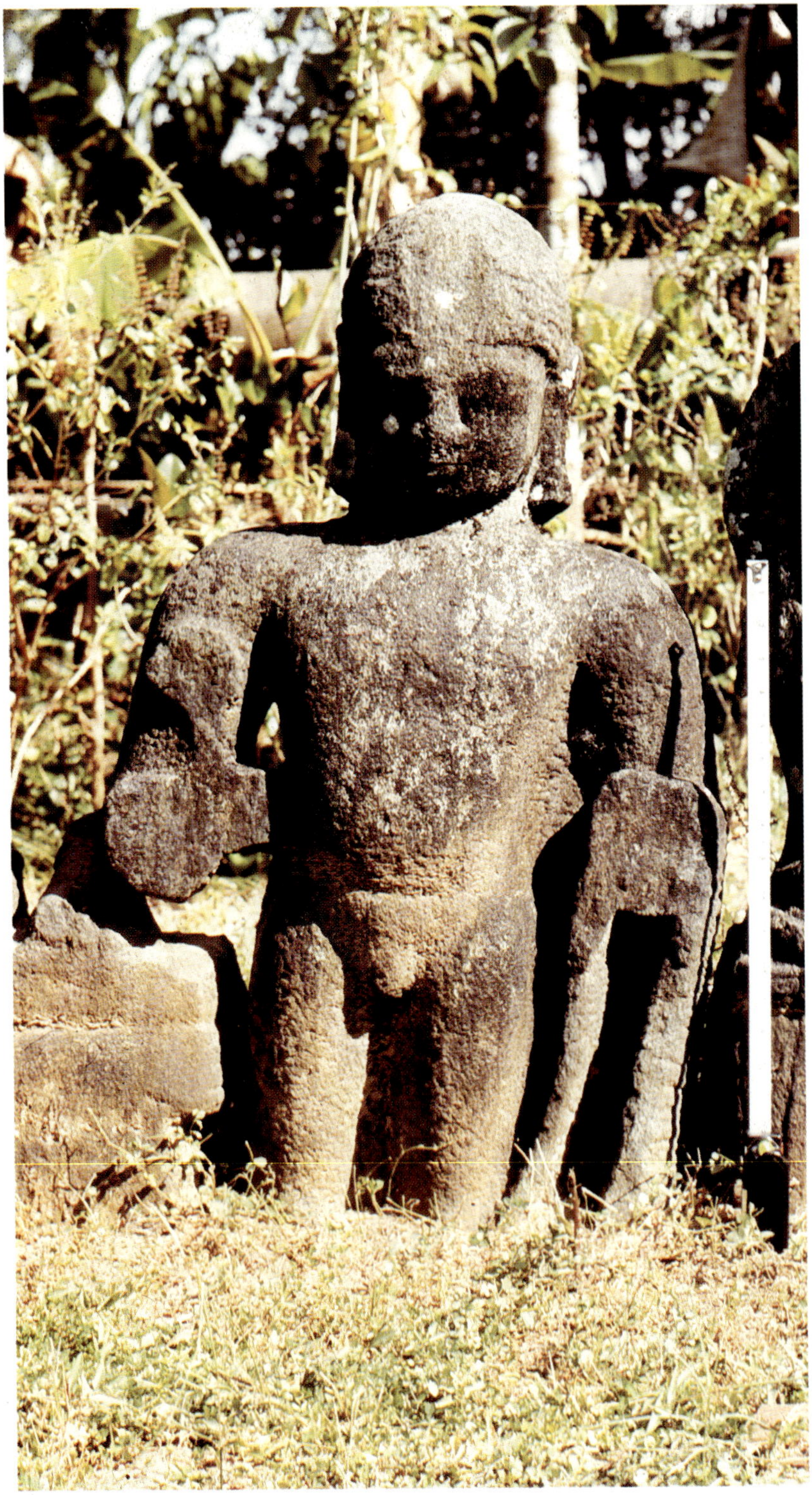

Pl. 33: Buddha image to the right of Viṣṇu figure, Haigunda Island in 5th-6th century CE.

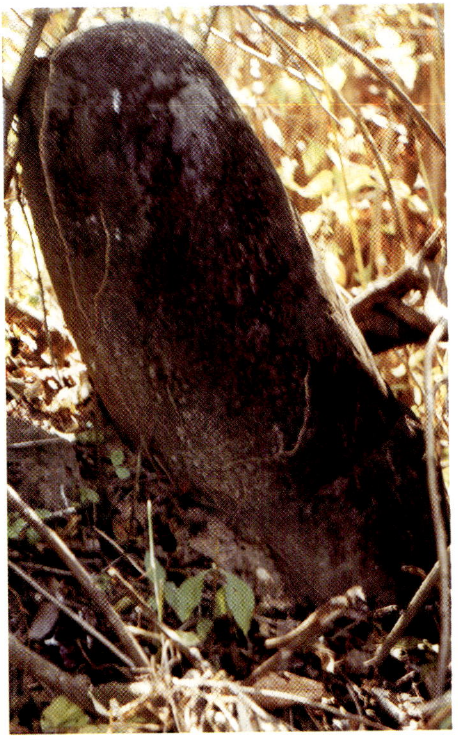

Pl. 34: Śivaliṅga found in a field in Haigunda Island, 5th century CE?

Pl. 35: View of Malpe creek as it opens into the Arabian Sea.

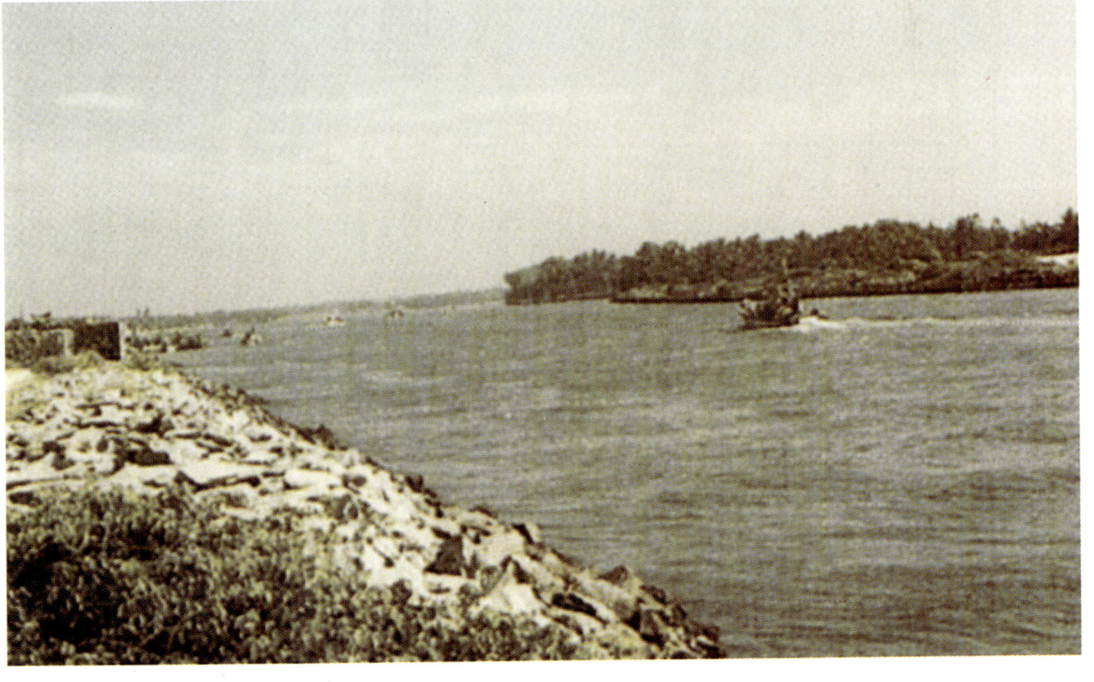

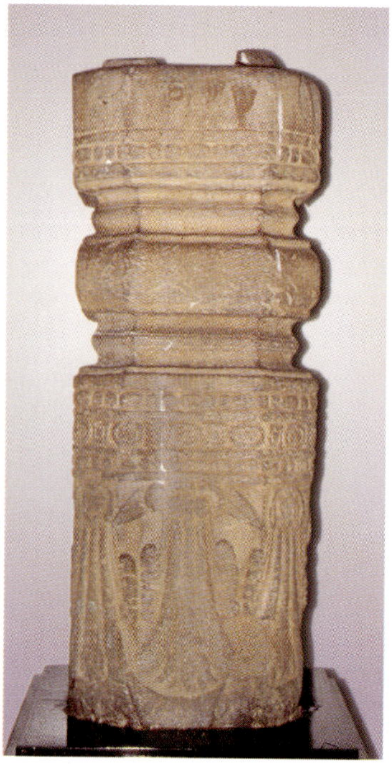

Pl. 39: Decorated stone column, Dvarāvatī period, 7th century CE.

Pl. 40: Bodhi tree carved on stone plaque, 6th century CE.

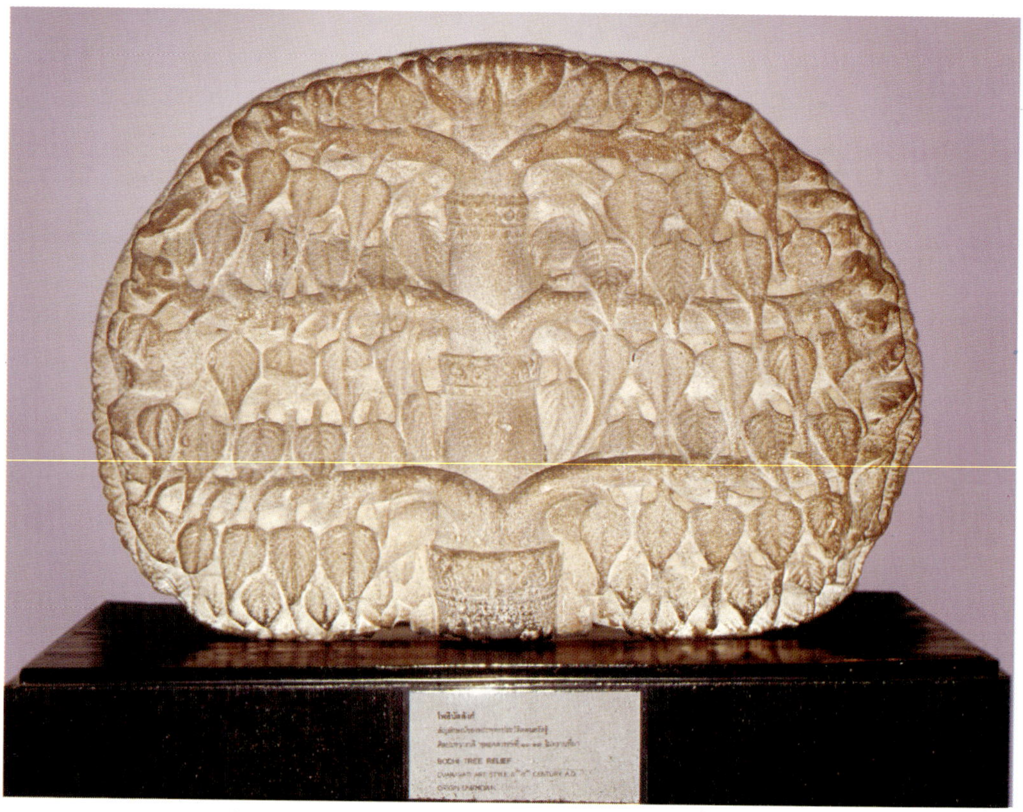

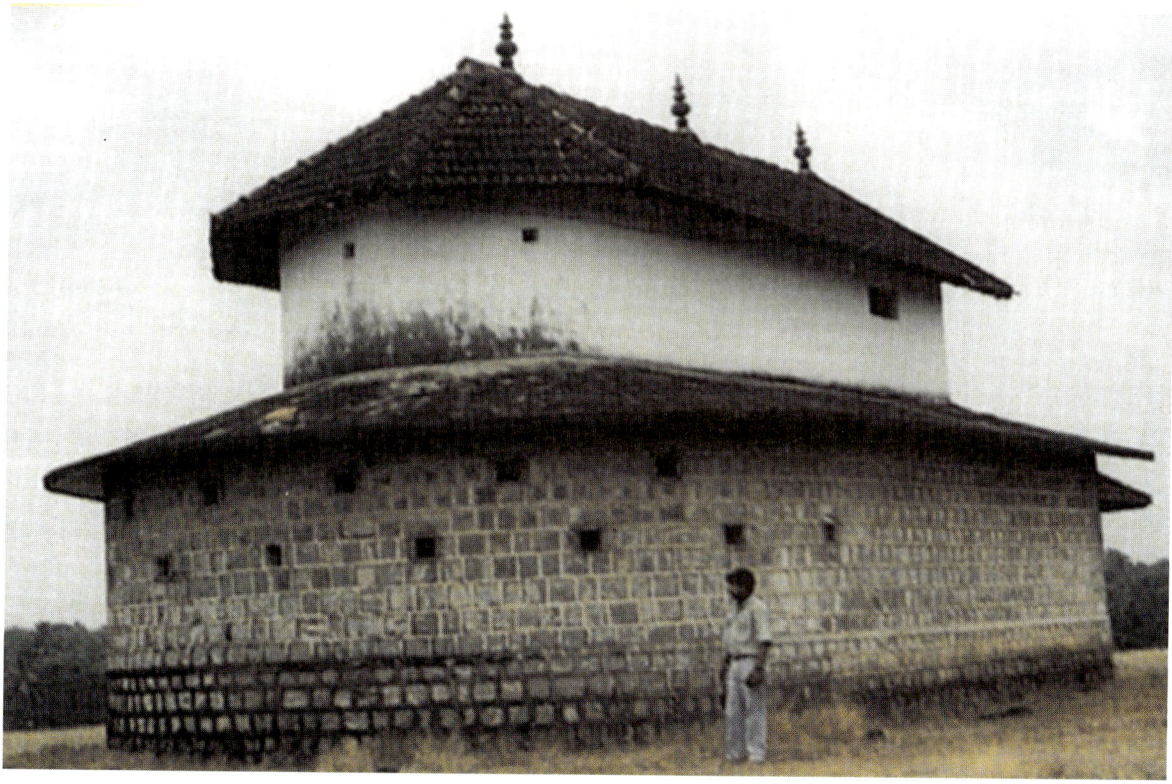

Pl. 36: Apsidal temple dedicated to Śiva,
Udyavara, Dakshin Kannada.

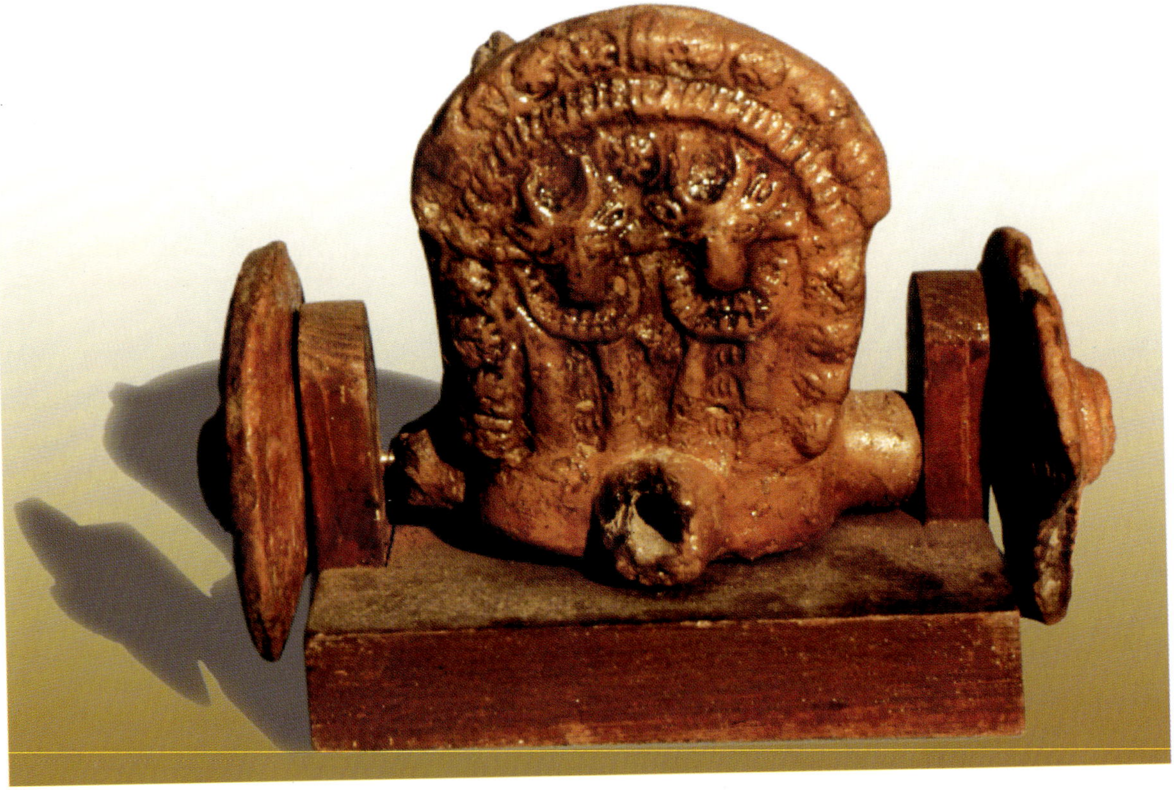

Pl. 37: Terracotta toy cart, Kauśāmbī, 1st century CE.

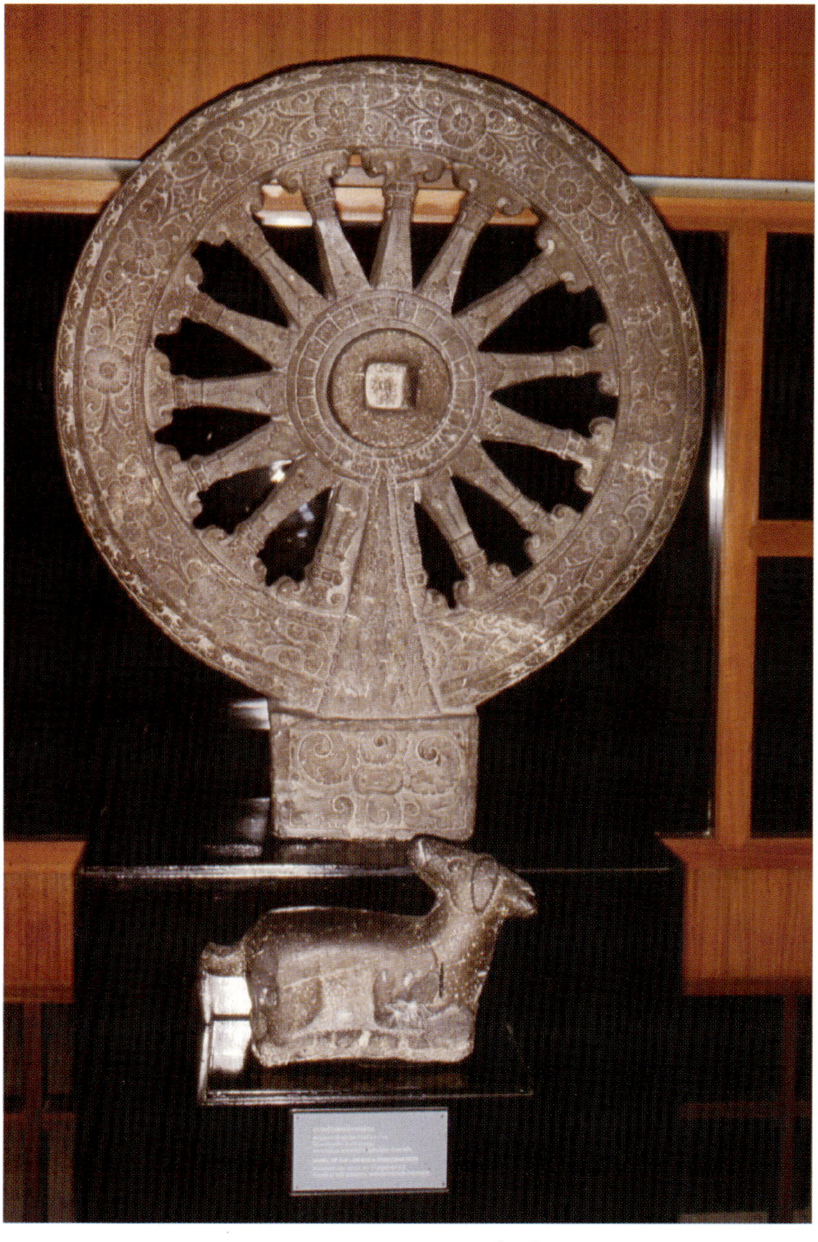

Pl. 38: *Dharmacakra* in stone, 7th-8th century CE, Bangkok National Museum.

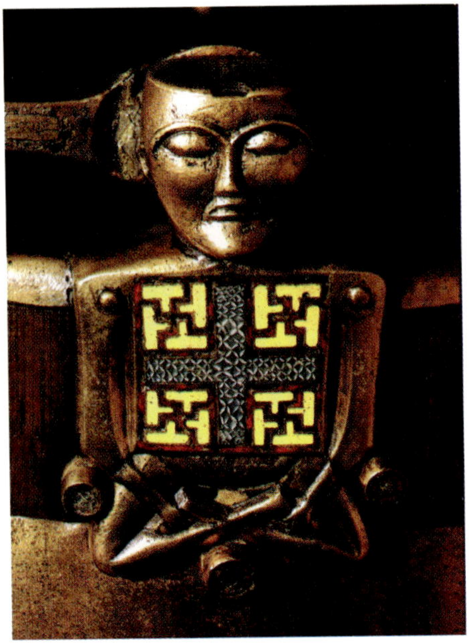

Pl. 41: Metal figure from Viking site in Norway resembling a Buddha figure.

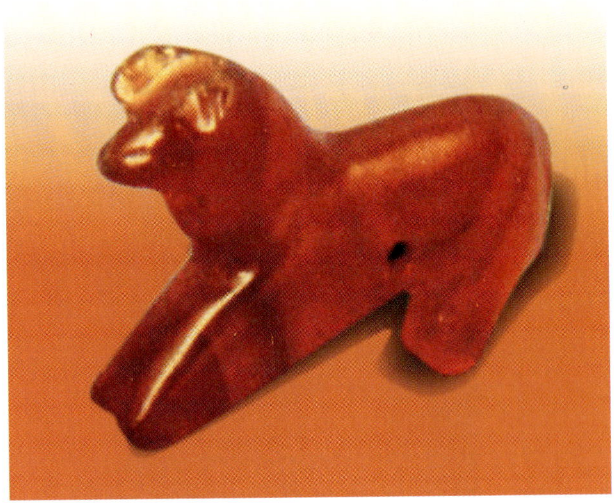

Pl. 42: Carnelian bead in shape of a dog from Kauśāmbī (Uttar Pradesh), early centuries CE.

Pl. 43: Agate beads from Ban Don Ta Phet, Thailand,. 4th-3rd century BCE.

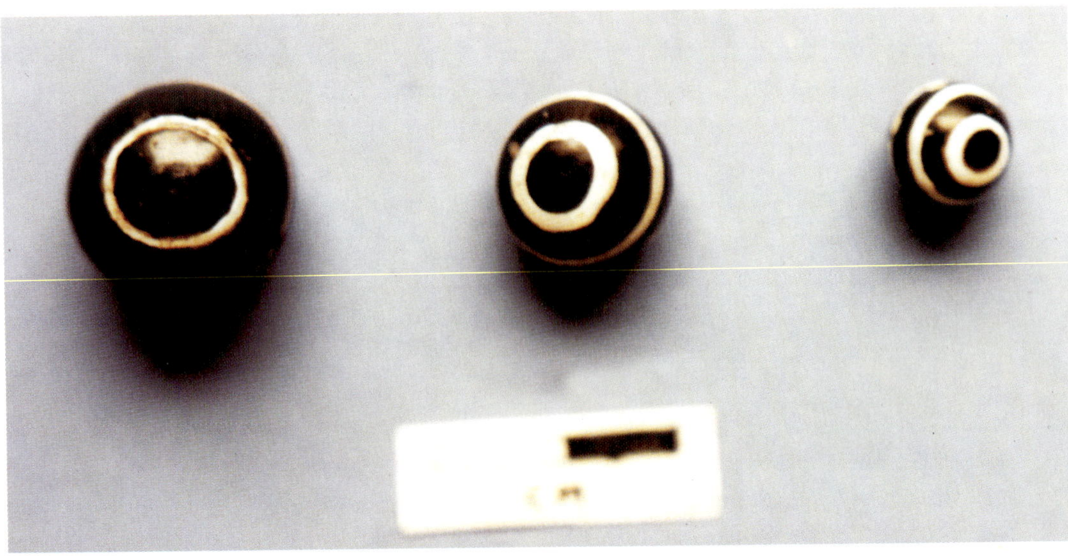

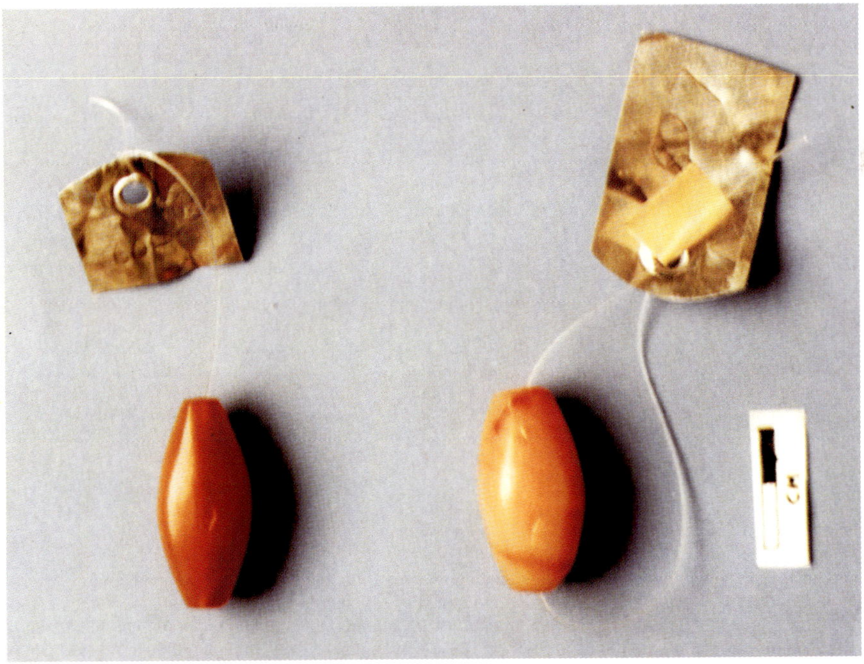

Pl. 44: Carnelian beads from Ban Don Ta Phet, Thailand, 4th-3rd century BCE.

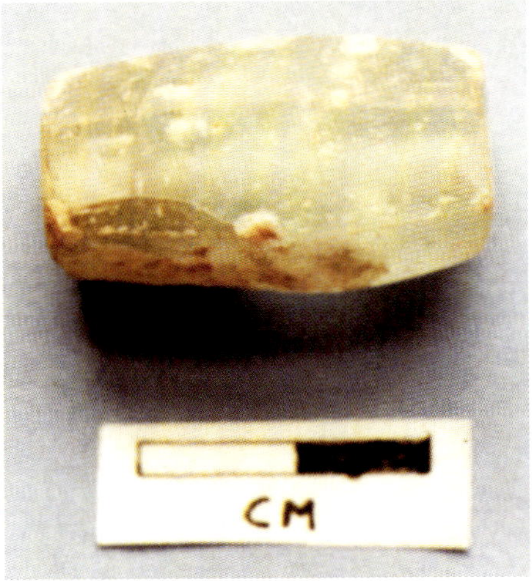

Pl. 45: A glass 'beryl' from Ban Don Ta Phet, Thailand, 4th-3rd century BCE.

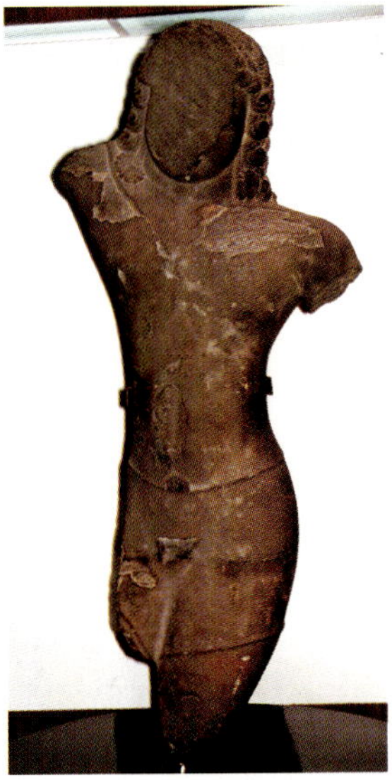

Pl. 46: Kṛṣṇa lifting mount Govardhana, stone, Bangkok National Museum, 6th century CE.

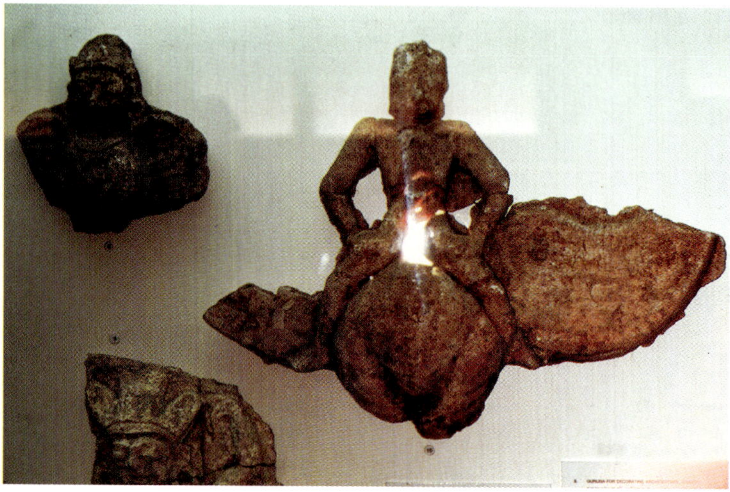

Pl. 47: Personification of Garuḍa. Stucco, Bangkok National Museum, 6th-7th century CE.

Pl. 48: Elephant in stone on Kayama Hill, Puri District, Orissa.

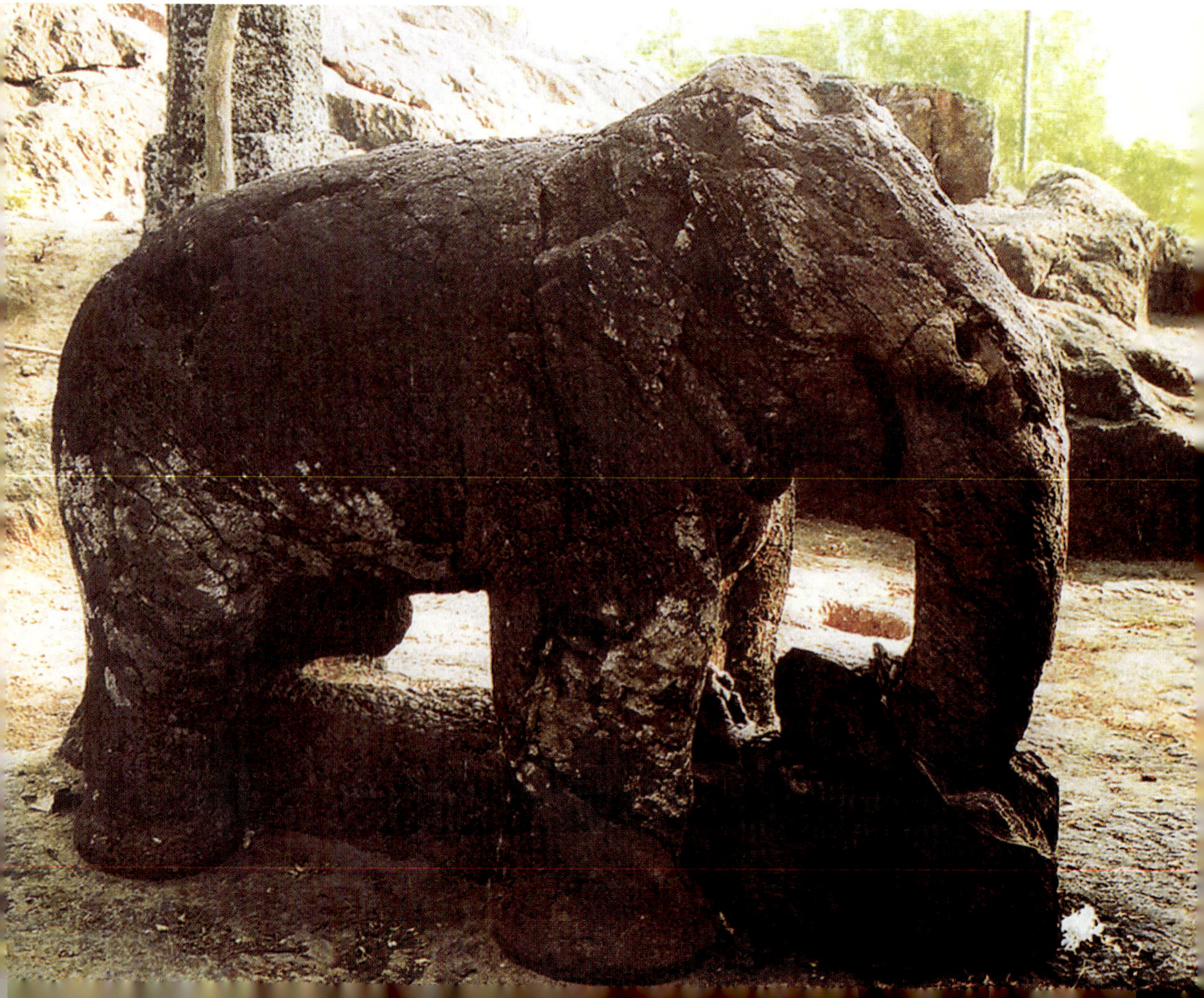

References

Agrawala, R.C., 1970, *Roman Figurines on Pottery Handles from India and allied problems*, Baroda: Dept. of Museums, Baroda State.

Agrawala, V.S., 1984, *The Heritage of Indian Art*, Delhi: Publications Division.

Ajit Kumar, 2003-04, New Identification of the so-called Surya and Indra panels in Bhaja Cave 22, *Kala* vol. II: 44-52.

Ardika, I.W. and P. Bellwood, 1991, "Sembiran: The Beginnings of Indian Contact with Bali" in: *Antiquity*, vol. 65, no. 247: 221-32.

Asher, F.M., 1980, *The Art of Eastern India*, 300-800, Delhi: Oxford University Press.

Asthana, S. and B. Jha, 1999, *Gāndhāra Sculptures of the Bharat Kala Bhawan*, Varanasi: Bharat Kala Bhawan.

Avazini, A., 1994, The Red Sea and Arabia, in *Ancient Rome and India*, (R.M. Cimino ed.), pp. 53-59, Delhi-Rome: Italian Embassy Cultural Centre and ISMEO.

Barrett, D., 1957, *A Guide to Karla Caves*. Bombay: Bhulabhai Memorial Institute.

Basa, K.K. 1992, "Early Glass Beads in India" in: *South Asian Studies*, vol. 8: 91-103.

———, I. Glover and J. Henderson, 1991, "The Relationship between Early South-East Asian and Indian Glass" in: *Bulletin of the Indo-Pacific Prehistory Association*, vol. 10: 351-65.

Biswas, S.S., 1981, *Terracotta Art of Bengal*, Delhi: Agam Kala Prakashan.

Bronson, B., 1990, "Glass and Beads at Khuan Lukpad, Southern Thailand" in: *South Asian Archaeology 1986*: 213-30.

Brown R.L., 1996, *The Dvaravati Wheels of the Law and the Indianization of South-East Asia*, Leiden: E.J. Brill.

Brown, P., 1983, (rpt.), *Indian Architecture (Buddhist and Hindu)*, Bombay: D.B. Taraporevala and Sons.

Chakrabarti, D.K. and R.K. Chattopadhyay, 1992, "Notes on the Archaeology of Maldaha and West Dinajpur Districts, West Bengal," *Journal of South Asian Studies*, 8: 135-53.

Chandra, P., 1966, *Stone Sculpture in the Allahabad Museum*, Delhi: American Institute of Indian Studies.

Chapekar, B.N., 1969, *Report on the Excavations at Ter*, Poona.

Cimino, R.M., 1994, "The Indian Ivory Statuette from Pompeii," in: *Ancient Rome and India* (R.M. Cimino ed.), pp. 119-21, Delhi: Italian Embassy Cultural Centre.

Coomaraswamy, A.K., 1972 [1927], *History of Indian and Indonesian Art,* Delhi: Munshiram Manoharlal.

Craven, C., 1986, *Indian Art,* London: Thames and Hudson.

Deo, S.B., 1974, *Excavations at Bhokardan 1973,* Nagpur: Nagpur University and Marathwada University.

———, and J.P. Joshi, 1972, *Pauni Excavation (1969-70),* Nagpur: The Nagpur Vidyapeeth.

Dofflemyer, V., 1999, "Viṣṇu Images from Ancient Thailand and the Concept of Kingship" in: *Marg,* vol. 51, no. 2: 38-52.

During-Caspers, E.C.L., 1981, "The Indian Ivory Figurine from Pompeii — A Reconsideration of its Functional Use," *South Asian Archaeology 1979*: 341-53.

Dussubieux, L. and B. Gratuze 2003, Non-Destructive Characterization of Glass Beads — An Application to the Study of Glass Trade between India and South-East Asia, in *Fishbones and Glittering Gems* (A. Karlstrom and A. Kallen eds.) pp. 135-148. Stockholm: Museum of Far Eastern Antiquities.

Fergusson, J. and J. Burgess, 1880/1988, *The Cave Temples of India,* Delhi: Munshiram Manoharlal.

Francis, P., 1982, *Indian Agate Beads,* Lake Placid, New York: Centre for Bead Research.

———, 1991, "Beadmaking at Arikamedu and Beyond" in: *World Archaeology,* vol. 23, no. 1: 28-43.

Ghosh, A., 1989, *Encyclopaedia of Indian Archaeology,* vol. I & II, Delhi: Indian Council of Historical Research.

Glover, I.C., 1996 "Recent Archaeological Evidences for Early Maritime Contacts between India and South-East Asia" in: Ray, H.P. & Salles, J-F (eds.), *Tradition and Archaeology — Early Maritime Contacts in the Indian Ocean,* New Delhi: Manohar Publishers and Distributors, pp. 129-158.

Glover, I.C., and B. Bellina, 2001, "Alkaline Etched Beads East of India in the Late Prehistoric and Early Historic Periods" in: *Bulletin De L'Ecole Francaise D'Extreme-Orient,* 88, 2001: 191-215.

Goetz, H., 1963, "An Indian Bronze from South Arabia," *Archaeology,* 16, 1963: 187-89.

Gogte, V., 1997, "The Chandraketugarh-Tamluk Region of Bengal: Source of the Early Historic Rouletted Ware from India and South-East Asia" in: *Man and Environment,* vol. XXII, no. 1: 69-85.

Gupta, M.C., 1997, *A Study of Beads from Kauśāmbī,* Allahabad: Swabha Prakashan.

Gupta, S., 1994, *The Art of Kausambhi,* Academic pamphlet brought out on the occasion of an exhibition in the Allahabad Museum, Allahabad: Allahabad Museum.

———, 1998a, Nevasa: A Type-site for the Study of Indo-Roman Trade in Western India, *Journal of South Asian Studies,* vol. 14.

———, 1998b, *Roman Egypt to Peninsular India: Archaeological Patterns of Trade, 1st century* BCE — *3rd century* CE, Unpublished PhD thesis submitted to the University of Pune.

———, 2003, From Archaeology to Art in the Material Record of South-East Asia, in *Fishbones and Glittering Emblems* (A. Karlstorm and A. Kallen eds.), pp. 391-405, Stockholm: Museum of Far Eastern Antiquties.

Gupta, S. and S.K. Aruni, 2005, Early Historic Kanārā: Was it Really Ptolemy's Pirate Coast?, *Journal of Indian Ocean Archaeology* no. 2: 42-54.

Gupta, S., D. Williams, and D. Peacock, 2001, Dressel 2-4 Amphorae and Roman Trade with India, the evidence from Nevasa, *Journal of South Asian Studies,* 17, 7-18.

Gupta, S.P., 1980, *Roots of Indian Art,* Delhi: BR Publishing Corporation.

Gupta, S.P., Sunil Gupta, Tejas Garge, Rohini Pandey, Anuja Geetali and Sonali Gupta 2004. On the fast Track of the Periplus: Excavations at Kamrej — 2003, the *Journal of Indian Ocean Archaeology,* no. 1, vol. 1: 67-79.

Gururaja Bhatt, P., 1969., *Antiquities of South Kanārā,* Udipi: Prabhakara Prakashan.

Hallade, M., 1968, *The Gandhāra Style and the Evolution of Buddhist Art,* London: Thames and Hudson.

Hegde, R. and G. Sarvamangala, 1997, Haigunda — an ancient river settlement of Karnataka, in *An Integrated Approach to Marine Archaeology* (S.R. Rao ed.), pp. 75-77, Goa: National Institute of Oceanography.

Holmqvist, W., 1956, *Excavations at Helgo, I. Report for 1954-56,* Stockholm (downloaded from internet).

Howell, J.R., 1995, *Excavations at Sannathi 1986-89,* New Delhi: Memoirs of the Archaeological Survey of India, no. 93.

Karttunen, K., 1997, "Wooden Tables with Ivory Legs," in: *South Asian Archaeology 1995,* vol. 2 (R. Allchin and B. Allchin, ed.), New Delhi: Oxford and IBH Publishing Co. Ltd., pp. 557-62.

Knox, R., 1992, *Amarāvatī,* London: The British Museum.

Kramrisch, S., 1939, "Indian Terracottas" in: *JISOA* vol. VII, 1939: 99-101.

———, 1960, *Indian Sculpture in the Philadelphia Museum of Art,* Philadelphia: University of Philadelphia Press.

Krishnan, Y., 1996, *The Buddha Image, Its Origin and Development,* Delhi: Munshiram Manoharlal.

Kuwayama, S., 1997, "A Hidden Import from Imperial Rome manifest in *Stūpas,*" in: *Gāndhāran Art in Context, East-West Exchanges at the Crossroads of Asia* (R. Allchin, B. Allchin, N. Krietman and E. Errington, eds.), Cambridge & Delhi: Ancient India and Iran Trust and Regency Publications, pp. 119-171.

Lahiri, N., 1992, *The Archaeology of Indian Trade Routes,* New Delhi: Oxford University Press.

Lal, B.B., 1949, Sisupalgarh 1948: An Early Historical Fort in Eastern India, *Ancient India,* no. 5: 62-105.

Lars, 2004, "Sacred Architecture, Sacred Landscape: Early Buddhism in North Coastal Andhra Pradesh," in: *Archaeology as History in Early South Asia* (H.P. Ray and C.M. Sinipoli, eds.), pp. 376-391, New Delhi: ICHR and Aryan Books International.

Le May, R., 1956, *The Culture of South-East Asia,* London: George Allen and Unwin.

Lohuizen de Leeuw, J.E. van, 1949/1995, Chapter titled "The Buddha and Jina Image in the Kusana Art of Mathura", in *The Scythian Period,* Delhi: Munshiram Manoharlal.

Lush, J., 1998, "Antiquities in the Aden Protectorate, 1935-40," *Journal of the British Yemeni Society,* 1998 (downloaded from internet).

Lyons, I and H. Ingholt, 1957, *Gāndhāra art in Pakistan,* New York: Pantheon Books.

Marshall, J., 1960, *The Buddhist Art of Gāndhāra,* Cambridge: Department of Archaeology in Pakistan at this University Press.

Mehta, R.N. and A.J. Patel, 1967, *Excavation at Shamalaji,* Baroda: M.S. University Archaeology Series no. 9.

Mitra, D., 1978, *Bhubaneshvar,* New Delhi: Archaeological Survey of India.

Mohamed, Naseema, 2002, "Pre-Islamic Maldives," in: *Man and Environment* vol. XXVII (2): 109-15.

Mukherjee, B.N., 1997, "The Impact of Gandhāra on the Art of Ancient Vanga: A Case of an Eastern Response" in: Allchin, R. Allchin, B. Krietman, N. and Errington, E. (eds.), *Gandhāran Art in Context, East-West Exchanges at the Crossroads of Asia,* Cambridge & Delhi: Ancient India and Iran Trust and Regency Publications (pp. 173-88).

Murthy, P.R., 1997/98, A Note on Two Sculptures from Chandravaram, *Kalā,* vol. IV, 1997-98: 106-108.

Narain, A.K., and P. Singh, 1977, *Excavations at Rajghat, Part III,* Varanasi: Banaras Hindu University.

Panigrahi, K.C., 1961, *Archaeological Remains at Bhubaneswar.,* Calcutta: Orient Longmans.

Petrie, Flinders, 1909 - 1996, *The Arts and Crafts of Ancient Egypt,* London: Bracken Books.

Poonacha, K.P. and M.S. Visweswara, 1991, Ancient Port-Towns of Karnataka with Special Reference to Honnavara, in *Recent Advances inMarine Archaeology, Proceedings of the Second Indian Conference on Marine Archaeology of Indian Ocean Countries* (S.R. Rao ed.), pp. 67-72, Goa: Society for Marine Archaeology, National Institute for Oceanography.

Prasad, Rajendra B., 1980, *Art of South India, Andhra Pradesh,* Delhi: Sundeep Prakashan.

Quagliotti, A.M., 1998, *Buddhapādas,* Kamakura: Institute of the Silk Road Studies.

Rao, K.P., 1994a, Kottapatnam: An Early Sea-Port in Southern Andhra, *Proceedings of the Indian History Congress,* Delhi: 829-831.

———, 1994b, New Archaeological Evidence revealing South India's Early Contacts with China. Paper included in theme volume on *Archaeology as an Indicator of Trade and Contact* issued by the Academic Committee of the Third World Archaeological Congress, New Delhi, December 4-11, 1994.

Rao, S.R., 1966, Excavations at Amreli, A Kshatrapa-Gupta Town, Special Issue of *Bulletin of Baroda Museum and Picture Gallery,* vol. XVIII.

Ray, H.P., 1991, "In Search of Suvarnabhumi: Early Sailing Networks in the Bay of Bengal" in: *Bulletin of the Indo-Pacific Prehistory Association* no. 10, 1991: 357-65.

Roy, Anamika, 1994, *Amarāvatī Stūpa, A Critical Comparison of Epigraphical, Archaeological and Sculptural Evidence,* Delhi: Agam Kala Prakashan.

Rydh, H., 1959, *Rangmahal,* Lund: CWK Gleerup Publishers.

Salles, J-F., 2004, "Archaeology and History of Bangladesh: Recent Perspectives," in *Archaeology as History in Early South Asia* (H.P. Ray and C.M. Sinopoli, eds.), pp. 185-218. New Delhi: ICHR and Aryan Books International.

Sankalia, H.D., B. Subbarao and S.B. Deo, 1958, *The Excavations at Maheshwar and Navdatoli 1952-53,* Baroda–Poona: Deccan College Research Institute and M.S. University Publication no. 1).

Sarkar, H.B., 1970, *Some Contributions of India to the Ancient Civilizations of Indonesia and Malaysia,* Kolkata: Punthi Pustak.

Sastri, S.M., 1927, *McCrindle's Ancient India as Described by Ptolemy,* Calcutta: Chuckervertty, Chatterjee and Co. Ltd.

Sharma, G.R., 1969, *Excavations at Kauśāmbī 1949-50,* Memoirs of the Archaeological Survey of India, no. 74, Delhi.

Sharma, R.C., 1984, *Buddhist Art of Mathurā,* Delhi: Agam Kala Prakashan.

Shinde, V.S., P.P. Joglekar, Ravi Jadhav and V. Naiknavare, 2004, A Satavahana Period Shrine of Laxmi-Parvati at Siddhapur, District Solapur, Maharashtra, *Man and Environment* vol. XXIX, no. 2 (July–Dec 2004): 117.

Sircar, D.C., 1998, *Inscriptions of Asoka.* New Delhi: Publications Division, Ministry of Information and Broadcasting, Government of India.

Smith, M.L., 1999, "Indianization from the Indian Point of View: Trade and Cultural Contacts with South-East Asia in the Early First Millennium CE." in: *Journal of the Economic and Social History of the Orient,* vol. 42, Part 1, February 1999: 1-26.

Soundara Rajan, K.V., 1985, *Junagadh,* New Delhi: Archaeological Survey of India.

Stone, E., 1994, *The Buddhist Art of Nāgārjunakoṇḍa,* Delhi: Motilal Banarsidass.

Subrahmanyam, B., 2004, *Buddhist Relic Caskets in South India,* Delhi: Bhartiya Kala Prakashan.

Sundara, A., 1990, Ancient Ports of Karnataka, *Journal of Marine Archaeology*, vol. 1, June 1990: 39-45.

———, 1992, Place Names, Traditions and Archaeology, *Puratattva*, no. 22: 97-101.

Thapar, R., 1961, *Asoka and the Decline of the Mauryas*, Oxford: OUP.

Theunissen, R., P. Grave and G. Bailey 2000 "Doubts on Diffusion: challenging the assumed Indian origin of Iron Age agate and carnelian beads in South-East Asia" In: *World Archaeology*. vol. 32 no. 1 (pp 84-105).

Tripathi, A., 2003, *The Buddhist Art of Kausambi (300 BC – AD 550)*, New Delhi: DK Printworld.

Tripati, S., 1999, "Marine Investigations in the Lakshadweep Islands, India," *Antiquity*, vol. 73, no. 282, December 1999: 827-35.

Veraprasert, M., 1987, "Khlong Thom: an ancient bead and manufacturing location and an ancient entrepot" in: *Seminar in Prehistory of South-East Asia*, SPAFA Final Report., SEAMEO, Bangkok, Project in Archaeology and Fine Arts, pp. 323-31.

Verma, S., 2004, "The Archaeology of the Early Temples of Saurāṣṭra," in: *Archaeology as History in Early South Asia* (H.P. Ray and C.M. Sinipoli, eds.), New Delhi: ICHR and Aryan Books International, pp. 185-218.

Wayman, A. 1989, "The Mathurā Set of Aṣṭamaṅgala (Eight Auspiciuos Symbols) in Early and Later Times," in: Srinivasan, Doris Meth (ed.), *Mathurā: the Cultural Heritage*, Delhi: Manohar Publishers, pp. 236-46.

Wheeler, R.E.M., A. Ghosh and Krishna Deva, 1946, Arikamedu: An Indo-Roman Trading Station on the East Coast of India, *Ancient India*, no. 2: 17-124.

Wicks, R.S., 1999, "Indian Symbols in a South-East Asian Setting: Coins and Medals of Ancient Dvaravati" in: *Marg*, vol. 51, no. 2: 12-22.

Williams, Joanna G., 1989, The Case of the Omitted Hundreds: Stylistic Development in the Mathura Sculpture of the Kusana Period, in *Mathura: The Cultural Heritage* (D.M. Srinivasan ed.), pp. 325-31, New Delhi: American Institute of Indian Studies and Manohar.

Wilson, H.H., 1983, (tr.), *The Matsyamahapurāṇam*, Delhi: Nag Publishers.

Index

abhaya-mudrā, 18-19, 46
Abysinnians, 43
Achaemenids, 94
Adam, 31
adhiṣṭhāna, 57
Aḍichallanur, 69
Aḍurru, 62
Agathocles, the Bactrian king, 2, 14, 119
Agni, the fire god, 78
Ahicchatra, 14
Ai Khanum, 14
Airāvata, 39, 78
Ajantā, 20, 38
Alexandria, 95
Allahabad, 14, 21, 35
Allahabad Museum, xiv, 14, 112
āmalaka, 97
Amarāvatī, xiii, 2, 4-5, 10, 12, 14, 19, 21, 28, 32, 35, 44, 46, 53, 55-56, 58-59, 61-62, 65-67, 85, 88-89, 92, 94, 103, 112, 117-20
  school 28
  stūpa, 19, 28
amphorae pieces, 23, 50
Amreli, 45-47, 50
Ānandeśvara Temple, 58
Ananta Gumphā, 84
aṇḍa (hemispherical top), 10, 38, 43-44
Andhra Pradesh, 10, 19, 35, 48-49, 53, 62-63, 65, 177
Androth island, 92
Antoninus Pius, 63
Anurādhapura, 12
apasmāra puruṣa, 57
Arab traders, 89
Arabian inscriptions, 95
Arabian Sea, 7, 23, 43, 55
Arabo-Roman, 121
Aravalli ranges, 23, 25
Ari Atoll, 91
Arikameḍu beadcraft industries, 67-69, 106, 108
art (Graeco–Roman, Parthian), 6
art and trade, 21
art of Gandhāra, 17, 25
Arthaśāstra, 53
Aśoka, 12-13, 82, 86
Aśokan pillar, 13, 55
aṣṭamaṅgala, 10, 63, 83-84, 112-13
Atlas, 120
Augustus, 63
Avalokiteśvara, 44, 82
Avantī, 34
āyaka, 63
āyudha, 46

Bacchanalian, 14
Balarāma, 2, 14, 119
Baluchistan, 1
Ban Don Ta Phet (BDTP), 104, 106, 108
Bangarh, 78
Bangladesh, 80, 82
Barābar, group of caves, 10, 35
Barābar-Nāgārjunī, 35

Baroua river, 65
Barygaza port, 26-28, 31
Basrur coast, 70
Bavikoṇḍa, 54, 62-63, 117
Bay of Bengal, xiii, 5, 7, 21, 34, 53, 63, 65, 105-06, 112, 115
Bedsā caves, 37-39, 41, 117
Begram, 59, 95
Bengal, 2, 21, 32, 34-35, 78, 80, 82, 117
beryls, 106, 108-09
Bhagavanpavam, 63
Bhairava, 82
Bhaja, xiv, 2, 10, 35, 37-39, 52, 78, 85, 117-18
Bharhut, 2, 10, 12-13, 16, 21, 26, 28 31, 37, 39-40, 59, 84, 94, 112-13, 118
Bharhut–Sāñcī, 13
Bharuch, 26-28, 37
Bhaṭṭiprolu, 61-62
Bhir Mound, 108
Bhītā, 14, 21
Bhokardan, 13, 26, 31, 51, 95
Bhṛgukaccha port, 26, 50
Bhubaneswar, 87
Bikaner, 25
Bimlipaṭnam, 63, 65
Black and Red Ware, 37
Black Polished Ware, 37
Boat Devī, xi
Bodh-Gayā, 2, 10, 12, 34-35
bodhi tree, 2, 55, 97
bodhisattva, 14, 16-17, 21, 119
bouleterion (a rectangular stepped assembly hall), 59
Brāhmanical, 2, 4, 10, 14, 16, 52, 73, 80, 84, 87, 103, 110-12, 119
  deities, 16
  images, 4
Brahmapurī, 31
Bronze Age, viii, 1
Buddha, xiii-xv, 2, 4, 6, 12-14, 16-21, 33-34, 40, 43-44, 52, 55-57, 66-69, 73-74, 77, 81-82, 86, 89, 91-92, 112, 119-21
  as a transcendental being, 4
  preached his sermon, 19
Buddha image of
  Ajantā, 20
  Amarāvatī, 5
  Gandhāra, 18
  Mathurā, 18
Buddha School of Art, xiv, 16, 18, 19, 21
buddhapāda, 63, 67, 83, 91-92, 111-14
Buddha's life, 12, 18
Buddhism, 17
Buddhist, 2, 9-10, 14, 19, 28, 103, 110-11, 119
  caves, 9, 26, 28, 37
  ideas migrating east, 28
  monastic complexes, 54
  sanctuaries, 37
  stūpa, 2, 26, 28
Buddhist art of
  Andhra, 19
  Gandhāra, 25
  Sārnāth, 34
Buxar, 14

caitya, 38, 42, 51-52, 54, 63
Caius Vibius Pansa, 91
cakra, 61, 92, 109
Campā, 32
Candraketugaṛh, 34, 78-79, 81, 110
Candravaram, 55, 66-67
Caracalla, 65
caves of
  Barābar, 10, 35
  Bedsā, 37-39, 41, 117
  Buddha, 9, 26, 28, 37
  Jayavijaya, 85
  Junnār, 28, 37-38, 41
  Kārle, 10, 28, 37-39, 60, 73, 117

Lomas Ṛṣi, 2, 9, 35
Naneghāṭ, 120
Nasik, 28-29, 37-38, 41
Pītalkhora, 10, 38
post-Mauryan times, 10
rock-cut, xiii, 2, 10, 22
Udayagiri-Khaṇḍagiri in Orissa, 10, 13, 35, 41, 78, 84, 86-87, 110, 117, 120
Uperkoṭ, 48-49, 120
Central Asia, 52
Central India, 18, 26
Ceras, 68
Chaiya, 103, 112
Viṣṇu image, 109
Chalcolithic communities, 22
chatarī, 38, 43-44
Chaul port, 31, 42-43, 117
China, 92
Chryse, 65
Cilkā lake, 62
Cittorgaṛh, 25
coast of
Basrur, 70
Gokarṇa, 70
Karwar, 70
Malabar, 68, 70
Malpe, 70
Coḷas, 68
Commodus, 65
Corinthian, 49
Coromandel, 62
Cupid, 58

Dachinabades, 53
Dakṣiṇāpatha, 53
Daṁtamitrī, 38
Deccan, 6, 26-28, 30-32, 37, 45, 53
devakula, 45
*devī*s, 87
Devnimorī, 23, 25-26, 50
Dhamma, 62
Dharaṇīkoṭa, 53
dharmacakra, 13, 60, 66
dharmacakra stambha, 96
dharmacakra-pravartana pose, 44
dharmaghoṣa, 13
Dhauli, 2, 82-84, 86, 88
Dhofar, 92
dhotī, 18-19, 46, 73, 79, 94
Dhūlikaṭṭa, 55
dhyāna, 67
Didārgañj *yakṣī*, 2, 6, 86
dohada pose, 16
Domitian, 63
dvārapāla, 10, 85, 88, 120
Dvāravatī, 96-97, 109, 113

Egypt, 45
Ekero Island, 97

Funan, 114

Gajalakṣmī, xi, 14, 32, 34, 40-41, 84
gaṇa figures, 26, 50
Gandhāra, xiii, 4-5, 14, 16-18, 21, 25-26, 28, 32, 35, 38, 44, 48-50, 52, 56, 59, 68, 80, 91, 98, 111, 118-22
Buddha, 18, 98
School, 61
Gandhāra–Bactria, 25
Gāndhāra/Gāndhāran, 6, 18, 33, 51, 97, 104, 121
Gāndhāra art, 17, 19, 26, 94
gandharva, 44, 49
Gaṇeśa Gumphā, 14, 26, 74, 78, 83-84, 86
Gaṅgā, images of, 14, 35
Gangetic
basin, 17, 22, 26, 32-34, 78, 109
Valley, xiv, 1, 10, 21, 32, 34, 51, 79, 81, 84, 110
Zone, 77
Garuḍa, 109
Geographia of Ptolemy, 65-66, 70

Gersoppa falls, 70
Ghaṇṭaśāla, 62, 66
Ghoṣitārāma monastery, 34, 56
Giluṇḍ, 25
Goa, viii, xi
Godāvarī river, 31, 53-54, 59, 61-63, 65
Gokarṇa coast, 70
Golī, 56
Graeco-Roman, 19, 26, 45-46, 48, 50, 58, 72, 85, 95, 120
Greek, 18, 27, 31, 89, 121
  art, xiv, 17
Guḍimallam, 2, 54, 57, 119
Guḍivaḍa, 55
Gujarat, 23, 25-26, 45, 47, 109
Gulf of Khambaṭ, 23, 49
Gumada, 63
Guṇṭupalli, 62, 65
Gupta period, 6, 16, 20, 32, 34, 46-47, 69, 73, 84, 87, 92-93

Hadhramaut, 121
Hadhrami, 121
Hadipur, 79
Hadrian, 63
Haiguṇḍa, 55, 71-73
Hīnayāna Buddhism, 32, 43, 52, 65, 117
Hanumān, 40
Haṛappan, 22
  civilization, 1, 13, 37, 107
  migrations, 22
  period, 106
Hārīti, a Buddhist deity, 34, 56
harmikā, 10, 38, 43-44
Haroā, 79
Hastināpura, 32
Helgo, 97-98
Hellenistic, 18, 25, 30-31, 50-52, 68, 81, 91, 93, 121
Hiṅgalāja Mātā, a local deity, 43
Hindu-Kush range, 17
Honnavara, 71

Ikṣvāku, 7, 19, 61
Indian Ocean, vii, xiii, xiv, 7, 91, 121
Indian Ocean Rim Countries, vii
Indianization, 7, 89, 99, 101-02, 105, 109, 114-15, 121
Indian sculptural art, xiii, 6
Indic sculptures, 109
Indo-Pacific beads, 106-09
Indo-Roman, 27
Indra, xiv, 2, 14, 37, 39, 78, 89, 118
Indus-Saraswatī Civilization, 1
Iranian, 17
Iron Age, 1, 37, 105, 114
Italy, 13, 50-51, 95

Jaggayyapeṭa, 55
Jaina, 2, 9-10, 13-14, 77, 111, 119
  caves, 13
  tīrthaṁkaras, 4, 16
Janārdana, 74
Jañjīrā creek, 42-43
Jātaka tales, 2, 19, 66
Jayavijaya cave, 85
Jhūsī, 14
Jina, 6
Jūnāgaṛh, 26, 45, 48, 62, 120
Junnar, 30
Junnār caves, 28, 37-38, 41

Kadamba period, 74
Kajur, xi
Kālidāsa drama, *Mālavikāgnimitram*, 16
Kaliṅga War, 13
Kaliṅgapaṭnam, 54, 63
Kaliṅgapaṭam or *Kalingoe* port, 63
Kalliena port, 29
kalpavṛkṣa, 112
Kalyāṇa port, 29, 31

Kamaya, 83
Kamrej, 27, 46
Kanārā, 69-71
Kāñcīpuram, 68
Kanheri, 29, 42-44, 52, 72-73, 87, 117
Kanheri port, 37
Kaniṣka, 17, 21, 49
Kaṅkālīṭīlā, 16
kapota, 57
Karaḍ, 31
Kārle caves, 10, 28, 37-39, 60, 73, 117
Kārttikeya, xi, 4, 16, 57, 84
Karvan, 47, 52, 87, 121
karwar coast, 70
Kāṭhiāwāṛ, 25
Kauśāmbī, 2, 21, 31-35, 51, 56, 97, 106, 108-10
  plaques, 33
Kauśāmbī–Vatsa, 32
Kāverī river, 67
Kāverīpaṭṭinam port, 67-68
Kayama Hill, 86
Kesarapalli, 55
*keyūra*s, 96
Khambaṭ, 109
Khao Sam Kieu, 113
khaḍga, 47
Khlong Thom, 104
Khoṛ Rorī *yakṣī*, 51, 89, 92, 94, 99
Khuan Lukpad, 113
Kinnarī Pot, 95
kirīṭa, 47
kodhi (hall), 29
Koḍumanal beadraft industries, 69
Koḷ community, 43
Kolhapur, 29, 120
Koṇḍapura, 27-28, 31, 50
Kondivte, 42, 44, 65, 87
Koṅkaṇ coast, 29-31, 37, 40-42, 44, 51, 65
Koṭapad, 63
Koṭṭapaṭnam, 67
Kottis port, 66
Kṛṣṇā
  basin, 55
  river, 7, 19, 21, 28, 31, 53-54, 57, 59, 61, 66-67, 120
  the deity, 2, 14, 119
  Valley, 12, 19, 53, 56, 58, 61, 94
Kṣatrapa
  coins, 25
  rulers, 27, 45-47, 49-50, 52, 120
Kubera, the deity of wealth, 16, 78
Kuḍa harbour, 29, 37, 42-44, 52, 87, 117
Kulavaka Jātaka, 40
Kuśāmba, the king, 32
Kuṣāṇa, 6, 14, 16-18, 20-21, 27, 32 34, 45-47, 50, 73, 81, 93-94, 120
  Art of Mathurā, 17
Kuṣāṇa–Gupta, 33, 81-82, 103, 109
Kuśāvatī river, viii
kuṭi (temple), 29

Lake Malaren, 97
Lakshadweep islands, xv, 53, 55, 69, 75, 92, 117, 120
Lakṣmī, 4, 78-79
Lakṣmī-Pārvatī, 31
Lakulīśa images, 52, 87
Lampascos, a dish from Turkey, 89, 91
Limyrike coastal areas, 53
Liṅgarājupalem, 63, 65
Lomas Ṛṣi caves, 2, 9, 35, 38, 52
Long An, 113

Magadh, 10
Mahābhārata, 32, 70
mahājanapada, 1, 32
Mahāsaṁghika sects, 4, 56
Mahāsthāngaṛh, 80, 82
Mahāyāna proselytization, 52, 87

Mahāyānists, 44
Maheśvar, 26
Mahiṣāsuramardinī, xi, 4
Mahiṣmatī, 26
Maia, 79
Maisolos, 66
Maitreya, 19
Majjhima Nikāya, 40
Malabar coast, 68, 70
mālavāhaka, 26, 48-49, 61, 94
Mālavikāgnimitram, a Kālidāsa drama, 16
Māldā, 82
Maldives, 55, 69, 74, 91, 117, 120
Malpe coast, 70
Malpe Udyavara, 71
Manakha (Yemen), 93
Manakha plaque, 94
Manara river, 66-67
Manarpha port, 66-67
Mandagora port/harbour, 29
maṇḍapa, 10
maṅgala symbolisms, 114
Marcus Aurelius, 63
Marib, 121
Maruti temple, 28
Mat, near Vṛndāvan, 17, 45, 120
Mathurā, xiii, 4-6, 14, 16-17, 20-21, 26-28, 32-35, 42, 44, 47-48, 50, 52, 56-57, 61, 69, 74, 80-81, 84, 89, 93-95, 110-11, 118-22
Matsya Purāṇa, 112
Mauryan, 2, 6, 9-10, 12-13, 32, 34, 41, 77, 80, 84, 110
Māyā, a goddess, 79
Mediterranean, 23, 31, 120
Megalithic, 69, 77
Megasthenes, 63
mekhalā, 46
Meshvo river, 23
Mhdei (= Mahādevī) river, xi
mithuna, 10, 28, 42, 44, 59, 93-94
Mount Vesuvius, 95
Mṛcchakaṭikam, ancient Sanskrit play, 14
Mucalinda, 55
  nāga, 63, 83
mudrā, 74
Murud, 43

Nagal, 37
Nagar, 25
Nagara, 23
Nāgarī, 25
Nāgārjunakoṇḍa, xiii, 7, 14, 19, 32, 51, 53-59, 61-62, 66-67, 85, 89, 93, 117, 119-20
  excavations, 19
nāgī-sculptures, 83
Nakhon Si Thammarat, 103
Nālandā-Rājgīr, 34
Nānāghāṭ pass, 29, 40
nandipāda, 110, 111
nandyāvartas, 92
Naneghāṭ caves, 120
Naples, 50
Narmadā river, 26
Nasik caves, 28-29, 37-38, 41
Nāva Devī, xi
Netravali river, 70
Nevāsā, 30-31, 50-51, 120
Nicakṣu, the King, 32
Norway, 97-98

Oc Eo, 103, 113
Oman, vii, xiv, 51, 89, 92
Orissa, 2, 10, 35, 41, 62, 77-78, 83, 111, 117
Osmanabad, 28
Oxyrhynchus, 79

Paiṭhan, 27-31
Pakistan, 25, 50, 98
Pāla style, 82

Palaepatmae, 29
Palembang, 103
Pallavaneśvaram, 67
Palshet, 29
P'an P'an, 103, 114
pañcacūḍa, goddess, 34, 79
Pāṇḍavas, 32
Pāṇḍurājārdhibi, 81
Pāṇḍyas, 68
Pansaimol, viii, xi
Papyrus Oxyrhynchus, 70, 79
Paraśurāma, 70
Paraśurāmeśvaraswāmī, 57
Parkham *yakṣa*, 16
Parthian, 18, 94
Parthian–Sassanian, 25
Pārvatī, 84
Pāṭaliputra, 12, 34, 41
Patna, 14, 32, 34
paṭṭa, 72
Pauni, 21, 31-32, 35, 59
Peninsular Malaya, 107
Pennar port, 66-67
Peḍḍagañjam, 62, 66
Periplus Maris Erythraei, 27-29, 31, 43, 53, 70, 94
Persian Gulf, 121
"Petroglyphs" or Rock Art, viii
Pīpal, 97
Piprahwa, 12, 107
Pirla mines, viii
Pītalkhora caves, 10, 38
pīṭha, 58
Pompei, 13, 51, 89, 95
Pondicherry, 53
Pong Tuk, 103
port/harbour of
  Barygaza, 26-28, 31
  Bhṛgukaccha, 26, 50
  Chaul, 31, 42-43, 117
  Kaliṅgapaṭam or *Kalingoe*, 63
  Kalliena, 29
  Kalyāṇa, 29, 31
  Kanheri, 37
  Kāverīpaṭṭinam, 67-68
  Kottis, 66
  Kuḍa, 29, 37, 42-44, 52, 87, 117
  Manarpha, 66-67
  Mandagora, 29
  Pennar, 67
  Qana, 94
  Sūrapāraka, 29
  Semylla, 29
  Soppārā, 31
Poseidon, 31
post-Gupta period, 32
post-Mauryan times *ghāṭ* caves, 10
Prabhāsa Paṭan, 37, 49
Prasenajit, 40
Pratiṣṭhanpatha, 30
Prayag, Allahabad, 1
Purāṇas, 32
puruṣa, form of Śiva, 54, 57

Qana port, 94

Radhanagar, 86
Raṅgamahal, 25, 35, 49
Rājataleka Paiṭhanapatha, 29
Rājghāṭ, 109
Rāma, xi
Rāmapūrvā pillar, 41
Rampurva, 13
Red Polished Ware, 23, 51
river
  Baroua, 65
  Godāvarī, 31, 53-54, 59, 61-63, 65
  Kāverī, 67
  Kṛṣṇā, 7, 19, 21, 28, 31, 53-54, 57, 59, 61, 66-67, 120
  Kuśāvatī, viii
  Manara, 66-67
  Meshvo, 23
  Mhdei (= Mahādevī), xi

Narmadā, 26
Netravali, 70
Śarāvatī, 70-72
Tāpī, 46
Yamunā, 14
rock-cut
architecture, 9
caves, xiii, 2, 10, 22
sanctuaries, xiv, 9, 10
Rohā creek, 42
Roma, a goddess, 18
Roman art, 17
Romanization, 121
Romans, sigillata wares of, 51
Romans/Rome, 18, 23, 30, 38, 49-52, 59-60, 63, 65, 67-69, 89
Rorī *yakṣī*, 99
Rouletted Ware, 67
Rudrapuruṣadatta Pillar, 58
Rupabas, 16

Saba, 121
Sahet-Mahet, 107
Śailodbhavas, 83
Śaka, 120
Śaka-Kuṣāṇa, 16
Śakra, 78
Śākya Clan, 113
śākya (lion), 113-14
śālabhañjikā, 93
Salihundam, 2, 54, 63
Salipeṭaka, 63
Salsette, 43
Śāmalājī excavation, 23
samapāda posture, 79
Sambhar, 25
Saṁghamitrā, 59
saṁghāti, 74, 98
Sanaa, 89
Sāñcī *stūpa*, xiv, 2, 10, 12-13, 16, 21, 26, 28, 31, 35, 37, 39-40, 51, 59, 84, 88, 93, 118
Saṅghol, 42, 61
Sanguem, viii, xi
Sankisa, 13
Sannathi, 21, 32, 59
Sanskrit, 14, 102
Śānta-Durgā, xi
sapatra-keyūras, 96
Saptamātṛkās, xi
Śarāvatī river, 70-72
Sārnāth, xiii, 2, 4, 13, 20, 34-35, 41, 44, 69, 74, 80-81, 111, 119, 122
School of Art, 19, 34
Sarnath Museum, 112
Sārnāth–Kauśāmbī, 4
Sassanian, 18, 94
Sātavāhana, 7, 28, 41-42, 45, 120
Saurāṣṭra, 21, 26, 45-46, 48, 51-52, 120
Scandinavia, 98
sculptural art of
Gandhāra, 4
India, 4
Kauśāmbī, 32
Mathurā, 5
Pāṭaliputra, 5
Scythian, 7, 18, 32, 45, 47-48, 72, 81, 85, 120
Semylla port/harbour, 29
Septimus Severus, 65
Shiveni Hill, 38
Siddhapura, 31
śikhara, 57
Sikri, 16
Silk Route trade, 77
Sindh, 1
Śiva, 2, 6, 14, 52, 54, 57, 87
śivaliṅga/śivaliṅgam, 54, 57-58, 72, 74
Skandamātā, 25
Soṅkh, 17
Soppārā port, 31
South-East Asia, 21, 89, 99, 101-09, 111, 113-14, 121
Souttekeny, 69

Sri Lanka, 10, 12, 62
Śrī-Lakṣmī, 78-79
Śrīkṣetra, 113
śrīvatsa, auspicious symbol, 67, 83, 112-14, 118
śrīvatsa-oriented, 92
Śṛṅgaverapura, 14, 17
sthānaka, 46
stūpa, 10, 12-13, 16, 19, 22, 25, 28, 31-32, 35, 37-38, 43-44, 54-55, 60, 63, 75, 91, 118
Svami Rudrasena III, 25, 50
svastika, auspicious symbol, 67, 83, 92, 96, 98, 110-12, 114, 118
Sūrya, xiv, 2, 16, 37, 39-40, 78, 82, 118
Sūrapāraka port, 29
Śuṅga age, 6, 14, 28, 32-33, 41, 79, 85
Śuṅga–Sātavāhana, 42
Swāt region, 98
Sweden, xiv, 89, 91, 97

Tagara, 27-28, 31
Tamil, 68-69
Tamil Saṅgam, 85, 120
Tamil–Brāhmī inscriptions, 10
Tamluk, 35, 79-81
Tāmralipti, 110
Tanesara-Mahādeva, 25
Tāpī river, 46
tīrthaṁkaras, 14, 16-17, 87, 111, 119
Taxila, 30, 50, 61, 107-08, 110
Ṭer, 13, 26-28, 31, 35, 50-51, 62, 95
terracotta figures, 13-14
Tha Chana, 113
Thaddoo island, 74, 91
Thailand, 103-04, 106-07
Thai–Malaysian isthmus, 103
Thotlakoṇḍa, 2, 54, 62-63, 117
Tiberius, 63
Tilda, 81
Tisa, 86
Tissamaharama, 12, 62
Topra Pillar, 13
trade routes, 21, 77
Tripurī, 31
triratna, 55, 112
Turkey, 89, 91

Udayagiri, 83
Udayagiri-Khaṇḍagiri cave groups in Orissa, 10, 13, 35, 41, 78, 84, 86-87, 110, 117, 120
Udayana, a king, 34
Udyavara, 74
Ujjain, 26-27, 31, 96, 118
Umā-Maheśvara, 84
Uperkoṭ caves, 48-49, 120
Uttar Kannada, 74
uṣṇīṣa, 44, 47, 89, 98

Vaiśālī, 2, 12, 35
Vaiṣṇavī/Vaiṣṇavite, 14, 48
vajra, 47, 112-14
vajrāsana worship, 66
Vallabhipura, 121
Vaḍgāon Mādhavapura, 31
Vaḍḍamanu, 75, 94
Varanasi, 34
Vāsavadattā, 34
Vatsa, 32
Vedas, 2, 118
Vedic
  idioms, 4
  tradition, 4, 9, 40, 111, 118
Vedic God
  Indra 9, 40
  Sūrya, 9, 40
Venus, 58
Vespasian, 63
Vidarbha, 31
Vidiśā, 26, 95
Vietnam, 103
vihāra, 51, 54, 62-63, 77

Viking, xiv, 98
Vinukoṇḍa, 63
Visakapatanam, 62
Viṣṇu, 4, 6, 14, 16, 46-47, 49, 73-74, 82, 103, 111-12, 120
Viṣṇukuṇḍin, 57
vṛkṣa-caitya, 55
Vṛndāvan, 17

West Asia, 25
Western Ghats, 37
Western Kṣatrapa dynasty, 7
Wima Khadphises images, 17, 50
worship,
 aniconic to iconic forms of worship, 2
 the Buddha, 12
 the *stūpa*, 12

yajñopavīta, 46
yakṣī, 10, 13-14, 16, 19, 26, 40, 51, 85, 89, 93, 95, 99, 110, 118
yakṣa, 19, 55, 72-73
yakṣīṇīs, 118
Yamunā river, 14
yavana, 38, 68, 85, 88, 120
Yavanikā, 59
Yelleswaram, 57
Yemen, xiii, 62, 89, 121